A Moment to Breathe

A Moment to Breathe

365 DEVOTIONS THAT MEET YOU IN YOUR EVERYDAY MESS

(in)courage editor
Denise J. Hughes

PUBLISHING GROUP

NASHVILLE, TENNESSEE

978-1-4627-6706-9

Published by B&H Publishing Group
Nashville, Tennessee

Dewey Decimal Classification: 242.643
Subject Heading: DEVOTIONAL LITERATURE
\ WOMEN \ MEDITATIONS

3 4 5 6 7 8 9 10 • 23 22 21 20 19

Introduction

OH, FRIEND, WE ARE so glad you're here. Come on in. Yes you. Even if you're still in your pajamas. And especially if you're still wearing yesterday's makeup. We like you just the way you are. Because here at (in)courage we're all about being real. Real about our struggles. Real about our messes. And real about Jesus, who welcomes us all with arms as wide as the heavens He made.

We may come from different places, but when we come together, we find one thing to be very true: Our heartaches may be different, but our hearts are the same. And that's what you'll find in these pages—stories from women in every season of life, women who have been there, women who understand.

We're so honored to include the beautiful voices of eighty writers, and you can find out more about each woman in the Author Bios in the back (p. 369).

As you turn each page, imagine a friend opening her door, welcoming you into her story.

This collection of everyday stories is where you can find yourself among friends—friends who'll lean in close and say, "Me too!" Through our stories the bonds of friendship deepen as we listen to each other, laugh with each other, and learn from each other. Because we're better when we're living this one beautiful life together.

We know life can be wonderful and wonderfully messy all at the same time. We also know that God often moves in unseen ways through our most ordinary days. Which is why we see each story as an offering of hope, from one heart to another. Sister to sister. Friend to friend.

With 365 readings, each day begins with a passage of Scripture, tells a story of everyday faith, and encourages you to take a moment to breathe with a simple but fun way to complete your day.

Start with Day 1 and read through the devotions daily for a whole year or go at your own pace. We've also included a Scripture Index (p. 377) so you can easily find a devotional by verse. Feel free to mark these pages with your own words too. Share them with friends. And let us know how God uses these words to bring hope and encouragement to your everyday.

So kick off your shoes and join us for a relaxing but special time, where friends come together and share the real stuff of everyday faith.

May the stories on these pages become the very place your soul can exhale . . . where you know that you know . . . you have a place here . . . a place with many voices, one heart.

We're All Worth a Second Look

BY HOLLEY GERTH

I am sure of this, that he who started a good work in you will carry it on to completion until the day of Christ Jesus. PHILIPPIANS 1:6

WE WANDER OVER TO our favorite fruit stand, to a table laden with discounted fruit labeled "seconds." A wiry woman says, "These are here because they have some kind of trouble."

I look at her and say with a half-grin, "Don't we all?"

My husband and I have bought these peaches before and we know what she means. There might be a bruise from a hard landing on unrelenting ground. There could be a tiny hole where a bug helped itself to dinner. I glance at the cousins of these peaches sitting on other tables inside the little stand. They're beautiful and unblemished as they sit proudly in their buckets waiting to be taken home by folks who will not settle for anything less. I think if I were a peach I'd rather be on the "seconds" table where the messy is allowed.

We choose our imperfect peaches and cart them home with anticipation. I set one on a small cream-colored plate and split it right down the side with a silver knife. I bring the piece to my mouth and take a bite. It's an explosion of sweet and tart and summer.

I look at it and whisper right to its skin, "Who would have thought you had that in you?" Then I think about how this rings true to life. Because we all have parts of our hearts or stories that we think don't measure up. We call them unworthy and less than and we put them to the side. But the longer I've walked this spinning earth, the more I find those are the places where the glory and the beauty are likely to show up and shout, "Surprise!" I had assumed "seconds" meant "not first, not best." Maybe it really just means "worth a second look."

A Moment to Breathe . . .

As you go through your day, look into the eyes of the cashier or the barista or the mailman and say hi. Learn their name. Give them a "second look" and a smile that says, "You matter."

Praying for Rain

BY LISA-JO BAKER

Ask the LORD for rain in the season of spring rain. The LORD
makes the rain clouds, and he will give them showers of
rain and crops in the field for everyone. ZECHARIAH 10:1

AT THE KITCHEN SINK there are only dishes and soap suds and
my thoughts. So late at night while the household sleeps, I straggle
into the kitchen to find peace in a sink full of waiting dishes. As
I rinse my bright red frying pan, I find myself praying desperate
dreams for the future. I pray for what I want but rarely for what I
have.

But recently, I was reminded of the verse in Zechariah that says:
In the season of rain, pray for rain. And suddenly I'm back in South
Africa on a dry game farm surrounded by farmers who haven't seen
rain in months. These sun-weathered men sit in their rough clothes
at a long table outside. The first course is cucumber soup. But with
first bites come cold, hard drops. Rain. I prepare to make a dash for
the inside of the lodge, but I'm the only one to move.

The men carry on with their meal as the rain falls down and
the soup splashes up. But their actions speak louder than words
and my father interprets them for me, "They won't leave the rain,
because they don't want it to leave them." In the season of rain,
they want more rain.

With soap suds up to my elbows, I lean on the sink, remembering.
What I have now is once what I wanted so desperately: healed
marriage, healthy children, the beginnings of meaningful work. I
don't want to lose sight of these in the chase after my next prayer
request. In the season of rain, still pray for rain. Because, once the
rain begins, it's tempting to walk away from the answered prayer
and move on to the next thing. But I do not want to do that. I want
to sit and revel in what God has given me here and now. Daily,
between soap suds and dirty dishes, I want to pray for what I have.

A Moment to Breathe . . .

Pray for the rain that's already falling, giving thanks
for the abundance He's already shown.

Dear John

BY ALIZA LATTA

Therefore accept one another, just as Christ also accepted you, to the glory of God. ROMANS 15:7

THE PLANE HAD JUST started to climb into the air when the man sitting next to me knocked his elbow against mine. I turned to him and smiled. (I always smile when I feel awkward.) "My name is John." He said each word painfully slow, his hand sort of flapping while pointing to his chest.

"Hi, John. It's nice to meet you. My dad's name is John, too."

He then asked, long and slow, each syllable a marathon, "What is your name?" I felt guilty when the word slipped quick and easy from my lips. "Aliza."

"Aliza," he repeated, nodding. He looked at me, his blue eyes sharp but kind. "I have to apologize. I haven't always been like this. I was in an accident." When I understood what he said, I felt this deep sinking in my gut. John felt he needed to apologize because I might think him different.

How many plane trips had he taken where people didn't talk to him because they thought he was different? How many days did he wake up wishing, praying, begging God to go back to the day when people didn't think him different? I saw the looks he was given on the plane and my heart hurt, because the truth is, John is no different than me.

We're both searching and hoping and laughing and struggling, and so yes, maybe those things don't look exactly the same for the two of us, but who is to say that he is different and I am normal?

John says he reads a lot of books and he loves Netflix, and he used to be a really good biker. Before we got off the plane, John elbowed me again. I turned to him, and I'll never forget the words he gave to me. And in the sincerest voice I've ever heard, "Aliza, I hope that you are able to do everything I can't."

A Moment to Breathe . . .

When you see someone who might seem a little different,
pause and say hello. Look into their eyes. Smile.
Give the simple, but important, gift of dignity.

The Hidden Stain

BY DENISE J. HUGHES

. . . Christ loved the church and gave himself for her. EPHESIANS 5:25

DRAPED IN WHITE LACE I stood ready, waiting. The room brimmed with busyness around me as the bridesmaids clutched their bouquets and the mothers adjusted their corsages. Then suddenly, an eerie silence descended. I searched the faces of my girlfriends while expressions of shock and horror stared back at me. "What happened? What is it?"

I followed their eyes to something behind me. The train of my bridal gown was several feet long—just how I always dreamt it would be. And there, kneeling by my train, my thirteen-year-old cousin held a steaming hot clothes iron; beneath it a dark orange triangle smoldered on the train of my dress. Apparently she tried to iron out the creases in the train, but the iron was too hot for the satin.

As the music began in the sanctuary, I looked up and said, "Quick! Somebody run to the church office and find some liquid Wite-Out!" I figured it might make the fabric clumpy and goopy, but at least it wouldn't be dark orange.

I told my cousin not to worry about it and plotted with my maid of honor how we could hide the stain. Instead of spreading out my train behind me, like she did at the rehearsal, I asked her to fold the fabric over to cover the stain. And down the aisle we went.

In Scripture, the church is the bride of Christ. By God's grace, the stain of our sin no longer marks us. We are cleansed and set free. The bride of Christ isn't perfect, none of us are, but Christ's forgiveness is complete.

On my wedding day, no one in the sanctuary knew the bride had a huge ugly stain on her dress. But one day, there will be another wedding, and the bride of Christ will appear . . . without spot or wrinkle.

A Moment to Breathe . . .

Look on the cover of this book. You'll see a faint stain from a coffee mug. It's there on purpose. Because we all have "stains" we want to hide, but Christ removes them when we ask Him to. And we've no better reason to exhale than that.

What Will the Neighbors Think?

BY MARY CARVER

For am I now trying to persuade people, or God? Or am I striving to please people? If I were still trying to please people, I would not be a servant of Christ. GALATIANS 1:10

"WOULD YOU PLEASE JUST be quiet?" I hissed as my daughter raised her voice once again. My eyes darted back and forth, searching for any movement on our street, any evidence that our neighbors were outside and within earshot of my noisy family. Life with a tween and a toddler is awfully loud a lot of the time, and it can be embarrassing. Between back talk from one and tantrums from the other, silence is a hot commodity around here.

Our street is a quiet one, which only highlights our not-so-quiet family. Since we moved here last summer, I've worried about what our neighbors must think of us. We arrived in this community excited to meet new people and share our lives and our faith with them. But insecurity and the need to please quickly eclipsed those good intentions.

One day, as I buckled my youngest into our car, I heard voices. I saw an open garage door and realized another mom was just as exasperated (and expressive) as I often find myself. I heard her holler at her kids to get in the car—and it hit me. I'd been wasting time hiding away and trying to control my family's appearance for people I'd never met when I could have been walking across the street to introduce myself (and my noisy kids). I'd neglected the chance to connect in my effort to impress.

It's impossible to love our neighbors when we're worrying about what those neighbors might think of us. Choosing love requires humility and honesty instead of perfection and protecting reputations. It might even mean letting my kids run wild in our front yard while I introduce myself to that mom across the street.

A Moment to Breathe . . .

Don't spend another minute worrying about what others might think. Let's be who we are and share who God is.

Trust the Path

BY ANNIE F. DOWNS

Make your ways known to me, LORD;
teach me your paths. PSALM 25:4

I WENT WALKING LAST week around a lake in Nashville, and because I was feeling particularly inspired by the cooler weather, I followed a new sign I had never seen to a path I had never walked. I looked at a map before heading out, even took a picture of it with my phone. I'm prone to getting lost—it's practically a spiritual gift of mine—so I know better than to just jump off the road and onto a path without a map of some sort.

My earbuds in, I walked on the dirt path for ten to fifteen minutes . . . thinking, praying, processing. Two particular situations were on my mind. Neither had a clear right or wrong answer to me—both were opportunities that may be worth taking. I was worried, though, that I was going to miss what God had for me. "Just show me, Lord," I said, "and I'll do what You want. I just don't know where either of these are going."

I looked down and realized I didn't know where I was, which was true in lots of areas of my life. A little lost, a little sure I was wrong, a little concerned that I was missing the right thing. I also thought I may be lost in these woods. In a blink, God stamped a statement onto my heart: *Trust the path.* I looked at my feet, at the path, and remembered the path would take me back to the road eventually. I had seen it on the map.

Trust the path. I knew God didn't just mean the one at the lake. He meant the questions in my heart. I don't have to know where things are going, I don't have to know the destination, I just have to trust the path. So I'm choosing, in my life and in my walk around the lake, to trust the next step. To trust that the path I'm on is going somewhere and wherever that is, God knows.

A Moment to Breathe . . .

Take a walk around a park or around your neighborhood.
Talk to God while you walk, maybe not out loud (although
that's fine too), but listen for His direction.

When You Need Permission to Let It Be

BY DEIDRA RIGGS

I lift my eyes toward the mountains.
Where will my help come from? PSALM 121:1

THE OTHER NIGHT, I sat on the couch, staring at the cursor on my laptop. Blinking. I was considering dressing up as a blinking curser the next time I get invited to a costume party. Thank goodness my husband broke into my reverie: "Let it rest," he said.

"Huh?" I said to him, trying to pull myself away from the hypnotic beat of the cursor.

"Let it rest," he said again. "Close the laptop, and let it be. It will still be there tomorrow," he said. "Nothing will have changed, and nothing is going to change, just because you sit here, staring at that screen."

He had a point. So I closed it. Let it rest. Let it be. And the whole entire world opened up in front of me. I remembered music and food and laughter and the sound of snow melting from the roof overhanging our front porch. I remembered fresh air and sunshine. My husband and I hopped on our bikes and rode a few miles to the lake nearby. We sat on a bench that faced the setting sun, and we talked about where we've been and what we hope will be.

On the way home, we stopped at a red light next to a young boy and his dad, also on their bikes. We waited for the light to turn green, and the little boy was saying, "There are millions of us, racing across the street!" He hunched low over his handlebars, imagining a throng of bike racers, waiting for the starting gun. "One! Two! Three! Four! Five!" he shouted above the whoosh of cars passing by, and then the light turned green and we were off! All five million of us, in the race of our lives. Once we crossed the street, the boy and his dad turned off, but my husband and I pedaled hard and we shouted into the wind, "One! Two! Three! Four! Five!" and laughed out loud as the sun spilled pink and orange across the horizon.

A Moment to Breathe . . .

Step away from the task demanding your immediate attention
and look up. Go outside and "lift your eyes to the mountains."

9

On Being the Truest Version of Me

BY ALIA JOY

The LORD will fulfill his purpose for me. LORD, your faithful love endures forever; do not abandon the work of your hands. PSALM 138:8

EVEN HER SWEAT WAS cute. Her cheeks flushed a blushing pink like a peony petal. Her hair curled in damp wisps around her face as she lifted a water bottle to her glossed lips and my gaze flicked away from her to the full-length mirrors lining the walls of the gym.

My face was cherry-splotched and my pony tail hung limp and greasy. My oversized T-shirt was soaked through and I could see where it was clinging to the bulges beneath my industrial-sized sports bra—one I struggled to wedge myself into with hooks and clasps and enough Velcro to stick a grown human to a wall, one that might require the jaws of life and some serious intervention to release me from. I won't be showering at the gym.

I went every day for two weeks and then never again. Years have passed since then, but I still remember gym girl. I remember the feeling of being way too much and not enough every time I went. There was a time when my skin was smooth like marble, and my body was strong and young. But I wasn't enough then either.

I see gym girl everywhere when I let envy dictate my dreams, my goals, my reality. I see her in all the ways I come up short. And I let it keep me away from the process. Not to change into a me that's good enough, but to believe that just showing up is part of the journey . . . not just to a fit self, but to a fit soul.

I am back to exercising. I pull on my oversized T-shirt and work myself into a fine ache, and when I look in the mirror bypassing the scale, I feel spent yet whole, flushed and alive. I'm not looking for a better version of myself, but a truer version of who I have always been: loved, cherished, beautiful, strong.

A Moment to Breathe . . .

*Be the truest version of who God created you
to be. Be that girl, today and always.*

If You Know Him

BY SARAH MAE

For by one offering he has perfected forever those who are sanctified. HEBREWS 10:14

HERE I AM, ON my couch crying, again. I will never get it together. I am such a failure. I am just so tired of making plans and lists and self-help do-overs that end right back where I started. I just can't do it. I can't fix myself.

It's been five years since I had a "failure" break down. I was done, over trying to be better, do better, get better. I just kept missing my mark, my perfectionist, pull-myself-up-by-the-bootstraps, get-it-together mark. So I sat on my couch and cried out to the Lord. I threw my hands up and said, "I'm done."

It was as though the Lord was waiting for those very words, because when I finally recognized my deep weakness, when I finally gave in, that is when I was able to grow and mature in Christ by relying on His strength. I am clay, and clay cannot mold itself. He is the molder and perfecter of my faith and my soul and all of me.

And the best, most wonderful life-giving news of all? As He's intimately molding me toward maturity, He doesn't look at me as a failure. He looks at me, His beloved daughter, and sees perfection, completeness, because of Jesus Christ. God has already perfected me because I know Him. Yeah, there's still work to be done with my humanity here on earth, and I'm certainly not perfect here, but where I'm going? Done deal. Perfect. Complete. Right now. What sweet freedom. What grace. What an exhale.

A Moment to Breathe . . .

Whatever you're holding on to today, give it to God. Let Him do the work as you put one foot in front of the other by faith in obedience. And breathe deep—He sees you as complete right now.

Because Life Is Hard

BY JEN SCHMIDT

. . . the one who is in you is greater than the
one who is in the world. 1 JOHN 4:4

I APPROACHED MY DOOR and tried to focus. Brown paper bags littered my sidewalk. Food, toiletries, diapers, and gift cards overflowed. It was all for my family. We were approaching a year without a paycheck, trying to keep our business afloat and avoid foreclosure on our home. But we were nearing the end of our rope. I begged God for clarity, but heard nothing. I cried out wondering how much longer this season would last, but answers weren't coming. Days felt like years, and in the midst of this, my mother-in-law—vibrant and healthy—was diagnosed with a brain tumor and given months to live.

I was done. But then He fed me. Literally.

With some bags of groceries and diapers, He reminded me that He is greater than the circumstances we face. My circumstances do not determine my peace. The world can neither give us peace, nor take it away. Life is hard. And it will probably get harder. Jesus said as much when He promised we'd have trials in this life (John 16:33). He wasn't trying to scare us. He was trying to prepare us.

God knows my pain and He understands my problems. But we have to trust Him, even when we can't trace Him. This is when I choose to fully lean into my Lord Jesus. It's a choice. In the midst of pain, it's a choice . . . to recognize truth, to believe in His sovereignty, and to find peace amidst heartbreak. I may never figure this all out, but He knows, He sees, and He wants to carry this burden for us. We can't do it alone, but we can be there for each other. And maybe bring a bag of groceries too.

A Moment to Breathe . . .

Sometimes God's sweetest blessings are in a bag of groceries. The next time you're at the store, grab an extra bag and fill it for a family.

Peace over Productivity

BY BECKY KEIFE

You will keep the mind that is dependent on you in
perfect peace, for it is trusting in you. ISAIAH 26:3

HAVE YOU EVER SEEN a hummingbird at rest? Even when she hovers over a flower, dipping her slender beak deep into the blossom for a nectar drink, even then her wings beat infinitely faster than my eyes can account for or my mind can understand. She is constantly in motion. Zipping to and fro—a creature to catch in mere glimpses. Flashes of blurry beauty and intrigue.

But today she sits on a telephone wire, a black silhouette against the pale blue sky of early morning. So tiny upon the wire. She could be an oversized acorn or balancing leaf; it would be difficult to discern were it not for the occasional slow turning of her fragile head revealing that needle beak.

In this moment she is not striving. No flying or trying. Just being.

Is every creature given the gift of pause? Is every living thing led to rest, if under the Creator's view alone?

I wake up early to steal a handful of quiet moments. There is email to check, a work task to attend to, and a Bible study lesson to complete for an upcoming meeting. I feel pressed on all sides and need productivity to triumph.

I look up again from my messy desk, window facing west, and my wire friend is gone. But I gaze upon her empty spot and know—a deep knowing that I deeply need to know—that she is cared for as part of God's precious creation. She is carried in the constant motion that will consume the remainder of her heart-wildly-beating, wings-frantically-fluttering day.

Her rest may be seldom. Hidden. But she is not unseen.

And I claim the truth again: It is worth putting aside my desire to be productive in order to take up the pen of paying attention.

A Moment to Breathe . . .

Look outside. Or look up. Notice a bird nearby, sitting on
a branch or wire, and find a seat yourself. Take a deep
breath and exhale, thanking God for the gift of rest.

It's a Bad Day, Not a Bad Life

BY KRISTEN WELCH

A human is like a breath; his days are like
a passing shadow. PSALM 144:4

I GAVE IN TO temptation and colored my hair right before bed. And then at 11:00 p.m. I washed my hair thirty-seven times because hair color called *Espresso* is named that for a reason. *Why are people like me allowed to use chemicals?* I fell into bed with my damaged pride and slept fitfully. When the alarm sounded the next morning for church, I was still in a bad hair mood with a tingly scalp, a stiff neck, and a gone-to-bed-too-late hangover. I went back to sleep. Yes, I skipped church because of hair. Please, don't judge.

The house was sluggish until after noon, our regular routine turned on its side. What started out as a simple "don't do that" to one of my kids ended up in a full-blown tantrum. Just like that, our day went from lazy Sunday to the end times. While my husband and I retreated to our bedroom to try and get on the same page, I could hear my kids arguing in the other room. The tension in our house was thick. I longed for a do-over, and I'm not just talking about my hair.

"Can we just pray together?" I asked my husband with tears right on the edge of spilling over. And what I really meant was . . . *Can my family just pray with me, for me?* We piled up on our bed, too many legs and arms and too little space and we held hands. It was an awkward *Little House on the Prairie* moment for sure. But no one pulled away or complained. Our kids wanted a do-over as much as we did.

Our youngest asked if she could pray first. And then my husband led us in a simple prayer. I couldn't hold my tears then because this is what I needed. My teen daughter rubbed my hand when she saw my tears and whispered, "It's okay, Mom." I nodded. Because now it was.

A Moment to Breathe . . .

Give yourself permission to have a do-over. On your couch or your bed or wherever, open your hands and bow your head and invite God into your day, asking Him for a fresh start.

The Difference between Asking and Doing

BY ROBIN DANCE

*And let us watch out for one another to provoke
love and good works.* HEBREWS 10:24

TIMING FOR A GIRLS' weekend couldn't have been more perfect. I'd been home from Germany only four weeks, and this group picked up right where we left off. Soon enough, conversation swirled in an easy-flowing meander. They wanted to know about Germany, so I gave a condensed, practiced response. But one of my girlfriends wanted to know more, not about Germany, but about me. Her eyes penetrated mine as she took hold of my heart and asked, "How are you doing with all the changes you've gone through the past year? How's your heart doing?"

I hadn't seen it coming. Buoyed by laughter and connection and stories, sitting on that bedroom floor with the wall holding me up, I didn't realize my guard was completely down. I shook my head slowly, unable to speak, tears burning my throat and stinging my eyes, my own body betraying me . . . revealing secret hurts. Relational void, disappointment, rejection, loss.

Her question was a match lighting a soggy fuse, and it didn't do me a bit of good to try to stop those blasted waterworks. "Come right here," she said, patting an empty spot on the bed next to her. "We're gonna pray for you." I shook my head again and whispered *I can't* and she gently insisted, "Yes you can, right here." (Pat. Pat. Pat.)

All the others gathered round and close. They touched me with their hands and their hearts and their words. They pressed blessing and understanding and healing deep into the marrow. How did they know exactly what to pray? I hadn't given them details, but in the beautiful, mysterious ways of God, He led them through the veins of my ache and ministered love through these heart sisters.

A Moment to Breathe . . .

Instead of saying, "I'll pray for you," become the kind of friend who stops to pray—right then! You don't need to know all the details. God knows. Just bring your friend into His presence and pray.

That Which We May Not Know

BY LISA WHITTLE

For we are his workmanship, created in Christ Jesus for good works, which God prepared ahead of time for us to do. EPHESIANS 2:10

ONE HOT HOUSTON NIGHT, a young father stood up from his padded pew to beg for prayers for his daughter. She was newly born, but far from thriving. The middle soft spot of her cranium was closed, and the doctors said his baby needed immediate neurosurgery plus two blood transfusions. The man carried this burden into a crowded gathering of believers on a Wednesday night. Church, they called it. And this was a night of prayer.

It didn't matter that this young father was a preacher himself. He traveled with Jesus' name on his lips, but on this night, that was not his role. He was, instead, silent with others on every side . . . broken in his heart . . . desperate to take care of his family . . . needing to believe his God would answer prayer.

He didn't know the man with hair far grayer and a wallet far fatter sitting in the crowd. He didn't know that man would hear his request and sense a stirring in his spirit to help a young father in need. And so it happened, that life in a secondhand sense, was given to me. I was that baby. Because in the sovereignty that can only be God, the man with the gray hair and fat wallet paid for my surgery. He was a man I would never get to meet.

This piece of my true-life story is a reminder that there are things we'll never know. We may never know the heart behind the words, the struggle behind the request, the private story that lives behind the eyes of the person. But today let's pause to honor those who respond without knowing. Let's give glory to the God who does see everything and works to bring the two together. For we may never know the life we can forever change.

A Moment to Breathe . . .

Ask God if there is someone in your community—perhaps even someone you don't know—who has a specific need you could meet. Then look throughout the day for a door of possibility.

Stepping Out of the Way

BY RENEE SWOPE

*I called to the LORD in my distress, and I cried to my
God for help. From his temple he heard my voice,
and my cry to him reached his ears.* PSALM 18:6

ONE EVENING AFTER AN intense "discussion," my husband told
me no matter what he did or how hard he tried, it was never enough
for me. He was right. I had a bad habit of finding fault with him as
a husband and as a dad. But when he implied I was impossible to
please . . . well, that sent my already-out-of-control emotions reeling.

I grabbed my coat and stormed out the front door. Hot tears
streamed down my cheeks as I replayed our conversation in my
head. Determined to figure out what J. J.'s problem was and get
Jesus to fix him, I started filing complaints against my husband
in what you might call a prayer. And I finally heard myself—all
the ugliness, all the anger. That's when I realized I needed help.
I needed God to help me figure out—after seven years of a happy
marriage—how we had gotten to this ugly place.

Instead of just crying, I found myself crying out to God for help.
When I stopped talking and started listening, I sensed God showing
me how I wanted J. J. to make up for all the ways my dad had
fallen short. Years as a child in a broken home with a broken heart
led to a significant loss and deep disappointment. Yet, I had never
grieved the happily-ever-after I longed for but didn't have.

My unfulfilled hopes had become bitter expectations, and I
became controlling and critical. Instead of expecting my husband
to make up for my losses, I needed to cry out to God with my hurts
and call on Him for help. As I continued to process what had happened in my childhood and how it affected my marriage, I learned
to ask God for help through each step of my healing journey. It took
time, prayer, and courage, but God was so very present and able to
help me, eventually, get to the other side.

A Moment to Breathe . . .

*Do a quick "analysis of expectations" in your closest
relationships. Those places in your heart, where a
disappointment would likely turn into resentment. Ask the
Lord to help you release those expectations today.*

The Good News

BY JENNIFER DUKES LEE

Then they said to each other, "We're not doing what is right. Today is a day of good news. If we are silent and wait until morning light, our punishment will catch up with us. So let's go tell the king's household." 2 KINGS 7:9

THE FIRST TIME THE gospel made sense to me wasn't the day the guy on the street corner handed me a tract. It was the day when a dear friend brought me a latte, a listening ear, and one of those small, personalized packs of facial tissues. I needed my friend that day. Life was running off the rails with my sixty-hour work weeks and my severe avoidance of anything spiritual. I had called my friend, overwhelmed with exhaustion. I clearly needed Jesus in my life, but I didn't know it yet.

She knew. So she did what friends do. She showed up. I don't remember exactly what she said about Jesus, but when she handed me those tissues, my heart instinctively knew that I needed what she had: Jesus Christ.

Years later, I ran across a story in 2 Kings 7, where lepers had discovered a deserted camp with lots of food, silver, gold, and clothing. At first, the lepers kept the good news to themselves. But then they remembered that others were starving. They couldn't keep the news to themselves so they went back and told the others. That's what my friend did for me. She knew where the feast was, so she gently led me to that feast. She couldn't keep it to herself.

This is one of the most important, joyous, and scary callings we have—to bring the Good News to weary friends. That day, my friend could have remained silent out of fear. But in her own way, with a frothy coffee from the corner shop, she brought hope to my doorstep. I'll never be the same.

A Moment to Breathe . . .

If you have a friend going through a hard time, reach out. You don't have to have all the answers, or know all the right Bible verses. Your friend simply needs to know you're there for her.

For the Love of God and Place

BY MARLENA GRAVES

"Pursue the well-being of the city I have deported you to. Pray to the LORD on its behalf, for when it thrives, you will thrive." JEREMIAH 29:7

NOT HERE. I DIDN'T want to be here. I wanted home. I wanted my friends and community back. I wanted to return to the way things were before people wrecked both our community and workplace. I wanted it to be the way it was before whole departments vanished, before the friends and coworkers my husband and I so dearly loved were forced to move away—before we too were forced to move away.

I sat on the couch and gazed out the window as portions of Psalm 137 floated around inside of me, "By the rivers of Babylon—there we sat down and wept when we remembered Zion. . . . How can we sing the LORD's song on foreign soil?" (Ps. 137:1, 4). I was a foreigner here, weeping—with no friends, no church, and no community when I needed them most.

Not only did I have to work to forgive those who had wrecked our community, I had to do it while wounded and left for dead. How does one escape such profound sadness and creeping bitterness? Slowly and painfully.

Little by little I forced my gaze off of myself and onto Jesus. I trained my eyes on Jeremiah 29:7: "Pursue the well-being of the city I have deported you to. Pray to the LORD on its behalf, for when it thrives, you will thrive." I feebly clung to this verse, trusting I'd eventually move through my grief as I sought this city's welfare.

Perhaps if it were up to you, you wouldn't be where you are today. Maybe you feel unknown, alone, and out of context. I understand. Yet while you're here, why not pray for friends to come along and ask the Lord how you can seek welfare of this place? Soon you'll find your welfare is wrapped up in the welfare of the people who are right around you, right here.

A Moment to Breathe . . .

Pray for the welfare of your town or city. Learn about the things your city is doing and ask God to show you how you might participate in the life of the city you live in.

The Gifting and Lifting of Grief

BY CHRISTIE PURIFOY

Give thanks to the LORD, call on his name; proclaim his deeds among the peoples. Sing to him, sing praise to him; tell about all his wondrous works! PSALM 105:1–2

I INDULGE IN SHOUTING some days, but mostly I respond by retreating into silence. When my children explode over cracked Legos and the last Popsicle, I struggle to stay with them in the noise. I want to slip away, to climb the stairs, to sit in the curve of the bow window noticing yellow leaves on the lawn outside.

As the world grows louder, I grow quieter. Sometimes this feels like wisdom, but I know it is also weakness. It requires strength to share our stories. To risk being misunderstood. It requires faith to tell small stories. To believe that what seems to be inadequate is of value.

When my fourth child was born, my body struggled to make milk for her. The hormonal peaks and valleys of that process seemed to switch a lever in my brain. I became depressed. I had so many reasons to be happy, but depression sucked all emotion from my mind and filled the emptiness with anxiety. I can remember sitting in my comfortable, soft rocking chair, holding my baby, and trying to remember why I had once cared about babies or repairing old farmhouses or ordering seeds for the spring garden or anything at all. I could no longer remember why it mattered if any of us ever got out of bed.

When I stopped trying to nurse my baby, and the last of my milk dried up, the depression lifted. A severe mercy. It meant that I knew happiness again. It meant that I knew sadness again. Healing looked like a renewed capacity for both joy and sorrow. When I read the words from Psalm 105, I remember what happened to me after my daughter's birth and that I have a song of praise. I tell Him thanks, for healing me enough to grieve.

A Moment to Breathe . . .

Tell a small story today—a story from a moment in time when the days seemed bleak, but then there was hope, and you learned to give thanks.

When Someone Hits the Pause Button on Your Life

BY KRISTEN STRONG

And when the chief Shepherd appears, you will receive the unfading crown of glory. 1 PETER 5:4

FOUR YEARS AGO THIS week, my daughter underwent surgery on her spine to repair a broken neck. My biggest question at the time was if the pediatric neurosurgeon would be able to correct her problem—a malformation of her second vertebrae—the more secure way or the less secure way. The more secure way—inserting a pin into the bone on each side of her vertebrae—would allow her to wear a neck brace post-op. But if her bones were too small and he had to use a less sturdy means of treating her, she would have to wear a halo. A halo is more restrictive; a type of headgear that attaches to the forehead through four pins and keeps the head and neck completely and totally still. Obviously, we prayed our girl would be able to wear the neck brace rather than the halo.

The neurosurgeon said a nurse would call us in the waiting room just as soon as he knew the viable option. So my husband and I sat in the waiting room, fidgeting and reading the same paragraphs of magazine articles over and over. That morning felt like a held breath, like someone hit the pause button on our lives. Finally the call came. The nurse told us, that by the tiniest of margins, the doctor was able to insert a pin on one side, so our girl could wear the neck brace during recovery.

When I think back to this time, the waiting wasn't long in the grand scheme of things. Just two or three hours. Heaven knows we've waited longer for other scary things, and I don't doubt you have too. Sometimes those times of waiting have ended favorably, and sometimes they haven't. But they have all ended. And if they haven't yet, they will one day, with a crown of unfading glory. It's a promise.

A Moment to Breathe . . .

When you find yourself holding your breath, know you're not alone, and these days will not last. Hope is the reason we keep going, keep trusting, keep believing, and yes, keep breathing.

To Work Quietly with My Hands

BY EMILY P. FREEMAN

*L ORD, my heart is not proud; my eyes are not haughty. I do
not get involved with things too great or too wondrous for me.
Instead, I have calmed and quieted my soul.* PSALM 131:1–2

I'M LEARNING TO CROCHET. Is that dorky? I have a feeling what
the hipsters do with yarn these days is knit. But I've heard that
takes two needles, which is completely intimidating. So for now,
it's crochet. I took a class with my daughters at a local craft store,
and after three hours we learned one stitch—if that's even what
you call it. We make rows in a line, turn, and make another line. It's
too narrow for a blanket, too wide for a scarf, and it doesn't matter
anyway because I don't know how to read a pattern or do anything,
really. I want it to be relaxing.

I like the idea of staying a beginner. I like moving my hands in
a predictable rhythm to make nothing in particular except maybe
some space for my soul to breathe. I like the absence of pressure,
the complete lack of temptation to show off or get arrogant. This
week, as I imperfectly practice this new craft, I'm discovering
the spiritual discipline hidden beneath the uneven rows of yarn.
Sometimes I need to engage in an activity for the single purpose of
disengaging from productivity.

There's an invisible world that lives inside our bodies, the inner
world of the soul. And this inner world needs our attention, but it
doesn't respond to programs, agendas, or hustle. The soul responds
to space, silence, and Jesus.

I'm discovering Christ in ordinary moments . . . both the ones
where I feel capable and the ones where I am out of my element.
I'm discovering Him, in the visible world I can see and the invisible one that lives within me. And sometimes I need to actively do
things I'm not good at in order to remember how desperately I need
Him. Sometimes I need to work quietly with my hands in order to
settle my soul.

A Moment to Breathe . . .

*What activity helps you cease the demands of productivity?
Set aside some time today to work quietly with your
hands, without the demand of being productive.*

Practicing True Hospitality

BY ANNA RENDELL

Be hospitable to one another without complaining. 1 PETER 4:9

LAST NIGHT WE HAD friends over to stay with us. We live near the airport and they had a morning flight, so it was a great excuse for a sleepover. We sat in the kitchen, talked until midnight, and shared crackers right out of the bag. Their room had clean sheets—and an avalanche behind the closet door. A package delivered earlier that day remained smack-dab in the middle of the kitchen floor. The dirty dishes were overflowing, and I wasn't even home when they arrived!

A couple weeks earlier I heard someone say, "True hospitality is when your guests leave your home feeling better about themselves, not feeling better about you." These words hit my heart. Too often I'm a hot mess before guests arrive. I whirl around the house, scrubbing and cleaning and arranging. I plan the meal and make a time chart so things are ready upon their arrival. I snap at my husband and plunk the kids in front of the TV so they're not in my way. But not this time.

The condition of my house was less than ideal, but it was our everyday. We were in the middle of a busy week, and they stepped right into the thick of it. The thing is, I didn't bat an eyelash and neither did they. The mess didn't matter because in that moment, being together mattered more. This is how I know that something is softening in me. That thing that would normally drive me to run myself ragged cleaning before company came? It's slowly dissolving.

Because if friends don't feel welcome in our homes, they won't feel welcome in our hearts. I'm releasing my too-high expectations and carefully plotted menus. And I'm releasing my family from the pressure cooker I've so often placed them in as we prepare for guests. By letting go of those things, my heart feels ready to receive, and that opens the door to true hospitality.

A Moment to Breathe . . .

Ask yourself the one thing you'd like to have "ready" when company comes over. Maybe it's an extra set of clean sheets folded and ready. Do that one thing and then release all the other expectations.

Seeing the Greatness of Who He Is

BY NASREEN FYNEWEVER

But ask the animals, and they will instruct you; ask the birds of the sky, and they will tell you. Or speak to the earth, and it will instruct you; let the fish of the sea inform you. Which of all these does not know that the hand of the LORD has done this? The life of every living thing is in his hand, as well as the breath of all mankind. JOB 12:7–10

BE STILL, I TOLD myself. The heavens were pausing the scurry of this world and the busy of the day. Slices of sunshine found their way through the branches to kiss the path in front of me. I knew at once that time in His creation would refill my soul.

I took a deep breath of air. Spring was still a few weeks away, but nature was clamoring to find expression for her Creator. Swaths of light danced across the earth while the whisper of the wind invited birds to sing. Leaves left behind from another season moved to brush against the dormant grass.

I paused to take it in. Yet my breathing began to shallow as my mind focused on to-do lists and the voices declaring I was not enough. Clouds moved in concert with the earth and soon shadows fell across my surroundings. My spirit chilled a bit at the invitation to be self-absorbed amidst His glory. I felt ashamed for losing my view of His splendor.

As I turned to walk home, I noticed two deer in the woods nearby. Together they walked gracefully until one froze as my shuffle caused a startle. The front deer slowed cautiously, but did not stop. Surveying the surroundings, the halted deer followed in step and joined the increasing scamper pace of the one who led.

This allowed my heart to skirt away from its inward focus. My God will lead me. I will freeze and falter, but just as the deer found their way, I will also be led toward safety and life. He wraps me in the lessons of skies and the animals, for they will display how great He is. My heart is learning to see Him. He will teach me to trust. Let everything that has breath and beauty testify.

A Moment to Breathe . . .

A quiet walk outside. A breath of fresh air. A singing bird nearby. Enjoy the beauty of God's creation this day. See how the wonders of the world He created testify to the greatness of who He is.

Against All Odds

BY RACHEL ANNE RIDGE

The wilderness and the dry land will be glad; the desert will rejoice and blossom like a wildflower. ISAIAH 35:1

I PLANTED IT MORE than a decade ago—my lavender plant in a four-inch pot that held a tiny dream. I was so hopeful back then. I'd moved to the country from our suburban neighborhood and imagined that someday I'd have a beautiful lavender farm. I could just see it: row after row of fragrant purple mounds that would be part of our new life and business. I knew it wouldn't be easy. People told me it didn't have a chance. But I chopped the rocky soil and planted the seed anyway.

Then life got tough. The economy tanked and I worked hard to make ends meet. At times the stress made my chest hurt and I lost sleep. I abandoned the lavender farm dream and went into survival mode. The little plant was forgotten in the years that followed, but somehow it hung on through blistering heat, record-setting drought, ice storms, and torrential rains. Every now and then I'd pass by it and see the small mound of silvery green foliage and marvel at its tenacity. Though alive, its growth was stunted by both the elements and my lack of care.

Not once did it flower. It just *survived*—as though its strength was used up simply to stay alive, and there wasn't a single drop left over for something as frivolous as a bloom. I understood, only too well. Sometimes, just *staying alive* is the best we can do. Surviving is victory. And it is victory enough.

Then one morning, my breath escaped in an awestruck sigh. Fresh purple blooms floated above the green mound like a tiara. The warm breeze made them dance, tethered on their stems lest they frolic away. I sank down in front of it and slowly rubbed the colorful florets between my fingers. The distinctive scent immediately permeated the air and lingered on my skin, and I had to smile. "Just look at you. You made it."

A Moment to Breathe . . .

Whatever season you find yourself in today, hold to the promise that by His grace there will come a day when you will blossom into all the beauty He has prepared for you. It's a promise.

When You Need to Step Away

BY KRIS CAMEALY

*The one who lives under the protection of the Most High
dwells in the shadow of the Almighty.* PSALM 91:1

THE OTHER DAY I told my friend, "Life is too short to do something that drains your soul." This bit of truth rolled off my tongue easily that day because, in that moment, I was deep in the midst of a social media break. A growing restlessness in my soul, coupled with the prompting of the Holy Spirit, whispered to my heart that I needed to pull way back from the unending chatter of the Internet. After trying to refill my tank with what a thousand of my closest "friends" had to say, God stepped in and invited me into a secret space—a sacred space, alone. With Him.

"It's like stepping into God's office to dump out all of my emotional garbage and let Him help me sort it," I told my friend. We laughed about the visual, but one of the struggles I often wrestle with is my own eagerness to share with others what God is doing in my heart, in those private moments. When I make this mistake, I stop focusing on God, and start looking around at others. I start listening to their stories, quickly forgetting that just hours before, God was working out some of the kinks in my own.

This time, however, I stepped fully and quietly into that secret place with Him and sat there in my mess and endured the month-long unwinding of a great many knots in my heart. Instead of anxiety about stepping away, I experienced relief. I came to God dirt-dry and found revival in His presence alone.

We are called to tell of His goodness and grace to all who will listen. But also we are called to the quiet, tucked-away place alone with Him, where the uncomfortable-but-necessary healing and growing can happen, away from the chatter and peering eyes of the waiting room. Alone with the Almighty, I tasted the sweetness of grace that could not—and cannot—be experienced anywhere else.

A Moment to Breathe . . .

*Step into that secret place with God, to a season of
hushed fellowship with God. Later, you can tell others
of the goodness He has done for you there.*

Welcome In

BY LORI HARRIS

"When you host a banquet, invite those who are poor, maimed, lame, or blind. And you will be blessed, because they cannot repay you; for you will be repaid at the resurrection of the righteous." LUKE 14:13–14

IF YOU WERE TO drive by my house, you'd likely take a second glance at all the life whirling around in the middle of what some would call the badlands. A dozen boys are shooting hoops in the side yard while three girls are eating animal crackers and drinking lemonade at the picnic table in the front yard. Two boys are swinging from the horse swing dangling from the oak tree while four more jump on the trampoline. My second oldest is in the kitchen baking brownies to share when the animal crackers are gone.

Our family lives in an impoverished part of town where mamas work odd jobs and daddies are absent from homes and hunger is as real as the drugs being pushed down the street. You could probably call our home a community center because our home is the hub of neighborhood activity. The yard and everything in it belongs to every one of us and every one of us comes to the table as equally needy family members.

But this gathering around the table as a family didn't happen overnight. It has taken five years of living among those on the margins of life and intentionally choosing to invite the poor, the addict, and the abused to our table. It has taken five years of standing in a lowly place in our city for us to find our place here. And it has taken five years of continually opening our hands wide enough to let the superabundance of kingdom resources flow through our fingers for God to remind us that we simply get to steward what He graciously gives us.

Jesus promises that our hospitality to the poor will be repaid at the resurrection of the righteous.

But friends, we can reap the blessings now. Let's open our homes and invite the poor to our tables.

A Moment to Breathe . . .

It doesn't have to be fancy or formal. Just an open door. A friendly wave. And an invitation to come in. Let's invite someone into our lives today and share a simple meal around a table together.

The Things We Say Yes To

BY AMBER C. HAINES

"But let your 'yes' mean 'yes,' and your 'no' mean 'no.'
Anything more than this is from the evil one." MATTHEW 5:37

I SAID YES TO a little green house with a big garden and two rows of fruit trees. It's like a mansion if your standard were teeny tiny houses. There's a clothesline here, and the breeze beneath my shade trees is a gentle one. We've been waiting for a gentle time. We've been waiting for our own space and for silence. We just didn't know how to find it until I learned how many no's it takes to make a yes.

I said yes to quiet. The drive into town is longer than I'm used to. I drive in silence. I come home and tell the boys to read. I sit beneath the ceiling fan or on the patio. I reach for my cell phone and jerk my hand back quickly. I sit and watch. Doves blow up from the harvested corn. The pears are beginning to fall.

These are little things that remind me that I am small: the silence and then the burst of insanely loud laughter and wrestling, a dish-stacked kitchen with no dishwasher, a hydrangea with heavy laid-down heads, four hall drawers to fit what used to go in an entire room. This one yes has taken at least a thousand no's. Only half my clothes fit in the closet. Half is all I needed. When half was all I had, it was all I wanted.

When we said yes to scaling, slowing, and quieting down, it wasn't really saying yes to less work. We said yes to better work. I said yes to picking squash and researching how to harvest hazel-nuts. These are things I love. I said yes to the work of closeness, the children always within the reach of a whisper.

These are little things we'll look back and remember. I said yes to living small. I said yes to what I call a beautiful life, and it surprises me. Work boots and scrub-gloves on, I can hear God in this place.

A Moment to Breathe . . .

Time for a little math. How many good no's will it take to make one great yes? Start with one. Perhaps say no to answering emails after 5:00, or to TV past 11:00 on a weekday.

A Sympathetic Heart

BY DAWN CAMP

For we do not have a high priest who is unable to sympathize with our weaknesses, but one who has been tempted in every way as we are, yet without sin. HEBREWS 4:15

MY GREAT-AUNT MAYME HAD an uncanny ability to empathize with children. When my kids did things that made me crazy, Aunt Mayme smiled in the face of my exasperation and reminisced about her own childhood. She not only remembered things she did as a child, but also how it felt. She could relate to my children in ways that set her apart from my ability as their mother. Although she lived for nearly ninety-four years, Aunt Mayme retained the ability to see the world through a child's eyes.

I learned that firsthand knowledge of pain grows empathy. Years ago we visited out-of-state family with our new baby boy, our second child. Another family member was there who had recently miscarried. I knew she was happy for us, but I also realized that being around our son reminded her of the baby she lost. As much as I wanted to comfort her, I didn't know how, so I remained silent and missed the chance.

The next year I experienced a miscarriage. I still remember the range of emotions I felt: overwhelming sadness, followed by guilt over the lack of excitement I experienced when I found out I was pregnant (our baby had just turned one), and finally anger. Never again have I remained silent when a woman I know miscarries a child. Not only can I sympathize, I can empathize. I know what to expect in the days and weeks following a miscarriage and how a television commercial for baby food can hit you like a punch in the gut.

Sympathy mingled with firsthand knowledge is a powerful combination. When we empathize, we can act with compassion, speak with wisdom, and listen with understanding. The lessons we learn in hard times can become holy gifts to other women, like beauty raised from ashes.

A Moment to Breathe . . .

Ask God to expand your heart for others—to mourn when others mourn, and rejoice when others rejoice. Be the kind of friend who truly empathizes with others.

A New Morning Routine

BY STEPHANIE BRYANT

*"Sacrifice a thank offering to God, and pay your vows
to the Most High. Call on me in a day of trouble; I will
rescue you, and you will honor me."* PSALM 50:14–15

MY BREATH FOGS UP the mirror as I swipe another coat of mascara on my lashes. *Thank You that my skin isn't broken out today.* I step back to examine my attempt at dreamy eyes. *Thank You that my hair doesn't look strange, even with all the humidity. Thank You for my dear friends. Thank You for sending them my way. I need each of them and You knew that.* God heard my prayers to send me real friends.

I check my phone for the time. *Thank You for sound sleep last night with no bad dreams. And the opportunity to serve You today. Oh, and that new opportunity that You brought out of the blue. That was amazing. I'm blown away by Your provision. Thank You, Lord.*

My morning routine has changed. Not with a new loofah or hairbrush, but with how I dress my mind. Instead of waking up asking for things, nervous about the day, trying to control my circumstances with rapid gunfire prayers toward heaven, I turn my heart toward grateful. I acknowledge the small that can break my day or make my attitude.

My goal is simple. To give God glory. But sometimes I make it more complicated than it needs to be. I love when He reveals to me how to do the desire of my heart. The one He planted there long ago. Not blood or sweat or try-hard sacrifice, but thankfulness. A thankful heart for the big, and most definitely the very small. That's all Jesus wants from me.

A Moment to Breathe . . .

*Give Him glory, friend. Begin a new morning routine, starting
right now, no matter what time of day it is. Share a sacrifice
of thankfulness to God. Tell Him what you're thankful for.*

Evidence of Beauty

BY ELISE HURD

A joyful heart makes a face cheerful, but a sad heart produces a broken spirit. A discerning mind seeks knowledge. PROVERBS 15:13–14

I THINK THEY WERE surprised at my response. After all, I am a makeup artist and hair stylist. The bride and her bridesmaids had been saying for a good half-hour how "mouth parentheses" and crow's feet around the eyes are so ugly, and since we have medical means to "erase" those signs of aging, it only made sense to use them. Then they asked me, "Don't you think so, too?"

I smiled, my own lines showing, "Well, I guess I don't have a traditional American view on wrinkles or beauty due to my mom. The main thing I remember about her is how she was always smiling at me and my siblings. She told me once that she read about the importance of smiling at your kids. It was important for kids to see the smile on your face when they entered the room to communicate that you were happy to see them, that you love them, and treasure their presence. I have always felt that from her, and when I think of her face, I think of her smiling at me. It would have been really sad for me if she had done something to erase all the beautiful evidence of her love for me."

The silence was full of teary memories, and the mother of the bride's smile settled softly in its familiar lines.

"And," I added honestly, "I've begun noticing that expression lines have started on my face, too, and it is very strange. But I pray that when my daughters think about my face toward them, they will mainly remember me smiling at them. And I plan on keeping the evidence. I have said it countless times: Beautiful is from the inside. When I do makeup and style hair, I'm just putting an occasion-appropriate personalized frame on the masterpiece that you already are."

A Moment to Breathe . . .

For real beauty, the kind that can't be bought, but that can be applied right now, remove years of soul-wrinkles, and smile at everyone you meet today. They'll notice and they'll remember.

From East to West

BY STACEY THACKER

As far as the east is from the west, so far has he removed our transgressions from us. PSALM 103:12

THE LOOK ON THEIR faces said it all. I was mad and they knew it. I couldn't get to a safe haven fast enough. But I made my way to the restroom a few feet away from where my undoing took place. I shut the door and slid down to the floor. Broken. Hot tears streamed down my face, "Lord, what is the matter with me?" Slowly it all poured out, every hurt feeling and overreaction. Jesus, patient as ever, received every last drop of my confession and whispered: *Loved, My daughter.*

Maybe you can relate. You might buy into the fact that you are loved. You might even begin to see that you are liked. You might even, just for a minute or two think: *Sure, I can put a couple of great days back-to-back, and I'm not so bad.*

But then, it happens. Like me, you have one of those no-good, awful, horrible bad days. And you blow it. You yell at your kids. Or maybe you lie to a friend or speak hurtfulness to your spouse. You judge. Or worse. And in the midst of it, you are shocked. Embarrassed. Angry. You don't like you right now. So you withdraw and hide in your own heart and hope and pray no one notices.

But Jesus does. And while you are swimming in the sea of your own guilt and shame, He is tenderly speaking truth from His Word to your heart: *I've removed your sin as far as the east is from the west. It is gone. I carried it away. So there would be nothing between us.* And somewhere in the middle of the mess, you start to believe it.

Is it like that for you? It can be. He wants you to know your sin is not greater than His power of forgiveness. You could try to measure it, but East to West will get you every time.

A Moment to Breathe . . .

God's forgiveness is real and available, every time. Just imagine it. How far the east is from the west. That's how far He has removed your sin from you.

Growing Confident

BY FRANCIE WINSLOW

Do not fear, for I am with you; do not be afraid,
for I am your God. ISAIAH 41:10

DURING A FABULOUS LUNCH with a dear friend, the light-heartedness of our time together changed when a sticky topic of conversation came up. Immediately, I felt the atmosphere shift with an undertone of tension. When I asked if she was okay, she said, "Of course!" with a tender smile. But on her drive home from lunch, she called to talk about how she was really doing and that, indeed, our conversation had hit an "insecurity button" in her life. She was gracious, humble, loving, and open. She was open to God's healing in her life and open to walking in true confidence. And her phone call resulted in a newfound freedom in our friendship.

In similar situations, there have been times when, instead of being real, I chose to say, "I'm fine," when really I was dying inside. Maybe I was too scared to be honest. Or maybe I wasn't sure how to express the insecurity I felt. When my friend called to clear things up with me (and I love her for that!), she set me on the path to more freedom in ways she didn't even know.

Growing into a woman of true confidence means we'll risk doing real life with real people—trusting God to build something beautiful in the midst of our mess and asking Him to change us and make us more gracious, humble, loving, and open.

We were created to pursue true confidence together. I know from experience that it's hard to find these kinds of friends. Friends who are trustworthy, safe, and caring. Friends who love you and want the very best for you and your family. It's so much better to do life with people, than alone. It's what we were made for and what we all crave. When we pursue wholeness in Christ, it paves the way for others to follow and find freedom for themselves. That's what my friend did for me.

A Moment to Breathe . . .

Be intentional today to connect on a heart level
with a friend you trust. Be the kind of friend who
answers honestly when you're really not fine.

DAY 32

When God Says No

BY KELLY BALARIE

*But as it is written, "What no eye has seen, no ear has heard,
and no human heart has conceived—God has prepared
these things for those who love him."* 1 CORINTHIANS 2:9

I WAS EXCITED FOR this big opportunity. I was going to be used by God for something magnificent, something meaningful. I could feel it. I could see it. And I could almost smell it . . . until, it happened. The phone rang and I heard, "There has been a change of plans." Have you ever received one of those calls? The type of call that takes away the good you were supposed to unwrap, hold, and then jump up and down over?

There was another woman, and I was asked to hand over the near once-in-a-lifetime dream. I didn't want to, but I relented. Nearly every part of me felt like kicking and screaming, but the other part of me trusted God would use this to speak to my heart. So I listened. And remembered the words of 1 Corinthians 2:9. We cannot fathom the things God has prepared for those who love Him. God loves me. God also loves her. He has plans for us both.

It's in moments like these we have to choose. We can choose to wallow in the idea of limited opportunity or we can choose to see the unlimited God we follow.

Not too long after I was passed over, I got word about the other woman. She was diagnosed with severe cancer. She noted how vital and encouraging this special event was in her life. How God had carved it out just for her soul. How others had blessed her in a way she would never forget.

To her, it was a cherished honor she could hold through hard times. She received her "something magnificent, something meaningful," but the thing is—so did I. He made my sacrifice count for her. And that is worth something.

A Moment to Breathe . . .

*Picture the face of a friend who received something you really,
really wanted. Ask God to fill your heart with gladness for her.
Then send her a note, telling her how happy you are for her.*

Small Home Hospitality

BY ANN SWINDELL

Share with the saints in their needs;
pursue hospitality. ROMANS 12:13

WE HAVE A SMALL home—a split-level condo with two bedrooms and a galley kitchen that never has enough counter space. In most places in the world, our home would be considered normal, perhaps even large. But here in affluent suburbia, our square footage is, comparatively, on the compact end of things. Any time we have more than a handful of people over, our guests sit on the stairs when the couches and chairs are full.

A couple of years ago we hosted a small group that grew to nearly thirty people. Before we were able to raise up new leaders for the group to split it into two, I prayed that God would literally make physical space for every person that came into our house. And God did. Yes, things were tight. Each stair doubled as a seat and many people sat on the floor. It was hot, even when the air conditioning was blowing as high as we could set it, and there was no real sense of personal space.

But we read the Bible together and sang together and prayed together, and people kept coming back—and bringing friends. And you know what? No one complained about having to sit on a stair rather than a seat. No one told us they thought our home was hindering what God was doing. That's when I got over apologizing for our home. That's when I stopped letting my hospitality button get pushed by what we didn't have and what I couldn't control.

I realized that if God could fit thirty people into our little house and that all those squished people could encounter His truth and His goodness when we were together, the size of our home didn't matter. It wasn't holding Him back. So until God moves us, this home is the one we have, and I will be grateful for it.

A Moment to Breathe . . .

Create a space, however small, where you can invite
a friend over. Into your home. Rediscover hospitality
outside the definitions we find on HGTV.

Your Gifts Revealed

BY KENDRA TILLMAN

He reveals the deep and hidden things . . . DANIEL 2:22

SEVERAL YEARS AGO I enrolled in a two-year program offered at our church for any member with an entrepreneurial spirit. The second year of the program included a Discovering Your Purpose class. The primary method for discovering your purpose in that class was learning about the spiritual gifts described in Romans 12. Through reading, instruction, and my own observations, I identified with the gift of teaching. A teacher loves to gather and share information with others, but there's always the potential of coming across as know-it-alls.

After our instructor explained this, I hesitantly raised my hand and said, "I'm a teacher who loves to motivate others, but I try hard to not come across as a know-it-all. I learned a long time ago how to keep my mouth shut." Her response was not at all what I expected.

Her first response was a question, "What happened?" She followed that up with another question, "Who squashed your gift?"

Immediately, the Holy Spirit brought to mind a memory from around the third grade. I was an excellent student academically, but I usually received a poor grade in "Conduct" because I could not stop talking. The result: I learned at the age of eight that in order to continue to be seen as good, I needed to keep my mouth shut. By the end of the school year, my "Conduct" grade improved. I didn't learn how to harness my gift, I only learned to suppress it.

Decades later I realized that my elementary experience was holding me back from the plans God had for me in the present. Only God could have revealed this to me and it has forever changed me. You also may have untapped gifts inside you, because of a well-meaning teacher, friend, or even a family member. Like Daniel, don't hesitate to ask God to reveal your gifts so that you may fully live out His purpose for your life and give Him praise for what He reveals.

A Moment to Breathe . . .

Name the passion that's a fire in your bones and consider one simple way you can express that gift today.

The Gift of Our Words

BY KAYLA AIMEE

A word spoken at the right time is like gold
apples in silver settings. PROVERBS 25:11

AT THE GROCERY STORE, my five-year-old was in full-on extrovert mode. She was literally dancing through the aisles. She, my Scarlette, does not walk. She hops and bops.

It was one of those days when I was exhausted. I had been up with the baby all night, and I was doing my level best to stay patient as I reminded Scarlette again to be mindful of other people who did not view the produce aisle as their personal stage.

As I perused the strawberries, someone tapped me on the shoulder and I turned to see an elderly woman with coiffed white hair smiling at me. We struck up a conversation and she absentmindedly stroked Scarlette's hair as she talked. "I was watching you with this one," she continued. "I can see she's a wild one, but you are such a good mama. You're so patient with her and I know you must be tired with this little boy here. But I can tell your kids are well-kept and well-loved."

She went on to tell me about the son she lost to cancer when he was thirteen years old. "Maybe if it happened today they could have saved him, but back then there wasn't anything they could do. So you just keep being grateful for your babies," she told me.

When I got home, I ugly cried. That particular morning had been full of noise and my heart was discouraged. But the kind woman in the grocery store gave me just the right word at just the right moment. She saw me weary that morning, under the weight of the world, and she noticed that I was doing my best and she spoke encouragement into my life with her words. They were sweetness to my soul.

That interaction touched me so deeply that I determined to speak encouragement aloud as much as possible. I want to say something uplifting to everyone I pass.

A Moment to Breathe . . .

Make your words a gift. To whomever you pass.
On the sidewalk. In the store aisle. Speak a kind
word of encouragement to everyone you meet.

The Mediator in My Mess

BY TERI LYNNE UNDERWOOD

For there is one God and one mediator between God and humanity, the man Christ Jesus. 1 TIMOTHY 2:5–6

FROM THE MOMENT MY feet hit the floor, I knew it wasn't going to be a banner day. I'd overslept. We were out of coffee. And both my husband and my daughter seemed determined to get on my last nerve. By 8:30 that morning, I had cried at least five times. I was ready to throw in the towel (or at least run away from home for a day or two). Honestly, I just wanted to give up.

Even as I sat down with my Bible and journal, the enemy's whispers echoed through my head: *You're not good enough, not godly enough.* And I nodded in assent, because, well, I knew those things were true.

I opened my Bible that morning to be reminded of a beautiful truth: Christ is my Mediator. He is ever-standing before the Father, interceding on my behalf, pleading my cause, and claiming His blood over my sin. Of course I'm not good or godly enough. Most days I'm just a hot mess trying to manage the chaos of life and hoping I don't ruin anything.

But there He is, Jesus Christ, leaning in to the Father saying: *She's mine. That one, with all the fears and anxieties, all the falling and fumbling, my blood was shed for her.*

If we could grasp this—that we don't have to do more or be more, we just have to be His—imagine how our thoughts and lives would look quite different.

Jesus was born in a dirty barn, traveled on dusty roads, died on a rugged cross, was buried in a borrowed tomb. He knows all about the mess of this life. He isn't turned off by our failings and foibles. He doesn't walk away from our doubts and difficulties.

And here's the best news of all—He isn't in that borrowed tomb anymore! He is standing now before the throne, interceding on our behalf, mediating for us.

A Moment to Breathe . . .

Just picture it! Jesus at the right hand of the Father, interceding on your behalf. That's the God we serve! Thank Him for being a God who cares about every detail of our lives—even the seemingly mundane moments.

The Fellowship of His Sufferings

BY DIANE W. BAILEY

My goal is to know him and the power of his resurrection and the fellowship of his sufferings, being conformed to his death. PHILIPPIANS 3:10

I HAD CRIED MYSELF into a hot-splotched mess during the prayer time of our Bible study. The sorrow over my irreparably damaged marriage left my emotions raw and easily triggered. As the prayer ended, I opened my eyes and realized an older woman had come to sit by me. "It's not fair," I sobbed, "I'm a Christian and I prayed for God to restore my marriage, but it ended in divorce anyway."

The older woman listened as I gasped for breath. When I became quiet, she asked, "Can you praise God even if He never tells you why?" I stared at her, unable to answer.

For years I have mulled over this question as sorrows would come trying to leach the happiness from my life. Praising Christ in the pain seems, at first, to increase my pain. But when I rejoice in who He is, more than the sorrows I mourn, something wonderful happens. Clarity comes.

At one point, Jesus' mother and brothers thought He was insane, the church leaders betrayed Him to the authorities, His friends turned their backs and ran when He was sentenced to death. There isn't one sorrow we have that Christ is not able to put His arm around us and say, "Yeah, Me too."

Suffering is never easy. But there's a fellowship that comes when we go through difficulties with Christ. We might not ever know why, but we know who is with us—Jesus Christ, our Lord and friend. It isn't until we are further down the road that we look up from our tears and realize His arm was around us the whole time.

A Moment to Breathe . . .

It's in trials and heartaches that His presence often seems strongest, for He promises to be near the brokenhearted. Whether your day ends with dismay or delight, look for Him to be near.

Purpose in a Quiet Life

BY GRACE CHO

Seek to lead a quiet life, to mind your own business, and to work with your own hands, as we commanded you. 1 THESSALONIANS 4:11

SHE'S GOING TO CHANGE the world. Those were the words I read on my seminary recommendation letter, the words I had heard growing up. They filled me. They fueled me. I was meant for greater things. I knew it, and others affirmed it. To me, greater meant glory. Greater sufferings and greater sacrifices all equaled glory. On the surface, it sounded right and good, but in the unseen depths of my heart, it wasn't for His glory; it was for mine.

Though I planned my life with sights set on bigger and more, God began the work of small and quiet. He dismantled my dreams for *my* kingdom, so He could bring *His* kingdom through me. Instead of sending me off to an unreached people group far away from comfort and security, He sent me back to the place I grew up, to the middle of suburbia, where I stay at home investing in the little ones He's set right in front of me. His is truly an upside-down kingdom.

It's in this season of being hidden and hushed that I'm learning death of self is the portal through which He brings Himself to others. It's here that God works out the faith He's started in me, transforming me toward Christlikeness. It's here that my faith is being matured, that my character is being honed into holiness.

I once despised the small, quiet life because it felt beneath me, but now I see its purpose. All the opportunities and all the platforms will amount to nothing if Christ in me can't be seen. So I stay grounded in the daily, in all the seemingly insignificant responsibilities, because in His upside-down kingdom, success and reward are found in the faithfulness of the small and quiet.

A Moment to Breathe . . .

He is Emmanuel even in the mundane. Experience His presence and His work in and through you in the little things He calls you to today.

Roadblocks and Signposts

BY ANGIE RYG

How happy is the one who does not walk in the advice
of the wicked or stand in the pathway with sinners
or sit in the company of mockers! PSALM 1:1

WHILE ATTENDING A GRADUATION party for a dear friend's son, I was struck by the prayer of his grandfather. The grandfather gave thanks for the roadblocks that kept him from sin and the signposts that led the way. The grandfather prayed for more roadblocks and signposts in the young man's journey.

I started to think about the roadblocks God had used in my life. The party I couldn't go to when I was younger. The unhealthy relationship that ended. And the job finishing that wasn't good for my family.

There were signposts too. The words of a friend that encouraged me to hunger for more of Christ. My small group that challenged me to serve and share the love of Jesus. My family that supported me with laughter and love.

How truly blessed we are that God uses roadblocks and signposts to protect us and draw us closer to Him.

In the same way, we can be a roadblock or a signpost for others. I can share about the dangers of sin and the consequences that have happened in my life because of them as a roadblock. For signposts, I can challenge my family and friends to pursue holiness as a standard rather than the world's sin. I can speak of God's grace, forgiveness, and unfailing love.

I'm thankful for the prayer of a grandfather, demonstrating pure love and encouraging all who heard him to live a life that points to Christ in everything we do. I pray that God will use my life as a roadblock for temptation and a signpost for His glory, that my actions will point others to Jesus and His gift of grace for us all.

A Moment to Breathe . . .

Reflect on seasons past and consider the ways that some
of the circumstances you've experienced might have been a
roadblock or a signpost. Give thanks to God for these moments.

Embracing the Imperfections

BY MYQUILLYN SMITH

[Be] hospitable, loving what is good, sensible,
righteous, holy, self-controlled. TITUS 1:8

I JUST NOTICED A new, growing hole in my sofa. I love this sofa but all of its edges are starting to wear dangerously thin. Now I regret not making sure those old lady-ish arm protectors were properly in their place over the past five years. And I admit, I even got a little teary-eyed thinking about how much I enjoy this sofa, and knowing that we can't afford a new one anytime soon. My sofa has holes and stains and is starting to fade in all the wrong places.

Somewhere deep in my twisted thoughts I ask myself *Why, why was I such a fool to allow it to be used so carelessly?* But there is a good side to having a not-so-perfect sofa. I can freely have friends over, friends with toddlers who eat melty chocolate-chip cookies on the sofa—and they don't gasp when a chip falls onto the fabric. And now when one of my boys isn't feeling too well, with threat of you-know-whatting their Spaghettios, I let them rest on the sofa without fear that it will be ruined. My husband can plop down in his favorite spot and if his greasy popcorn hands happen to fall onto the arm of my precious sofa, well, there's no threat of me shooting him a disapproving look.

Then it dawned on me. There is something worse than a falling-apart, used-up, five-year-old sofa. A perfectly unused five-year-old sofa. It would be such a tragedy if my five-year-old sofa were in mint condition. Not only do I think the sofa (which I realize is an inanimate object but for the sake of this point let's pretend) is thrilled to be fulfilling its sofa purpose, but we are actually so much freer to enjoy it because of its imperfections. Once again, I realize that my unconscious quest for perfection is thwarted. And I am actually thankful for the daily reminder that it doesn't have to be perfect to be beautiful.

A Moment to Breathe . . .

Designate a space—even if it's just a comfy chair—that welcomes
everyone. A space you're not afraid to get messy or stained.
A space that says, "You can relax here and be yourself."

DAY 41

Do It Afraid

BY SUZANNE ELLER

*The LORD is for me; I will not be afraid. What can
a mere mortal do to me?* PSALM 118:6

CHEEK TO CHEEK, MY eight-month-old grandson, Josiah, and I dance in the pool. When his feet dip in the cold water he sucks in his breath and scrunches his face to cry. I pull him close and he smiles. We dance again. Somehow my presence is enough, in spite of his fear.

Years ago when I was a young mom, I was afraid. Afraid I'd never get it right. Afraid that I had been so damaged that, like a banged-up old suitcase, I'd carry the clutter of my chaotic childhood into the lives of my babies. There were times I sat on the floor with a child in my arms, tears brimming as I rocked and prayed: *Lord, how can I be a good mom if no one showed me how? I'm so afraid I'll mess this up.*

One day these words whispered somewhere deep in response: *Do it afraid, Suzie.*

Looking back, I believe that God wasn't asking me to embrace my fears, but to trust that He could somehow use this ill-equipped, work-in-progress woman to love and shape three human beings. It meant that it was okay to say that I didn't have all the answers all the time, because no one has all the answers all the time. It meant that I could stop comparing. It meant that on those hard days when I felt like I didn't have a clue, when my knees hit the carpet, I was met with mercy and a fresh start for the next day.

And every time I did it afraid, the layers of the past peeled back to reveal who I was today, separate from my childhood. At some point, *fear* shifted to quiet assurance. And somehow *His* presence was enough, in spite of my fear.

A Moment to Breathe . . .

*Will you do it afraid . . . whatever the Lord is calling you
to do right now? Whatever fear might be holding you
back today, give it to God and rely on His strength.*

SEGMENT

The Difference Our Words Make

BY JESSICA TURNER

. . . a timely word—how good that is! PROVERBS 15:23

SHE CAME TO OUR first meeting prepared, with half a dozen legal pages full of notes. It was clear she had taken a lot of time to ready herself for this meeting. The same was true for the next meeting, and the next, and the next. As our group divided and conquered for a big presentation, she was always the one going the extra mile, making phone calls and doing additional research to make us better. So a few days before our next meeting, I went to her cubicle and thanked her for her work. I don't remember my words, but I wanted to let her know that she was appreciated and made a difference.

The next day we happened to arrive at work at the same time and she said to me, "You know, I was thinking about what you said to me last night." Did you catch that? She went home that night, hours after I spoke to her, and thought about my words. The next morning, when I saw her for the first time, they were still on her heart, while I had not thought of them since I walked away from her desk.

Kind words are balm for our souls. Too often I find myself going about my day so quickly that I miss opportunities to extend a simple kind word. My colleague's response reminded me that all it takes is a few seconds to say *Thank you, you matter. You helped me, you made a difference.*

Now I look for opportunities to say kind words and verbally acknowledge people's good work, what they mean to me, or even just how they look. I don't know why this was such an aha moment for me. Of course, kind words leave an impact. So many times in my own life, a person's words have stuck with me, long after a conversation ended. So today, let's makes someone's day and share a kind word.

A Moment to Breathe . . .

Make someone's day with a kind word, and then take a moment to let it make yours, too.

The Key to Giving In to Rest

BY KATIE ORR

"Stop your fighting, and know that I am God, exalted among the nations, exalted on the earth." PSALM 46:10

MY FRIEND'S FIVE-MONTH-OLD IS in a stage lately where he fights the inevitable nap. At this age, he's taking in every detail of the world around him. The sounds, the smells, and the sights of all the fascinating people and activities around him. Once he begins to get sleepy, he knows what's coming and he fights it every step of the way. No amount of rocking, swaddling, or bouncing will do, especially if there's a conversation going on around him. He simply doesn't want to miss a thing.

He doesn't understand that sleep is the best thing for him. His mommy knows best. Naptime is a necessity. Rest is what will help him grow so he can experience even more of the world around him.

I tend to be a fighter of rest, too. I don't want to miss out on opportunities or experiences. I long to see more, do more, and be in the middle of the excitement of all the people who fascinate me. But like the five-month-old, I sometimes lack the needed perspective that leads to giving in to rest.

The beginning of Psalm 46:10 is also translated "Be still" and "Cease striving." These are difficult tasks for an achiever. I like to be busy climbing ladders and completing my checklist. Waiting and resting are not my strong suit.

The command, however, is not simply to "stop your fighting," it is also to "know that I am God." This is the key to giving in to rest: To remember that my loving, personal, and faithful Father is orchestrating my day. To let His peace wash over me, knowing everything does not depend on me. He has a good, abundant, and specific plan for my life. Amidst all my activity, I can trust in Him enough to include a rhythm of rest into my busy days

A Moment to Breathe . . .

No matter what time of the day it might be, spend just five minutes lying down in a quiet room. Just five minutes.

Unloading the Stones

BY ELISA PULLIAM

*"I will give you a new heart and put
a new spirit within you; I will remove your heart
of stone and give you a heart of flesh."* EZEKIEL 36:26

I'VE ALWAYS HAD A thing for stones. I know that may seem strange, but for me they bring to mind one of my favorite places on earth—this sliver of a beach nestled along the north shore of Long Island. Oh, the countless evenings I spent on that stony beach, watching the sun go down while my children splashed out in the sandbar. There I sat, thinking and pondering, as I'd scoop up the stones in my hand and admire their uniqueness and their story. Soft and smooth. Hard and impermeable. Dark and light. Speckled and spotted.

Each stone was a poignant reminder of my life—of all our lives. Because we, too, can be soft and smooth while also being hard and impermeable. We may long to reflect the light of Christ as our lives are turned in His hand, and yet we've been dulled by the beat down from the storms. Maybe there's not even a glint of shine, as our hardened hearts ooze bitterness and pain.

I confess my heart was hardened, even a decade after coming to know Jesus as my Savior. I was lugging around guilt, shame, and anger. Once I got honest with God and gave Him access to my heart, He moved in and emptied out all the stony parts formed by wounds.

God turned my heart of stone to flesh. He made my heart His dwelling place as He wrote a new story upon the stones of my life. And He wants to do that in you.

A Moment to Breathe . . .

*Give God the stones stored up in your heart so that He can
turn your heart more fully into His dwelling place.*

Toward Transparency

BY MEI L. AU

*"There is nothing covered that won't be uncovered,
nothing hidden that won't be made known."* LUKE 12:2

HELLO, MY NAME IS Mei and I'm a recovering perfectionist. Left to my own devices, my pantry would be color-coded, labeled, and organized by height, expiration date, and food group.

But I have a confession to make. I'm a fraud. Other than my immediate family, most people think I'm super-organized and I admit, as a newlywed, that was my goal. I tried so hard to emulate the home decorating magazines, but trying to maintain this façade was exhausting. Overwhelmed, I would fall into a pit of depression—a pit I personally dug. I was in bondage to a lie—that my value and self-worth were tied to how beautiful and immaculately maintained my home was.

Jesus criticized the religious leaders of His day for being more concerned about the appearance of righteousness than being internally transformed by the love of God. The religious leaders were more interested in outward appearances, from hand-washing ceremonies to tithing the smallest amount from their herb gardens. They were attempting to gain God's favor with rules and rituals. And they made God's Word a duty, not a delight—a burden, not a blessing.

But God wants us to seek Him, not be self-seeking.

We can try to hide our messiness behind doors of self-righteousness, but it's all a pretense. God sees our inner self—our motives, desires, and thoughts. And He wants to do an inward work, conforming our hearts into the image of Christ. It's His grace poured into us that will ultimately produce the outward manifestation of a beautiful heart, a heart that exalts our Creator. And by His grace, we are given permission to be transparent and authentic. We are allowed to open a few cabinet doors and permit others to see the messiness of our broken lives.

A Moment to Breathe . . .

*Go ahead and open a cupboard, open a drawer. Whether
it's organized or messy inside, it doesn't reflect who you are.
Open the door to your heart today and share a part of you
that you normally keep concealed with a trusted friend.*

The One Thing That's Impossible to Lose

BY BONNIE GRAY

*"For wisdom is better than jewels, and nothing
desirable can equal it."* PROVERBS 8:11

I DON'T KNOW HOW I could have lost it, but I did. My wallet. When I got home from shopping, I realized I couldn't find it—a pink wristlet that was a special birthday gift from a friend. An hour later, after zooming back to the store, looking in all the shopping carts and turning my car inside out, I had to accept the truth: my wallet was gone.

There are moments in life when we may be at a loss for what to do or say. No matter how much we try to come up with pros and cons, real life can't be planned. But God's wisdom is always there in the midst of the unexpected. Our names are written on His heart and He desires to meet us in the midst of our challenges, disappointments, and losses.

God's love for us never grows old. And He promises to give us the help we need. It's His promise. We may need courage to speak words in a new way. We may make mistakes. Yet, God longs for us to rest in His embrace. He understands our needs better than we do. When we're uncertain about our next steps, we can be certain that God's not letting go.

Let's choose God's love as our guide this week. May His whispers of love awaken our hearts with hope for the journey. Let's choose to be still and listen. God is called Emmanuel, God with us, because He really is with us. As is. We are close to His heart. And we can confide in Jesus, friend to friend.

Even when things don't work out as planned—I never did find my wallet—let's quietly make space in our day for Him, and for each other. Let's offer our words as prayer. Because together we are among kindreds in this quiet space.

A Moment to Breathe . . .

*You can never lose the grace of God. It's His gift. And
He never revokes His gifts. Tell Him how thankful
you are that His gifts can't be lost or forgotten.*

A Place of Your Own

BY MELISSA MICHAELS

"I will meet with you there above the mercy seat,
between the two cherubim that are over the ark
of the testimony; I will speak with you from there about
all that I command you regarding the Israelites." EXODUS 25:22

I REMEMBER A SEASON of life where I felt really down and discouraged. I needed to connect with God and sense His presence. So one morning I quietly stepped into my yard and started a garden. You know what? God met me there. I had set everything else aside to be alone and make time to hear from Him. Now I see gardens as a very special place for meeting up with God.

Do you have somewhere set aside where you go to be alone, a place where you can shut out the world and hear God's voice? A quiet place where you look forward to meeting God and where God is invited in to meet you?

It's easy to slip into only meeting God at church on Sundays. But to really grow and get to know Him, we need to set aside a time and place of our own—a place where we can be intentional about meeting up with God as a part of our day-to-day life. Maybe you have a special chair, a comfy blanket, a Bible, and a journal on a table designating that is your place. Or maybe you go to a local coffee shop filled with the hustle and bustle of voices, but you tune them out when you begin to sip your coffee in the corner booth, open your Bible, and begin to read God's Word.

It really doesn't matter where your "place" is. The important thing is that we're deliberate in our intent to meet Him somewhere regularly. While the beach is a great place to meet God, if it takes you hours to get there, you might want to find somewhere within walking distance so you can meet Him daily. And then once you have that place set aside, don't forget Him or get distracted by the things of the world. He's there, waiting for us to show up and invite Him in.

A Moment to Breathe . . .

If you don't already have a designated time and place to meet with
God, create a space today and commit to meeting Him there daily.

Freedom from Perfection

BY ABBY MCDONALD

*For freedom, Christ set us free. Stand firm then and
don't submit again to a yoke of slavery.* GALATIANS 5:1

AS I TURN MY face toward the glow of the digital alarm clock, I can almost hear the seconds ticking away. I will myself not to look at the time, not wanting to know the limited hours until sunrise. Instead of counting sheep, I talk to the Shepherd, but my thoughts are too jumbled to make sense in the unnamed hours.

Untouched, the laundry sits piled in the basket. Uncompleted, my to-do list of projects grows. Why can't I pull it together? Christ came so that I could have freedom, but I'm not free. I'm trapped in an unending chaos of everyday life, trying to find balance between the pursuit of a dream and the reality of responsibility.

In the stillness of the morning, I find a space to breathe. I hear the faint whisper of the Spirit calling ever so gently: *Come to Me and rest.* I reluctantly oblige. And when I open my Bible, my guilt collides with truth. God's grace is sufficient for me. I'm struck by the simplicity of it. God never intended for me to be perfect. His strength is enough for us both when I say, "God, I'm worn out. I'm a mess. Please give me the strength I lack."

Freedom in Christ comes when I relinquish my need for perfection and rest in Him. By holding myself to a standard only Christ can attain, I am fooling myself. But when I let Him fill the spaces and the shortcomings with the glory that is His, and only His, I find rest. Sweet, soul-quenching rest.

So today, I'm making a promise to myself, which I may need to make again tomorrow. Not to let myself be burdened any longer with the yoke of perfection. If I could attain this lofty standard, Christ would never have come. For the sake of weary perfectionists everywhere, I'm so glad He did.

A Moment to Breathe . . .

*Tell Jesus how grateful you are that He is enough. You
don't have to be perfect. Because He already is.*

The Little Foxes We Find

BY BRITTA ELLIS LAFONT

Catch the foxes for us—the little foxes that ruin the vineyards—
for our vineyards are in bloom. SONG OF SONGS 2:15

ONE SATURDAY WE WOKE up to a sunny kitchen crawling with black ants. We hadn't been in our new house long, but we knew moving back to the deep South, after years away, would mean dealing with bugs. From that moment on, we had a close partnership with pest control. Within six months we were visited no fewer than ten times to exterminate those pesky ants. They started in the kitchen and then popped up on the second floor in our bathroom. I was discouraged. Somehow, the ants had spoiled our new house excitement.

The little things can really get you down sometimes, you know? Like little foxes spoiling a vineyard, life's trials—even petty annoyances—can prevent us from resting in Jesus. Simple, everyday struggles can squash the perfect fruit of relationship with Him. When I'm tired. When I'm overscheduled. When I'm disappointed because life has not met my expectations. These "small" things are like little foxes, threatening to steal the fruit of joy, hope, and peace that Jesus says is already ours.

How easily I forget that this life is just a whisper in the light of eternity. I forget that God is on top of things—He's got this. So instead of dwelling on the little foxes, we can look to Him. We can rejoice, knowing that in spite of the mess swirling around us, God has chosen us to be a light in the world. If we can't see any good in the ordinary, if we're struggling to find joy in the everyday . . . these earthly reminders of struggle reveal Jesus at His best. Because He has overturned them all. Jesus came to give us peace with God. He can and will accomplish His purpose in your life, and in mine. He is the reason we have joy and hope and peace. And there isn't a fox anywhere that can steal that away.

A Moment to Breathe . . .

Name the "little foxes" in your everyday world that threaten
to steal your joy, your hope, and your peace. Ask God to
help you keep your eyes on Him, and not on them.

Fit for Glory

BY KIM HYLAND

Now we have this treasure in clay jars, so that this extraordinary
power may be from God and not from us. 2 CORINTHIANS 4:7

WHEN I THINK ABOUT a treasure, I think of buried things. Things that have been secretly stored in a locked chest and hidden safe away from any who would dare to steal what's mine. What doesn't come to mind is a fragile jar of clay.

Treasures are typically placed in strong things, because strong things—like a safe or vault—have the inherent ability to protect what they contain. Yet God chose to place the treasure of the gospel in weak, fragile "clay jars." In us.

At first, this seems counterintuitive, as if maybe God didn't think this plan through. When I consider the incredible beauty and power of the gospel, I don't know that I'd trust myself with such a treasure. I'm acutely aware of my weaknesses and failures, and try as I might, I'm unable to perfect myself. A fragile clay jar really is an apt description of me.

But God wasn't being careless. He had a definite purpose in His decision to entrust the treasure of the gospel to us—so the source of the gospel's power would be clear and God's glory would be revealed in our weakness. We are fragile by design! This is a huge relief, because it's consistent with my reality. I am weak, cracked, broken, and sorely lacking in any inherent strength. But it's right in the middle of that humble reality that I am most fit to reveal God's glory.

I used to despise my weaknesses and exert tons of effort trying to fix myself and hide my flaws. But understanding the truth of God's design has truly renewed my mind. Rather than being places of shame and frustration, my liabilities have the potential to draw me into the security and safety found only in deep dependence on God. And that sweet place is where I can reveal His glory best.

A Moment to Breathe . . .

Find a fragile jar or vase or even a dish somewhere in your home.
Set it on a windowsill or fireplace mantle—somewhere you can see it
every day. When you see it, remember that we are clay jars, but we
carry the gospel inside us, revealing God's glory, everywhere we go.

Chosen by God

BY KIMBERLY COYLE

Instead, God has chosen what is foolish in the world to shame the wise, and God has chosen what is weak in the world to shame the strong. 1 CORINTHIANS 1:27

THROUGH THE RESTAURANT WINDOWS, the lights of New York City glittered against a backdrop of velvet sky. I stared outside in silence while the rest of the table talked law, politics, and business ventures.

We sat around a table cluttered with half-empty glasses and plates smeared with the remnants of butter, potatoes, and steak. The waiter slipped in and out with a fresh basket of bread with such ease it appeared as if the table magically replenished itself. He made himself invisible, and as I sat surrounded by my husband's colleagues, I faded into the shadows too. I could add nothing to the conversation, and I spent the evening wondering what I would say if anyone asked about my work—the quotidian tasks of raising small people and tidying up. No one ever asked.

I walked away feeling malnourished and hungry for recognition. As we parted ways and everyone said their goodbyes, I hooked my hand around my husband's arm and tried not to cry. On the drive home, I remained silent. While it hurts to feel invisible to the movers and shakers of this world, I'm learning to let go of my need for their validation. Like Hagar wandering in the wilderness, I serve a God who sees what others don't see. In my smallness and my lack of worldly influence, I remain His chosen.

When I look at the disciples, I find myself in good company. God glories in choosing the unexpected to do the work of His kingdom. Jesus chose salt-of-the-earth laborers. They were radicals and zealots, doubters and unknowns. And despite this, they embodied the message of the gospel. Like the disciples, I am an ambassador of the Good News. Chosen, cherished, and wholly known.

A Moment to Breathe . . .

Think about each of the disciples Jesus handpicked. Worldly status or achievement didn't matter. Because Jesus looks at the heart. Thank Him today for choosing you.

Held by God

BY ALECIA SIMERSKY

He reached down from on high and took hold of me;
he pulled me out of deep water. PSALM 18:16

I REMEMBER WHEN MY kids were young and they wanted to hold my hand when they were unsure of their next step; they were wee-bits learning to walk. Looking at me with their sweet, round eyes so full of expectancy and trust, they'd reach up with their chubby fingers and wait for my hand to grasp onto theirs.

Once they felt my hand, they happily and confidently took their next step forward because they knew I was there. They knew I wouldn't let go. I wouldn't let them fall. That is how I picture God with us. He's waiting for us to reach up and grab hold of His hand. He's always there, with an outstretched hand, waiting for us. He's there to guide us through the unknown future.

I've always been the girl that begged God for a sign, anything to let me know I was on the right path. But maybe all I've really needed to do is draw close and take the hand that's waiting to be held. In the silence. In the whisper. That's when I sense His presence. That's when I know. It doesn't matter what the future holds or if I'm on the right track. He's there. He's right there with me.

Being close to the One who holds my heart—who has named the stars and counted my hairs (even the gray ones)—is what really matters in this life. And so I take His hand and my breathing slows. My heart fills with knowing. I am held. And I can trust He won't let go of me, just as I won't let go of my new little walker.

A Moment to Breathe . . .

God promises to draw near to you as you draw near to Him. Talk to Him. Tell Him about the ways you're afraid of stumbling. Ask Him to steady your spiritual gait, as you walk in faith each day.

Be Astonished

BY HILARY YANCEY

Look at the nations and observe—be utterly astounded!
For I am doing something in your days that you will not
believe when you hear about it. HABAKKUK 1:5

LORD JESUS, WHAT ARE *You doing?* The MRI hummed and whirred. A fetal MRI is a delicate and lengthy procedure; it requires lying still and praying with the feel of sweat dripping onto the pillow and your hair slowly clumping at the nape of your neck, praying that they will see a miracle. Praying that they will see something they could not believe. I imagined myself hearing the story whispered between nurses, the MRI technician, our OB/GYN. Surely this is the kind of astounding thing that the prophet talks about? Surely this would be our miracle?

God brought my family into the bright, new world of parenting our son Jack, just as he was formed. God brought me into the bright, astonishing goodness of Jack's first smile with his wide cleft and the second smile with the tiniest ghost of a scar on his upper lip. God astonished me, astounded me. God did something I would not have believed if I had been told in that sweaty, white tube lying on that pillow with clumps of hair sticking to my neck.

Perhaps it is not the miracles we expect, but the ones that God astonishes us with, that draw us nearer. I've learned to spend less time trapped in my own tunnel of imagination and planning for what might happen. And instead, trust that He is writing the story and can do immeasurably more than I can imagine.

A Moment to Breathe . . .

Think of a story in your life that turned out differently than you
hoped and prayed it might. How did God reveal Himself specifically
to you during that season? Ask Him to grow your faith in Him.

Because a Little Goes a Long Way

BY LOGAN WOLFRAM

Your boasting is not good. Don't you know that a little leaven leavens the whole batch of dough? Clean out the old leaven so that you may be a new unleavened batch, as indeed you are. For Christ our Passover lamb has been sacrificed. Therefore, let us observe the feast, not with old leaven or with the leaven of malice and evil, but with the unleavened bread of sincerity and truth. 1 CORINTHIANS 5:6–8

THE HOUSE SMELLED AMAZING as all of the ladies arrived to pray for our children's school. I opened the oven to remove the banana bread, excited that I'd woken early enough to make them all a treat served warm from the oven. It looked odd though. The entire middle was sunken inward where it should have made a rounded dome across the top.

I jiggled the pan and while it seemed firm enough, one slice in and I realized that something was terribly wrong. It was mushy and gooey, but not the kind that makes something more delicious. What did I do wrong?

Oh, mercy! I forgot the eggs! I tripled the batch to make more for later and I'd forgotten every single egg for every single loaf! Those six eggs would have risen the entire batch to spongy perfection, but as it was, leaving them out impacted every crumb. And so it goes . . . when we add or leave out the right ingredients, the entire batch can end up completely impacted and often inedible.

It goes much the same when we place our faith in Christ. He gives us a new identity. When we try to do things our own old way, or when we leave out the fresh new ingredients that we have been given in Him, the whole lot is affected. Out with the old, in with the new. In Christ we are made new. In Him, we have the recipe to live the very best life. He neither adds too much of one thing or leaves out another, so let us learn to live for Him, and with Him, and in Him—to cast off the old ways and, instead, operate with the ingredients of His goodness and truth.

A Moment to Breathe . . .

Bake a loaf of banana bread for a friend. Or buy a sweet loaf at the bakery and tie a ribbon around it. Give a friend some sweet goodness today.

The Only Way

BY MELISSA AARON

"Your kingdom come.
Your will be done." MATTHEW 6:10

I GOT SAVED WHEN I was five years old. Which is code for: I did all my sinning while I was saved. My biggest obstacle in this journey has not been giving my life to Christ. That was a done deal from a very early age. My difficulty was in submitting my will to His.

I remember adults asking me throughout my entire youth what I wanted to do when I grew up. They encouraged me to follow my heart when it came to decisions about where I'd go to college, or what career I'd pursue, or who I'd marry. And for so long I got stuck there, trying to follow my heart and my dreams. And when I prayed, it wasn't, "Thy will be done," it was always, "Lord, please let my will be done."

But we've often worked so hard for our dreams and waited so long for our plans that we don't want to give them up. His will may not be what we had in mind, or worse, an undisclosed will requires us to wait and simply trust in His plan. Ick. Waiting is the worst!

Yet, God is asking us to release our plans, and sometimes it takes something pretty major to get our attention. But when all has been stripped away, He presents His will as an alternative to the "path of me."

I realize now there was only ever one way: His way. All other roads were a distraction. His will is where I can stop chasing my plans and rest in the knowledge that I am walking in the good deeds He set in advance for me to do. Daily praying, "Your kingdom come, Your will be done."

A Moment to Breathe . . .

Open your Bible and read the "Lord's Prayer" in
Matthew 6:9–13. Make these words your own and
pray them from your heart, today and always.

The Day I Stopped Believing

BY KIMBERLY GILLESPIE

Answer me quickly, LORD; my spirit fails. Don't hide your face from me, or I will be like those going down to the Pit. PSALM 143:7

OCTOBER 8, 1991. THAT'S the day I stopped believing. After seventeen months of praying. The woman who wrapped me in her womb for nine months, the five-foot-tall ball of feistiness I called "Momma"—lost. Beaten by the faceless, cruel devil of a disease that didn't care that she had fourteen- and seventeen-year-old daughters who still needed her for guidance, love, support, and encouragement. Cancer didn't care. And on that day I decided that God didn't either. Sure, I kept up the façade. I still attended church. I still taught Sunday school. Heck, I even went on to seminary.

I believed in God, but I didn't trust Him. I believed He was able, and that He could. I simply didn't believe He would—for me. Sure, He loved me enough to let me into heaven after believing in His Son. But did He care enough to answer the prayers of my heart on earth? So I stopped believing in prayer, its purpose and its power. Why pray when God is going to do what He wants anyway?

Honestly, I still go there sometimes. When life is difficult, circumstances aren't as I would like them, and I feel as though my prayers hit a reinforced concrete wall, that seventeen-year-old girl returns. She still questions. But then I recall the lessons that the years have taught me.

Eventually I'd meet the man who would become the supporter, encourager, cover, and cheerleader that my mom never had the chance to be. Together, in times of joblessness and homelessness and hopelessness, with bills and babies, we learned that God is a faithful provider. We saw Him deliver and direct. And we learned to pray more, cling tighter, and trust harder. In the darkest of moments, He provided just enough light to keep us on the path. And He'll do the same for you.

A Moment to Breathe . . .

Can you name a day you were tempted to stop believing too? You can tell Him about it, you know. Because He already knows. And He understands more than we know. Turn to Him today, with all your doubts and fears.

Because We All Need Somewhere to Belong

BY JACQUE WATKINS

*And let us . . . not [neglect] to gather together, as some are
in the habit of doing, but encouraging each other, and all the
more as you see the day approaching.* HEBREWS 10:24–25

I FIRST MET THEM last year, while walking the downtown streets of San Juan. Pigeons. Hundreds of them, everywhere. I tiptoed among them, and one step must have been too firm, because dozens of them flew into the sky at once, almost on cue. But no sooner had they taken off, they landed right back on the plaza, returning to the exact spot where they began. They did this over and over, no matter how many footsteps interrupted them, they returned. This was their community.

I'm longing for community like that. I think we all are. To find our people and hang together. To fly together when we hear threatening "footsteps" coming. To stick together and return again to "our place."

As women we tend to be flighty. And sometimes it's just easier to leave the flock; it's less of a hassle to occupy the same space. We get threatened when everyone wants to eat out of the same hand, because we forget there's plenty to go around. We compare and measure ourselves short. We decide to quit risking. We decide to leave everyone behind, to become isolated and alone. Except alone won't work. Because we need each other.

We need the one who's perched in the tree. And the one whose view is from the ground. We need the older one and the younger one. And the gray-and-white-spotted one. Everyone has something unique to offer. And what would community be if there were no diversity at all?

Few things are as lovely as synchronous teamwork, pulling together and cheering each other on. Few things are as wonderful as giving our strengths and receiving from others what we lack. Few things are as sacred as protecting, trusting, and caring for one another. Building a place we're known for. A place that's ours. A community where we belong.

A Moment to Breathe . . .

Ask the Lord to put someone on your heart. Someone who tends to keep to the sidelines. Someone who'd love an invitation to join.

On the Other Side of Impossible

BY LOVELLE GERTH-MYERS

*Blessed is the one who endures trials, because when he
has stood the test he will receive the crown of life that
God has promised to those who love him.* JAMES 1:12

I WALK TO THE stage in amazement. I never believed I would make it to this place. They announce my name and hand me a diploma. I can hardly hold back the tears. So many times I almost gave up. But I worked so hard I to get to this place right here, right now.

Six years ago I was isolated and alone. I had dropped out of high school. College seemed too good for a girl like me. That's where the smart people went. You know, the ones with parents who believed in them and actually prepared them for it. By God's grace I finished high school and went to a community college. I felt so different and stupid compared to the other kids. There were so many nights with little sleep because school and my full-time schedule at work didn't always mix. I continued on and pushed myself forward, looking toward the finish line, uncertain of my future.

The Lord is so faithful. At age twenty-one, I was adopted. Now I have parents and a huge support system cheering me on. Somehow they knew I could do it even when I didn't think I could. They never let me give up. They listened to my cries and cheered me on all the way to the finish line.

Now with my cap and gown on, and a bachelor's degree in my hands, I am so full of thankfulness. I am thankful the Lord took a broken girl and did the impossible. He saw something in her that she didn't know existed. He pursued her and constantly reminded her that His ways are not limited by her circumstances. He healed her. He gave her parents. And He proved to her that she isn't stupid. Most of all, He showed her that she is worthy because her worthiness is found in Christ alone. Everything that was taken from her, God in His gracious love has redeemed.

A Moment to Breathe . . .

*Think of a moment in your life when you crossed a finish
line you didn't think you could. Tell God how grateful
you are that He was with you through it all.*

Starting Small

BY SHELLY WILDMAN

"For who despises the day
of small things?" ZECHARIAH 4:10

I HAVE AN EMBARRASSING confession to make: I used to want to be famous. I thought that if I could just plan that huge event, speak on a gigantic stage, or write that best-selling book, I'd somehow make God happy.

But then I had kids and devoted years doing the not-so-glamorous work of laundry, diaper changing, and runny-nose wiping. Unfortunately, I also spent a lot of time resenting the mundane work of raising children, thinking that somehow this wasn't the "it" that God had planned for me.

One day, sitting in my living room amid toys scattered about and children clambering for my attention, I cried out to God for help. I confessed that I didn't like who I had become—a whiney, resentful, complaining mother who was unsatisfied with God's provision for her. God heard my cry, and slowly began to show me that this life is exactly the life He would use to shape my character, to help me become the woman He wanted me to be.

And so the work began. Through small beginnings, God showed me that He wanted my heart so much more than the sacrifices I was making by staying home with my children. He gently helped me see that it's not what I do that pleases Him, but who I am.

I wouldn't trade those early years with my daughters for anything, not just because of the fun we had together or the joy I experienced watching them grow into adulthood, but because of what God did in me during those years. He patiently took a miserable, frustrated young woman and pointed her to grace.

A Moment to Breathe . . .

Think of a "small beginning" in your own life—whether in
your past or your present—and see that small beginning as the
shaping of your character, trusting that God is faithful to bring
the good work He has for you to completion in His timing.

The Friend I Didn't Know I Needed

BY JENNIFER J. CAMP

*Love one another deeply as brothers and sisters. Outdo
one another in showing honor.* ROMANS 12:10

WHILE STANDING IN THE rain, my friend handed to me a small square canvas, colored turquoise and green with yellow-orange bursts of flowers brushed with her hand. We had just finished a hike, our tennis shoes and black yoga pants splattered with mud, our faces dripping with water, hoods fastened tight around our heads. "I made this for you," she said.

The week before, after another muddy hike, she had played me a song on her phone as we tucked in, warm and dry, in the front seat of her car. The water pelted the windows, clouds thick and dark. It was a song of longing and healing—of feeling weary and missing God, of faith and knowing He is near. My heart beat fast, my face hot, as each word sung spoke straight to my heart.

I received the painting and the song, the conversations and the time together, as the gifts they were—God pursuing me in the flesh, a dear friend who loves with wide-open generosity and bold vulnerability. And that was just the beginning of our friendship. I had never met a person like her. It is no small thing to show honor to one another; to show respect and love. It's risky to offer oneself and give without reservation so that another person feels valued and seen.

On the back of her painting my friend wrote, "For His Flower." She knew my heart for God, the way He was wooing me to Himself, and she was letting God use her, too. The actions we take in honoring the people in our lives show us the face of God. And I want to see that face. I need that more than anything.

A Moment to Breathe . . .

*Ask God to show you one specific, tangible way you
can honor a friend today. Then bless that person
with your time, your talent, and your words.*

When God Turns Your Kicking and Screaming into Beauty

BY HANNAH VAN DYK

He has sent me to heal the brokenhearted, to proclaim liberty to the captives and freedom to the prisoners; to proclaim the year of the LORD's favor, and the day of our God's vengeance; to comfort all who mourn, to provide for those who mourn in Zion; to give them a crown of beauty instead of ashes, festive oil instead of mourning, and splendid clothes instead of despair. ISAIAH 61:1b–3a

I LIVE IN A sleepy town with one stoplight to its name. It would be the understatement of the year to say I did not want to move here. At age fifteen, it felt like too much. So I kicked and screamed. The kicking is metaphorical. The screaming? Well, that is literal. I threw a lot of teenage tantrums and whined about how life wasn't fair. I holed up in my room, wrote letters to people who were gone, and tried to figure out how I could make them stay. I cried a lot. And I refused to paint my bedroom walls until there was a ring on my mother's finger. But then there was a summer of pausing, reflecting, and growing. Then a ring came, and a beautiful wedding, and finally, the move.

I look at my life now, and I can see what happens when God turns all of your kicking and screaming into beauty. I'm thankful God doesn't always listen to immediate me but is always looking out for the long-term me. I didn't think I would find beauty or comfort or peace in a silly one-stop town, but I did. I didn't think I would learn about humility or hard work or sacrifice while living on a smelly farm, but I did. I didn't think I would watch the sun light up the sky with golden hues and savor the feeling of being home with a family that finally feels stable and whole, but I do.

I wasn't expecting to find beauty here. But I did. And I think that speaks to a God who hides beauty in the most unexpected of places. I know we go through different seasons in life, and there will be seasons of kicking and screaming. But I also know there's beauty at the end of it, when we trust Him with all of it.

A Moment to Breathe . . .

Think back to a season in your life when it felt like you were kicking and screaming. How has God—with time and grace—brought beauty from those ashes?

Deep Roots

BY KAITLYN BOUCHILLON

*The person who trusts in the L*ORD*, whose confidence indeed is the L*ORD*, is blessed. He will be like a tree planted by water: it sends its roots out toward a stream, it doesn't fear when heat comes, and its foliage remains green. It will not worry in a year of drought or cease producing fruit.* JEREMIAH 17:7–8

THE FLOWER BULB WAS wrapped in tissue paper, placed gently inside a gift bag. Just as fall began to exit and winter announced its arrival, I found myself shopping for soil. The bulb, a thoughtful gift from a dear friend, wouldn't survive the coming season without careful planting. I scooped soil by the handful into a gray pot, lining the bottom. Next, the bulb. Then another handful of soil on each side. Finally, I stood back in admiration of a project completed. Really, though, it had only just begun.

Each morning I filled a regular drinking glass and slowly watered around the bulb. At first just a few drops would flood the pot. The bulb had yet to settle into its surroundings and the soil wasn't ready to accept the very thing that would bring about new life. Yet day after day, I filled the glass. It wasn't long before a few drops were no longer enough. The bulb took root and after several weeks of faithful watering and tending, I woke to a green shoot emerging from the soil.

It wasn't much to look at, certainly, but I cheered and clapped so loudly you would have thought I won the lottery. Days turned into weeks as the green shoot grew to several feet in height. And then, seemingly overnight, the flowers bloomed big and bright. The natural result of careful watering was beauty, growth, and new life.

The brilliance of unfurling petals was unmistakable, but the incremental growth was too miniscule for my human eyes to see. Our personal growth often feels the same way. Yet as we stay close to the Source, and as He is faithful to water and tend, our roots sink into Him as our lives grow upward and outward.

A Moment to Breathe . . .

Be intentional with at least one friend to spy the growth in each other, spurring one another on in the faith.

The Gratitude Train

BY ARLENE PELLICANE

Let us enter his presence with thanksgiving; let us shout triumphantly to him in song. For the Lord is a great God, a great King above all gods. PSALM 95:2–3

WHEN I VISITED THE Virginia War Museum with my family, I was delighted when my son said, "Mom, look there's the Gratitude Train. It was given to the U.S. by the French filled with gifts to say thank you for sending aid in World War I."

How did you know that? I wondered. Ethan is fascinated with history and his enthusiasm for the museum is infectious. Coming home, I thought about that Gratitude Train. Wouldn't it be nice to have gratitude running steadily through our lives, like a train riding on a sturdy track?

Scripture tells us to live with hearts of gratitude, but sometimes we forget. We may forget the battles of the past, which purchased the life of freedom we enjoy each day in America. But when we take time to remember the courage of soldiers and their families, we are filled with gratitude. We can also forget in our homes. We seem to be able to remember the wrongs committed against us pretty well, but what about the rights?

So the next time I'm not feeling too grateful for my spouse (he snores!) or for my kids (they're on my last nerve!), I want to picture a Gratitude Train rolling down the tracks right through my family room. Not the little engine that could. Not Thomas the Tank Engine. The full-size Gratitude Train! And inside each boxcar, there are treasures to be remembered. Like the day I met Christ. Or that time a job offer came just in the nick of time.

Today let's take time to remember. When we remember the goodness of the living God through the years, we won't ever run out of things to say thank you for.

A Moment to Breathe . . .

Picture a train running through your living room. Yep, a train. Your job is to fill each "boxcar" with something you're grateful for today.

Steadfast and Sure

BY ERIKA DAWSON

"As the Father has loved me, I have also loved you. Remain in my love. If you keep my commands you will remain in my love, just as I have kept my Father's commands and remain in his love." JOHN 15:9–10

"NOBODY LOVES ME!" SHE cried, hot tears spilling from her little girl heart.

Of course her words weren't true, but *feeling* trounced reality, and her perception became what she believed. I know this has been true of me and probably true for so many of you. We're hungry for love and acceptance, approval and admiration. Our feelings often lie, telling us we're unloved and unlovable, but the truth never changes—you and I are loved by God.

How deeply are you loved? You are loved with the same intensity and consistency that God loves Jesus. No matter how you feel, the truth is that you are loved completely, profoundly, unwaveringly! Nothing can separate you from His love! But here lies the crux. After telling us how much we are loved, Jesus instructs us to "remain" in His love, which He says is done by keeping His commandments. Will we? To keep His commandments is to love God with all our hearts and souls and minds, and to love our neighbor as ourselves.

This isn't a list of doing more or trying harder. As we draw near to the heart of God, we can live out of His immense love for us. Jesus doesn't ask us to do anything He hasn't already done. Jesus' life is characterized by serving, humbling, giving, obeying—even unto death. Are we willing to live like Jesus? To obey, to follow when it means denying ourselves? In this age of indulgence, can we abstain? In a culture of right now, can we wait? When others get, can we give? Instead of others looking at us, can we point them to Him? Will we surrender, serve, give?

May we remain in His love, resting our lives on the love of Christ, so we can authentically give our lives away to love God and love others well.

A Moment to Breathe . . .

Feelings don't always reflect reality. Remind your heart that God is truth and God is love. And His love for you is steadfast and sure.

When All Isn't Calm

BY CAROLINE TESELLE

I will listen to what God will say; surely the LORD will
declare peace to his people, his faithful ones. PSALM 85:8

THIS MAY SURPRISE YOU. It surprises me to admit it . . . at least out loud. I'm an anxious person.

I've been pushing this down, deep inside me for a long time now. I'd rather pass the blame on other things or people. I hate to admit that I have anxiety. Feeling weak and ashamed, my mind screams, "Keep that curtain closed!"

I hate for people to know that my husband is married to an anxious wife. I hate for people to know that my kids have an anxious mom. I hate for my friends to know that they have an anxious friend.

When it hits me, it's out of the blue. Over the years, I found the things that normally calm me down: writing, going for a walk, listening to music, taking deep breaths, reciting verses or song lyrics. Eventually, all is calm again. But this year, the anxiety began to *seep* instead of being sudden. Regaining the calm and suppressing the anxiety became more difficult.

And here's the hard truth: The only way I can breathe freely is to admit the truth that I'm an anxious person; I don't have to suppress my anxiety and face it alone. When those exasperating moments threaten to seep in, when all isn't calm, I will face those anxious moments by trusting in God's promises and listening to the words of encouragement from family and friends.

If you are facing an anxious moment (or moments) and you need to breathe freely again, join me in the trusting, embracing, clinging, cherishing, and listening.

A Moment to Breathe . . .

Take a deep breath. Then another. Ask God to fill you with His
peace and thank Him for His faithfulness to keep His promises.

Singing for Joy

BY MEL SCHROEDER

You are my helper; I will rejoice in the
shadow of your wings. PSALM 63:7

I GREW UP WITH two girls who became my best friends. We share a lot of memories—some sweet and sappy, others hilarious and embarrassing. But there's one memory that stands out more than the rest.

We were about six years old and had just discovered our gorgeous singing voices. Crowding around the piano while their older sister played, we belted out the song, "Let There Be Peace on Earth" for the entire neighborhood to hear. Believe me when I say there was no peace on earth that day! As the song went on, our singing turned to almost screaming as we each tried to outdo the others.

I've often thought of that day and how lovely our rendition of that song was. For all the screechy loudness that took place, we sure sang that song with joy . . . overflowing amounts of it. Even if it made everyone else in the house cover their ears. My own six-year-old daughter is the same way. She'll sing a tune and dance around the house, exploding with joy for absolutely no reason at all other than the fact that she loves life and she loves Jesus and He shines through her. That inspires me . . . not only in the singing or the dancing of my days, but also in how I live.

Regardless of the day's challenges or life's circumstances that lie ahead, there's always a reason for joy because of all my Father has done for me. The singing kind. The dancing kind. The living-it-out-because-I've-got-Jesus kind. So if you catch me doing a little dance or singing a silly opera tune with my girl, well, that's why.

A Moment to Breathe . . . .

Find a way to sing, or dance, or live with joy. Because He loves
you, friend . . . so, so much. And that's worth singing about.

He Calls the Broken

BY KRISTIN A. SMITH

Falling to the ground, he heard a voice saying
to him, "Saul, Saul, why are you persecuting me?"
"Who are you, Lord?" Saul said.
"I am Jesus, the one you are persecuting," he replied.
"But get up and go into the city, and you will
be told what you must do." ACTS 9:4–6

EVERY SUNDAY I STEP onto the stage as part of our church's worship team. While I love the practices and the people, the stage part still terrifies me. But I do it because I love entering into God's presence by singing His praises.

I used to believe I needed to have my life all together before I had the "right" to be up there singing. I wanted to be involved, but I knew I was a failure, a hypocrite, and a sinner. God only calls the perfect, right? At least that is what the enemy likes to whisper to me, and for a long time I believed it. Finally I heard someone say: *God doesn't call the perfect; He perfects the called.* Oh, this is such sweet music to this broken girl's heart.

I don't have to have it all together. And I can guarantee that I have a lot of growing and refining to do. But knowing that God has called me to a specific purpose, and knowing that He will equip me along the way is enough for me right now. It gives me the courage to say "yes" to being a part of something that is for His glory and not my own.

Saul's conversion on the road to Damascus is another reminder that God calls the broken. He called Saul. He even called him by name—a man set on murdering believers. Well, if God could use a man like that, He can certainly use you and me. I don't know what your past looks like. I don't know what secrets may be hiding that are trying to convince you of your limitations. But God is enough for all of us, and it is through Him and by Him that we are redeemed. God uses the redeemed. And that is you and me!

A Moment to Breathe . . .

You know that thing in your past? That thing you think
makes you unqualified? Yeah, that. It's washed away by
the blood of Christ when you've asked for His forgiveness.
He is calling you today, even calling you by name.

She Scares Me

BY MELANIE DAVIS PORTER

*But the LORD said to Samuel, "Do not look at his appearance
or his stature because I have rejected him. Humans
do not see what the LORD sees, for humans see what is
visible, but the LORD sees the heart." 1 SAMUEL 16:7*

"SHE SCARES ME," THE young lady said as she pointed to a name on the Bible study sign-up sheet. I burst out laughing because the name belonged to a dear friend. This "scary" friend is bold in spirit, but has a heart the size of Texas. I could see how the young lady might be intimidated by my friend's larger-than-life persona. But then I started thinking about all the times we miss out on friendship opportunities because we perceive something different than reality.

The quiet lady who sits to your left in worship may be introverted, not haughty. The young mom brushing past you in a hurry may be at the end of her momma rope with three little ones in tow. The quiet girl who looks away when you catch her eye may be drowning in grief or depression. The truth is, we all come to the table with our own hang-ups. We all have broken, raw places.

I grew up believing first impressions are lasting impressions, especially in the professional world, but we should have a different view based on God's reply to Samuel when seeking the new king of Israel. While people look at outward appearances, God looks at the heart. And we should do the same. Let's take time to get to know the hearts belonging to all the faces around us.

Everyone has a bad day every once in a while. Besides, the beautiful lady dressed to the hilt with all the diamonds might be the most humble person in the room. The super chatty girl may not be so bad once you get to know her and realize her infectious zeal for life. Given the opportunity to engage my "scary" friend, the young lady soon fell in love with her. We just never know what God has waiting for us on the other side of a friendly conversation.

A Moment to Breathe . . .

*Think of one person in your life who seems a little intimidating.
Make a plan to go out of your way to greet her the next time
you see her. In fact, say a little prayer for her right now.*

For When You're the New Girl

BY SANDY HAFEEZ

Do nothing out of selfish ambition or conceit, but in humility consider others as more important than yourselves. PHILIPPIANS 2:3

WE HAD JUST MOVED to Atlanta and I was the new girl. I was meeting new people left and right—something I normally enjoy—but this time it just felt exhausting.

I was afraid of saying something silly or perhaps laughing when it wasn't intended to be funny. Afraid of not wearing the right outfit and coming off too stiff, too loose, or not age-appropriate enough. Afraid of not meeting expectations or not knowing the Scripture reference or not having wise words of counsel. Afraid of . . . rejection.

Fear needs approval, but love needs you. Love agrees with God about who we are and who He is—that He is sovereign and will orchestrate our relationships whether they will end up being casual acquaintances or deep connections.

Fear says I cannot be my true self, but love says I want you to know the true me. I make plenty of mistakes, but by the grace of God, I get a few things right too. When I walk in love for others and the grace that covers me through Jesus, I can open myself up to people—flaws and all. I can love others by being a safe place for them to be who they are. Because it's exhausting trying to act perfect.

Fear is self-focused, but love is others-focused. When we walk in fear in our relationships, we are thinking too much about ourselves. And in my experience, when I spend too much time in my own head, I don't love others well, because I'm not thinking about them. I'm too absorbed with me. I want to come across as a great person, so I talk too much because I want to explain to you how great I am through my conversation.

But love listens and focuses on getting to know others. With God's grace, I'm clinging to love and investing in the relationships I'm building.

A Moment to Breathe . . .

The next time you find yourself the new girl, find one person you can begin getting to know. If you know of a new girl right now, strike up a conversation and get to know her story.

God's Word Is Our Compass

BY SHEILA DAILIE

Then the men of Israel took some of their provisions,
but did not seek the LORD's decision. JOSHUA 9:14

"SO WHAT DIRECTION ARE we headed now?" my farmer dad would ask on a Sunday country drive. "Who lives on that farm?" my school-teacher mom would quiz. Growing up in the country meant that most car drives became geography, genealogy, and directional lessons. As a result, my sense of direction is well-developed.

But when we went to Washington, DC, my internal map stopped working. Even after studying a city map, my compass was broken. Nothing seemed to help. I had to trust our daughter knew the city. Even though she had learned to drive in the country, she was now a sophisticated city driver, with an accurate inner road map.

Similarly, Joshua finds himself in new territory, uncertain of the direction to take. The people of Israel had been making inroads in Canaan, defeating the nations. And the Gibeonites were next, so they used their wits to save their tribe. They brought moldy bread, worn-out sandals, and thread-bare clothing to persuade Joshua they had come a far distance. Joshua wasn't supposed to make treaties with anyone who lived close by, but since the Gibeonites appeared to live far away, Joshua made a treaty with them. He neglected to ask God for wisdom in this situation.

Just as I rely on my inner compass for directions, the Gibeonites relied on their wit. While they saved their lives, hauling wood and water for the children of Israel would be their fate. And like Joshua, when I fail to seek God's direction, the outcome is like a stone dropped in a puddle, with an ever-widening ring of consequences. When we're tempted to take action without consulting God, we're wise to remember both the Gibeonites and Joshua. Our wits, though sharp, and our hearts, though set to follow after Christ, can be fooled. This is why being grounded in God's Word is so vital. Better than any earthly compass, God's Word guides us and leads us in the way of God's wisdom and grace.

A Moment to Breathe . . .

Read the entire story of Joshua and the Gibeonites in Joshua 9 in the Bible. Because the best compass in the world is the Word.

True Rest

BY RACHEL C. SWANSON

"Come to me, all of you who are weary and burdened,
and I will give you rest." MATTHEW 11:28

IT WAS JUST ANOTHER day—changing diapers, shuttling kids, and rearranging Tasmanian devil sized messes in my house. It was also another mom-boss kind of day—approximately 1,000 unread emails, prepping for an event, trying to focus as I finish the project before me.

My to-do list, home, and work responsibilities overwhelmed me. Everywhere, voices seemed to shout: *You can't do this. There's not enough time. Just give up. You're such a failure. You're such a bad mom. Bad wife. Bad friend.*

I jump on Instagram. Just a few minutes to quiet my thoughts. But the world is even louder as I scroll and scroll and scroll. Next thing I know an hour has passed and my brain is ready to implode. Ugh! Okay, time to get back to my to-do list. I jump on Amazon to buy new shoes for my kids. Their current holey ones—not to be confused with "holy," because shoes and kids are far from it—give the appearance of homelessness. Just sayin'.

One click from purchasing I notice eight other unplanned items in my cart! How'd that happen? Hmm. Scanning them, I justify the need even though I know I shouldn't. But it's too easy. Click—BAM—it's on my doorstep in two days. Hopefully my husband isn't home when they deliver.

When life feels overwhelming, why don't we run directly to the One who will give us true rest? Instead we settle for temporary relief in the form of Netflix, Instagram, chocolate chip cookie dough . . . you can fill in the blank. While these things may not be inherently bad, the provided solace is fleeting, never fully satisfying. In fact, it often leaves us aching even more. If you're feeling weary and empty, His Word is clear. Jesus will give us rest. Seek Jesus. Pray to Him, right now. He is the peace and rest your soul is longing for.

A Moment to Breathe . . .

What are your favorite distractions? Take a moment and ask Jesus to be your rest today. Right now in this moment. Invite Him into your day.

Finding God in a Deserted Heart

BY JOLENE UNDERWOOD

This is what the LORD says: The people who survived the
sword found favor in the wilderness. When Israel went
to find rest, the LORD appeared to him from far away. I
have loved you with an everlasting love; therefore, I have
continued to extend faithful love to you. JEREMIAH 31:2–3

I LAY ON THE bed pregnant and screaming. My son wouldn't be born for several months, still I labored through a different kind of pain. "No! No! No!" I threw a tantrum in an empty room. The God I'd loved as a child had become too distant, demanded too much. He wanted me to love Him—and Him alone. He wanted my heart committed to Him fully. But everything inside me rebelled in fear.

I longed for a man to love me and never leave me. So many times I tried to get one and keep one. Nothing worked. What was wrong with me that I was alone again? Me—a broke, single mother with a second child on the way—without friends or family nearby.

Loneliness spilled over. I couldn't contain my wounded heart any longer. I thought of my sister in college whose growing faith made me question mine. She had shared a poem with me; it spoke of surrender and satisfaction in God alone. Not what I wanted to hear, but what I needed to experience. God knew. He spoke to my heart tenderly though I recoiled fiercely.

Eventually, my dry heart could take no more. The Spirit nudged me into one honest step forward. "God, I confess I don't truly want You. Help me to want to want You." More tears came and the process began. My struggling turned into surrender. This crisis of faith sent grasping hands in search of His loving grip.

Wrestling in this wasteland led me to know God in a deeper way. Day by day I came to trust the kind of love that never fails and never leaves. And this same love is yours in Christ too. Even when we're afraid, God is faithful to grow a new love in us. A love that never fails and never leaves.

A Moment to Breathe . . .

Take a moment and pray this simple prayer: Lord,
help me to want to want You more.

When God Fills the Gap

BY KARINA ALLEN

Even if my father and mother abandon me,
the Lord cares for me. PSALM 27:10

I HAVE A BIOLOGICAL father, but unfortunately, there isn't much to tell. He and my mother were never married. When I was nine, he gave me a purple and white 10-speed bike with matching colored streamers attached to the handle bars. He died before I turned ten. That is the sum of what I know. Had it not been for a picture that I have of him, I wouldn't have been able pick him out of a crowd. My mother never talked about him and I never asked. *Welcome to my family.*

Rather than mourning the loss of my father, I mourn the loss of what should have been. I should have had a lifetime of memories with him. He should have both wanted to play and actually played a significant role in my life. One of the toughest facts to reconcile is that he either didn't desire to play a role in my life, or he was incapable of doing so.

A lifetime of growing up fatherless stirs up a well of insecurities that I can barely put to words. These insecurities have been an underlying motivation in many of the decisions I've made. It hasn't been easy, but I know that God has been with me. He has been ever so faithful to extend His grace to me at times when I've been unaware of Him or even when I've been far from Him.

Unlike the many spiritual mothers the Lord has given me, I haven't really had any spiritual fathers in my life. Maybe He decided to fill that gap with Himself; which floods my soul with hope, peace, and joy. God chose me—just as He chose you—to be His beloved daughter. There is no end to His love and grace toward us.

A Moment to Breathe . . .

Thank Him for being such a good Father. Thank Him for
being there, even when no one else was. Thank Him for the
love and grace He so lavishly gives to His children.

When It Appears That All Is Lost

BY ALYSSA DELOSSANTOS

We know that all things work together for the good of those who love God, who are called according to his purpose. ROMANS 8:28

MY FRIEND IS A painter, and we happened into a conversation about her process. As she taught me her steps, I reached for a pen and paper to record her every word. She showed me a picture of her canvas and spoke of the "under painting." First she painted the basic images in terms of lights and darks. To me, it looked like a sketch in a sepia filter. She went on to say the painting would emerge out of these initial details. She said it's easy to get lost in this phase and giving up comes easily. As she spoke, I knew God was stirring in my heart to pay close attention to her words.

You see, in the middle of my hardest seasons, I've looked at the canvas of my life and felt like maybe God had gotten lost, or perhaps skipped over me. That He indeed had good plans for many, but somehow I wasn't included. I want to see a finished work, but I get discouraged when it appears my canvas is just lights and darks—seemingly colorless.

For a vivid picture to emerge, lights and darks have to be painted. Lights and darks add tone value to the painting. A painting has to have both. My "dark" or hard seasons are the first I want to dismiss or hide. But God desires to use my experience to point to His work as the Creator. He uses the darks and lights to create a vivid image of Himself in and through the lives of those who call Him Lord. With strokes of a wide and gracious Father, He has given me eyes to see His work through the experiences of my life.

God is painting on the canvas of my life . . . and yours. Let's choose to trust the Artist. Because the picture is still in process.

A Moment to Breathe . . .

Think of the lighter and darker moments you've experienced. Imagine them painting a picture of your life. Somehow God will bring them all together to form something beautiful in you.

Lavished with Grace

BY BEV RIHTARCHIK

In him we have redemption through his blood, the forgiveness of our trespasses, according to the riches of his grace that he richly poured out on us with all wisdom and understanding. EPHESIANS 1:7–8

WHEN I GOT MARRIED, I remember feeling very blessed, in part, because of the multitude of gifts lavished upon us by family and friends. Over time, however, those gifts ceased working or they outgrew their usefulness. In contrast, God blesses us with spiritual blessings, including His mercy and grace, which are eternal.

I especially love how God didn't just give us His grace, no, He richly poured His grace upon us. His grace simply doesn't run out. Never do we have to worry that His grace will dry up. When we think we've used up our allotment, there will still be grace to spare.

Picture yourself standing under a rushing, roaring waterfall—with all of His grace pouring down upon you, completely soaking you. God, in His great love for us, drenches us in His grace. That's a picture of His grace. Unlike human gifts that will eventually turn to dust, the gift of His grace will carry us from here to eternity.

In order for us to live with freedom in this world—to free us from the bondage of our sin—God had to pay a huge price. The ransom price for our lives was death upon a cross. If giving one's life is not the ultimate act of grace, I don't know what is! He did this specifically for you, and for me. And His grace will never, ever run out.

A Moment to Breathe . . .

Picture yourself standing under a waterfall. With the rushing water pouring over you. Thank God for His lavish grace that He so freely gives.

Face-Down and in Need of Forgiveness

BY EVI WUSK

I will make known the LORD's faithful love and the LORD's praiseworthy acts, because of all the LORD has done for us—even the many good things he has done for the house of Israel, which he did for them based on his compassion and the abundance of his faithful love. ISAIAH 63:7

"YOU AND YOU ARE out of here! Follow me!" I bellowed as I flung the classroom door open, leaving my students in my angry wake. The voice that came out of my mouth did not seem to be my own.

As I tromped down the hallway toward the office, leading these two young men to their doom, I had a moment of clarity. Thank goodness the boys were behind me and couldn't see me almost giggle. What was I doing? Now, don't get me wrong, I do think that my middle school students can behave with a certain level of maturity, but I knew my tantrum wasn't really going to fix anything. In my attempts to get the class back on track, I had come up empty one too many times, so I grasped for control the only remaining way I knew how. I yelled and anyone who disagreed could just get out.

I might have giggled in embarrassment on the walk to the office, but I cried in shame on the drive home from work. How could I have let things get so out of control? Didn't I know better? Apparently on this day, I didn't. And at the end of the day I needed forgiveness for stepping onto the easier path that I knew to be wrong.

When we're face-down in a pile of the mess that we've made, it's hard to remember that the failure we feel is not the failure we are. Quite the opposite. Repentance is a sign of God's deep goodness within all of us, this "made in the image of God" part of us that can't be eclipsed by our bad behavior.

These face-down moments, while terrible, are also weirdly comforting. I am reminded, yet again, that it's not my job to have everything together, to never screw up. God's got that covered. And for that, I say thanks.

A Moment to Breathe . . .

Think of a time when you blew it and wished you could have a do-over. Thank the Giver of grace for the opportunity to turn and return yet again.

Rooted and Grounded

BY JUDY WU DOMINICK

I pray that he may grant you, according to the riches of his glory, to be strengthened with power in your inner being through his Spirit. EPHESIANS 3:16

WHILE WORKING IN THE yard, I saw a young crepe myrtle shoot sticking out at the edge of a flowerbed. I thought it would be easy to yank it out of the ground. As soon as I started pulling, though, it became apparent that it was going to take more effort than a hard tug. So I grabbed my hand axe and started digging up the dirt around the base of the shoot. This revealed a surprisingly hefty root system. Before I knew it, I was pulling up dirt and grass with this root along a seemingly endless path.

I stared at this thing after it came out of the ground. That little shoot seemed utterly unimpressive on its own. It had no height, no flowers, no additional branches. But its root system was substantial.

It made me realize that we too often judge others by what we can see and measure. *I wish she were more patient. I wish God would help her overcome this addiction. She needs to learn to control her temper.* But these "shoots" that are troublesome to behold, with their sickly leaves, are remnant shoots of an old root system that is in the process of being discarded. It's not that the leaves and branches just need reforming. The entire root system must be displaced by a new one.

We get distracted from this reality when we focus solely on fixing (or asking God to fix) the problems that we see above ground. Every problem stems from an unhealthy, unseen root system. But a strong, fruitful tree will develop naturally from a healthy root system.

In a similar way, we are to be rooted and grounded in the love of Christ. As we drink from the infinite well of Christ's love and encourage each other to do so, our roots will grow stronger, healthier, and more established. We will in turn become rooted, grounded, and ultimately, transformed.

A Moment to Breathe . . .

Ask God to show you the things in your life that are connected to unhealthy "root systems" and invite His love to become the new root in your life.

What You Say Really Matters

BY DONNA JONES

No foul language should come from your mouth, but only
what is good for building up someone in need, so that
it gives grace to those who hear. EPHESIANS 4:29

I LOVED TUESDAYS. EVERY girl in my second-grade class was a member of Brownies, which made it the place to be. Excitedly, I buttoned up my uniform and placed the matching beanie on my head, ready for my meeting. After filing into the room with the other girls, I took a seat on the floor.

Our troop leader—an imposing woman with a commanding voice—stood and began barking instructions. Something she said seemed unclear so I raised my hand. She rolled her eyes, clearly annoyed. "Would you please put your hand down, Donna? You always have a question. Sometimes I'd like to flush you down the toilet!" She chuckled, clearly amused with her words, causing a ripple of giggles throughout the room.

I thought: *Well, that was a mean thing to say.* In retrospect, my childlike assessment was an understatement. Her words were downright rotten. My Brownie leader's words remain etched in my brain to this day, but all these years later, I'm grateful her cruel comments didn't stick. Sure, they caused surface embarrassment, but thankfully, no permanent damage. Looking back, I realize why her words stung but didn't scar. Often—daily, in fact—I heard words of life-giving affirmation from the lips of my parents.

Words like . . . I love you. We're proud of you. Thanks for being so kind.

Words of consistent blessing build more than confidence or courage; they build a wall of protection, preventing permanent wounding from hurtful, discouraging, or critical words spoken by uncaring people. Words benefit when words build. Not everyone grows up with parents who build like this. My mother didn't. But despite her upbringing, she took the words of Ephesians to heart. And by doing so, she protected mine.

A Moment to Breathe . . .

Each word we speak either builds up or tears down.
Let's use our words to build others up today.

When It's Time to Move

BY KIM MARQUETTE

These all died in faith, although they had not received the
things that were promised. But they saw them from a distance,
greeted them, and confessed that they were foreigners
and temporary residents on the earth. HEBREWS 11:13

WHEN WE MOVED FROM Kansas to Arkansas, it was our choice, but it meant change—a lot of change. We now lived in Small Town USA where there were few chain restaurants and no second floor at the mall. For an urban girl like me, I thought I had reached the end of the earth. When we pulled into the driveway of our new rental house, we were excited to start this new life in a new place at a new company. But we were also sad to have left our families, friends, and all that was familiar.

Moving means change and conflicting emotions and sometimes chaos, but God is never surprised by any of it. In fact, He's been in the business of moving people since the beginning. Adam and Eve were evicted from the Garden of Eden. It was a necessary downsize for them. Noah and his family were moved by torrents of rain. Abram was told, not only to move, but also to change his name.

All of them were still living by faith when they died. They did not receive the things promised; they only saw them and welcomed them from a distance. They knew they were aliens and strangers on earth, yet every one of them remembered how God had been faithful in the past, and that He promised them a future.

Whether we're in the midst of a move or not, we must view God the same way—remember how God has been faithful to us in the past and that He has promised a future to us as well. God promises that our King is coming back one day. Until then, we can live with our hands open—going where He goes, staying where He stays.

A Moment to Breathe . . .

Start a list, perhaps somewhere in your Bible, of the times
the Lord has shown Himself faithful in your life. And
when you have moments of wavering, return to the list
and remember the good things He's already done.

Hope Falling

BY CARI TROTTER

Purify me with hyssop, and I will be clean; wash me,
and I will be whiter than snow. PSALM 51:7

QUIET FLAKES OF SNOW—EACH unique and untouched by the harshness of earth—descend from the heavens. As each crystal lands safely, the earth seems tranquil, hushed. The snow changes our plans though. It interrupts our day that was prearranged with adventures and running. At first glance, an unexpected bother has sabotaged my momentum. I'm stopped by an uncontrollable circumstance and irritated. But then I listen. I lean in to hear the falling snow. Hope is free falling to earth.

As winter white blankets earth, I let the snow fall. I don't stop it, adjust it, change it, manipulate it, or grieve it. I allow the snow to fall and let it change everything—to script a new plan for today. Because I sense Him saying: *Let my grace not be an interruption, but a divine appointment. Let hope fall all around you today.*

Finding hope in life has become my soul's desperation, begging for something to rise from the ashes that have made me crumble in weakness. The lonely, the poured out, the caregivers, the risk takers, the dreamers . . . with souls sore, and yet, God is always enough. This truth is a confession because it's a yielding, an attempt to take one more step, one more act of faith, with little guarantee that this act will provide the results we desire.

Yet here today I sense His quiet encouragement, not just for me, for but all of us. To keep hoping for that job of your dreams. To keep hoping that loving others counts. To keep hoping that each deposit made in this life has eternal significance.

It's the quiet things that can't quite find the space to fall when life is busy and the world around us is loud. But the snow finds us in the quiet as He finds our hearts and whispers hope.

A Moment to Breathe . . .

Whatever unforeseen delay you may encounter today
or this week, see it as a gift, a chance to listen, to
lean in and hear Him calling you to Himself.

When All You Want to Do Is Eat a Cheeseburger and Cry

BY DENISE J. HUGHES

*Blessed are those who hunger and thirst for
righteousness, for they will be filled.* MATTHEW 5:6

OUT OF DESPERATION I call my husband at work. But I hear his voicemail instead. Here I am, at home with two screaming babies while he's in a quiet conference room with other adults. So I decide to leave a message but I don't say anything. For forty-five seconds I let his voicemail record the shrill cries of two infants.

I hang up and try everything in my mommy-arsenal to soothe the shrieking cherubs. I feed them, change them, bathe them, and dress them. When that doesn't work, I swaddle and bounce, sway and burble. Still, nothing. As a last resort I buckle my babies in their car seats and take them for a drive around the neighborhood. A ride in the minivan usually quiets both of them. Then I have a brilliant idea. I know where we can go, and it won't even require getting out of the car.

I find the nearest drive-thru and whisper "thank you" to the girl who hands me a paper bag with my cheeseburger and fries. I pull into a nearby parking space, and with both babies finally asleep, I eat my happy meal and cry.

Several years have passed since I left the now-infamous message on my husband's voicemail at work. But even now, whenever I feel down, guess where I'm tempted to go? Not to my knees. Not to God's Word. But to the nearest drive-thru altar.

This isn't what I want to be true of me. I want to hunger and thirst for righteousness more than a cheeseburger and fries. Because only God can fill a hungry heart. The deep hunger I feel inside can never be truly satisfied with food or anything else. Only when we come to the banquet of the King and dine in His presence, feasting on the goodness of His Word, are we truly filled.

A Moment to Breathe . . .

*Open God's Word to drink from the living water, for it's the only
thing that will ever truly satisfy. Not just when times are chaotic,
but even in the quiet mundane of the everyday, seek Him.*

When You Feel Unusable

BY TERI LYNNE UNDERWOOD

An account of the genealogy of Jesus Christ, the Son of David, the Son of Abraham: Abraham fathered Isaac . . . Judah fathered Perez and Zerah by Tamar . . . Salmon fathered Boaz by Rahab, Boaz fathered Obed by Ruth, Obed fathered Jesse, and Jesse fathered King David. David fathered Solomon by Uriah's wife. MATTHEW 1:1–6

"THANK YOU," SHE WHISPERED through her tears. I squeezed her hand and smiled, my own tears falling to my lap. I didn't really know her. But there in the sanctuary, I saw the loneliness, the sorrow, in her eyes. When we bowed our heads to pray, I wrapped my arms around her, not knowing her story.

After the service, she looked at me and the story of a husband's betrayal, of losing what she'd thought was true and forever, poured out. She hadn't been able to share the weight of her loss, her fears, her anger, her brokenness with anyone. But that day, all it took was an arm wrapped around her during a prayer for the dam to break open. I looked into her eyes and told her the one thing I knew was absolutely true: God loves her and nothing in her story rendered her less precious to the God of all creation.

I wish I'd had time that day to share with my new friend about the women in Jesus' genealogy: Tamar. Rahab. Ruth. Bathsheba. Mary. These women, the ones named in the ancestry of Christ, were each broken, imperfect. Tamar pretended to be a prostitute and seduced her father-in-law. Rahab really was a prostitute. Ruth was a foreigner. Bathsheba, Uriah's wife, was an adulteress. And finally Mary, an unwed, teenage mother.

I don't know your story—the parts of your past that make you feel unusable by God, but I know this: the very same truth I shared with my friend is true for you as well. The God who chose to include these five women in the family tree of His Son, looks at you and sees potential, possibility, and promise. And His plan for you is good, very good.

A Moment to Breathe . . .

The sting of betrayal is like no other, and yet, Jesus came to bind the brokenhearted with His forgiveness and grace. When you hear a story of betrayal, purpose your heart to respond with the same forgiveness and grace that God has shown to you.

Taking Care of Each Other

BY ANN SWINDELL

"I give you a new command: Love one another. Just as I have loved you, you are also to love one another." JOHN 13:34

WHEN I TURNED THE key to our front door, what I found surprised me. My house was cleaner than I'd left it! I opened a card on the table and discovered why: my friend had cleaned my house, left dinner in the fridge, and placed notes around my home—notes that reminded me of my value in Christ and His love for me.

Her thoughtfulness overwhelmed me. Because I felt—how else can I say it?—I felt taken care of. Most of my days are spent taking care of others. I rub backs, prepare meals, kiss cheeks, tie shoes, wash dishes, mentor students, write checks, grade papers, and give lectures—along with a hundred other things. I can guess your plate is similarly full. You're probably caring for others too. As women we're used to being nurturers, the ones who take care of others. But how often do we let others take care of us?

It feels foreign and vulnerable to be taken care of by others. When my friend came into my house and cleaned (*ack!*) my bathroom, she saw things I didn't want anyone to see. When she put things away, she learned how unorganized I really am. But you know what? If she had asked if she could help, my knee-jerk reaction would have been to say no. Because I should be able to take care of everything on my own, right?

Instead, my friend loved me by taking care of me before I asked. She did something tangible that relieved stress from my life. And I experienced Christ's love through her that day. Taking care of each other is one of the sweetest gifts we can give our friends. But that might mean taking care of one another before asking permission to do so. We won't bulldoze each other, but we might need to smother one another—with love and care.

A Moment to Breathe . . .

Be that loving friend today. Take a meal. Or perhaps a basket of fresh fruit. Offer to pick up your friend's kids from school and take them to the park. Or stop by to say hi . . . and do the dishes.

The Very Best Kind of Rest

BY HOLLEY GERTH

My love calls to me: Arise, my darling. Come away,
my beautiful one. SONG OF SONGS 2:10

I SIT ACROSS THE table from my husband on a cold snowy morning. "I've been trying to rest," I say, "and I don't think it's working."

He looks up at me, "Maybe your idea of rest isn't really rest." I nod. I've been thinking about that too. When I felt like I needed to slow down, I took that literally. I spent more time on the couch. I crossed items off my to-do list. And I felt worse. "You're a dreamer," my husband goes on, "you need to be free to chase ideas, move toward the future, try new things. That's what renews you."

He's a wise one, my man. I'm coming to see that when God asked me to rest it was actually more about my heart. Learning to trust instead of strive. Learning to enjoy rather than push so hard. Learning to focus on the moment instead of results. I think of the verse God put on my heart when all this began . . . a call to arise, to come away with Him. It's an intimate invitation—not to step away from life but to embrace the Giver of it.

I read once that the word *rest* is actually closely related to the word *celebration*. That puts it all in a whole different light, doesn't it? What if God's invitation to rest is really an invitation to joy—to experience life to the full?

I feel the hope seep back into my bones, the peace find its way to my soul again. Yes, I'm made to dream. And to love the Dreamer. So are you. What if we think about rest differently—not as simply the absence of work but instead as the presence of a Person? To be with the One who made us, who formed our hearts, and who places dreams within us, like seeds that grow into all He has for us.

A Moment to Breathe . . .

What does rest look like for you? What's restful for one person
might look differently for another. Write down seven different
ways you can rest. Yep. Seven. Then try one today.

Making Old Things New

BY LISA-JO BAKER

For I will create a new heaven and a new earth . . . ISAIAH 65:17

THIS WEEK I DID something I've been too scared to try for decades. I painted a piece of furniture! I'm not sure why the idea of painting a piece of furniture seems so intimidating to me. Painting something that's old and beat-up and you really don't like anyway is hardly a risk.

We have this old dresser. It's very pine and very dated and very bumped and bruised. I've thought about getting rid of it. But I decided to try painting it instead. I bought the cheapest paintbrush and drop cloth (because I really wanted to be sure I didn't stain the floor in this rental). I picked out some pretty new hardware for the drawers. And then it was time to crank up the music. I barely sanded. It's such an old piece of furniture that it didn't have any real shine left to it. And then I just went to work. It was ridiculous how much fun it was. And sister! It's ridiculous how proud I am of myself.

I wasn't paranoid about perfection. I just focused on the fun of making something old new again. I wasn't sure if it needed a second coat or not. So I texted a friend. Her response made me laugh out loud because, of course, there are no paint police. "Paint it till you like it," she said. Isn't that just the best advice? Sand it till you like it. Pick the color till you like it. Paint it till you like it. Our homes should be safe places. Why do we allow them to boss us around? No ma'am. Make like this newbie decorator and just move it, paint it, redecorate it till you like it.

And I like it, very much. It's so pretty. I keep walking over to pet it and admire it from different angles in the room. My only regret is that I didn't try this a decade ago.

A Moment to Breathe . . .

Don't let your home be the boss of you. Try that thing you've wanted to do for years. And while you're at it, remember, we serve a God who specializes in making old things new.

When That Thing Is Too Hard

BY LISA WHITTLE

*But Moses replied to the L*ORD*, "Please, Lord, I have never been eloquent—either in the past or recently or since you have been speaking to your servant—because my mouth and my tongue are sluggish."* EXODUS 4:10

I AM NOT A man, nor have I crossed paths with a burning bush, but today I feel like Moses. I am swallowed up in my inability to string wise sentences together, inspire a strong moment, or lead anyone to the heart of God. Tomorrow morning, I will stand behind a cross of wood and honor my beautiful friend, Jennifer, who now lives in heaven. And the only thing I'm sure of is that I can't do it.

I can't speak words that will adequately cover the vastness of her life. I can't paint the love and soul and passion of this woman in vivid enough colors. I can't stand before those grieving and tell them something that will be good enough to justify her being gone. I can't not become a blubbery mess, since what I most want to do is curl up in a corner, doing the ugly cry, while mourning my own sense of loss. I can't pretend I feel worthy of the honor to speak when so many other people loved her, too. I can't say the right thing. I can't say enough. I can't say anything, at all. I can't. It will have to be Him.

> The LORD said to him, "Who placed a mouth on humans? Who makes a person mute or deaf, seeing or blind? Is it not I, the LORD? Now go! I will help you speak and I will teach you what to say." (Exod. 4:11–12)

I do not care what all the inspirational books in the world say about the vast abilities of humans to create life-changing moments for ourselves. It's simply not true. All those really good, right, lasting, awesome, moving, important, inspiring, not-a-train-wreck, not-making-it-about-ourselves moments in life will not come from you or me. When the *too-big thing that is not able to be humanly done* is in front of us, it will only be Him.

A Moment to Breathe . . .

Never worry about what you might say, today or any day. Instead, invite Him to speak through you. Give Him the reins of your heart and trust Him in every situation.

The Truth about Comparison

BY KELLY BALARIE

*For we don't dare classify or compare ourselves with some
who commend themselves. But in measuring themselves
by themselves and comparing themselves to themselves,
they lack understanding.* 2 CORINTHIANS 10:12

I REMEMBER THE SCHOOL bell ringing. As I opened my Care
Bears lunchbox, my mind dreamed the possibilities. Pudding?
Crackers? Chocolate milk? Oreos? I relished in the anticipation of
"what could be." (I'm not sure why I did this since I knew exactly
what my lunchbox held—a peanut butter and jelly sandwich with a
side of banana. My usual.)

I peered from lunchbox to lunchbox. What did they get? Pudding?
Oreos? Is a banana trade-able? Do they think I'm lame because I have
nothing to trade? Who notices that I eat the same thing every day?

Underneath the questions around the peanut butter and jelly
sandwich in my lunchbox. I was really asking questions that were
much deeper. What I really wanted to know: Do I measure up? I
was looking for confirmation of my worth. I was looking to see if
others counted me less valuable because I didn't have what they
had. I was looking to be seen as a contributor. I was looking to be
appreciated. I was looking to feel special.

Even today, these feelings don't go away. Even if we aren't
comparing ourselves to others, don't we all desire to feel valuable,
worthy, appreciated, admired, acknowledged? These desires are not
intrinsically wrong. But God has more for us than jealous eyes that
constantly size up the quality of the "lunchbox" sitting next to us. He
wants us to see more. To live greater. To discover life in a richer sense.

God wants us to live abundantly in the identity He has uniquely
given us—not in one set by the standard of others. When we keep
our eyes on Him—not on others—He will show us the life He
designed—a life of joy, contentment, and peace.

A Moment to Breathe . . .

*The next time you find yourself tempted to look to the right
or the left—to compare what you have with what someone
else has—pause instead and ask God to fill your heart with
a deep gratitude for everything you already have.*

The Truth Is I Am Tired

BY ALIA JOY

*I said, "If only I had wings like a dove! I would fly away and find rest.
How far away I would flee; I would stay in the wilderness. . . . I would
hurry to my shelter from the raging wind and the storm."* PSALM 55:6–8

WE SIT ON BARSTOOLS, waiting for the hostess to clear a table.
We catch up on the funny things our children have done, we people
watch in the busy restaurant, and with my straw I stab at the lime
that's sunk to the bottom of my glass. She asks how I'm doing, and
I'm relieved that today I can tell her the truth without her eyebrows
knitting together concerned.

The truth is I'm tired. My need gapes wide, a constant devour-
ing hunger, and I've not the strength to pretend anything less.
I've filled it with lesser things, always to be bloated and sick and
more ravenous than before. I long to be filled, yet I find the most
beautiful presence of God when I am the most wretched. It feels
like nourishment, like amazing grace. I've been discouraged and
battered but not without hope.

Sometimes obedience feels exhausting. Sometimes doing the
thing He calls us to do doesn't mean it all works out how we
thought. Sometimes we realize in the failing how much we longed
for a tiny taste of our own glory, and it dies bitter on our tongues
like the poison it is. Sometimes we thirst for living water to wash it
from our throats and make us clean again.

"I am tired, but good," I tell her and I mean it. I smile wide, and
it feels foreign spreading through my cheeks up into my eyes. My
circumstances haven't changed, but I feel hope that God is at work
in the midst of the tilled and filthy soil of my heart.

I know I may be tossed ragged, but at this moment I realize I've
never been unanchored. I'm tethered to the grace that lets me
breathe under the weight of the tempest. I stretch my limbs like
deep roots and inhale freedom. It is a moment. And it is enough. It
is the blossom of hope unfurling toward the light.

A Moment to Breathe . . .

*It's okay to be real. It's okay to be tired. Our anchor
in Christ will hold. Because even when you break,
He is still good. Hold to this truth today.*

That Hidden Place

BY SUZANNE ELLER

*In him we have boldness and confident access
through faith in him.* EPHESIANS 3:12

YEARS AGO I WAS in Europe on a ministry trip. Our hosts brought us into the beautiful city of Vienna. I stood outside a church that had been in Vienna since the 16th century. Some people stood outside with cameras, angling for beautiful shots of the Gothic architecture. Others lined up to see the painted ceilings.

But right next to the front doors a man sat cross-legged. His face, downcast. His feet, dirty. His clothes, ragged. He held his palms up hoping for alms. But no one saw him. He was lost in the crush of the crowd, at their feet, to the side.

My heart became heavy with the irony. We were surrounded by beauty and a symbol of the Ancient of Days, and a hungry man was lost in the tradition and adoration of a building.

Sometimes we find ourselves in that very place—surrounded by the beautiful exterior trappings of our faith, but failing to see the poverty of our own need. We are that beggar, living in hidden spiritual poverty. So how do we fill the emptiness inside? His presence. We go into our secret place with God and empty ourselves. Of fear and striving and comparison and worry. Because we are poor in self, but rich in Him.

It's a bold move in a sense, but one that Scripture teaches. Because of Christ and our faith in Him, we can now come boldly and confidently into God's presence. So I ask myself: If my palms were held up, what would Jesus pour into them today?

A Moment to Breathe . . .

*Fill up in His presence by soaking in His Word. Read
all of Ephesians 3, then write out Ephesians 3:12.*

How It Feels to Be Held by God

BY KRISTEN WELCH

*"And whoever gives even a cup of cold water to one of
these little ones because he is a disciple, truly I tell you,
he will never lose his reward."* MATTHEW 10:42

WE PULLED UP IN our driveway, exhausted. Our unplanned trip to my sister-in-law's bedside and subsequent funeral left our little family emotionally empty. Raw. Familiar cars parked in front of our house. They quietly filled in the gaps our journey left, doing what needed to be done. As I dropped bags of dirty laundry in the laundry room, I saw bags of groceries on the countertop. Ten minutes home and there was dinner at the front door. The mailbox held condolence cards, the phone had messages. Family and friends, neighbors and community, all holding us.

The first Sunday back at church we heard whispers of condolence and knowing looks. Compassion. I believe this dinner-serving, grocery-giving, and burden-bearing is what Jesus had in mind when He said we should love one another. We wonder how to change the world, how to leave a mark, move the hand of God? We change the world when we simply meet the needs of another. When we love others more than ourselves, not expecting anything in return.

Because no matter the troubled road we journey (and we all walk it at some point), life goes on. Laundry piles up and bellies need to be fed. When we rake the yard of one who can't, we see God. It's love.

We've been doing a lot of holding in our house. I hold my husband as he grieves his dear sister who died far too young. He holds our children as they try to grasp death and eternity. Our children hold the hand of God with their simple faith. Our immediate and extended family is held by community. And it feels like the arms of God.

A Moment to Breathe . . .

*Make it a point to hug one person today. Or two or three.
Make today a day you hold someone close, if only for the
briefest of moments, and tell them how much you care.*

When You're Waiting on God in a Lonely Season

BY KRISTEN STRONG

For now we see only a reflection as in a mirror, but then face to face. Now I know in part, but then I will know fully, as I am fully known. 1 CORINTHIANS 13:12

FROM MY SPOT ON the front porch, I never heard them coming until the driver tapped his car horn. My eyes bounced from my laptop to the white car driving by, and I immediately recognized the two friends inside. I sprang up and pumped my arm so hard waving that I nearly took flight right off the porch. When the car rounded the corner out of sight, my tears came out of nowhere.

What is my problem? I scolded myself. *So now passing cars make me cry?* I knew exactly what my problem was. Once again I found myself in a season of changing friendships, and it took a mad wave at friends in a passing car to make me realize just how long I've gone without solid, in-person girlfriend time.

A few months ago, one of my friends went back to work full-time. Soon after, two other friends moved away. And just like that, my community up and left the building, and it felt like our family had moved again even though we hadn't gone anywhere. I mulled this over and whispered, *Lord, whomever I'm meant to be friends with, please just work it out.*

As the words of my prayer soar upward, I trust He catches them. You can trust He catches your prayers too. If you find yourself in a season of waiting on friends, please know this: Every component of your life—including your need for friendship—is tucked inside God's care.

Yes, I could be in a season of waiting on friends because He wants my attention elsewhere. But God is a God of follow-through and finishes, and I'm learning to live in each friendship season with hope-filled contentment. We don't yet see things clearly. But it won't be long before the weather clears and the sun shines bright.

A Moment to Breathe . . .

Few things are sweeter than to be fully known and loved—just as you are. It's why genuine friendships are so valuable. Reach out to a friend you haven't connected with in a while and tell her you care.

On Prayers That Permeate His Heart

BY ANNA RENDELL

This is the confidence we have before him: If we ask anything according to his will, he hears us. And if we know that he hears whatever we ask, we know that we have what we have asked of him. 1 JOHN 5:14–15

I'VE FOUND THAT MY most important conversations happen in the most mundane places. The car. The hallway. Even the bathroom. My preschool-age son is super proud that he is potty-trained. I mean, it is a big accomplishment. He's now moving into the phase where he prefers that I wait behind the closed door while he does his business, and we often talk through the door. One day last week he said, "Jesus lives in my heart. God lives in the sky. And sometimes God cannot hear us when we pray."

Let me tell you . . . I jumped on that one and a good long bathroom-door-between-us heart to heart ensued. Even at three years old, I want him to know that God always hears us. In the every-moment chatter. In the impassioned and pleading, tear-filled prayers. In the muttered-under-our-breath asks for patience. In the silent moments when the Spirit intercedes for us. In the joyful praises. In the desperate pleas for a swift answer. He hears them all.

I was once taught that there are three answers to prayer: *yes*, *no*, and *not yet*. This may be theologically simplistic, but it brings me peace to know that "unheard" isn't an option. No matter where we pray or how we pray—the eloquence of our words notwithstanding—He hears. Our words don't fall on emptiness but go right to the throne room, rising like incense.

Revelation tells us that an angel in the throne room offers incense at the altar, and together with the prayers of the people, it rises together to God's heart (Rev. 8:3–5). He hears and He cares. Our prayers might not be answered with rumbling thunder and flashes of lightning, but they never go unheard. I want my little boy to know this. I want my own heart, and yours, to know this too, and for us to rest in the peace of knowing that each word spoken to Him is delivered.

A Moment to Breathe . . .

Tell God about your day. Just talk to Him. He hears you. Like incense rising, your prayers reach God's heart. Every time.

When It Feels like You're Wilting

BY ALIZA LATTA

*"The LORD is just; he is my rock, and there is no
unrighteousness in him."* PSALM 92:15

THESE PAST FEW WEEKS I haven't been praying. I've wanted to, but I haven't. *I'm just so busy right now*, I told myself. I haven't been reading my Bible either. I saw it, sitting there on my nightstand, but it had been covered up by other things—glasses of water, notebooks, textbooks . . . my laptop. I had a list of reasons the length of my arm for why I wasn't praying or spending time with Jesus. I just had surgery, my second art show is quickly approaching, and the amount of ongoing college schoolwork is still somewhat shocking to me. As legitimate as these reasons may be, without spending time with Jesus, all of these things empty me.

A few days ago I was sitting on my bed and started crying. "I can't do this anymore, Jesus," I told Him. "I'm too tired. I'm too overwhelmed. I think I said yes to too many things. I think I'm going to have to pull all-nighters for the next month to finish everything I need to do. I feel like I'm drowning. No, not even drowning. I feel like I'm withering, like I'm shriveling right up."

If I was a flower, I was a wilted one. Because I'm a verbal processor, I was trying to fill up on people. I would talk to people about how I was feeling—overwhelmed, worried, and anxious—about all the things I needed to do. Unfortunately, no human was satisfying enough for me.

Jesus is the One who takes my shriveled-up self and breathes life into me. Without Him, I am empty. Only when I lay myself down, when I give Him my worries and fears and anxieties—including the things that I think must appear so petty to Him—can I finally be full.

So I started to pray again. I also began reading Hebrews. And this has made all the difference.

A Moment to Breathe . . .

*Oh, the to-do list seeks to make a slave of the heart.
Instead, talk to Jesus and listen to Him speak through
His Word. Perhaps start with Psalm 92.*

The Lord Is Our Defender

BY JEN SCHMIDT

"The LORD will fight for you,
and you must be quiet." EXODUS 14:14

AS I TIPTOED INTO the kitchen, I overheard my parents in the living room, interceding on behalf of a horrible man. A man bent on ruining my father's reputation, lying in order to restore his financial success, and in the process, destroying ours. I stood behind the wall eavesdropping, all the while becoming more upset with what I heard. "We pray blessing over their family . . . reconciliation . . . harmony . . . forgiveness." How could they pray for our enemy? How could my parents not be outraged?

My justice-oriented nature wanted to gather the troops and defend at all cost—my mother's simple retort rocked my world, "The Lord is the defender of our reputation." But what about right now? This isn't fair. Let's call everyone. Let's gather the assembly. Let's tell them what he's done. We can create a community with a common adversary and it's completely within our right.

Decades later, I can still feel the emotions of that day. Pivotal moments do that to you. They imprint your heart in untold ways. It took me years to understand that their choice was not done out of weakness, but with a strong conviction and strength of character. And I'll be honest, I don't always get this right.

In painful situations, there's nothing I want more than to rally the troops, but I'm continually reminded of my parents' early morning intercession. For years they offered their blessing to an enemy. I've come to realize how futile it is to worry about a reputation. If I live my life wholly abandoned to my Savior, He's got me right where He wants me. As my kids would say, "He's got my back." And friend, He's got yours too.

A Moment to Breathe . . .

That time you were misunderstood. That time you were accused.
That time you were maligned. Give it all to Him. Thank Him for
being your defender. Entrust your reputation to His care.

Don't Give Up on That Girl

BY SARAH MAE

[You took] off your former way of life, the old self that is corrupted
by deceitful desires, to be renewed in the spirit of your minds,
and to put on the new self, the one created according to God's
likeness in righteousness and purity of the truth. EPHESIANS 4:22–24

"GO AHEAD, I *DARE* you." Like venom, those words struck poison right in my heart. I held the razor blade, inched deeper into the lukewarm water, and sobbed. I couldn't do it. I lost the dare. Mom dared me to plunge those razors into my wrist after I threatened I could. My whole teenage spirit hurt desperately; I only wanted her to stop me, to plead for my life, to tell me I was worth more, to show me she loved me.

Alone in my hormonal, awkward, adolescent world, I felt comfort in the only place it was offered. And then, I got pregnant. I had an abortion. I got a trailer and played grown-up. I had a string of boyfriends. Life hurt and felt out of control. I eventually moved back in with my dad, who lived about six states away from my mom, and tried to regain "normal." New clothes, homework, and a curfew. Normal.

When I allow myself to ponder the memories of that time, I almost think it was another life, one completely foreign to me. I'm now sitting in my nice suburban home, with my good husband and three healthy, well-fed, well-clothed, much-loved babes. We live "normal."

But I was "that" girl. She was hurting and desperate and just wanted to be loved. She just wanted to be held and comforted. She just wanted the me that is here now. And she wants you. She needs you. If you see her in your child's school, or in your neighborhood, talk to her. Be kind and open. Show her love and grace. Show her the Savior. She's an outsider, the bad girl, the one it would be so easy to give up on. Don't give up on her. She just might have something worth saying one day.

A Moment to Breathe . . .

You know her. You've seen her. That girl. The one who probably
wouldn't fit in on a Sunday morning, sitting in a church pew.
But don't give up on her. Love her. Invite her. Include her.

You Don't Have to Hide Your Scars

BY JENNIFER DUKES LEE

"I tell you: get up, take your mat, and go home." MARK 2:11

I HAVE A SCAR on my left leg, an accidental souvenir from a head-on car collision in 2009. The insurance company offered to pay for plastic surgery, but I declined. I wanted to keep my scar because I needed to remember what I'd been saved from. When the doctors sewed up my leg, the stitched wound was in the shape of a Y. To me, the single letter stood for Yahweh. I felt as if I'd been marked by God's first initial.

My scar reminds me to thank God for rescuing me. I have other scars too . . . ones you can't see, but if we sat down face-to-face, I'd tell you more. My voice might tremble when I tell you the stories behind the scars. But our scars remind us that, though we were wounded, we've been healed. I know it's not healthy to live in the past, but that doesn't mean we ought to completely forget what has happened to us. Every once in a while, Jesus wants us to remember.

We see this in the Gospel of Mark. Do you remember what happened when some friends bring a buddy to the feet of Jesus? After healing him, Jesus tells him to pick up his mat and go home. Imagine the condition of that ratty, dirty mat. Yet Jesus tells the man to take the mat with him, like a wretched souvenir. That man's mat is like a scar. It's a reminder of who he had been, and what he was rescued from. I think that Jesus is asking the same of us.

Friend, keep your mat. I get it: Maybe you'd rather forget your past. But your mats—your scars—they're part of your story. Someday, you will cross paths with someone who will have the same kind of wound you once had. They'll need to know your story. Your voice might shake a little when you pull out your mat, or show them your scar, but don't be afraid. It doesn't mean you failed. It means you were healed.

A Moment to Breathe . . .

Think of the scars you carry—the ones both seen and unseen. There's a story with each one. Ask God to reveal to you someone who needs to hear your story today.

We Are Carried

BY BECKY KEIFE

He redeemed them because of his love and compassion; he lifted
them up and carried them all the days of the past. ISAIAH 63:9b

THE *BING-BONG* REVEALED A friend reaching out for prayer. I paused in my morning hustle of spreading peanut butter on sandwich bread and prayed. I sensed the Spirit giving me a word for my friend. I texted back, "Ask Jesus who He says you are."

A bit later my phone flashed her response, "Carried. Jesus says I am carried. Carried by the Holy Spirit." I smiled and gave thanks in my heart for such a poignant word gifted to my friend who carries a very heavy load. Yes, she is carried.

My day bustled forward with tasks big and small. Near noon, I buckled my four-year-old into his car seat and picked up his brothers from school—it was dentist day. The dentist isn't my favorite destination, but six months prior marked a successful trip with three well-behaved boys and zero cavities. I smiled walking into the brightly painted office, expecting another bright experience. What happened next left me sorely disappointed.

My youngest son—the most naturally compliant one—flipped a switch from cooperative to heels-dug-in defiant. The next hour was a battle of the wills. (This battle is difficult on its own, but excruciating when required in public.) After much pleading, bribing, FaceTiming with Daddy, and help from a fantastic staff, I'm relieved to say my boy got his teeth cleaned. But back in the minivan after the ordeal, relief spilled over in hot, angry, embarrassed tears.

I felt totally defeated. Hadn't we moved past this stage? What triggered this? How could I have prevented it? The heat of my frustration permeated the rest of the day. Until I reread the message from my friend. Jesus says that I am carried.

I took a deep breath and realized that as mad as I felt, God had empowered me to act with love, patience, and gentleness. I hadn't lost my cool. I had neither shamed my son nor given into his defiance. The Spirit whispered to my heart: *I carried you.*

A Moment to Breathe . . .

Carried. You are carried. Right now. This minute. Rest in the
assurance that Jesus has you, close to His heart, held in His hand.

Hope for the Rejected

BY AMBER C. HAINES

This hope will not disappoint us, because God's love has been poured out in our hearts through the Holy Spirit who was given to us. ROMANS 5:5

MY GREAT-GRANDMOTHER WAS A young maid for a wealthy farm owner, and she got pregnant, just a young thing, before she was married. That baby, head full of curly red hair, was my grandmother, and she lived with her own grandmother instead of with her young mama. Nine years later, she finally moved into the house with her mama and daddy and all her younger sisters. She was gorgeous, grew long legs, and became a majorette with a wit and beauty that snagged a handsome country boy. The country boy played a mean game of basketball. Together they had my mama and my aunt, but he didn't stay.

It makes me wonder if shame can be learned from our parents as well as it being in this world as a result of the Fall. Something in every one of us has felt the sting of rejection. Some of us hold back all our beauty for fear of coming under the shame of rejection. I know my grandmother has had a hard time passing down the beauty instead.

I knew what I was supposed to do. Go into all the world and share the gospel with every creature. But something in me held back. I was asking for His kingdom to come, but then it terrified me, because I knew I was hindered in my walk. I began to work through all the things that kept me from loving others.

So much of the world that I had tried to control began to crumble when I finally named it: a spirit of fear and rejection. When I finally named it, called it an idol, and saw what lies it had fed me, I couldn't help but turn and run in the opposite direction. The walls I've built, they are crumbling. Sometimes we just haven't yet believed how much we are loved. What I'm finding in this freedom is completely new. It's a race, and I'm finally running. I am full-on running toward hope.

A Moment to Breathe . . .

Whatever shame you battle, lay it down. Ask Jesus to take it all. And receive the unconditional love He has for you. Then run. Yes, run in the freedom you've found in Christ.

The Kingdom of Heaven Is like a Mustard Seed

BY HILARY YANCEY

He presented another parable to them: "The kingdom of heaven is like a mustard seed that a man took and sowed in his field. It's the smallest of all the seeds, but when grown, it's taller than the garden plants and becomes a tree, so that the birds of the sky come and nest in its branches." MATTHEW 13:31–32

ONE YEAR I BOUGHT my husband a Meyer lemon tree. It's the first time I've attempted to keep any plant alive, and I wanted—I needed—to see the fruit of my labor. Perhaps not surprisingly, my patience wore thin early, despite my promises to the woman in the greenhouse where I bought the tree. She had warned me that the tree needs time and care—that it can be years before they blossom with fruit, and that in the seasons where you tend without reward, your care should not waver. But mine did.

One morning I sat on the couch with the tree—thirsty for water behind me—and I read Matthew 13:31–32, where Jesus said the kingdom of heaven is like a mustard seed. It's strange, isn't it, that He asks us to think of the seed but not the tree? I once imagined that His purpose was to teach us to look for the kingdom of heaven in the small, unexpected things. But on this morning, as I reread this passage, I no longer heard Jesus telling me that the kingdom of heaven is in small or unexpected things.

Instead I sensed Jesus telling me to look at the tree: *Look closely. The kingdom of heaven is the care that a seed requires. The kingdom of heaven is working in the company of the unseen, watering when you see no flowers and pruning when you see no fruit.*

In this life, we won't always see the fruits of our labor. We're making investments that impact eternity. Like the care for the tree, we care for what the Lord has put in front of us, knowing that it honors Him and honors others. And we trust there will be fruit whether we see it or not.

A Moment to Breathe . . .

Whatever task you're facing, whatever job needs doing, continue in faith, knowing that your work is never unseen by the One who matters most.

When You Have to Say the Hard Thing

BY ANNIE F. DOWNS

But speaking the truth in love, let us grow in every way into him who is the head—Christ. EPHESIANS 4:15

MY PALMS WERE A little bit sweaty as I sat at the coffee shop just a few minutes from my house. The walk on that particular day felt much longer than usual. A friend had hurt my feelings and we needed to talk about it. To be fair, I had hurt hers as well.

I wasn't preparing for an argument or a fight; she and I are great friends. And because I value the friendship, I wasn't willing to sweep my feelings, or hers, under the rug. But hard conversations are still hard, even if there's lots of love in the mix.

For years I thought it was easier to stay quiet, avoid confrontation, and never share my feelings if they were negative. *If I loved my friends,* I thought, *I should just keep my hurt or sadness to myself, and move on.* I just don't like saying the hard thing. It's not fun for me. My personality tends to lean toward "Let's have a great time!" not "Let's have a hard conversation!"

But the older I get, the more I recognize that the hard conversations are actually what make for the great time. I mean, not in the moment, but later, when voices have been heard and the hard things have been said and the feelings have been shared.

So there we sat, face-to-face, and we said the things that hurt. It wasn't easy. I cried. She did too. But we didn't yell or scream, and we didn't walk away before we were done. We both said what hurt, we both apologized (it doesn't always work that way, I know), and we both walked away a little wounded and a little healed.

But here's why we have to do it, in love. Because truth in love leads to health and life. Truth in love doesn't kill, it resurrects. Truth in love may hurt, but it will also heal.

A Moment to Breathe . . .

Love. Wrap every truth in love. Love doesn't change the truth, but when we really love someone, we tell them the truth in love, so the truth can be received, and the relationship restored.

Margin of Error

BY MARY CARVER

Be kind and compassionate to one another, forgiving one another, just as God also forgave you in Christ. EPHESIANS 4:32

MY PASTOR USED A term in a completely different way than I'd heard it used, and it made me sit back in my seat. As he continued to talk about interacting with others, I scrambled to open my notebook and write down exactly what he'd said. I knew I didn't want to forget it.

He defined patience as having margin in your heart for other people's errors.

For a brief time in college I majored in psychology. It took exactly one semester of required math and science courses to cure me of that particular career option, but that doesn't mean I didn't learn anything. One concept I learned in that challenging semester was the margin of error, or as I call it in my non-scientific mind, wiggle room. That use of the phrase was more about research studies and sample sizes and credible, scientific results. But this was something different, something vital to my understanding of the way God calls us to love others, of the way He loves us.

Through much of my life, I've struggled with perfectionism. And not content to simply demand perfection from myself, I've held my friends and family up to exacting standards as well. I've loved fiercely, but at the first sign of weakness, I've become devastated by their inability to live up to my unrealistic expectations.

God has shown me over time how this tendency is hurtful, both to me and to the ones I love. But this encouragement to allow margin for other people's errors—to save some wiggle room for my people to be human—showed me how to live (and love) differently.

A Moment to Breathe . . .

Be intentional to create margin in your heart for other people's errors. Extend the grace to others we so greatly need ourselves. Yes?

You'll Never Be Perfect
(and That's a Good Thing)

BY RENEE SWOPE

Her mouth speaks wisdom, and loving instruction
is on her tongue. PROVERBS 31:26

AN EMAIL FILLED WITH criticism had slipped into my inbox that week and it hurt my feelings . . . for days. That one email set off a storm of self-doubting emotions. It's amazing what one person's criticism can do. When someone criticizes me as a mom, I'll doubt myself as a mother. When someone criticizes me as a friend, I'll doubt my ability to be a good friend. Ten people could say something nice to me or about me, but what I'll remember most is that one person's criticism.

I called a friend to process the harsh email and my emotions. With wisdom she told me, "Renee, you'll never be perfect. And if you ever get to where you are perfect, you will be all alone!" Boy, she was right! I'm definitely not perfect, and I'm sure I'll never be perfect. And I'm thankful because I don't want to be all alone.

Sweet friend, here is what I know . . . Jesus was the only perfect Person to walk this earth, yet He was constantly criticized. But, guess what? Nowhere is it recorded in Scripture that Jesus ever doubted Himself. No matter what, He stayed secure in His purpose and confident in His calling. That day, my friend spoke reality into my feelings. And God used her wisdom to remind me: Jesus depended solely on His Father's approval.

What His Father said was all that mattered. And that is what He wants for us, too. He is there in the midst of our less-than-perfect lives, when disappointments and failures leave us empty and make us doubt our worth and purpose. He is there when we're criticizing ourselves and questioning whether we have what it takes to be a godly woman. He sees us, and He's pursuing us with the gift of His perfect love.

A Moment to Breathe . . .

Let God be perfect. And embrace the less-than-perfect
reality of your life, your day and learn to see both as
normal because, after all, only God is perfect.

Sandpaper People

BY ROBIN DANCE

Pursue peace with everyone, and holiness—without it no one will see the Lord. HEBREWS 12:14

AS A YOUNG MOM, I was struggling through a difficult season with a strong-willed child. I read all the parenting books and plumbed the depths of Scripture for wisdom. But then my father-in-law posed an inflammatory question, "What if this is about you?"

How dare he suggest my son's behavior was my fault! I hurled a half-dozen recent incidents to illustrate how wrong he was. He listened but then gently continued, "I didn't say how he's acting is your fault. I said maybe this is about you. Maybe God is allowing the dynamics of the relationship with your son to do a refining work in your life." My father-in-law, the prophet.

A few days later, his words still lingering, I was strolling down the toy aisle while shopping. I came across one of my favorite childhood toys—a Rock Tumbler set. This set could take a bag of ordinary rocks and transform them into extraordinary polished stones, just by adding water and grit and spinning them for a few weeks in a tumbler.

Looking at that Rock Tumbler, I suddenly understood what my father-in-law had been saying. A rock will remain a regular old rock until it's rubbed the right way. Different kinds of grit produce different results and all are necessary to produce a polished stone. Like rocks tumbled or rough wood sanded, a person changes over time when external forces rub up against them.

This "rub" forever changed the way I viewed difficult people and circumstances—beginning with my son. My perspective realigned to consider what God might be teaching me through challenging relationships and situations. Rather than give in to defeat or frustration, I decided to embrace each opportunity to mature in faith and grow in wisdom. I began to ask the question, "What does God have for me in this?" This didn't make the difficulties go away, but it did give purpose to every situation I faced.

A Moment to Breathe . . .

Think of a challenging relationship in your life and ask God what He might be trying to teach you through this situation.

Fancy's Feathers

BY STEPHANIE BRYANT

Rest in God alone, my soul, for my hope comes from him. He alone is my rock and my salvation, my stronghold; I will not be shaken. PSALM 62:5–6

WE'D LIVED ON OUR farm for only a few months when I had to take one of our hens, Fancy, to the vet. We thought Fancy was sick. She ate ravenously, while the other chickens pecked normally, but she kept getting thinner and she was losing her feathers. Come to find out, she was being picked on.

We didn't understand all of the signs at the time, but pecking order is real. Chickens establish rank, and everyone wants to be over someone else. The vet showed me where the other chickens had been pecking her on the back of the neck, pulling out her feathers. But on her stomach, she was almost bald where she was pulling out her *own* feathers. Fancy was down to three pounds, which is tiny for a mature hen, because she had stopped fighting back for her right to be nourished.

At this point, the other chickens didn't have to convince Fancy she didn't deserve the same as the others. They didn't have to intimidate her, chase her away from the flock, or not let her rest on her nest. She believed what they dished out. She had convinced herself how they treated her was true. She had turned on herself. We took the vet's advice and rehabilitated her with time away from the flock and extra special nutrition. I call it the "chicken spa."

How many of us have felt the same as Fancy? Beat up. Worn out. And needing a safe place to heal and recover. Let's stop pulling out our own feathers, believing the lies that the enemy spews about us. Rather, let's replace each lie with the truth of God's immeasurable love and grace for each of us. I'm happy to report that within a few weeks Fancy recovered fully and was placed back into the flock, thriving as if nothing had happened.

A Moment to Breathe . . .

*Take a deep breath, slow walk, and a long bath.
Create space in your day, however briefly, to separate
from all the weariness of everyday demands.*

It's Not Always Easy
for Nice Girls to Be Nice

BY DONNA JONES

All of you be like-minded and sympathetic, love one another, and
be compassionate and humble, not paying back evil for evil or insult
for insult but, on the contrary, giving a blessing, since you were
called for this, so that you may inherit a blessing. 1 PETER 3:8–9

I WAS TIRED, HUNGRY, and hot—definitely in no mood to be put on hold by customer service. By the time the customer service rep answered the line, I'd heard their mindless elevator music so long my last nerve was shot. I was snippy, maybe even a bit rude.

And to tell you the truth, I didn't care. I was weary of the incompetent service I'd gotten so far and ready to give the young man who had the misfortune of having me as a customer a piece of my mind. I half expected my unresolved issue to be met with a list of justifications and maybe even a "you'll just have to deal with it, lady" attitude, which is what happened the last time I called.

But I detected something different in this young man's voice. Could it possibly be kindness? Even so, his kindness wasn't going to deter me from my rant. No sir, this company needed to know they had a very dissatisfied customer. And by golly, I was just the gal to tell them. But the longer I ranted, the nicer he got. Wouldn't you know I'd get the one competent professional the company employed just when I was all geared up to give him a piece of my mind?

Pretty soon I couldn't justify my behavior any longer. His kindness melted my harshness until I found myself awash in a pool of humility. While my intent had been to change his company's actions, his actions changed mine.

I chuckle when I think about how 1 Peter 3:9 says, "you were called for this"; what an apt picture of a customer service rep's daily routine! And I'm reminded, ultimately, that God is the one who calls us to kindness. Blessing others should be a part of our daily routine, even—or maybe especially—when others don't bless us.

A Moment to Breathe . . .

Be ready to bless someone today,
even if they don't bless you.

The Spiritual Gift of Cheerleading

BY DEIDRA RIGGS

When Moses's hands grew heavy, they took a stone and put it under him, and he sat down on it. Then Aaron and Hur supported his hands, one on one side and one on the other so that his hands remained steady until the sun went down. EXODUS 17:12

IN HIGH SCHOOL, I was a cheerleader. But cheerleading was never considered a sport. Maybe it was the skirts that threw people off. But let me tell you, being a cheerleader is every bit as athletic and important as running the 400-meter relay. Each summer, just like the soccer team, we rose early to rehearse and worked hard at our sport. We invested in the success of our team as if we were holding the line ourselves. When our team won, we celebrated their success. And when they lost, we carried the burden, right along with the players.

These days, I'm still a cheerleader. In fact, I think cheering may be one of my spiritual gifts. I take great pleasure in watching my family and friends see their dreams come true. It's as if their dreams take up residence in my heart. I cheer and do cartwheels when they succeed, and I cry and pray and feel disappointment for them when roadblocks stand in their way.

Perhaps you can relate. Maybe you find great pleasure in cheering the success of others. Or, maybe you find yourself frustrated with a role that many consider a non-sport. You wonder why God seems to have called you to the sidelines, instead of the main stage or center court. Take heart, girlfriend! In God's great manuscript, there is no such thing as "sidelines." Every single role, every season, every assignment matters, and has great significance in the kingdom of God.

Like Moses, every person needs an Aaron and Hur. Sometimes, we get to be Moses, and other times we get to be—yes, *get* to be— the ones who help carry the load. There is nothing quite like being a cheerleader in the body of Christ.

A Moment to Breathe . . .

Think of one person in your life who could use a little cheer today. Devote yourself to being their cheerleader. Send her notes or texts with encouragement. Let them know you are FOR her.

Waiting for God's Gifts

BY KRIS CAMEALY

Take delight in the LORD, and he will give you your heart's desires.
Commit your way to the LORD; trust in him, and he will act. PSALM 37:4–5

I GATHER THE TINY pieces into a well-worn freezer bag. Barbie shoes and random matchbox wheels, Lincoln logs and a teensy set of fairy wings. Items potentially dangerous. This "Piece Bag" is a coveted thing around our house. The kids climb on chairs and pull at the cabinet, "Can we please look in it?"

I say *no* often because I *know* what happens when they look in the bag. They begin to covet, they long for things they're not ready for yet. I know what it's like. So many things in my life have remained out of reach, tucked away on the reserve shelf, not suitable for my handling, *or mishandling* as it might be. I have longed for, and occasionally whined, for things I wasn't ready to handle.

As I tuck my middle boy into bed, he looks droopy-eyed at me and asks for something he cannot yet have. I smile weakly because I empathize with his wanting and I understand the challenge of waiting. I brush his shimmery gold-brown hair aside and remind him about the piece bag in the cupboard. We talk about how God has a "piece bag" of His own, for each of us, and though the one in our cupboard contains mostly hazardous odds and ends, God's "piece bag" is infinitely more awesome, a treasure chest, overflowing with gifts that He will hand down, in His perfect timing.

We whisper there, in the bottom bunk, and then he asks in all seriousness, "Does God really have special gifts for me?" Without hesitation I choke out, "Yes, my sweet boy, with only your name on it." He rolls over and closes his eyes. I stand to leave, but his hand finds mine, "I'm really happy now," he says.

I pray his joy lasts. I pray he remembers this night. Because when God opens His hands, He will give the perfect, appropriate gift, at just the time, with all of His love.

A Moment to Breathe . . .

When you find yourself waiting for a special something you
deeply desire, remember that whatever God desires for you is
infinitely greater. Ask Him to birth His desires inside your heart.

He's Never Too Busy for Me

BY MELISSA AARON

*"Even before they call, I will answer; while they
are still speaking, I will hear."* ISAIAH 65:24

MY BROTHERS AND I were latchkey kids. Meaning, we were home alone after school and all day long during the summer. I was the baby of the family—and the resident snitch. My mom worked in the next town over, and I would call her every day, multiple times, to tattle on my brothers. You can imagine how much it must have thrilled my mom to receive those phone calls from me.

It wasn't as if my calls were ever truly necessary. They were usually about someone hogging the remote control, asking what she thought we should have for a snack, or to complain about our level of boredom.

One day I called one too many times. The next thing we knew she was walking through the door in the middle of the day. She'd had it with our shenanigans and told us to get into the car. She was taking us back to work with her so we couldn't call and bug her anymore. We sat in the car in the parking lot of her job that afternoon. All of us too angry with each other to speak.

We stopped the excessive calls and it's now a funny story we tell about our youth. What I can appreciate about this story now, especially as a parent with my own kids who call me multiple times a day while I'm at work, is that our Father is a God who never gets tired of us. He's never too busy and He loves for us to share all the things, big or small, on our hearts. I love that about Him. He waits for us and promises to be found when we are seeking Him. He vows to hear us when we call, to listen while we're speaking, and to respond to our prayers.

A Moment to Breathe . . .

*Take a moment and "call" Him now. Tell Him about
your day, and ask Him to guide your steps.*

Removing the Remnants

BY JACQUE WATKINS

For we know that our old self was crucified with him so that the body ruled by sin might be rendered powerless so that we may no longer be enslaved to sin. ROMANS 6:6

WITH A GRUMBLING HEART, I pulled into the parking lot . . . the heat of the day pressing down. My body is here to serve, while my heart is somewhere else altogether. An abandoned lot, ridden with weeds is the project before me. For my discipleship class, we were given a service mission assignment to cultivate humility. One full hour of pulling weeds. Just God, the weeds, the heat, and me.

As I pulled one dead weed after another, it amazed me that although they were dead, they were everywhere with deep and stubborn roots. And even some that looked dead, still had the greenness of life in the deepest part of their root, in a sort of dormant state.

Amidst my grumbling, God pursued, with a message for my heart, straight from His. These dead weeds are just like our sin we've allowed to creep into the soil of our hearts. Our past can be so ridden with remnants of weeds, that even when they appear to be dead, upon further inspection, their roots still contain life. To really heal from past sin, we must go back to those ugly remnants and remove their stubborn roots . . . to excise them once and for all.

As the hour ended, I looked back on the cleared stretch of soil—the result of my solo effort—and I was satisfied. The dirt was bare and even, boasting of its potential. A soil ready for something new that won't be disgraced or choked out by the ugliness of dead weeds.

Driving away I gave thanks—remembering that in spite of the wretchedness of my attitude, He met me. In my service, I was changed.

A Moment to Breathe . . .

Examine the soil of your heart for any remnants of lingering sin. Ask the One who gives new life for forgiveness and freedom. Because a forgiven heart is a heart that can exhale.

Choosing Change

BY KIMBERLY COYLE

*In the spring when kings march out to war, David sent Joab with
his officers and all Israel. They destroyed the Ammonites and
besieged Rabbah, but David remained in Jerusalem.* 2 SAMUEL 11:1

I'M STILL LEARNING HOW to live a life in rhythm with the advent
of each new life season. When I fool myself into thinking I've mastered the needs of my family or my own needs during a particular
season, the winds of change stir and blow away this theory.

I struggle most not at the onset of change, but when I set my shoulder like a stone and lean against it. When I wrestle with the season in
which God has placed me, I find myself making poor decisions out of
a fearful and reactionary heart. I choose self over others, distraction
over commitment, or my desires over God's desires for me.

In 2 Samuel, King David chose to stay behind in the city during
the season where kings are called to battle. Rather than leading
his people, defending his land, and conquering old boundaries, he
remained in Jerusalem. There, he fought an even greater battle
against his own flesh.

In the latter part of 2 Samuel 11, we see David—in the wrong
place in the wrong season with the wrong woman. It awakened a
desire in his heart that eventually led him down a path of adultery
and murder. David's experience reminds us to be focused on the
still, small voice of our Father. To what is He calling us? If we refuse
the direction of this season because it is painful or wounding or it
strains against our own desires, where will it lead us?

God continually calls us forward into new seasons of growth. The
Christian life is not stagnant; it is ever changing, ever growing.
When we bind ourselves to the past and refuse to fight new battles,
we become deaf to the voice of victory calling to us from the future.
To everything there is a season. Let's move with the wind and the
waters and learn how to embrace every hard and holy moment we
find in it.

A Moment to Breathe . . .

*Regardless of the season you may find yourself in,
learn how to embrace change and find holy moments
among the everyday parts of your life.*

Building Bridges with Our Stories

BY KAITLYN BOUCHILLON

He comforts us in all our affliction, so that we may be able to comfort those who are in any kind of affliction, through the comfort we ourselves receive from God. 2 CORINTHIANS 1:4

SOMETIMES GOD ASKS US to turn the page, but occasionally we get to look back. Recently I returned to the hospital where I had brain surgery. Every room holds a memory, and when I go back for tests I'm tempted to look the other way as I pass the railings where I pushed my legs to walk again. But these pages in my story are the moments when God proved Himself faithful and strong.

Our stories are like dandelions. They spread farther than we'll ever know when we breathe out and share. You have one, you know. A story. As simple or messy as your day in and day out may feel right now, God is weaving a tapestry of beauty into your story that will tell of His faithfulness when generations to come read the pages of your life.

Inviting someone into your story is not easy. To speak of His faithfulness might mean you need to reveal a few scars. I'm reminded of broken places as I walk the hospital hallways and await the latest test results, but I'm also reminded of this truth: these walls give Him glory.

Jesus said if people keep quiet, the stones will cry out in praise (Luke 19:40). But there's no need for the rocks to cry out when we share our stories with each other. Tell me of your mess, and I will feel less alone. Open your door and allow me to sit and hold your hand as you share bad news. Call me on the phone and we'll have a dance party, miles away from each other, as you tell me God has opened another door to your dream.

Be generous with your story. Let's be a community that shares our stories, gives Him the glory, and remembers that He is still writing. The story isn't over yet.

A Moment to Breathe . . .

Nothing binds two friends so fast as the power of story. Share a part of your story today with a trusted friend. It's in the sharing of our stories that we find community in one another.

How to Measure the Size of the Waves

BY DIANE W. BAILEY

Jesus said, "Leave the children alone, and don't try to keep them from coming to me, because the kingdom of heaven belongs to such as these." MATTHEW 19:14

MY GRANDCHILDREN STAND AT the water's edge watching small shells disappear into the surf-washed sand. Waves bigger than life pound at their feet, but they have no fear, not as long as Granddaddy is near. Their mother and I stand to the side, far enough to allow them a sporty adventure, yet close enough to pick them up should the adventure make sport of them. Their souls live free because they trust us. They don't know about bacteria or sharks. Fear is foreign to them. They simply know the joy of discovery and play.

Eventually we grow older and we hear news of tragedy, so we build walls to protect ourselves and our families. We build as if salvation, protection, and provision are ours alone to fight for and achieve. We devote time and energy trying to hide from danger and fear, instead of facing it, knowing we are held in God's right hand. The truth is, we sacrifice our freedom on the altar of fear when we measure the size of the waves instead of the size of His hands.

In God's hands we find our freedom from fear by the work done on the cross of Christ. When we measure the waves by the size of our hands, fear will always have the upper hand. But when we measure the waves by the Word, we discover fear's impact is little more than a ripple in the water and not a huge wave after all.

I marvel at our little ones in the waves and wonder when I lost part of my freedom. When did worry become more important than wonder? Can I go back to the days of laughter and light-hearted joy?

I step into the cool of the water's edge all the way up to my waist, and I begin to allow the waves to push me higher.

A Moment to Breathe . . .

Determine to walk through this day with your eyes and heart open to the beauty around you. Notice the way a bloom turns its face toward the sun. Become a noticer of wonder today.

Now or Never

BY JESSICA TURNER

Pleasant words are a honeycomb: sweet to the taste
and health to the body. PROVERBS 16:24

LAST SUNDAY I SENT a text message during church. Don't judge. Our pastor told us to. You see, we're in the middle of this series where we're talking about living a life filled with intention, relationships, love, faith, and joy. Our pastor has been pushing us to think about what we'd do if we had a week left to live and to do those things now. To have those conversations now. To not wait.

As an illustration, our pastor had our congregation pull out our phones and send a text message to a friend, a family member, anyone that we felt led to reach out to. As I thought of the people in my life, an old friend popped in my mind. So I texted her: *Just wanted to tell you how much your friendship means to me. Your encouragement, laugh, and ability to truly listen is such a gift. Though we don't talk often, when we do I leave feeling filled up. You truly are one of the greatest blessings of my college experience. Love you.*

She responded: *These words reached the depth of my heart! Thanks so much, Jess, for taking the time to say this. Means the world.*

A few days later, I called her on my way home from work. Toward the end of the conversation she said, "By the way, thanks for that text. I don't know what prompted it, but it meant a lot to me." Her words made me think about people in my life who need a word of encouragement. Who else simply needs a kind word?

So once a week I plan to write cards to ten friends to let them know that they matter to me, how they have impacted my story. Like the text, my messages won't be long, but they will be heartfelt. My prayer is that, when they reach my friends' mailboxes, the simple card will be like honey to their souls.

A Moment to Breathe . . .

Take a moment to tell a friend how much you appreciate her.
Write a few words of encouragement. Text a few uplifting
words. Speak truth and love into someone's life today.

At the End

BY KIM MARQUETTE

*So he answered me, "This is the word of the L*ORD *to Zerubbabel: 'Not by strength or by might, but by my Spirit,' says the L*ORD *of Armies."* ZECHARIAH 4:6

I USUALLY FIND MYSELF "at the end." Growing up, my last name began with a "W" so I was always at the end of every roll call. And it's uncanny how often I enter a bathroom only to find a toilet paper roll with six or fewer remaining squares. Somehow I regularly find myself standing in front of the company water cooler as the bottle reaches its end. Then I'm socially obliged to replace it by lifting a twenty-five-pound jug of water on top of the receptacle.

This isn't just a physical occurrence either. I tend to find myself at the end of my proverbial rope, too, on a frequent basis. What's in this for me to learn? Why am I always at the end of things, situations, and supplies? Perhaps the true lesson is this: I desperately need to get to the end of myself.

It's a lot harder, though, to replace me than a new roll of toilet paper or a heavy water jug. What does it mean to get to the end of oneself? To say, "Enough!" to one's self? Where do I even begin? It's always been about me. I'm an only child with a driven, gregarious personality. My unique design seems too perfectly positioned to feed the me-monster.

Graciously I've been given several heaping doses of humility, but still the me-monster will not die once and for all. So . . . I must rise daily to slay the me-monster. Some days are easier than others, but that me-monster continues to resurrect itself. It's a constant battle—a constant death to self. I should be discouraged, but alas, I'm a radical optimist. I take heart, put to death the me-monster once again, start over, and relish in the truth that God's compassion never fails. His mercies are new every morning. The me-monster is not going down without a fight. But Christ in me wins in the end.

A Moment to Breathe . . .

Can you identify your me-monster? If not, ask the Lord to reveal it to you. And take heart, the same power that raised Jesus from the grave lives inside every believer.

He Just Keeps Giving

BY SANDY HAFEEZ

I pray that the God of our Lord Jesus Christ, the glorious Father,
would give you the Spirit of wisdom and revelation in the knowledge
of him. I pray that the eyes of your heart may be enlightened so
that you may know what is the hope of his calling, what is the
wealth of his glorious inheritance in the saints. EPHESIANS 1:17–18

MY SON ASKED ME if God had ever given me a gift. And like a good mother, I gleamed and said, "Yes, son, He gave me you and your brother."

My son responded, "Mom, He gave you Jesus."

Well, there you have it, schooled by a seven-year-old on the greatest gift of God ever.

Yeah, it was cool, even tweet-worthy, to have my child drop truth on me like that. But afterward, with a little more introspection, came the conviction and the searing question of this: Do I genuinely see Jesus as the gift He is? The gift for my soul salvation and every single day?

When that same son is faced with challenging interactions with peers at school, and my mama heart naturally fears and wants to control things, God gives peace—and the restraint not to do or say anything crazy. God reminds me that He is sovereign over my son's challenges.

When friends are all busy and there is no one to verbally process with, God gives us the gift of prayer and a listening ear that's always available. He also gives us grace when we fail to turn to Him first.

When the world is too loud, God reminds me of truth in His Word.

All of that can happen in the span of a couple hours. He keeps on giving of Himself throughout the day, the week, and eventually the years.

I'm so grateful I get to count my kids, friends, house, and the food on my table as blessings—all gifts from His hand and worthy of our thanks. But no gift is as precious as Jesus Himself. All those things will indeed pass away but my dear Jesus is with me now; He is my treasure, He has gone before me and will be my eternal inheritance.

A Moment to Breathe . . .

Take time today to notice the ways God is giving you Himself.

The Way It's Supposed to Be

BY BRITTA ELLIS LAFONT

My lips will glorify you because your faithful love is better than life. So I will bless you as long as I live; at your name, I will lift up my hands. PSALM 63:3–4

ONE MORNING I LEFT my two-year old daughter with my mother-in-law. I drove to the hospital, parked, carried my suitcase, and checked in, alone. My husband was deployed and it was time to have my baby. Scott was on the phone, from Japan, when our baby was born. Motherhood wasn't supposed to be this lonely.

Later, another "birth"—the completion of a project I'd worked tirelessly on. I was exhausted and thrilled and feeling vulnerable, and I shared my little treasure with a close friend and she seemed to like it. Then she turned sharply, saying, "But don't forget, there's nothing new under the sun." Her motive might have been good—to keep me humble—but the words seemed out of place and mean-spirited. Friendship wasn't supposed to feel so raw.

Friendship should be the place where you serve, encourage, and help carry each other, but sometimes there's nothing you can do. One dear friend has rheumatoid arthritis and another has multiple sclerosis. My husband has Crohn's disease.

We live in a broken world. Some days, life seems to crumble around us. Family can't, or won't, be there for us. Friends disappoint us. Our bodies fail us. Everyone and everything on earth will let us down, but God never does. He has been weaving His trustworthy and faithful love into our stories from the beginning of time.

God has a special love for His people. In Hebrew, God's faithful love is called *hesed*. Today, we know this as God's grace. God pours out *hesed* through Jesus, whom He sent to rescue, redeem, and renew us. Jesus is living proof of God's faithful love. He is God's promise to us, made flesh.

A Moment to Breathe . . .

Soak this in: Your heavenly Father really loves you. For real. Forever. Nothing can ever separate you from His faithful love.

The Marching of Time

BY SHELLY WILDMAN

The boundary lines have fallen for me in pleasant places;
indeed, I have a beautiful inheritance. PSALM 16:6

I'M WATCHING HISTORY BEING cut down. A large maple tree, which has probably stood in the middle of my backyard as long as this house has stood on our street, is being removed. Problem is, the trunk was half dead. Full of rotting wood that crumbled at the touch.

I also just learned that one of our favorite restaurants closed. It was a tiny French restaurant we discovered years ago in a neighboring town. An unassuming place with cheesy décor, twinkling lights, and oilcloth covering the tables, yet the food was amazing. Years of family celebrations took place at that little French restaurant. It had become like home to us, with a warm meal on a winter's night. Now it's gone, memories never again to be made there.

Our youngest just graduated from high school. So we celebrated. Family drove and flew in from across the country. The weekend was grand and fun (and also exhausting), but it was also another closing of the books as we will never again have a child in school here. The empty nest is looming.

Sometimes I'd like to hold on to those "good old" days when everything seemed simpler and sweeter and more serene, but that's not possible. Time marches on. Trees are cut down. Favorite chefs retire. Our children move on. Yet our hearts are forever tied to those memories, those places, those experiences.

I admit there are days when I struggle just a little with putting the past behind me. But I know the days ahead will be just fine—with or without that tree in our backyard, with or without the amazing food we occasionally got to enjoy, with or without my children running through my house—because I know my life is more than the past. I've been promised a future. And so have you.

A Moment to Breathe . . .

Go ahead. Take a stroll down memory lane. Our memories make us
rich, and they become fertile soil for us to plant seeds of gratitude.
Tell God how thankful you are for some of your dearest memories.

When You Feel like You're the Only One with Yuck

BY ANGIE RYG

But you are a chosen race, a royal priesthood, a holy nation, a people for his possession, so that you may proclaim the praises of the one who called you out of darkness into his marvelous light. 1 PETER 2:9

STANDING HAND IN HAND, with India's heat sweltering us both, she takes me aside and whispers, "Thank you for making me know I am not alone." Her dark hair is swept up into a beautiful braid and wisps are sticking to the side of her face as she leans in again, "I like that you shared your yuck with us."

Earlier in the day I had shared with a group of women how God takes our mess and turns it into His masterpiece. No matter what we've been through, we are chosen, forgiven, and called Holy daughters of the King. I shared my yuck—my insecurities and my constant seeking for approval. I shared how I sometimes lose my temper, and well, sometimes I don't always like my job as a mother.

At one point in my sharing, my translator, a Hindi woman, looked at me and asked, "How do you translate 'yuck'?" I thought about it and, with deep spiritual and theological insight, I made a gagging noise with my throat and pretty soon we had over fifty women making gagging sounds to explain what the word *yuck* meant.

Yuck is a universal problem. It started way back in the garden when Adam and Eve desired yuck more than God's best for them. They gave up the beauty of the garden and a pure relationship with God for selfish pride. But when we let go of our yuck, God replaces it with a crown of beauty.

It's okay to have a past you'd rather forget. It's okay to have broken dreams. Real beauty isn't found in looking perfect or being perfect; real beauty is found in the romance of being loved by a perfect God. In spite of our yuck, God calls us His beloved. We are wanted, chosen, and so dearly loved.

A Moment to Breathe . . .

We all have our yuck, but thankfully, God's grace is greater than all our yuck combined. Take a moment and thank Him for the sweet grace He freely gives.

You May Never Know

BY EVI WUSK

Humble yourselves, therefore, under the mighty hand of God,
so that he may exalt you at the proper time, casting all your
cares on him, because he cares about you. 1 PETER 5:6–7

I'VE HAD SIX JOBS in the past ten years. My lifelong farmer father cringes at the thought. No, actually my father has a genuine way of loving me regardless. Maybe I'm the one who cringes. Why can't I find the thing I'm made for and stick with it? Why wasn't I one of those girls who knew she was a teacher from the moment she played school with her dolls? Why can't my résumé be simpler and show a sense of commitment?

A friend's words recently stopped me short in a discussion about call and vocation. "Well, you may never know," she said. "Think of all the people in the Bible who came to the end of their lives not having any sense of whether their ministry truly made a difference."

This thought had never occurred to me. Somewhere in my search for vocation, I got the message that this was all figure-out-able if I just tried hard enough. The thing is, God cares about us ridiculously. Whether we're jiving in the job of our dreams or wondering how we dreamed this life up, God's got us. He's with us in the uncertainty, in the joy, and even in the pain. Right next to us—as close as breathing.

What if, instead of striving and searching and worrying about the thing I was made to do, I look around for a thing that needs doing today? Sometimes my children are literally calling. While I might not know my one true calling, I do know I am called to follow the way of Christ. What would it look like to answer the small calls of my life wholeheartedly, as if I were serving Jesus through other people? What if that is enough? What if it is more than enough?

A Moment to Breathe . . .

The people you serve today . . . they are your ministry, your calling.
And they are enough. Enough for today. And for all your todays.

When It's Hard to Take a Family Photo

BY KATIE ORR

Where, death, is your victory? Where, death,
is your sting? 1 CORINTHIANS 15:55

TWO YEARS AGO THIS evening I received the news. I'm pretty sure I was the last to find out. My twenty-nine-year-old brother, James, had died. My husband and I frantically packed our family of five and left for home the next morning. During that eight-hour drive, tears came often and sporadically. *This can't be real. He's really not dead. He'll be there when we get home. He will.* It felt like a really bad dream. Completely surreal.

I stood shaking in the funeral room parlor with my mom and dad, brother and sister. We sobbed for what seemed like hours as we said our final goodbyes to James. My eyes played tricks on me as I looked into the casket. His chest seemed to raise and lower. But it couldn't be. He'd been dead for days. My eyes saw what my heart longed for. Breath. Life. A second chance. My hand touched his cold face and I kissed his forehead.

Goodbye, James.

Back at my parents' home it felt as if he should be home for dinner any minute now. Still, to this day, I expect him to walk around the corner and make his appearance. But he never does. He never will. How I long to see him again. To be a better sister. To store up and savor every moment we had together. There's a place in my heart that will continually long for him to pull up in the driveway, to join us for dinner. That grief-filled room will forever be imprinted in my memory.

As a family, we are completely incomplete without James. We have yet to take any new pictures together. It's not that we've made a pact not to. We've not even talked about it. It just doesn't seem natural anymore; it doesn't seem right to take a family picture with one of us missing.

Maybe we'll be able to this year. Maybe.

A Moment to Breathe . . .

Saying goodbye makes it hard to breathe. Our only
hope is in Christ alone. Find a friend today and
share a favorite memory of your loved one.

The Rhythm of Thanksgiving

BY KAYLA AIMEE

*The Spirit of God had made me, and the breath
of the Almighty gives me life.* JOB 33:4

AS MY CHILD WAS born I fought against nature and attempted to hold her in. This is not how the baby books tell you to approach labor. Quite the opposite, actually. I was supposed to work with the contraction, breathing out and letting it deliver my baby into the world. Instead I gripped bed rails and held every breath attempting to stop her from slipping away from me, in both body and spirit.

They took her anyway, through an incision, making that effort to fight my own body all for naught. At twenty-five weeks gestation she was born near Thanksgiving rather than Valentine's Day. Many thanksgivings have left my lips but none so full of truth than the day I whispered it over her softly, as a nurse cleared away the tubes from her nose and mouth. I could see her heartbeats on a monitor and I counted every one.

Another heartbeat. Thank You, Lord. Another heartbeat. Thank You, Lord. She forgot to breathe. Let her breathe. Please breathe. She took a breath. Thank You, Lord.

Elsewhere, other families broke bread and bowed heads while I sat in the dark and uncovered a Thanksgiving I didn't know could exist in such suffering. I don't need a calendar for Thanksgiving now, all orange and brown, marked by apple cider and falling leaves. When she rolled over, it was Thanksgiving. When she spoke a single syllable, it was Thanksgiving. When she took shaky steps toward us, it was Thanksgiving.

I know our story could have ended differently and I'm still counting the Thanksgivings with heartbeats, a new rhythm of life where the smallest things really do call for rejoicing. And at night, when I tuck her in with the tulip blanket and feel her chest rise and fall with breath and pulse of a heartbeat underneath my hand, I can see it in the flesh. Thank You, Lord.

A Moment to Breathe . . .

*Look for all the small Thanksgivings in your day today.
Another heartbeat. Another breath. And give Him thanks.*

The Friends Who Pursue Us

BY ABBY MCDONALD

He reached down from on high and took hold of me;
he pulled me out of deep water. 2 SAMUEL 22:17

"YEP, I COULD HANG out with you." I chuckled at my new friend's words. She seemed so confident in our budding relationship. But a month later I was thrown into the world of unfamiliar. After having an emergency C-section, I learned my grandmother died. I tried to care for my newborn, mourn, and take care of myself, but I was drowning. I sank into a depression I thought would never end.

I rarely left the confines of our home as I navigated my new roles as a wife and mother. One day while doing housework in a zombie-like state, I heard a knock at our door. My new friend was standing there with her two kids. She held a bag of homemade treats in one hand and her daughter's tiny fingers in the other—not going to leave until I let her inside. She didn't care that I was still in my PJs. After feeding the baby while I rested, she insisted we go for a walk. I walked outside in the brisk air for the first time in days and drank it in. It was exactly what I needed, and I hadn't even realized it.

Sometimes it's only in hindsight that we can look back and see the mercies of God. With new perspective we see His hand through a friend reaching out and a word of encouragement received. Even though I continued to be a recluse after that day, my friend kept showing up. She introduced me to other moms of littles, and she brought me to Bible study. She didn't give up on me.

Little by little I came out of the darkness and embraced the Light. The more I reached out and embraced the community around me, the more I realized I wasn't alone. Through those moments, when we throw off the façade of perfection and embrace the real, God reaches down and says, "I'm here."

A Moment to Breathe . . .

Be that friend who shows up. Instead of waiting, be
the one to make the call. Knock on the door of a friend,
bringing a smile and maybe a bag of treats.

Spiritual Daughters

BY MEI L. AU

Shepherd God's flock among you, not overseeing out of compulsion but willingly, as God would have you; not out of greed for money but eagerly; not lording it over those entrusted to you, but being examples to the flock. 1 PETER 5:2–3

THE ELEMENTARY CHILDREN HAD picked fresh strawberries and made pies for a fundraiser for Mother's Day. "Can we buy the ones I made?" my son asked.

Immediately Mrs. Sizemore's face popped into my mind. I thought: *We can buy the pies and take them to her.* Shortly after I accepted Christ, God brought this sweet, gray-haired lady into my life. We'd only shared a few brief conversations at church but there was something about her kindness I felt drawn to.

"Happy Mother's Day!" we beamed as we gave her the pie. She started to cry. At the time, I didn't know she and her husband didn't have any children because they married late in life. This was the beginning of a special relationship with this dear woman of God; the first person I knew who had memorized Bible verses. She taught me to love all things Southern, including homemade butter pecan ice cream. Above all, Mrs. Sizemore showed me how she loved Jesus. So when my son's school had grandparents' day, it seemed apropos to invite Mrs. Sizemore and her husband.

One day, she said to me, "You are like a daughter to me!" This time, I cried. The rewards of a spiritual lineage are birthed when we risk vulnerability, when we pour ourselves into the lives of others.

Recently, I was asked to help lead a senior high girls' small group. Watching Jesus ignite their passion for His Word brings me great joy. I have been blessed to raise one son, but these precious girls have become my spiritual daughters, much like Mrs. Sizemore has been a spiritual mother to me.

God knows our deepest longings, and sometimes He fills them in completely unexpected ways.

A Moment to Breathe . . .

Look around on Sunday morning at church. Say hello to a woman older than you and a woman younger than you. Then press beyond the hello. Ignite new relationships within your congregation.

Embracing Life Change

BY ELISA PULLIAM

I, the LORD, examine the mind, I test the heart to
give to each according to his way, according to
what his actions deserve. JEREMIAH 17:10

DURING A KITCHEN RENOVATION, we pulled up the fake-brick linoleum only to discover another layer of flooring underneath it. This second layer was a flowery pattern. Below that was a darker version, and yep, below that one was a lighter one. The former homeowners swung from one extreme to the other, much like we do when we make vows about our future.

Yes, I was guilty of making vows about how my grown-up life would look different than my childhood, long before God got ahold of my heart in college. When I put my faith in Jesus Christ as my Savior, those vows changed and morphed into new ones. I vowed I wouldn't let anger, worry, and fear ruin my testimony, but no matter how hard I tried to change, nothing worked. Praying, going to church, and attending Bible study didn't fix my temper or mind-set one bit.

I was so intent on my "top layer" that I couldn't see what was happening below the surface. By God's grace, He used a dear friend to challenge me to get help to deal with the "bottom layer" issues. I met with a counselor who gently led me through the process of seeking the Lord about the layers-upon-layers hidden in my life.

Getting honest with God was like removing the old linoleum in order to build upon a solid foundation for the future. He didn't change my past, but He transformed my understanding of His faithfulness and forgiveness, His mercy and grace. Through that process, I learned how to walk in His truth, and His truth is what changed me at the core of my thinking and thereby my living. Embracing life change isn't about waking up one morning and being totally different. It's about inviting God to transform us over the long haul, one belief at a time.

A Moment to Breathe . . .

Oh, friend, allow God to go deep, beneath the layers of anger
and worry and fear. Invite Him to examine your heart and mind
and reveal to you the mercy and grace that is yours in Christ.

When the Door Closes

BY KIMBERLY GILLESPIE

To him be glory in the church and in Christ Jesus to all generations, forever and ever. Amen. EPHESIANS 3:21

I JUST KNEW HE was "the one." On paper it seemed logical. We appeared to have the same interests, similar passions. We could talk for hours, enjoyed one another's company. It just seemed "right." Then one day, we had the talk. You know, the "what are we doing?" one.

"What if I told you I found my wife?"

"Wait. What?!" Verbal sucker punch. Closed door. What happened immediately after that is insignificant. It's what God has revealed in the years since that is relevant. Over the years, I've prayed a number of prayers—both answered, and unanswered. There are times when I've celebrated because God not only provided what I was asking, but did so in ways far beyond my dreams and expectations. Other times, I've been so devastated by His "no" that I struggled to believe Him, or believe in Him and His goodness, deciding I would never ask Him for anything else.

In those times, He has been gracious and patient. The years have taught me, however, that often times a closed door is a blessing. That job that I didn't get? There was another one better suited for my personality and passion. That closed door to the city that I wanted to move to? It was a timing thing. It would take another ten years before the door opened, and this time I was better suited to thrive and commit to the calling God has given me. That man I didn't marry? It's not because he wasn't a good guy. He just wasn't the best for me. After almost ten years of marriage, I know that to be true. But God knew the whole time . . . and He provided.

Closed doors. They're painful. But, I am often reminded God doesn't promise that all things will feel good, but He does promise to bless beyond anything we could ever imagine.

A Moment to Breathe . . .

Can you look back over your life and see a closed door that eventually led to something more beautiful than you imagined? Tell Him how grateful you are for the way He moves in ways, often unseen, on your behalf.

Friendship Is Worth the Fight

BY DAWN CAMP

Two are better than one because they have a good
reward for their efforts. ECCLESIASTES 4:9

SOMETIMES GOD PLACES THE right people in our paths for a day or even for an hour. Recently a woman waved me to her table in a crowded mall food court when she saw I couldn't find a place to sit. I enjoyed forty-five minutes of conversation with her and her friend. I heard words that I needed to hear and shared a lovely lunch with two ladies I'll probably never see again. God moved in the middle, aware that I needed connection more than solitude.

Some women possess a gift for encouraging others to open up more than they would otherwise. Sometimes you have to gently probe to take a relationship beyond shallow waters. I want to be that girl. I'm a peacemaker by nature—a keeper of secrets, a respecter of privacy. My awareness of boundaries and personal privacy sometimes keeps people at a distance. Yes, sadly, even friends. But I want to be that friend who's not afraid to ask hard questions and dig deeper and lean in close and listen long to words heart-spoken. I want to be the kind of friend who inspires trust, encourages truth, and welcomes honesty. Differences in opinion may divide, but friendship is worth the effort. *Friendship is worth fighting for.*

Perhaps you're in a season where friendships are abundant. Or perhaps you're in a season where friendships seem scarce. Maybe you're new to your area. Maybe you're tangled in toddlers. Maybe you work long hours outside the home. Or maybe you're self-suffi-cient and tend to keep to yourself. But even the most independent among us need community.

Some relationships are ready-made. Maybe your kids play for the same team, or you attend the same Bible study. Still other relationships require work, especially when distance and sched-ules separate rather than connect. But the effort it takes to grow a friendship is always, always worth it.

A Moment to Breathe . . .

God endows His children with gifts that can be expressed within the
bonds of friendship. How can you best serve your friends today?

Lost in the Details

BY ALYSSA DELOSSANTOS

"How can I know this?" Zechariah asked the angel. "For I am an old man, and my wife is well along in years." LUKE 1:18

AS WE WALKED THROUGH the crowded church foyer, our youngest picked up unexpected momentum. He barreled his way through a sea of knees, a good five steps ahead of the rest of us. We kept a close eye on his location while he moved toward the exit with great gusto.

What happened next will come as no surprise; he smacked right into a pair of legs. He looked up and immediately realized he was not with his parents. In an instant, doubt and fear overwhelmed him and he began sobbing. His daddy, with eyes set on him, reached in and scooped him up in his arms and quieted his fears.

We never lost sight of him that day in the foyer because our vantage point was higher than his. He saw knees, we saw him. He felt lost, though he was never out of our sight. He could not make sense of his surroundings, yet we were only a few steps away. Doubt descended and fear took the driver's seat.

Laced with doubt, Zechariah's response to the angel makes sense to me. I come by doubt honestly. When words don't align with what my eyes can see, skepticism leads me to discount the likelihood altogether. Doubt is the hesitation to believe, and doubt's travel companion is usually fear. When I defer to doubt and fear, asking "How?" becomes my guiding principle. Unfortunately, getting lost in the details of "how" leaves me with "faith paralysis."

Faith is the assurance of things I cannot see. When I rely on my nearsightedness, the details I can see leave me swallowed in doubt and paralyzed by fear. Things won't always add up, circumstances won't always make sense, but my confidence is in my Father, whose eyes see me when I can't see Him, and who is assuredly working in ways I cannot see.

A Moment to Breathe . . .

Wherever you are right now, imagine your Father with His vantage point. Then exhale a prayer of thanks today, knowing He can see everything.

But God

BY KRISTIN A. SMITH

But God, who is rich in mercy, because of his great love that
he had for us, made us alive with Christ even though we were
dead in trespasses. You are saved by grace! EPHESIANS 2:4–5

WHEN LIFE IS RUNNING smoothly, it's easy to be grateful and praise God. But when things go south, as they inevitably do, I often find myself grumbling, "Why God?" instead of praying, "I trust You, Lord."

Have you ever found yourself at this crossroad? Knowing your heart is leaning in the wrong direction?

But God. Two simple, yet powerful words we find in Ephesians. Paul's words are a sweet reminder that God is a God of gracious detours. His grace steers us back to the path that leads to light and life. If anyone understood this grace, it was Paul. Paul was a man who spent years persecuting those who believed in God. A man who some may say didn't deserve the kind of scandalous grace that God offers.

But God. What a generous reminder that it's because of Christ we have freedom. The best of my best is but dirty rags to our Holy God. And yet, despite all my failings, God loves me. Most days I can't wrap my head around this kind of love. Even when I was so deep in my sin, He wanted life for me.

But God. God knew the witness Paul would become. Paul's conversion story is a powerful reminder that even when we fail or run away from God, He can and will use us for His purposes. In the book of Ephesians we find Paul in prison. Enduring what must have been incredibly difficult trials, yet Paul's response was to write a letter that would encourage other believers. Paul obviously understood, in a deep way, the immense grace that only God could give and he wanted us to understand it as well.

God's gift of grace is undeserved but always a balm to our over-striving, weary hearts. We don't have to be perfect. We are perfected because of Him.

A Moment to Breathe . . .

Write a letter to a friend—a real letter, with ink on paper,
written by your own hand, to a friend who lives far away.

Finding Joy

BY JOLENE UNDERWOOD

For his anger lasts only a moment, but his favor, a lifetime. Weeping may stay overnight, but there is joy in the morning. PSALM 30:5

FOR MUCH OF MY life, the word *joy* hung ever before me. Taunting me like a dangling carrot I could never grasp. Joy seemed foreign. Exclusive, and most definitely, elusive.

In the Psalms, David speaks honestly and with great emotion. He expresses anger, fear, hurt, and sadness—all emotions I relate to very well. In Psalm 30:5 he also says joy comes in the morning. So I've often wondered: *When will it be morning?* Or, more specifically: *Dear God, when will it be* my *morning?*

I cried out in tears, "Are You there?" I grew more honest, with myself and with God, about what I felt deep in my heart. I felt abandoned, and with trepidation I admitted I was angry with God.

Even so, I knew God wanted more for me than what I was experiencing. My heart wanted to find joy, yet I couldn't see it. Joy is hard to find when you can't see Jesus.

The more honest I became, the more I realized how desperately I needed Him. In the darkest places, I found Him tending to me. Caring for my hurts and speaking life into dead places. I've learned that joy doesn't come and go with our circumstances. Rather, joy can be experienced despite our circumstances. Because joy comes in knowing Jesus and experiencing His presence. Joy comes when we fall more in love with the One who loves us most. To experience joy is to experience Jesus.

Yes, I want joy, not trials. I want steadfastness, not testing. Maybe you too? Yet, God often uses the hard to refine us. To continue to transform us into the person we were created to be . . . more like Christ. As absurd as it may sound, God allows the hard to make us more holy. Christ is the hope lying ever before us, ever behind us, and ever with us.

A Moment to Breathe . . .

Does joy feel like a carrot dangling ever before you? Or maybe something else? Remove that "carrot" and see Jesus as the One who is ever before you, behind you, and with you.

All for One

BY KIM HYLAND

So if one member suffers, all the members suffer with it; if one member is honored, all the members rejoice with it. 1 CORINTHIANS 12:26

THIS VERSE SOUNDS GOOD, doesn't it? Sort of like a Christian version of the Three Musketeers' oath: "All for one, and one for all!" But living it out in our faith communities seems much harder than it looked for the cavalier trio we watched in the movies. Nevertheless, it's what we're called to do.

These verses and their directive come to us in the context of Paul's comparison of the followers of Christ to a body. Elsewhere in the Bible, we are often referred to as a family. But Paul makes it more personal, and its effect is profound if we don't miss it. Every Christian is a member of one body.

Consider your own body for a minute and see the ramifications of that. When one part of a body hurts, the entire body pays attention and does what it can to relieve and care for the hurting member.

Our youngest son was born premature and very ill. Fast-forward a few years, and Sam began to have dental issues. We couldn't understand, since we hadn't had any teeth troubles with his older siblings. Finally, a pediatric dentist explained to us that during Sam's early days the energy that would have normally gone to forming strong teeth was diverted to fighting illness and literally saving his life. His body "rearranged" its priorities to care for the weak, sick, and suffering parts at the expense of another "member."

In these days of increasing conflict in the church, this principle can help us avoid division and reunite the body of Christ. I may not understand why you hurt. My perspective as one member of the body is limited. But the fact that you do hurt is reason enough for me to care and do what I can to relieve your pain. We're a body, and that's what a body does.

A Moment to Breathe . . .

Think of someone in your local church body who is hurting right now. Ask God to show you how you can care for that person today.

The Gift of Spiritual Hunger

BY FRANCIE WINSLOW

*Taste and see that the LORD is good. How happy is the
person who takes refuge in him!* PSALM 34:8

FROM A VERY YOUNG age, God gently cupped my face with His hands and turned my gaze toward heaven. One of the most formative things I learned during those early years was the power of spiritual hunger. I was hungry and He filled me. Day after day after day. God loves to meet the hungry with abundance that, in turn, produces an even deeper hunger. God honors and blesses spiritual hunger.

When I speak of spiritual desire, I don't mean being shamed into a bunch of religious "shoulds." I *should* have my quiet time, I *should* go to church, I *should* read my Bible, I *should* share my faith. Rather, I'm talking about having an undeniable hunger for more of God—a desire for God that releases heaven's fullness to overflow into your life.

Here are three keys to understanding spiritual hunger:

1. Spiritual hunger is a gift. When we sense a tugging to know Him more, to read the Bible, to ask questions about Him, to just be near people who know Him, it's not a random emotion or a passing phase. It's the drawing of the Holy Spirit.
2. Hunger must be acted upon or it will fade. If we feed the hunger, it will grow. If we ignore the hunger, it will fade.
3. Hunger begets hunger. The more we taste, the more we want. The opposite is also true. The less spiritually hungry we are, the less we'll desire God, and the less we'll be filled.

God loves to stir within us a desire that takes us past a faint awareness of Him and into a lifestyle of walking with Him as our source of fulfillment. This is my prayer for us . . . that our hearts would be consumed with a spiritual hunger for more of Him. That our awareness of Him would increase. And that we would come to Him and be filled. Again and again.

A Moment to Breathe . . .

*Pray for God to increase your spiritual hunger for more of Him
and then open His Word and feast on the goodness you find.*

Every Step of the Way

BY KAITLYN BOUCHILLON

*"Haven't I commanded you: be strong and courageous?
Do not be afraid or discouraged, for the LORD your
God is with you wherever you go."* JOSHUA 1:9

THE THING ABOUT THE words "run your own race" is that I hate running. Walking, however, I can do—tennis shoes laced, earbuds in, and a trail through the trees encouraging me onward. Even with music playing, I can hear the crunch of gravel beneath my feet. Step after step, one and then another, steady and sure. A few times each week, my friend and I spend five minutes chit-chatting before she takes off and I watch her disappear around the bend. I don't rush after her and I don't stop. I just keep going, walking at my own pace, showing up.

Joshua did this and when I think of him, I can walk another lap around the lake and back through the trees. Before leading the Israelites into battle, God instructed Joshua to tell the people to walk. Not "fight" or "get ready" or "bring a sacrifice." He didn't ask them to write a blog post or tweet an encouraging verse. Just walk. Be strong and courageous. Stay with it. For six days, thousands of Israelites walked in obedience. And yet from their perspective, there was no progress, no result to show for the time put in.

Life feels this way sometimes. We walk through joys and struggles, heartache and confusion. And although we know God is with us, nothing seems to be happening around us. But I imagine God's words echoing inside, playing in their ears like the worship music pushing me just a little bit further: Be strong and courageous.

Even when it doesn't make sense and the road is long. Even when we can't see past the next step. We carry the truth with us and eventually, day seven arrives and the walls fall. We walk, He wins, and the gravel crunches beneath our feet. Step after step, one and then another, steady and sure.

A Moment to Breathe . . .

*If you're able, and weather permitting, take a brisk walk
outside. With each step ask God to join you in the choices
you'll make this very day. Be strong and courageous,
because He's with you every step of the way.*

The Stories We Live

BY JENNIFER J. CAMP

They conquered him by the blood of the Lamb and by
the word of their testimony; for they did not love their
lives to the point of death. REVELATION 12:11

I RETREAT TO THE living room, my feet up on our old pine bench, trying to read a book. Sitting here with a book gets me thinking about story—about the impact of another person's life on our own. Stories are more than just words. They're the choices we make and the experiences that shape us.

We don't have to write down our stories to be a storyteller, for our stories to shine wide and loud. We take in each other's stories just by living our own. Our experiences with other people shape the way we live—and live out—our own story. Sometimes we learn stories through books. And sometimes we learn stories from what someone told us. But for a story to be truly taken in by another person, it needs to be shared, through the sharing of a life. For a story to be told, we need to be among people . . . live alongside one another. For how we live—what we say and don't say, what we do and don't do—is the telling of a story that shapes the listener too.

Consider the story you write with your life. These are the stories of the body of Christ, the children of God. Our stories are pages of hope and light in the larger story God is telling. How we live and share our story affects the story of everyone around us.

Let us understand our own story better by walking alongside others, learning how our stories are similar and true and different too. Let us live our unique stories, with the stamp of the Holy Spirit on us. For that's the story we want written, the story the community around us needs to read. *Help us, God, to tell a good story this day.*

A Moment to Breathe . . .

Consider how your story is shaping the people around
you, and how their stories are shaping you. Ask God how
He wants to help you write your story—how, this day, the
choices that make up your story can be for His glory.

The Gift of Quiet

BY CAROLINE TESELLE

*There is an occasion for everything . . . a time to be
silent and a time to speak.* ECCLESIASTES 3:1, 7

GROWING UP WE HAD a family friend who would always tease me about being quiet. He would always come up to me and say, "No talking." He was teasing and he meant it in the nicest way. He was and still is one of the kindest persons I know. He was simply pointing out the obvious: I was a quiet girl. Looking back as an adult, I believe he was pointing out one of my strengths.

It took me years to embrace my quiet. There have been moments when being quiet has bothered me. I didn't like to be known as the "quiet one." This was especially true during my teenage and early college years. I didn't like being known as "sweet, quiet Caroline." Maybe because I'm surrounded by loud. The loud get attention. The loud get noticed. The loud get picked first. While the quiet are quickly forgotten.

As I've gotten older, I've learned it's okay to be quiet. Quiet wants to spend some time with you. Quiet wants you to take a few deep breaths and sit awhile. Quiet wants you to lean in and listen. Quiet wants you to step away from the computer screen, put down your mobile device, and turn off the television. Quiet wants you to call that friend that you've been too busy to talk to and invite them over for coffee or dinner. Quiet wants you to pay attention. Quiet wants you to give yourself permission to say, "No talking."

What's the quiet saying to you? Because when you've taken the time to listen—truly listen—you'll have a better idea of what you're supposed to say.

A Moment to Breathe . . .

*Turn off all the devices in the room you're in. Unplug from all
the noise for just five minutes. Simply sit and savor the quiet.*

On Being a Soft Place to Land

BY MARY CARVER

For those of you who were baptized into Christ have been clothed with Christ. There is no Jew or Greek, slave or free, male and female; since you are all one in Christ Jesus. GALATIANS 3:27–28

I ASKED MY FRIEND how she was doing. "No, really," I said, "How are you?" Her child had been sick—scary sick—and I could only imagine how scared and stressed and exhausted she must have felt. Though I'd offered help in various ways, she'd politely refused.

She told me that she was okay, although not good. She admitted that when friends had asked her the same question at church the day before, she had tried to describe the anxiety and the fear she was experiencing, but they looked at her blankly. As if they had no idea what she was talking about. As if they'd never felt a little crazy themselves. I hugged my friend and told her firmly, because I meant it deeply, "If someone says they've never felt a little crazy, they're either lying or boring." She laughed and thanked me for understanding. We hugged again, and I eventually walked out her front door.

When I think about my various friends and the crises we've endured together—or watched each other face—over the years, I can't help but think of the body of Christ. We are all one, but we each have a different part to play. I have friends who love kids and will offer to watch other friends' kids anytime an emergency or difficult situation comes up. I have friends who are handy and can fix things. I have friends who are great listeners and, when asked, can offer sound advice for most any situation. I have friends who are experts at making casseroles and driving moving trucks and folding a friend's laundry without feeling awkward.

I'm not like those friends. Those aren't my gifts. I make exactly one meal-to-go. I can count the number of times I've babysat friends' kids on one hand, and I can definitely make laundry (or an offer to help) awkward. But if you need someone who will understand when you feel a little crazy? I'm your girl.

A Moment to Breathe . . .

Go ahead and list your strengths—the things you do that make you a good friend. Then do one of those things you're especially good at today.

Choosing Joy

BY ARLENE PELLICANE

Let your eyes look forward;
fix your gaze straight ahead. PROVERBS 4:25

BEFORE I WAS MARRIED, I reluctantly went mountain biking with my husband. We were dating at the time, and I didn't know how to ride a mountain bike. He had to keep me from crashing into the poles—on both sides of the dirt trail. He taught me about steering in five words: *You go where you focus.* I needed to keep my eyes on the path, not on the poles. "Focus," he said, "on where you want to go. Don't focus on the obstacles."

Fast-forward a few years, and well, since we've had kids, there hasn't been a whole lot of mountain biking going on. But guess what we did earlier this month? Yep. We were in New York City, staying with his brother and sister-in-law who happen to be hard-core mountain bikers. So there I was, back on a mountain bike after a long hiatus. As the trail got narrower and switched back and forth, I had to stop before wiping out. I hissed to James (if you can picture me hissing), "I hate this!"

You see, the first five minutes of the ride happened to be the most challenging. I thought: *If the whole trail is like this, I'll never make it!* To my relief, it opened up a bit and wasn't as difficult. I did okay. But before you're too impressed . . . it was a beginner loop.

There were parts of the trail that led between two really big tree trunks. As I approached the trees, I thought, *Oh no! I'm going to hit that tree trunk!* But then I'd remember James's advice. *You go where you focus.* So I forced myself to look straight at the trail and not the trees. And you know what? I made it through, every time.

A Moment to Breathe . . .

Focus on the one thing—just one!—that you want to
do today. When obstacles threaten to get in the way,
choose to exhale, then refocus on the path.

The Days We Doubt

BY ALECIA SIMERSKY

Now without faith it is impossible to please God, since the one who draws near to him must believe that he exists and that he rewards those who seek him. HEBREWS 11:6

WE HAD JUST FINISHED reading our morning devotional. That's when my daughter looked at me and said, "Sometimes I don't know if God is real, I mean, I want to, but sometimes I just don't know."

I didn't say anything at first. She had just revealed a piece of her heart, and I wanted to stop time for just a moment. The truth is, I've doubted sometimes too. There have been days when I've struggled to see God in anything. And I just wasn't sure anymore. I've whispered, "God help me believe, increase my faith" more times than I can count.

There have been days when the doubt threatened to consume me for good and left me wanting to give up Christianity. So many times I've asked God to reveal Himself to me; I've felt like an Israelite begging for a sign. There were some nights I remember reading my kids a Bible story and thinking to myself: *Did this really happen? How can I teach them, when I feel so uncertain?*

Thankfully, God heard my cry. He didn't zap me with a ton of faith overnight; instead, He made me walk through some long, dark valleys. It was in those valley moments—when I didn't see a way out or through—that He revealed Himself the most.

Two years ago our home in Alabama wouldn't sell. Then a tornado ripped through town destroying everything in its path, except my neighborhood. Another family needed a home and ours was available. It's as if God had been keeping our house on hold, just for this family.

It's hard explaining to a twelve-year-old that sometimes we see God best when trials—or even tornados!—come our way. He reveals Himself in the most unexpected ways. So when my little girl tells me she just isn't sure, I tell her it's okay. We'll figure it out together.

A Moment to Breathe . . .

Take a moment and confess your doubts to God. It's okay. We've all had them. He understands too. Then ask God to reveal Himself to you in an unexpected way today.

May We Wrestle and May We Overcome

BY HANNAH VAN DYK

*"Your name will no longer be Jacob," he said. "It will
be Israel because you have struggled with God and
with men and have prevailed."* GENESIS 32:28

RIGHT BEFORE I BEGAN my fifth year of university, I felt paralyzed. Every time someone asked me, "What are your plans after school?" I would shrivel up, avoid eye contact, and say, "I don't know," which was the most truthful answer I had at the time. Part of me thought that, after five straight years of school, God's calling for my life would have been revealed to me—complete with a time line, good salary, and a job title attached to it. It was not.

I walked through hallways lined with lockers, knowing I had options for life after graduation, many of which offered safety, comfort, job titles, and time lines. And yet, there was this constant whisper in my heart that said, "Hannah, not this. Not this." So like any mature twenty-two-year-old, I began to fight. I fought what everyone told me I should do. I fought against the tugs of different passions. And more than that, I fought the God-whispers in my heart, telling me I needed to do something uncomfortable.

Eventually, I grew tired of fighting and wrestling. Isn't that the way it goes? It's like playing tug-of-war, and finally saying, "I can't keep tugging. I give up. I'm putting the rope down." I couldn't shake the discomfort I felt about life after graduation, so I went for a walk to a favorite park, ready to give up the fight. I sat under a tall tree on a red fleece blanket, warm in Toronto's summer humidity. I took out my journal and said, "Okay, God, we're doing this. I'm done fighting with everyone, and I'm done fighting with You."

We can wrestle. We can meet God in the desert and fight all night long, but at some point, we have to stop the fighting, listen to the whispers, receive the blessing, and receive a new name and a renewed calling.

A Moment to Breathe . . .

*Name the place in your heart where you're most tempted
to wrestle with God. Give it to Him. All of it. Lean in and
listen close as He shows you the plans He has for you.*

The Delight in Her Eyes

BY STACEY THACKER

Every good and perfect gift is from above, coming down from the
Father of lights, who does not change like shifting shadows. JAMES 1:17

"I'LL CALL A TAXI," Grandma said. "We'll go on Saturday." And so we did. This amuses me now, because we lived in a one-stoplight town. I'm sure there was only one taxi as well. Lucky for us, that day, it was available. We went by way of Brooksie's Diner. Being all of seven, I ordered a grilled cheese sandwich and a real vanilla cola.

After lunch, we walked to the five-and-dime. I normally strolled those aisles with only a wish and a prayer. But this day was different.

Grandma said, "You can pick out anything you like."

"Anything?" I knew what I wanted. A white baby doll seat, with a floral print cushion. It lay down. It sat up. It was awesome. I smiled taking it in my hands and squealed, "Thank you, Grandma!"

"Is that all you want?"

Her response stunned me. "I can get more than one thing?"

"Yes," she said, "whatever you want."

An hour later I climbed back into that taxi holding onto a new doll, disappearing milk bottles, and the beloved doll carrier. But the thing I remember most was the look in her eyes. Her eyes smiled with delight. So here I sit now, all grown up and sentimental for a real vanilla cola and just one more afternoon with my grandma.

As great as that would be, I have something even better . . . a Father in heaven who loves nothing more than to give good gifts. And I'm not talking about the stuff you can buy at the local five-and-dime. His gifts are good and complete. The best part: the Giver does not change. He's the same God who gave us the stars in the sky to light our way and His Son on Calvary to purchase our freedom. Do you see His eyes? They are smiling with delight. And His delight is for eternity.

A Moment to Breathe . . .

Make a list. Either on paper or just in your mind's eye. A
list of the good gifts your Father has given you. Then close
your eyes and imagine His, smiling with delight.

How Beautiful You Are

BY MELISSA MICHAELS

How beautiful you are, my darling. How very beautiful!
Behind your veil, your eyes are doves. SONG OF SONGS 4:1

THE OTHER DAY I asked my husband to come into our backyard so I could show him where I needed help with a project. As he walked behind me, I cringed a little remembering that I was still wearing the old pair of jeans I had pulled on earlier that morning when I let the dogs out. I've always been self-conscious about my curves, so I found myself wishing I had thrown on a long sweater to try to disguise from his view what I felt was an unflattering fit.

Even though I'm learning to be more accepting of my curves, I still succumb sometimes to a more destructive commentary in my head over what I feel are my physical imperfections. With every step I took, I imagined that my husband was thinking the same thing about me that I was thinking about myself.

Then he said, "You have such a cute little walk." What? I made him repeat himself to make sure I heard him right. "You have such a cute little walk." He wasn't behind me assessing my faults like I was in my own head, he was simply finding and appreciating something of beauty he saw in me as he walked with me.

The example of love my husband set that day (and many other days) inspired me. His words weren't just a reflection of what he saw in me, but they spoke volumes to me about who he is and how he walks, too. Through all the curves and ups and downs and challenges we've navigated over nearly three decades together, I see his daily decisions to still find beauty in me as his wife and to choose to love me as a reflection of his ultimate commitment to live and love like Christ.

A commitment to pursue love in spite of imperfections can help refine us and inspire others when they see Christ working in us.

A Moment to Breathe . . .

Be a noticer of beauty today. Instead of noticing the
imperfections in others, look for beauty and call it out in others.

To Linger at the Table

BY LORI HARRIS

It was as he reclined at the table with them that he took the bread, blessed and broke it, and gave it to them. Then their eyes were opened. LUKE 24:30–31a

LAST YEAR, I PICKED out some new sheets and new pillows for the twin bed at the end of our noisy hallway upstairs. I even bought some new towels for the bathroom and a window unit to cool the space. The closet was filled with totes of personal belongings and the fridge with small bottles of lemonade. We had a houseguest and our home was feeling the weight of one more person.

A house once buzzing with normal chaos morphed into a house swarming with abnormal chaos, emotional outbursts, and post-drunken rages. Mornings became a balancing act of people coming and going. Middays became a blur of job interviews and public servant drop-ins and lawyer visits. The phone rang off the hook. Child visitations took up Saturdays and Sundays. Quiet evenings became prime time for late-night counseling and truth-telling and gut-wrenching sobs.

Nine lives living under one roof—with six kids, two parents, and one houseguest—was enough to make my head spin and my heart ache, but not enough to make me see anything but the cost of my hospitality. Doing for her was inhibiting my ability to see her. That is, until I got the wild hair to treat her to lunch at my favorite restaurant.

After a long day in court and one dismissed charge against her, we ate guacamole and fish tacos and celebrated like old friends. And somewhere between the chips and salsa and mutual vulnerability and closeness at the table, I caught sight of the person instead of the work. She looked like Jesus. The cost of hospitality, the death to self to give another life, only serves to pave the way to real encounters with Jesus who is the Bread of Life. May we choose to be with our neighbors and linger at the table long enough to see the image of Jesus reflected back at us.

A Moment to Breathe . . .

Ask God to open your eyes to see the hearts of those He's placed in your life that you might love them with the love of Christ.

Radical Hospitality, Extravagant Love

BY MEI L. AU

*Then he said to me, "Write: Blessed are those invited
to the marriage feast of the Lamb!" He also said to me,
"These words of God are true."* REVELATION 19:9

"WHAT PUNISHMENT DO YOU think the young man deserves?" the police officer asked my mother-in-law. A troubled teenage boy had broken into her car and stolen her purse.

"I think he should be required to come to my house for Sunday dinner," she said. The police officer was shocked. So was her family. It was grace exemplified. Radical hospitality extended. An invitation to a new life.

Sunday dinners were always interesting at my in-laws. Before she would leave for church, my mother-in-law would put a roast in the oven and a large pot of vegetables on her stove to simmer slowly. You never knew who would be there; neither did she. If she knew anyone was eating alone or who just needed to be loved on, she'd invite them to dinner. Somehow, there was always enough food for everyone as we all squeezed into her small dining room.

For the young transgressor, Grace reached down and pardoned his crime. He deserved punishment, but he dined with forgiveness. When we openly welcome strangers, outcasts, and the neglected, we're showing them their value and worth in Christ. This is the heart of true hospitality.

My mother-in-law lived the gospel until her final breath. At her funeral, the church overflowed with mourners whose lives were touched by her generous and gracious spirit.

I know that one day we'll be reunited again, around another table for supper—at the great heavenly banquet, the glorious feast with our Redeemer, the wedding supper of the Lamb. It will be a joyous celebration of His divine kingdom, a new heaven and a new earth. There will be no more death, no more tears, and no more suffering. Together we will gaze upon the Bridegroom and behold the full radiance of His glory.

A Moment to Breathe . . .

*Think of someone you can invite to dinner this
week—someone who might be completely surprised
by the invitation, in the dearest sort of way.*

The Everyday Woman

BY KATIE ORR

"A thief comes only to steal and kill and destroy. I have come so that they may have life and have it in abundance." JOHN 10:10

OUR CULTURE IS CONSUMED with having it all. Oftentimes I buy into this lie that I can do it all. Have it all. Be it all. I begin to believe I can be Superwoman. I can take on more work today. I can be the ideal wife, mom, church member, and friend. And I can capture the perfect image of my moments to show everyone online how I am living the dream. When in reality, I'm a mess.

I get into trouble when I try to be everything. The toxic "I'm-not-enough" thoughts leave me emotionally unstable. The oppressive "I-ought-to" expectations of others paralyze my decision-making ability. The constant pressure of my "I-should" ideals squeeze every ounce of joy out of my moments.

These pitfalls bring humility—for the obvious reasons—and clarity, because I want a new vision of living my moments free from the not-enough's and the ought-to's and the should've's. In Christ we are promised abundant living. Not paralyzed living. Not terrified living. Not guilt-ridden living. *Abundant living.*

Everyday Christian living isn't meant to be confusing and crippling, but we make it such when we set our sights on being Miss Everything. Rather, we can direct our efforts toward Spirit-led obedience in simple everyday moments: working and watching, cooking and cleaning, teaching and training, sleeping and stirring. Because the promised abundant life is cultivated best when we are living out the everyday life God has planned specifically for each of us to live.

Whether we're a mom, a single woman, an empty nester, or a newlywed, we are everyday women made in the image of God. Every woman is an extraordinary masterpiece with layers of beauty and strength. We're each a piece in a God-sized puzzle, and our unique everyday pieces fit together to display the image of Christ to the world around us.

A Moment to Breathe . . .

For every not-enough feeling or ought-to expectation, match it with a truth or a promise found in God's Word. Like the truth in Ephesians 2:10 and the promise in Philippians 1:6.

Why Rest Takes Courage

BY EMILY P. FREEMAN

I am at rest in God alone;
my salvation comes from him. PSALM 62:1

"PRISON IS STARTING TO sound really good." My friend wasn't in danger of being convicted of anything, unless exhaustion is considered a crime. She was so tired that even the idea of prison didn't repel her if it meant she could be on a mattress and read a book alone. We laughed, shaking our heads at ourselves.

When a desert island, a hospital, and prison start to sound like a vacation, you know you need to take a rest on purpose. When you begin to fill empty hours of weekends and holidays with one more productive thing, you may not realize it's time to take a day off, but your spouse does. And so do your kids. And maybe so do your arteries.

Taking regular time off is not a punishment or a dare or a rule. It's a gift. It's taking a day to open your hands toward heaven and acknowledge you don't make the world go around. It takes courage to choose rest because you know what you are letting go of, but you do not know what you are stepping into. Rest can feel like a risk.

Maybe a break means a time to listen without the pressure to hear something profound; a time to read without the pressure to learn something interesting; a time to receive without the pressure to turn the gift into something more useful.

But just because you take a break from something doesn't mean you're resting. What I need even more than a break is rest—the kind that sticks around even after all the sand and chlorine is washed out of my bathing suit, the kind that softens the shadows of my soul even after I return to the dishes, the kind that comforts and sings in the midst of the same old routines. What I need, what we all need, is to find rest for our souls.

A Moment to Breathe . . .

Set aside some time for soul rest today. It likely includes some
combination of silence, solitude, nature, your people, and the
willingness to come into the presence of Christ and simply be yourself.

The Blessing of Endurance

BY GRACE CHO

Therefore, since we also have such a large cloud of witnesses surrounding us, let us lay aside every hindrance and the sin that so easily ensnares us. Let us run with endurance the race that lies before us, keeping our eyes on Jesus, the source and perfecter of our faith. For the joy that lay before him, he endured the cross, despising the shame, and sat down at the right hand of the throne of God. HEBREWS 12:1–2

I WANT TO RUN a marathon. The spiritual connection, the life lessons, the satisfaction of crossing it off my bucket list. Yes! Yes! Yes! I pump myself up with these thoughts, lace up my running shoes, and start jogging. I can see it in my mind's eye—I'm smiling, running 26.2 miles without trouble, and it's beautiful, really.

But I barely finish a lap around the track before my side starts to hurt and the picture changes . . . I'm sweating from every pore, my legs are burning, my face is red. There's no beauty in this picture, only struggle. I lose all motivation, and my jog slows to a defeated walk.

I get like this with everything. Whenever something gets hard, I want to run away from responsibility because I'm scared to fail *and* scared to succeed. If I fail, there's shame, but if I succeed, there's pressure to go further to the next level, the next success. It's easier to stay low, to get busy with things that don't matter, and to avoid the work I need to do for my soul's good.

To endure means being in it for the long haul—even when it gets boring or you feel like quitting. It's putting one foot in front of the other and taking the next step, whether it's running a marathon or walking in obedience. And maybe that's the point because easy doesn't grow us much. It doesn't force us to live a faith-requiring life.

I tell myself this when I want to quit running or quit doing any hard thing. When I take the next step, I lay the foundation to the path ahead. And in the long run, it will be beautiful and powerful in ways I never could've foreseen.

A Moment to Breathe . . .

Think of one thing in your life right now that's just plain hard—something that makes you feel like giving up. What does the next step look like? Not ten steps or twenty. Take the next step today.

The Woman in the Mirror

BY ANGIE RYG

Because if anyone is a hearer of the word and not a doer,
he is like someone looking at his own face in a mirror.
For he looks at himself, goes away, and immediately
forgets what kind of person he was. JAMES 1:23–24

I RETURNED FROM THE women's conference refreshed, but time gave way to something else. Most of the sessions were filled with strategies, charts, and procedures that I never got around to doing. It's not that I didn't know what to do. But, you know, sometimes I don't want to get up early to read my Bible. I want to stay in bed a few more minutes, one more snooze, and one more dream. I want my special sleep time. Basically, I want my own way.

The Bible says that when we listen to the Word but don't do what it says, we are like people who look at our faces in a mirror and, after looking at ourselves, we go away and immediately forget what we look like. That's what I do. Except I'll take it a step further. I'll put on glossy lipstick, sparkly eye shadow, and a touch of plum blush. Then I'll forget what I look like.

I read the books that tell me how to pray for my children and hear the message on how the gospel can truly change my life, and then I'll just go on and not do anything about it. It pains me to write that, but so often it is true.

The fact is, without the Holy Spirit encouraging us and using His power to change us, we would never ever want to do what the Word says. It's by His amazing grace that He gives us the desire to grow more and more in His Word every day so our actions may bring glory to Him.

He's the one who gives us a hunger for His Word, and when we abide in His Word, He gives us the strength we need, not just to read about change, but to actually experience change. Then we'll no longer be mere hearers of the Word, but also doers.

A Moment to Breathe . . .

Open your Bible today and read the first chapter in James. Ask
God to grant you the grace to do what He commands in Scripture.
Then give thanks that He'll empower you to do what He asks.

It Starts with a Yes

BY JUDY WU DOMINICK

*Don't neglect to do what is good and to share, for God
is pleased with such sacrifices.* HEBREWS 13:16

WHEN MY HUSBAND PETER and I bought our first house together, we prepared two guest bedrooms for out-of-town visitors. Once we felt reasonably settled, we started having people over for dinner. Although we're both introverts, we shared a desire to steward our resources well and to learn how to practice biblical hospitality.

We prayed, "Lord, help us be a blessing to others through what You've given us."

Soon after that, a missionary we knew returned home unexpectedly when she couldn't get her visa renewed. We invited her to live with us as she figured out her next steps. A few months into her stay, we took in a young mother and her son for three weeks as they worked through a family crisis. Facing terrible circumstances, our guests required more than clean sheets and towels. So we learned how to be advocates and provide emotional and spiritual presence.

Peter and I have hosted more people over the years, weaving in another move and the birth of our daughter. Each time we've said yes, God has tested and stretched our limits. But He has also given us glimpses of His heart for the poor, the orphan, and the widow while expanding our hearts in ways we couldn't have imagined.

Biblical hospitality looks different for all of us, but it starts with a yes. God then takes the seeds of our yeses and transforms them into unimagined possibilities—including us along the way.

A Moment to Breathe . . .

*Ask God to show you one person today you could invite over
for lunch. It doesn't have to be anything fancy, just lunch.
Hospitality is at its best when it's kept casual and simple.*

Waiting for Someday

BY DAWN CAMP

Since a person's days are determined and the number of his months depends on you, and since you have set limits he cannot pass, look away from him and let him rest so that he can enjoy his day. JOB 14:5–6

YEARS AGO MY YOUNG children and I arrived at an early morning homeschool event. This season consisted of nursing babies, sleepless nights, and endless diaper changes. But on that particular morning I'd fixed my hair and makeup and all of the kids wore shoes and clean clothes. Victory! Afterward a couple of young mothers told me of their struggle: they desired more children, but didn't know if they could do it, if they could handle the strain of the day-to-day and still hang onto their sanity. My family's presence that day—the fact that the kids and I looked happy and reasonably put together—was just what they needed to see. It gave them hope that the seemingly impossible might be possible after all.

God used me to encourage these women when I was knee-deep in financial worries, sleep deprivation, living in a state of minute-to-minute dependence on Him, and dreaming of those mythical "somedays" ahead. You know the ones. Someday I'll make a workable cleaning schedule and we'll have company more often. Someday I'll become a morning person and have quiet devotions before anyone else wakes up. Someday I'll take a class on graphic design and create the ideas floating around in my head.

Do you wait for "somedays"? What do yours look like? Someday we'll have a house that's big enough for entertaining. Someday I'll have children. Someday the kids will be grown and I'll do all those things I've kept in a holding pattern.

Planning ahead isn't a bad thing. Even God has plans for us. But even though God has a future planned for us, I don't think we're supposed to be waiting for those "somedays" before we dive in and do the work He's put in front of us today. God has given us today—right here, right now—for us to use for His glory.

A Moment to Breathe . . .

*List your "somedays." The things you hope to do someday.
Then look at today and see it as a day to do something you
might not have anticipated when you woke up this morning.*

A Cure for If Only

BY BEV RIHTARCHIK

But Joseph said to them, "Don't be afraid. Am I in the place of God? You planned evil against me; God planned it for good to bring about the present result—the survival of many people." GENESIS 50:19–20

I HAVE SO MANY bookshelves in my home that are overflowing. I have even more books—boxes of them—in the attic. In an attempt to pare down and simplify, I started going through the boxes to see which books I should give away.

Meanwhile, some conversations—and some arguments—had been taking place with one of my adult children. All of this had me wondering: *If only I had done something different, perhaps things would be different now.* I was plagued with "if only this . . ." or "if only that . . ."

As I sorted old books in the attic, a sheet of paper fell out of one of them. Tears welled up in my eyes as I looked at my father's words written in block print—typical of an engineer. My dad had passed away five years earlier, and there had been many instances when I wished I could ask him what he'd do in a given situation. And here in front of me was the answer to my mulling. My father's handwriting revealed some sermon notes from years before. The title of the sermon was "A Cure for If Only."

With his words on paper, my father reminded me that, indeed, God is at work fulfilling His plan through the failure and regret. Just as Joseph's hardships eventually brought him to a place where he could serve an entire nation, God has a plan and He's in control. No matter how badly I screw up, no matter how many mistakes I make, no matter how many "if only's" I have, God can redeem them. Our mistakes can never thwart the sovereign will of God. And in this we find great hope and deep peace.

A Moment to Breathe . . .

Whatever "if only" you find yourself pondering today, give it to God. Give it all to Him—every last worry and fear. Then thank Him that He is, indeed, working every circumstance in your life to come together for good.

A Season of Waiting

BY KIMBERLY COYLE

I am certain that I will see the LORD's goodness
in the land of the living. PSALM 27:13

I SAT IN THE same cramped seats I'd been in for eight hours when the message came over the speakers. A delay on the runway would keep us circling the airport for a "short period of time." I felt travel weary already, but another snack from my bag helped distract me from the delay to my destination. This strategy worked for the first two announcements. By the third announcement, I got anxious. By the fourth, I felt downright angry.

Holding patterns tend to have this effect on me. The seat feels more constricting than before. The noises become louder, the seat-belt chafes, and everyone around me seems hell-bent on behavior I find extremely annoying—like handling the situation with grace, unlike myself.

I'm currently in a season of waiting. I'd describe it as a holding pattern of sorts, as if God broadcasted over the speaker of my life: *Delay ahead. Grab a snack and a settle in for that movie. All those things you planned for at your destination? Forget them for the foreseeable future. We're holding.*

This season of waiting squeezes uncomfortably tight on a heart that wants room to land, room to stretch, room to run wild and free. It's caused me to step back and revisit my decisions, to dig deeper into my motives, to question my plans, and lean harder into my prayers. I sense very little in the way of divine intervention, and it seems as if the connection's gone silent. While waiting I wonder if it holds any meaning.

As I wait, I place my hope in the fact that this holding pattern is in itself a destination. Every decision made led to this place here, and I remain confident that regardless of how long it takes, I have seen the goodness of the Lord in the land of the living. Even when He's silent, I know more goodness lies ahead.

A Moment to Breathe . . .

When you find yourself in a holding pattern—in a season
of waiting—look for God's goodness, for the ways He's
showing Himself faithful, even as you wait.

Giving out of Excess Isn't Equivalent to Sacrifice

BY ALYSSA DELOSSANTOS

Each person should do as he has decided in his heart—not reluctantly or out of compulsion, since God loves a cheerful giver. 2 CORINTHIANS 9:7

WE GATHERED IN A circle to pray over the women who would be the recipients of the piles of donations collected. The prayers offered were thoughtful and heartfelt, but as the time of prayer tarried, I had a growing conviction. While I could hear the sounds of prayers spoken and held tightly to the hands on either side of me, my own thoughts overwhelmed me.

I thought to myself: *What we're doing isn't heroic.* We had gone to our closets, most of which were overrun with excess, and plucked out a few items we really didn't like anyway. This wasn't a sacrifice. As I glanced at the piles, I saw items pruned from the "has no value" section. We didn't pull out our favorite sweater as an act of love for the woman escaping abuse, nor did we give our best handbag. The items in our midst would be quickly forgotten.

Giving out of excess isn't the same as sacrificial giving. Sacrifice is the act of surrendering something prized. Our "giving" wasn't an act of courage or bravery.

Conviction and tears welled up in equal amounts. When it was my turn to pray, I spoke back to the Lord the words He had placed on my heart: *Forgive me for giving out of my abundance and then getting puffed up in arrogance about my good work. This act is not heroic. Refine me, Lord. Help me learn to give sacrificially.*

That moment will not escape my memory. I won't regret saying those words aloud. I am truly grateful for the conviction I experienced that day, while standing in the midst of excess, in the circle of community prayer. I pray that moment of refining lasts a lifetime. *Please, Lord, continue to draw out the impurities in me.*

A Moment to Breathe . . .

Where condemnation brings shame, conviction from the Lord brings opportunity for refinement, which leads to freedom. Thank Him for pursuing your heart and refining you.

Making Room for More

BY KAYLA AIMEE

And may the Lord cause you to increase and overflow with love for one another and for everyone, just as we do for you. 1 THESSALONIANS 3:12

MY WEDDING WAS GOING to be a small affair, with about fifty people or so. Partly because we had a tiny budget and partly because the venue said "we can comfortably seat about fifty people." I'm extraordinarily good at math, so I sent out exactly fifty invitations. If you've ever planned any sort of shindig, you see my mistake here. I assumed fifty invitations equal fifty people. So I was completely confused as to how I ended up with one hundred people on my RSVP guest list. When my groom-to-be walked in to find me perplexed while staring at the seating arrangements, he explained to me how multiplication works.

In the end it all worked out. I mean, I had to cut out almost my entire flower budget, return my fancy shoes, and hand-make my wedding programs in order to afford the extra food I inadvertently added to the budget, but what I remember the most about that day isn't the flowers or the footwear or the stationery. What I remember the most is how much love filled that room. Pictures from my wedding show everyone standing during the entire ceremony—and not because it's customary when the bride walks down the aisle. It's because there was standing room only.

I remember dancing with our guests under garlands strung with lights. I remember clasping hands with family and friends who came to witness the start of our new life together. I remember that our love was multiplied by the gift of their presence. And that is my hope for all of us, not just on special occasions, but every day—that we measure our moments, not with finite numbers, but with the love we share. Because that is the best kind of multiplication.

A Moment to Breathe . . .

As you walk through your day, consider the ways you can bless others with your presence, and with the love you share, because the best moments are always shared with loved ones who care.

Kingdom Ways

BY MARLENA GRAVES

For the kingdom of God is not eating and drinking, but
righteousness, peace, and joy in the Holy Spirit. ROMANS 14:17

WHEN I LOG ON to social media, I am quickly reminded how much I'm polarized by politics and theology. My instinct is to jump in and either defend or attack depending on the situation. It's as if God's commandments for how we're to lovingly treat one another don't apply to our political and theological differences. I don't want my theo-political allegiances to override my neighborly obligations. But how?

In 1 John 4:20, we read, "If anyone says, 'I love God,' and yet hates his brother or sister, he is a liar. For the person who does not love his brother or sister whom he has seen cannot love God whom he has not seen."

While many of us wouldn't want to describe our posture toward another as hateful, how many of us harbor contempt, dislike, or ill will toward our political opponents? If we do, honesty demands we admit we are guilty of hate. It's only in confessing our sin of hatred that we will be healed and set free in Christ to better love others.

It makes one wonder how on earth Jesus' twelve disciples grew in their love for one another given the likelihood they held different political views. I have a hunch that through the power of the Holy Spirit, fellowship with one another, suffering together, observing Jesus' life, and by personally experiencing Christ's love, they saw that their obligation to love one another was more important than their political disagreements.

As they spent time with Jesus, they discovered the nature of the kingdom is not centered on political and theological tribalism, one-upping one another, or constant division. Instead as Paul says in Romans 14:17b, the kingdom of God is characterized by "righteousness, peace, and joy in the Holy Spirit"—what they saw in Jesus.

A Moment to Breathe . . .

Be intentional with your words. Speak words that encourage and uplift those around you, including those who may believe differently.

All In

BY ELISA PULLIAM

"Love the Lord your God with all your heart, with all your soul, and with all your strength." DEUTERONOMY 6:5

THE FIRST TIME I used the expression "all in" was during a card game called Tripoley. As the game unfolds, it's not uncommon to reach a point in which you push all your chips to the center and declare "all in" as your strategic move to win the game.

Every single time I've played "all in" in a round of Tripoley, I've experienced this convicting twinge in my spirit. While I might be choosing to risk "all in" in a card game, was I living my life "all in" for God's glory? Do my "moves" demonstrate a whole-hearted commitment to God? Am I totally invested in obeying God's Word to love Him with all my heart, soul, and strength, and live for His glory? Does God have access to all of me? Or am I devoted to someone or something else more than God?

I confess there have been too many times when my "moves" convey that I've made an idol out of a relationship or responsibility, a pursuit or project, a title or an award. I've fallen into the trap of loving "the created thing" more than my God who created me!

As awesome as it is to win a game of Tripoley with an "all in" move, how much more rewarding will it be when I'm face-to-face with God and can confidently say to Him, "Lord, I was 'all in' for You."

A Moment to Breathe . . .

Declare that you're "all in" for God's glory—right now, today. Then live each moment committed to following His Word with your whole heart, soul, and strength.

The Sisterhood of Messy Hearts

BY MELANIE DAVIS PORTER

For by the grace given to me, I tell everyone among you not to think of himself more highly than he should think. Instead, think sensibly, as God has distributed a measure of faith to each one. ROMANS 12:3

SHE WAS THE FUNNIEST girl in school with the coolest clothes. Everyone wanted to sit by her at lunch, but she made that decision herself. She formed a club and the chosen members met on Friday nights at the skating rink. Then . . . her parents got a divorce. She told fewer jokes. The trips to the skating rink stopped. I found her crying one day and my sixth-grade heart hurt because her world was falling apart. I wanted to be a good friend, but she wouldn't let me.

Just like the popular girl back in the sixth grade, us big girls have holes in our hearts too. We all have secrets, heartaches, and betrayals. Wary of trust, walls go up, separating sisters in Christ. So what's the solution? What can we do? If we really want change, we have to be willing to change. Scripture says we should put others first, thinking of their needs ahead of our own.

This also means taking the lead in loving our sisters first . . . before they love me. What if we put away all unfavorable perceptions and choose to think only the best about our sister? What if we forget previous clashes and choose to start with a clean slate? What if we keep confidences in perfect trust and choose to speak only positively about her? And when we fail, what if we humbly ask for forgiveness and choose to forgive when hurts come our way?

In order for this sisterhood of messy hearts to flourish in Christ, grace must go both ways. Beauty is found in grace. Hope is exchanged in love. Redemption is mined from humility. And the meekness of a messy sisterhood can be a beautiful tapestry of merciful grace . . . if only we'll take the lead to love first.

A Moment to Breathe . . .

Take a deep breath and choose today to take the lead. You know that girl on the periphery? The one who keeps to the outer edges of circles and friends? Seek her out. Be the first to love.

To Be Brought Near

BY SANDY HAFEEZ

*But now in Christ Jesus, you who were far away have been
brought near by the blood of Christ.* EPHESIANS 2:13

MY HUSBAND WAS OUT of town while my oldest and I found
ourselves in the midst of a duel. Who will give in first? At first I
was calmly answering his questions, but there he was, all at the
tender age of four, spewing disrespectful words. I was on the brink
of spewing some back when out of nowhere he flung himself into
my arms for a massive embrace with tears flowing. I wrapped my
mama-arms around him and brought him near into my embrace.

With a front row seat to my son's sin, I am reminded again about
my own. I see his wrestle—fighting a strong desire to do what he
wants versus obeying what I've said. Even at my "tender" age of
thirty-five I sometimes think I know what's best and make my own
decisions apart from God. There are days I battle with Him over why
I don't understand His decision or why I don't understand His plan.

With tears of my own, sometimes all I can do is fling myself into
His arms—into the sovereignty and security of His arms, and once
again, I was brought near. Being reminded I am His and He is mine.

There's something about "being brought near" that floods my
heart with emotions. Maybe it's from my past of being rejected and
not really fitting in with people. Maybe it's because I've worn so
many different identities in my lifetime and none of them made me
feel at home. Or maybe it's because, once I found my true acceptance and identity in Christ, I still ran to other things for a sense of
shallow affirmation or worth.

But every time those things leave me empty. And I run to the
arms of the One who shed His blood for me, the One who gives me
true worth. My son reminded me of that when he threw himself
into my arms. When I was once far off, and dead in my sin, I was
brought near. And I am still brought near today.

A Moment to Breathe . . .

*Imagine yourself being brought near today. His arms, wide and
welcoming. His embrace, loving and tender. What better reason
to exhale? He's calling you to Himself. Each and every day.*

Jesus at My Kitchen Table

BY SHELLY WILDMAN

The chief priests and the scribes stood by,
vehemently accusing him. LUKE 23:10

WHEN I READ ABOUT Jesus before Pilate, I'm struck by how Jesus stood silently, not answering His accusers. He was put on trial, first before Pilate, then to Herod who mocked Him and sent Him back to Pilate, who could find no wrong in Him. Because Pilate bowed to the angry crowd, he ordered Jesus to be flogged and killed, releasing a thief and a murderer instead of Jesus.

And the whole time, Jesus stood silently, not saying a word to defend Himself. I think about how quickly I jump to defend myself, especially when I feel backed into a corner. If anyone was backed into a corner, it was Jesus. False accusations flew all around Him, yet He did not respond in any retaliatory way.

Why did He just stand there and take it? Why didn't He bring the temple crashing down on them all? Why didn't He at least laugh at them and tell them their day is coming? Humility. Jesus knew this was His time. He knew He was the only one who could set the world free, but in order to do that, He had to endure their mocking and torture.

I wonder what it might be like to have Jesus sitting at my kitchen table with me. His physical scars healed, yet still visible. His compassion showing through His eyes. His love overflowing. And I wonder what I'd say to Jesus.

I think I would ask Him to help my friends—the ones suffering and struggling. Surely He knows the people I love who are hurting. He knows all of my hurts too. But we could also talk for hours about the many blessings in my life as well. Then I'd take His hand, open His palm, trace the scars, and whisper, "Thank You."

A Moment to Breathe . . .

In those moments when you're tempted to defend yourself or justify
your actions, pray for God to give you wisdom and ask Him if this
might be the right time to practice the discipline of silence.

He Goes with You

BY MEL SCHROEDER

*"The LORD is the one who will go before you. He will
be with you; he will not leave you or abandon you. Do
not be afraid or discouraged."* DEUTERONOMY 31:8

PASSPORT, CHECK. SHOTS, CHECK. Bag, check. Deep breath,
check. A few months earlier I'd joined a team of college students
headed to the Amazon jungles of Peru. It was a long flight to a
faraway place, and someone kept mentioning anacondas and a
dumb movie about giant water-slithering snakes. But since I'm not
one to chicken out, I whispered a prayer and off we flew.

We hit the ground running in a jungle city in the northern part
of the country. We spent our first days hanging out with street kids,
holding baby alligators, practicing our Spanish, and getting ready
to lead Vacation Bible School. It was the most fun this small-town
girl had ever had.

Then we climbed onto that houseboat for two weeks, and oh,
the adventures that followed. Stopping in villages where people
had never heard about Jesus was the most eye-opening, humbling
experience. Falling in love with the sweetest kids in the world, only
to say goodbye until heaven, broke my heart in ways it never had
before. Learning to love another country was completely and unexpectedly wonderful. And God was with us every step of the way.

He was there the night we led a church service without electricity
and the day we climbed off the boat into knee-deep mud, laughing
ourselves silly as we tried to climb the hill to a village. He was there
when we traveled the ins and outs of the Amazon and in the leper
colony, giving hope to those with little of it. He was there when the
sweet woman in that tiny village prayed to ask Jesus into her life.

Every single, little part . . . He was there. And if He was there for
all of that, then He's there for all of our moments, too. No matter
how ordinary the day may seem. Take a deep breath, friend. He
goes with you.

A Moment to Breathe . . .

*Imagine the most faraway place you'd like to visit. Then
look around you right now. Tell God how grateful you
are that He is with you, no matter where you go.*

Connecting the Dots

BY KIMBERLY GILLESPIE

Therefore encourage one another and build each other up as you are already doing. 1 THESSALONIANS 5:11

"YOU ARE ONLY A dot on a dot." I have heard this statement plenty of times. Compared to the solar system, the size of the earth is but a dot. And me on earth? A dot on a dot. The universe, this world, our society, does not revolve around my dot, and yet, ironically, mysteriously, my dot, my life—your life—matters. Consider a child's simple dot-to-dot puzzle: missing a number does not prevent you from seeing the big picture. You can still tell what it is, but even a child knows, something is just not quite right.

Here are a few examples of the "dots" that connected in my life: Twenty years ago, a mentor suggested I attend seminary . . . (connecting) . . . I had visited a city years earlier that I fell in love with and determined I would love to relocate. As it turned out, I found a seminary there, attended, met and befriended many wonderful people—more dots—who impacted my life. One of those "dots" said she knew an organization that would be a perfect fit for me . . . (connecting) . . . I ended up working for this organization, and six months later, met my husband. Ten years, three children, and three states later, we've connected many more dots.

Would any of these events have occurred without the connection of each dot mentioned? I'll never know. And that's the point. We never know how our dot might impact someone else. Our actions matter. Our words matter. How we raise our children, treat our family and friends and random strangers on the street . . . it all matters.

So, as you go through your day, week, month, life, remember your significance to the dots around you. Yes, you may be merely "a dot on a dot," but the bigger picture is not quite right without you.

A Moment to Breathe . . .

Trace the "dots" in your life. Thank God for those encouraging influences in your life, then ask Him how you can be that kind of encourager to someone else today.

Can I Just Have a Normal Life?

BY JOLENE UNDERWOOD

"For the LORD your God is the God of gods and Lord of lords, the great, mighty, and awe-inspiring God, showing no partiality and taking no bribe." DEUTERONOMY 10:17

RECENTLY, I SHARED SEVERAL hard things happening in my life with a friend. Then I blurted out, "Ugh! Can I just have a normal life?" I took a deep breath and immediately said, "Whatever. Does anyone really have a normal life?" We both laughed. Because we realized the ridiculous nature of our expectations. While our situations are different, neither of our circumstances comply with our vision of "normal."

Maybe you've had these thoughts too? When life hits hard and you wonder why your life isn't like so-and-so's life, do you ever want to burst out with a similar plea?

Chronic illness. Financial blows. Parenting challenges. Deep loneliness. The list is seemingly endless. What is normal anyway? I tend to think of normal as a life free of hardships and long-standing challenges. This kind of normal says there will always be money to pay the bills. No one is sick. No one injured. Fear, anxiety, and sadness never hang around. Relationships don't break and people continually live in harmony. But you know what? Normal isn't a life absent of everything that is normal.

If normal is what's common to all people, then normal is the reality of living in a world where sin, death, decay, and a prowling enemy surround us. Normal is the reality that this world is not our home.

Our current normal changes because life ebbs and flows. The only One who stays the same is Jesus. He is our constant. He is the source of knowing how to navigate our current normal, even when that looks like making hard decisions. In our normal living, we find a God who is anything but. Nothing compares to Him and nothing ever will.

A Moment to Breathe . . .

Define your "normal." Then invite the all-powerful Maker of heaven and earth into your normal. Let Him be the one, steady constant in your life. He promises never to fail you.

Lovingkindness Poured Down

BY JACQUE WATKINS

The tongue of the wise brings healing. PROVERBS 12:18

THE WINDSHIELD INTERSECTED THE raindrops as the wipers cleared the remnants away in a steady, rhythmic strumming sound. Amidst their mesmerizing cadence, my thoughts continued on, filled with all I needed to accomplish that day. In the drizzling rain, I bolted out the car door to get the mail, and little did I know that the cold metal mailbox held a priceless gift—a treasure that's rare amidst these cyber-heavy days. A notecard, hand-addressed to me!

This timely word had dropped out of nowhere, and in the seat of my car with the rain pattering down, the sweet words of a friend poured down like rain on my parched and cracked soul, soaking in deep. And they brought the rain of flowing tears.

Overwhelmed by the kindness of a friend, I found myself enjoying the rain. I unloaded the groceries and put them away, and my phone chimed with a random text: *Have a wonderful day!* I paused, my heart full from the goodness of it all. This wet day was a gift to me, straight from the Father's heart to mine—from my Abba to me.

For a long time, He alone has known what we've talked about in our times together. How I've been floundering . . . wondering . . . where is my place? Do I really have friends? Does what I say, or do, really matter? And He sent His nourishing, reviving water to me this day, through the faithfulness and kindness of friends who know His heart well. They responded to His promptings, becoming His hands and feet to me, bringing me the affirming message of His heart . . . *You, my child, are loved.* And the lovingkindness of our God overwhelms.

A Moment to Breathe . . .

The lovingkindness of God and sweet friends are like rain to the soul. Be that kind of friend today. Write a note by hand or maybe just text a friend, telling her how much you care.

The Good News: This Is Only the Beginning

BY CHRISTIE PURIFOY

Then the one seated on the throne said, "Look, I am making everything new." REVELATION 21:5

IF YOU WALKED THROUGH my front door today, you would be greeted by three large green splotches. We were testing paint colors. We even chose one. But in between the choosing and the painting, five-hundred little tasks elbowed their way in. Last Saturday, my husband, having just cleaned up all the breakfast dishes, started murmuring about the floor. Would now be a good time to pull out the steam mop? Loving wife that I am, I shrieked and said, "No! Now would be a good time to get out the paint can!"

He sees the crumbs and dirt, I see the unpainted walls. In our house, someone always has their eye on the details and someone else on the big picture. So when each Saturday (with its ever-growing list of to-dos) comes around, I often find myself repeating these words, "This is only the beginning." These words remind me that I am exactly where I need to be. That something good is starting. That in God's story, the best is *always* yet to come.

We're all at the beginning of things. This is as true for the newborn as it is for aging parents. Our life on this planet is just the beginning. It's chapter one. Or better yet—only the prologue. It's where we begin to experience the work, play, rest, and worship we will enjoy *forever*.

I think "the beginning" matters much more and much less than we typically imagine. It matters more because the world we are experiencing now is not moving toward destruction. It is moving toward renewal. It matters less because the petty annoyances, the illnesses, the losses, and even the tragedies we suffer are *passing away*. The sin and evil and general brokenness that leave us breathless with fear and anger? They have already been defeated. They are on the way out.

A Moment to Breathe . . .

Locate an "unfinished project" and see it with fresh eyes, as something that's only now beginning. Relabel it as a new project, beginning today.

Because Hope Wins

BY NASREEN FYNEWEVER

Now this is what the LORD says—the one who created you, Jacob, and the one who formed you, Israel—"Do not fear, for I have redeemed you; I have called you by your name; you are mine." ISAIAH 43:1

I MOVED FROM THE fluorescent lights to the crisp cold of the outdoors. I beheld a new ceiling, a canopy of heaven stretched over the snowy floor. Colors and splays of nature beautifully enveloped me. Yet, depression clung to my every step. It seeped into my pores and crisscrossed my face, leaving hollow eyes and an unrelenting somber sheen. Life did not wait for me; no, it created a tide of expectations and a current of must-dos. I parceled out my energy to see others, to meet requirements, to do right by a career, family, friends, and a future. My smile, real enough to some and the shallow clear to others.

This week a colleague laid his beloved wife to rest after a torment of days and a life journey with mental illness. This week a student could not stay where bridges were built and allies found. Depression robs us. It thieves from many. Yet this I know, when strangle felt close, my lungs still filled. One more breath, one more day. I cannot do all of life the way I wish or take away others' pain. I cannot belong in all the ways an orphan girl is supposed to once adopted. I cannot change the color of my skin or how I fit into people's constructs. I cannot unlearn my trauma or forget my twisting of perception.

But as sorrow lies near—I live. To love. To teach. To lead. To write. To whisper. I do not know who will follow or who will listen, but my steady foundation of faith and the formation of friends and family remind me, to be me to the world. Who I am, whether small and in a ball, tired from the day, or strong and tall, knowing my purpose, I am alive.

One more day, friends. To tasks and talents, give what you can. Allow others to lend you hope when yours is low and depression is real. Let's walk together. Another day, yes, the light still shines.

A Moment to Breathe . . .

Step outside and breathe fresh air. Look to the sky and see His handiwork splayed in color. And tell your soul you are here for a reason. You are wanted. And you are so deeply loved.

Living with Less While Giving More

BY SHEILA DAILIE

"Give to him, and don't have a stingy heart when you give, and because of this the LORD your God will bless you in all your work and in everything you do." DEUTERONOMY 15:10

OVER LUNCH MY FRIEND tells me that she's challenging herself to limit her spending on groceries. She wants to simplify, to cut the excess. To me, her actions seem like a burden, but her enthusiasm spurs me to consider my own spending habits. And I determine not to enter a store unless I know exactly what I'm planning to purchase and hold myself to those items.

Months later, I'm surprised by how much this has impacted even the daily task of sorting mail as I toss the coupons directly into the trash. This decision has also made me more aware of the time I would normally spend dilly-dallying in a store, hauling my purchases into the house, and finding a place for them.

This discipline of intentional frugality has helped me realize how often I was purchasing an item for its beauty, even when I had no use for it, nor a place for it. My closets and cupboards are already full.

Recently, I've had to sort and disperse all the household items in my parents' home. They had plenty of stuff. Indeed, we kept the things that had sentimental value, but the process helped me realize that our children already have many things to disperse when we eventually move out of our current house. My goal for my husband and me is for our children to know why we had things and how we used them.

By finding ways to simplify our lives, we make room for God to use us as channels of His good. We are stewards of the wealth He gives us. He wants us to be like a river, our wealth flowing in and flowing out, not like the Dead Sea, accumulating salty mineral deposits, choking out life. When we choose to live more simply, with less to care for, we open the opportunity to give more generously.

A Moment to Breathe . . .

Practice the art of frugality today. Choose to spend much less than you would normally spend on groceries or eating take-out. Then watch what the Lord does with the margin created in both time and resources.

When God's Faithfulness
Sounds like Silence

BY KARINA ALLEN

God is my helper; the Lord is the sustainer of my life. PSALM 54:4

A RECENT FLOOD IN Baton Rouge has become the "gift that keeps on giving." I'm regularly dealing with new effects from it and the reality of wondering how I'll replace my belongings, how I'll replace my vehicle, and then most recently, how I'll find a new place to live. These thoughts have crept into my rest, keeping me awake at night.

The harder I try not to question God, the more the questions come. It feels as though His still small voice has faded into absolute silence. I'm at a loss as to what step to take next or even what direction to move toward. This is my reality. And it's okay. I rest in the fact that He can handle my questions and my doubts. He can handle my worries and my fears. Because He is God.

So when life feels like a flood that you might not survive, here are three things I've learned to do in this season:

1. Lean on what I know to be true. *Nothing* comes as a surprise to God. This truth brings me much comfort. Every morning there is a new opportunity for Him to move on our behalf. He is a provider for *every* need. He holds us.

2. Surround myself with faithful friends. God has blessed me with an abundance of friends who have sat with me, cried with me, and prayed for me. That is what a spiritual family does.

3. Choose to believe God's best for my life. Recently, I've decided I want to do a better job at believing He will bring about good from my circumstances. Because I also remember this: He's been faithful in the past, and He'll be faithful in my present and future. This is a truth we can stand on today.

A Moment to Breathe . . .

*Whatever circumstances you may be facing today,
run past your worries, doubts, and fears and run
straight to the One who can move mountains.*

Living the In-Between

BY EVI WUSK

This is the day the LORD has made; let us
rejoice and be glad in it. PSALM 118:24

IT FEELS LIKE THIS week has lasted fifteen days. My students are writing their names on my marker board during study hall, all wound-up after state and unit testing. Ten minutes to the bell, and I don't have the energy to remind them one more time to sit down. The last days of school can seem like a hoop to jump through before real-world living begins. But as long as it is today, this hour, I have to remind myself I am living a day that matters.

Today is a day to encourage someone. Today will be etched in eternity. This can be hard to remember as we anticipate weddings, new babies, grandchildren, retirement, events, or the end of the school year. But these days of waiting, these in-between days matter.

On these days that seem like mere checks on the to-do list of life, I am tempted to rush things, to jump from one activity to the next. With that attitude we have the total capacity to turn away from living our own life if we aren't mindful. Maybe you're there now, feeling God's presence and call on your life. Maybe you're a step off the path, or maybe you're so far away you've forgotten what your path was even supposed to look like. No matter where our choices have taken us, God is here. We might miss it, but God won't miss us.

So live this day, not some far-off day in the future when you're finally rich enough, or free-scheduled enough, or good enough, or graduated enough, but live right here, right now where you are already enough in the eyes of God.

When I go looking for the good, it finds me, usually in an unexpected place. Even now in a crazy study hall I not only see rambunctious students, but I notice the beautiful mess on my marker board. It was really so boring just minutes ago.

A Moment to Breathe . . .

Think of a day—in the not-so-distant future—that you're looking
forward to with anticipation. Now think of today and look around
you. Notice the daily grace that's here, in these in-between days.

Rooted in Him

BY KRISTIN A. SMITH

So then, just as you have received Christ Jesus as Lord,
continue to live in him, being rooted and built up in him
and established in the faith, just as you were taught,
and overflowing with gratitude. COLOSSIANS 2:6–7

I RECENTLY TURNED FORTY-TWO, and in the past few years I have seen some "changes" in my body. People warned me this would happen after turning forty, but I hoped I might be one of the lucky ones that would have a super metabolism and who could continue binge eating chocolate and see minimal effects.

Well, suffice it to say . . . I wasn't one of the lucky ones, so I started a new workout program. I joined an accountability group and every day I take some time to push myself toward better health. If there was a magic pill that would make it easier, I might be inclined to try it. But there isn't a quick fix for good health, and I'm realizing that it will be a lifestyle change for me long term, so I've established a new routine.

It's the same with my faith life as well. Over the years I've become complacent in my relationship with God. I don't invest the time needed to develop a solid connection with my Father, and when trouble hits, I'm filled with doubt and fears. Colossians 2:6–7 reminds us that we need to walk with God, we need to be rooted in Him and established in faith. An established relationship is one that takes time. If I'm unwavering in my pursuit to know God and seek Him in all things, when the storms come doubts may creep in, but my faith in Christ will overcome. I will be able to stand firm, confident in His plans for me.

When I commit to spending time with God on a daily basis, my spiritual muscles are built. Just as exercise energizes my physical body, time in His Word benefits my spiritual health. Making God a priority brings me joy. He is my strength, my shield. And I am grateful for the opportunity each day to know Him more.

A Moment to Breathe . . .

Take some time today and work on building your spiritual muscles.
Read the rest of Colossians. It's just four short chapters. Pray that God
would increase your faith so you'll be strong and rooted in Him.

Holding It Together

BY DIANE W. BAILEY

He is before all things, and by him all things
hold together. COLOSSIANS 1:17

EVEN IF I HAD been blindfolded, I would have known we had entered a hospital. The sterile smell of antiseptic filled the early morning air. It was the smell of healing in a place of hurting. We had walked through the familiar routine of registering my husband for what would be his seventh procedure under anesthesia in less than a year. It was not clear if this would be his last. Our initial resolve for victory with smiles had waxed and waned over the months. Tempers had snapped over trivial things, and hugs gave support when unfavorable reports returned.

The prayers of a weary soul could be reduced to only one word to keep it together—Jesus. This whispered one-word prayer can make the enemy tremble. Jesus—the name of the One who trumps death and is above all names. The name for which all knees will bow and all tongues confess that Jesus is Lord. I know this is true. I know with just a nod of the head, Christ could have previously healed my husband. But I know that going through these various trials has shown me the love of Christ in ways I could have not known in a perfect life.

Christ showed His love for me through the nurses who quietly joined in when we prayed, or hugged me when tears threatened to fall. I don't understand suffering and famine and evil that roams looking for whom it can devour. I have to accept that there will be struggles in this life. We live in a world that needs to be washed in the antiseptic cleansing of the blood of Jesus—the only One who can save us, heal us, and hold all things together.

My husband wakes in recovery asking for some ice to chew, and I am able to whisper three words of prayer this time. "Thank You, Jesus."

A Moment to Breathe . . .

When you don't know how to pray or what to say, you can always
whisper the most powerful one-word prayer—Jesus. Invite Him
into your day—into both the mundane and the marvelous.

Who You Really Are

BY ABBY MCDONALD

You did not receive a spirit of slavery to fall back into
fear. Instead, you received the Spirit of adoption, by
whom we cry out, "Abba, Father!" ROMANS 8:15

OUR FIVE-YEAR-OLD IS GOING through an identity crisis. He feels the need to remind us who he is by telling us his name. A lot. As though we might forget or something.

Nicknames are not allowed. When he's goofing off and acting silly, I sometimes grab him and say, "Come here, little turkey!"

Like clockwork he exclaims, "I'm not a turkey, I'm Gabe!" Ah, yes, I forgot. As if the memory of the child I carried for nine months could be erased in a moment of play.

As crazy as his thought process seems, I assure him that I know who he is. Yes, he is Gabe. He is my son and I haven't forgotten. To be honest, I'm not so different than he is. My wandering heart gets distracted by the things of this world. And before I know it, I forget who (and whose) I am. Instead of coming to God, I let the voice of condemnation whisper lies saying, "You'll never be a true follower of Christ."

I top off an afternoon of guilt by losing my temper and yelling at my kids over something trivial. Because when we forget who (and whose) we are, it doesn't just affect us. The ugliness seeps into the relationships around us.

Thankfully, there's a sure remedy for this identity crisis: God's Word. It lives and breathes life into the dry bones that shame tries to condemn. When I sit in a brief moment of quiet, He reminds me. His Spirit within me confirms I'm His. He tells me I have nothing to fear because He has sealed me as His own. Just like my persistent reminders to my five-year-old, God tells me as many times as I need Him to. I simply have to go to Him. I have to let the voice of truth drown out the voices of the world.

A Moment to Breathe . . .

Write out your full name. Then, just as you'd write a definition
next to a vocabulary word, write the following next to your name:
Daughter of the King. Because that's precisely who you are.

Singing the Words by Heart

BY CARI TROTTER

Let the word of Christ dwell richly among you, in all wisdom teaching and admonishing one another through psalms, hymns, and spiritual songs, singing to God with gratitude in your hearts. COLOSSIANS 3:16

MY SWEET EIGHT-YEAR-OLD POPPED in the car with rosy flush cheeks after a smoldering, hot Texas school pick-up and announced, "Today I heard one of my favorite songs, but it was just the instruments playing. It didn't have the words, but I knew the words by heart so I sang them anyway."

Her words rang through my entire being. There are seasons in life when we have only the strength to hold on with white knuckles to the Anchor as life crashes relentlessly over our souls. But even when we don't hear the words to the song we're so desperate to hear in our hours of deep need, let us know the words by heart and sing along anyway.

Some days I feel like the apostle Paul when he was "the least of the apostles" (see 1 Corinthians 15:9). But I do know this: Life is hard and every last one of us is overcoming something. Each in her own measure of faithful obedience is overcoming something just to make it to the next day, the next hour, or maybe even her next breath.

And here is the other thing I know: God's Word dwelling richly in us will save our souls if we brand it over our lives and scribble it all over our journals. Because knowing His Word by heart begs the song to sing itself out into our realities. We may have days when we don't know a lick of anything about how to live through it, but if we can whisper out those memorized words, sentences, and strung together paragraphs that tell the story of redemption, we are going to make it through.

So if you don't hear the words today and all you can hear are the faint recollections of an instrumental background? Sing the words of the Word by heart.

A Moment to Breathe . . .

Sing your favorite worship song by heart. In fact, look up the lyrics to three or four of your favorite worship songs and begin singing them every day.

God Uses You Every Day

BY JESSICA TURNER

"The Son of Man did not come to be served, but to serve,
and to give his life as a ransom for many." MATTHEW 20:28

AT LUNCH, MY NEW friend opened up and shared some struggles going on in her life, and I was able to speak truth into her life. When I got home, I shared with my husband about our time together. "It was the first time in a very long time I felt like God had used me," I told him.

He looked at me and solemnly said, "God uses you in this family every day, baby." His words meant the world to me. I have been thinking about them for months. Chances are, you need to hear the same thing.

God uses you every day.

When you cook dinner for a group of friends, He uses you. When you are sitting in a cubicle, answering emails, He uses you. When you get up in the middle of the night to rock your crying daughter, He uses you.

Sometimes in life's mundane moments, it can be difficult to see that, can't it? But it's true. God created us in His image for such a time as this. And so today, right where you are, I want you to pray and ask God to show you how He is using you. Because, if you are like me, you don't think of God using you when you are wiping snotty noses and trying to get dinner on the table after working all day. But He is. He uses you every day.

A Moment to Breathe . . .

See your day—this very day—as a fresh opportunity for God to
use you in a special way. A smile here. An encouraging word
there. Invite God to use you as you interact with others today.

The Gifts to Be Discovered

BY LOGAN WOLFRAM

So, whether you eat or drink, or whatever you do, do
everything for the glory of God. 1 CORINTHIANS 10:31

"HOW ARE THERE MORE dirty clothes? I just washed everything you brought down! Wait, these were clean, why are they back in the washer when you haven't worn them? Are you putting clean clothes back in the dirty pile because you're too lazy to put them away?" I ask my sons the same questions and I'm often met with the same sheepish expressions from them both.

I'm beyond thankful I don't have to scrub clothes in a bucket and hang them to dry on a line, but still somehow I find myself entangled in this never-ending battle of never being finished.

Some days feel like I'm rolling the same boulder up the same unending hill. And it can make me feel so tired . . . so defeated.

The daily things are so cyclical—cooking, cleaning, laundry, bedtimes, and then again with the cooking, cleaning, laundry, bedtimes. Sometimes we feel, which is true, as though there are always more tasks to complete, whether it's laundry at home or a pile of paperwork at the office. Our work is never done, and in that never-done place, it can be easy to grow oh-so-weary. It's easy to lose the joy and desire to do all things to the glory of God.

In a recent season of extreme busyness, I felt the Lord remind me in these spaces of never-ending chores there can be joy hidden in the mundane. I was reminded of the simplicity of sameness when engaging the expected. While repetition sometimes felt defeating, I also found myself relieved by the comfort of familiarity. The Lord reminded me that in all of the things we do, there are hidden gifts to be discovered. And in places where we might be tempted to grumble or complain, His glory still shines and invites us into praise and thanksgiving.

A Moment to Breathe . . .

Yeah, laundry can feel like that sometimes. What if you choose
to see that pile of work or laundry a little differently? Choose
to see it as an invitation to the sweet comfort of familiarity.

Cultivating the Good

BY RACHEL ANNE RIDGE

The point is this: The person who sows sparingly will
also reap sparingly, and the person who sows generously
will also reap generously. 2 CORINTHIANS 9:6

ONE OF MY FAVORITE scenes in life is the acres and acres of green corn and beans on the rolling hills of Nebraska. If you've ever driven through the Midwest in spring time, you've probably seen farmers in gigantic tractors, tilling their land in preparation for planting. They know a crop doesn't begin with planting seeds. It begins long before that—with planning soil management months in advance. And once the crop is underway, there's a whole science of tending, watering, fertilizing, and harvesting at precise moments for the best yield.

The same is true for our lives too. It's our job to cultivate the good in our lives with intentionality. We're laying the groundwork for the kind of crop we'll harvest someday. Preparation and cultivation are activities that help to create an atmosphere for growth and health, not only in our lives, but also in the lives of those around us.

What kind of harvest do we want to reap? Here are some ideas to get us started: If we want peace and quiet, maybe set boundaries on noise levels and set aside a space for quieter activities. For a healthier lifestyle, create a meal that features an array of vegetables. For spiritual growth, plan to memorize Scripture or commit to joining a Bible study. For a deeper relationship with a friend, ask her how she's really doing and be prepared to love her even if her answer shocks you.

Today, let's think about the kind of life we want to live and the kinds of relationships we want to have, and then let's take the necessary steps to cultivate that life. A crop will never grow out of rocky, untended soil. But with the hard work of preparation and cultivation we'll reap the benefits many times over.

A Moment to Breathe . . .

Take one small step today to cultivate the good in your life.
Maybe it's an added helping of green vegetables on your plate.
Maybe it's memorizing a Scripture passage you love. Or maybe
it's taking a few extra minutes on the phone with a friend.

A Good Fix

BY KIM HYLAND

"Am I a God who is only near"—this is the LORD's declaration—"and not a God who is far away?" JEREMIAH 23:23

I WAS BORN TO fix things, problems, and people. As the oldest child, I slipped right into my role as dutiful daughter and older sister. When my mom and dad argued, I'd lay in bed strategizing how I could fix it. When my little sister got hit by a neighborhood bully, I was out the door with fire and vengeance. In school, I loved the tests where the teacher would give you partial credit if you corrected—a.k.a. fixed—the problems you got wrong.

My fixing ways deepened as I grew. When my husband and I fought, I'd lay in bed strategizing how I could fix *us*. When my kids started running into trouble, I worked overtime to fix them too. Fixing became a full-time job. Before long I was headed for a life of overwhelmed delusion or the white flag of surrender. Thankfully, I chose surrender, and I began to learn the value of broken things . . . and broken people.

Now when I'm faced with broken things, I see opportunity. There's a time for fixing, but a premature fix can be more damaging than a break. The God who was willing to be broken Himself can do amazing things with our surrender in broken places.

So much of our growth and character have arisen from our broken places. Nobody really wants a quick fix. It is as worthless as it is inauthentic. Aching hearts long for empathy not simple solutions.

Watching a loved one struggle is painful. But how often is my desire to "fix" their problem, really a desire to protect my own heart from their pain? Might real love be willing to simply *be* with a friend in the breaking? To walk in the dark valley, holding up the lantern of hope until the light dawns? In the broken places of life, encouraging words and the reassurance of constant love may just be the best fix we can offer.

A Moment to Breathe . . .

Name the broken thing—or broken relationship—in your life that needs "fixing." Invite God into that broken place and ask Him to deepen your character and help you grow through it.

The Legacy We Leave

BY KIM MARQUETTE

*"His master said to him, 'Well done, good and
faithful servant!'"* MATTHEW 25:21

I ATTENDED A FUNERAL recently and was surprised by the tears that would not stop. Why should tears surprise me, especially at a funeral? At age ninety-three, Mr. Wallace went home to be with the Lord, and I was overjoyed for him; he was with his Savior, Creator, and King. No reason to weep over that good news!

Instead I wept in confession. I always knew there was something remarkable about Mr. Wallace. Behind all the outward appearances was a man who lived and loved sacrificially. He was all about service to his country, his family, and his Lord. He loved his wife of sixty-seven years, and he wrote letters and cards to remind her of his devotion.

I could be inspired by his commitment to write letters and cards . . . and I am. I could be encouraged to love, honor, and appreciate my husband more . . . and I am. I could be overjoyed that Mr. Wallace is home, free from the pain of this world . . . and I am.

But I also realized some ugly truths about myself and it brought tears. Because I get in the way. I get in the way when it comes to living and loving sacrificially. I get in the way when it comes to taking time to write a letter or a card. I get in the way when it comes to loving and honoring my spouse. I get in the way when it comes to growing deeper in relationship with my Lord.

My insecurities and worldly desires. My self-protection and self-exaltation. It all gets in the way. Mr. Wallace wasn't published, well known, wealthy, elected, sought after, or followed on social media. He wasn't famous, except with the Famous One—who I am certain welcomed him with, "Well done, good and faithful servant."

A Moment to Breathe . . .

Take a moment and think about the legacy you want to leave. Then choose today to live and love sacrificially to become a person of legacy.

The One Short Prayer That Will Change Your Life

BY ELISE HURD

"If you then, who are evil, know how to give good gifts to your children, how much more will the heavenly Father give the Holy Spirit to those who ask him?" LUKE 11:13

WE WERE ON THE way to church; I was so angry I couldn't speak. The outfits had been cried over and breakfast was a train wreck. We were so late it almost wasn't worth going. Plus my leaky, lumpy post-baby body couldn't squeeze into any clothing that didn't make me feel like a slouchy mess, and my hair looked greasy—even though I had just washed it. All legit reasons to cry.

My two go-to responses when emotions become overwhelming: either cry *or* get angry. I usually chose anger because at least I can function with anger. Tears have to be explained and leave puffy evidence all over your face that you're struggling. But neither option would work for this particular morning, because it was our first day back at church since I'd had the baby and I knew people would come see our new little one and ask me how I was doing.

I prayed silently: *Lord, please fill me with Your Spirit of power, Your Spirit of love, Your Spirit of self-control, and of a completely sound mind.*

A shift began in my emotion, and the thought of God preparing a table for me in the presence of my enemies came to mind, and I prayed further, deeper: *Lord, please fill me so full of Your Spirit that my cup overflows, that Your Spirit overflows onto everyone I interact with at church. On my children. On my husband.*

As we stopped at the red light, at the intersection just before church, I knew God had just parted a Red Sea in me and led me into a powerful truth. Instead of all that pain and anger, I had joy and peace. I was able to walk into church and worship. I was free to focus on others, and not myself. I was *free*.

A Moment to Breathe . . .

Pray the same prayer today: *Lord, please fill me so full of Your Spirit that my cup overflows, that Your Spirit overflows onto everyone I interact with.*

Finding the Missing Peace

BY BRITTA ELLIS LAFONT

Therefore, since we have been declared righteous by faith, we
have peace with God through our Lord Jesus Christ. ROMANS 5:1

MY BIG SISTER WAS the first-chair clarinet in junior high band and a cheerleader in high school. Even before Pinterest, she kept her room neat and organized. This girl was a straight-A student in honors classes, with a part-time job at Baskin-Robbins.

I was a daydreamer. I ran late for everything. I hid notes from the teacher in my desk and spent time figuring out how to skimp on my homework. My first day with glasses, some big boys teased me so mercilessly that the bus driver threatened to put them off the bus. I scrunched those glasses into my desk, behind all the half-done worksheets and notes to my parents.

I spent my childhood and adolescence comparing myself to my stellar big sister, and I couldn't measure up to her no matter how hard I tried. Looking around at other girls, my eyes went to the places where I fell short. My identity became a long list of needed improvements.

Then I brought my brokenness into my life of faith. I awoke every day feeling like a failure. Being a Christian was exhausting. No one told me that I wasn't "holy" enough, but that's what I believed. Then, God showed me in His Word: holiness isn't about me. It's about Him. Paul says we've been declared righteous by faith and we are at peace with God. It's a done deal. Jesus made peace between God and us and this harmony is constant, not something we undo with each mistake we make.

We aren't made righteous by what we have done, but by our faith. Faith is recognizing what Jesus has done and knowing that He will continue to keep the peace between God and us, even when we can't.

A Moment to Breathe . . .

Cease all comparisons and put your eyes solely
on Jesus and His holiness. Because His holiness
is enough to cover each of us completely.

Other Women

BY ALIA JOY

I have fought the good fight, I have finished the race, I have kept the faith. 2 TIMOTHY 4:7

WHEN I GOT MARRIED and had kids, everyone else seemed to remember to put the laundry from the washer to the dryer without having to rerun it three times. Other women managed to keep their houses clean and artfully decorated to look like a Pottery Barn catalog.

Other women served in children's ministry with healthy home-made snacks and hand-sewn puppets. Other women ran marathons and started nonprofits and had careers. Other women had degrees and letters dangling off their names from prestigious universities. Other women threw their heads back when they laughed; they didn't hunker down on the sofa and pull the throw pillow over their belly while trying to think of something to say.

Other women matched ankle booties to skinny jeans and layered infinity scarves without strangulation of any kind. Other women mastered the messy bun without looking like a small woodland creature was nesting in their hair. Other women rose at 5:00 a.m. to have quiet times next to their vases of fresh cut poppies grown in their gardens, which they'd Instagram next to their journaling Bibles with handwriting that looked like a custom font. Other women did all this all while starting a clothing company from fair-trade-organically-sourced ministries in their spare time.

Other women do it better, other women are better, I thought to myself and have believed it for far too long. But today I sow grace for myself. To be where I am, to be who I am. Today I reap grace for others, to excel at what God called them to do in all the excellent ways He's gifted them. They are running their own races. No one can outpace me when my route is different.

I breathe deep and bear my heart before God and feel the width of my soul stretching out like limbs hungry for a race. I look to what is set before me, and I take my place in the lineup.

A Moment to Breathe . . .

Ask God to give you the grace to run the race to which He's called you. If you do look around, cheer on the other person who is trying to do the same.

Wherever I Am, God Is Enough

BY LOVELLE GERTH-MYERS

And whatever you do, in word or in deed, do everything
in the name of the Lord Jesus, giving thanks to God
the Father through him. COLOSSIANS 3:17

I HAD JUST GRADUATED college. I worked so hard to get to that place and I was finally done. I thought to myself, *Surely, I will get hired quickly. I will figure out what to do with my life.* I had dreams and goals that I wanted to achieve immediately, but God doesn't work in my timing, so there I was stuck in-between jobs. It seemed like God was completely silent. Doors to potential jobs closed in every direction.

To make some money and occupy my time I began working at a thrift store where I had previously been employed. As I sat there cleaning the dusty area filled with trinkets and vintage items, I couldn't help but cry out to God, "Surely I am called for more than this?" I asked that question a lot. Every time I cleaned the bathrooms and sorted through used clothes, I would ask Him again.

As time went on, God began a refining work in me. He whispered into my heart: *Lovelle, I am enough.* Regardless of my current job— garbage person, a cashier, the CEO of a prestigious company, or a stay-at-home momma—He is enough. I can do everything my heart desires, but if God isn't my contentment then nothing I do will ever be enough. My life will be empty because only God is enough.

As time went on I did in fact get a job offer. It's not my ending point but it's going to give me the tools I need for the future, and I get to make a difference. Where God has placed me for now is enough. And friends, He has you right where He wants you too. So when discouragement tries to seep in, hold on to these words: God is enough. He is always enough.

A Moment to Breathe . . .

Wherever you are, right now in this very moment, you can trust that God knows what He's doing, and He has you where you are for a reason. Thank Him for being enough. Today and always.

Cast All on Him

BY RACHEL C. SWANSON

Cast your burden on the LORD, and he will sustain you; he will never allow the righteous to be shaken. PSALM 55:22

THE NOISY ENGINES DROWNED out the hammering in my chest. I yanked on the straps to double check—secured. Only moments away now from my release. The hatch opened. "Are you ready?" I knew only what he said by reading his lips. The chaotic wind screaming past the hatch opening made all other noise barely audible. Here I was, only a few steps away from miles of open space, about to cast my body out of a plane to experience the thrill of plummeting 12,000 feet through the air. For fun. Who does this? But cast myself I must. Time to trust the process and proceed.

It can feel scary to cast our burdens onto the Lord. Will He still love me no matter what I've done? Will He really come through for me? Can I trust Him to catch me when I fall?

Wind smacked my face and body at surprising speed. But even more surprising was the exhilarating feeling of weightlessness. Even though I was rushing at 120 miles per hour to the ground below, it felt like I was floating. Everything moved in slow motion—the horizon, the mountains in the distance, the landscape beneath me. A laugh escaped me as I felt incredibly free!

There was a tap on my shoulder. I nearly forgot I was attached to my instructor—my tandem guide and protector from imminent death—now signaling me to pull the cord.

Shwooosh! The parachute exploded open above us and we floated gently toward solid ground. I was safe.

Let's not be afraid to cast every single weight onto Jesus. Let's experience the exhilaration of burdens lifted. Nothing is too heavy for Him to hold and He will secure your fall.

A Moment to Breathe . . .

Close your eyes and imaging flying—okay, parachuting. Imagine the weightlessness. The freedom. Now picture Jesus there with you, tapping you on the shoulder, reminding you that you are never alone. Not ever.

The Joy of Pressing Through

BY KENDRA TILLMAN

Consider it a great joy, my brothers and sisters, whenever you experience various trials, because you know that the testing of your faith produces endurance. And let endurance have its full effect, so that you may be mature and complete, lacking nothing. JAMES 1:2–4

I LOVE THE SUMMER Olympics. Oh, the thrill of victory and the agony of defeat! I'm mostly a fan of track and field, but I also enjoy watching swimming, diving, gymnastics, and beach volleyball.

For two weeks the world watches and cheers on the best of the best. We listen to their stories. We celebrate. We grimace. But mostly we sit in awe of the magnificence that is possible with passion, focus, and persistence. Seriously, how is it possible for someone to run a mile in less time than it takes me to walk out my front door to my mailbox? How do you fall down during your race, get up, and finish as the winner? How do you break records in two weeks that seemed unbreakable for years? Amazing!

I've been thinking lately about what makes athletic competition so captivating and inspiring. I admire athletes for the sacrifices they make to reach the pinnacle of their profession. The lessons they've learned about themselves on their journey is something no one can take from them.

For Christ followers, this life of faith we live is the ultimate test of endurance and our training never ends. On those days—when the hurdles of life have the potential not just to slow us down, but to knock us off our feet—the book of James encourages us to hold on to joy, even amidst the trials of life.

Consider it a great joy whenever we experience various trials? Really?! How can God ask so much of us?

We hold on to joy in times of pressure, because when we do, the end result is a deeper faith and a greater joy that can't be taken from us.

A Moment to Breathe . . .

Like an athlete, every trial is the opportunity to stretch and grow. What area of your life is stretching you right now? Ask God to show you how to find joy, even in the midst of everyday trials.

The Truth about the Dark Days

BY SARAH MAE

*Why, my soul, are you so dejected? Why are you in
such turmoil? Put your hope in God, for I will still
praise him, my Savior and my God.* PSALM 42:5

I LOOKED AT MY iPod. Which playlist should I pick to listen to while I wash my dishes? My eyes went back and forth between my "Cleaning" and my "Rend Collective" playlists. I decided on the latter playlist with praise music because it had been a dark day. I propped my iPod up on my kitchen windowsill, pressed play, and as the words came out, something in me opened up.

I turned around, slid down to the floor on my knees, and cried. I thought: *I think I'm in a bit of a depression.* Depression is this weird thing that you can't really explain or give reason for. It just is. I get this way from time to time; it's just a darkness, and it seems to be a rhythm of my life, and I know it will lift.

I'm kind of a functioning depressive. I can be mostly okay, but in my home, going about the hours, everything is a mountain. I remember a professor once saying in class that when you find yourself in a depressed place, when everything feels hard, just do something small. Maybe you can make the bed. Do that. My small thing, right now, is writing this down, because there is something in the writing that helps.

Something about vulnerability and honesty allows the process to take its course. So while I am sharing that I'm depressed, I'm also hopeful because God is with me, and He knows all of my heart and every bit of my soul, and He will be kind and tender with me through this. I've been here before. You may have been here before too. Today, let's agree to be gentle with ourselves, slowly doing the dishes, and keep knowing we aren't alone. Because of Jesus, we are free, and we trust the healing in the heaviness.

A Moment to Breathe . . .

*Do one small thing today. Maybe it's the dishes. Maybe it's making
the bed. Making it's smiling at the clerk behind a counter. Maybe
it's smiling at the person in the mirror. Do this one thing.*

Peace in My Place

BY KRIS CAMEALY

Better a day in your courts than a thousand anywhere else.
I would rather stand at the threshold of the house of my
God than live in the tents of wicked people. PSALM 84:10

SURVEYING THE TOYS SCATTERED from one end of the room to the other, I sigh over the mess that makes up my daily life. While the kids nap, I read an article about a woman accomplishing her dreams; assuming a position in leadership at a well-known organization whose work I admire. Looking around the room again at the clutter, I slump back into the couch. There is no telling how much of my life I've wasted longing to be somewhere or someone other than where and who I am. Anytime someone else seems to be living the dream I dreamed for myself, I quickly forget the joy of living in God's presence, right where I am.

During a hard season of coming to terms with my place and my season, God whispered to my heart, "Hold the door." God gave me a vision of an open door, of a greeter, of someone who makes room for others, someone who invites. In that moment of conviction, I realized that my perspective of my current life was terribly skewed. Until that moment, I had viewed door holding as janitorial work—underappreciated, overlooked, insignificant. In my disillusionment, I'd lost sight of my calling. Convicted, I had to confess that what I craved was recognition, acknowledgment, and admiration. I longed for significance.

How had I forgotten that God sees me already? How much joy had I forsaken in my longing for a life other than the one I was living? I don't actually want to be anywhere else. I know the best place to be is where God calls me, doing whatever it is He has chosen for me. The best place to live is in the presence of the Lord. Our work in the Kingdom is whatever we do in His presence, for His glory alone. Making peace with our place is where we find the better life.

A Moment to Breathe . . .

Look at the floor—or the ground—beneath your feet. The very spot where you find yourself today may look simple, maybe even mundane, but you are there for a reason. Tell God how grateful you are for the place where He's planted you right now, for this season.

Hospitality Redefined

BY DENISE J. HUGHES

*He brought them into his house, set a meal before
them, and rejoiced because he had come to believe
in God with his entire household.* ACTS 16:34

WITH GLOVED HANDS I pull the chicken casserole from the oven.
To my own amazement, I didn't burn it. Relief fills me. I have only
fifteen minutes before our guests arrive, so I take a special packet
of seasoning and carefully sprinkle a fine layer over the casserole.
Then I step back to admire my handiwork. For the first time in my
life, I've actually cooked something edible.

My husband rounds the corner and gasps, "Why did you cover it
with that seasoning? You've ruined it!"

"What are you talking about? It's perfect!"

"Denise, the family had one request: *No MSG.* And that seasoning is full of MSG."

"What in the world is MSG?"

He rattles off some multi-syllabic word that resembles something from biology class a couple decades ago. Apparently, it's
a chemical. The family I'm cooking for is allergic to it. And I've
dusted the entire casserole with it. So we order pasta to-go from
Olive Garden and welcome our guests with the latest story of my
cooking failures.

When it comes to hospitality, I used to think I didn't have much
to offer. Because cooking just isn't my thing. But over time I learned
that real hospitality is about making others feel welcome, not
impressing them with my culinary prowess. While some folks have
an obvious knack for cooking, hospitality is something we can all
do. Hospitality can include a wonderful spread of food that's been
prepared by hands that delight to serve in that way, but more than
anything, hospitality is about creating a space to make others feel
welcomed and know they're wanted. And that's what I love doing
most.

A Moment to Breathe . . .

*Consider your own definition of hospitality. The only
requirements are open arms and a welcoming heart. Think
of one person you can show hospitality to today.*

When You Wish That Hard Thing Would Just Go Away

BY KRISTEN STRONG

Therefore, he is able to save completely those who come to God through him, since he always lives to intercede for them. HEBREWS 7:25

AS I CHATTED ON the phone with a friend, we swapped snapshots of what's going on in our lives. Then she asked me those four plain but powerful words: "How are you doing?" And because she isn't interested in the over-sifted "I'm fine!" answers, I knew she wouldn't settle for less than total honesty.

So I told her the straight-up truth: "I feel endlessly tired, ridiculously so. And really, I've been saying this for a long time. Why can't I just snap out of it?" She asked me to tell her more, so I said, "Ya know, I have several hard things coming at me from different angles, and many of them just aren't going away. I'm realizing that the lingering is just a fact of life. I don't anticipate the weight lifting anytime soon, and I'm worn out from the load."

She warmly listened and agreed with me that I had good reason to be tired. That's when I noticed my tears slipping south. What a kindness it is to have someone listen to you and say, "You know, given all that, you have good reason to feel the way you do." What a relief it is to find a heart advocate who hears you and validates what you're feeling.

I don't know what difficulties you faced yesterday, or the ones you may face today. But if they're totally wearing you out, let me whisper to your heart today, "You have good reason to feel the way you do." There will be seasons when hard things hang on even after you try to shove them out the door. Just don't shove hope out instead. Because while the wind howls and the lion roars, the Lamb reigns. Jesus isn't our adversary, He's our advocate. And if He never expected us to get worn out, we wouldn't ever need to be reminded that He is interceding on our behalf this very moment.

A Moment to Breathe . . .

Just picture it. Jesus in heaven, praying to the Father for you. Yes, you. What an amazing God we serve! Thank Him for being there, for interceding on your behalf today.

The Ministry of Tears

BY ROBIN DANCE

You yourself have recorded my wanderings. Put my tears
in your bottle. Are they not in your book? PSALM 56:8

I HAVE CRIED MORE in the past three weeks than I have since my mother's death, and that was a long time ago. Emotions? Threadbare. Sleep? Fitful at best. And it's embarrassing to admit the "why" of it, because if I play the Comparison Game, it's not a good enough reason to justify my fragility. I'm not facing illness or financial trouble, my marriage and my children are doing well. In fact, the "why" of it is ultimately good: We sold our house. But packing up and purging the house my children will remember as home—the place destined to inhabit their dreams when their minds drift back to childhood—undid me.

We've been married thirty years now—our babies are grown. Downsizing to a much smaller house forced decisions I didn't want to have to make. To toss any "thing" felt personal, as if I were saying that memory didn't matter. Suddenly everything mattered and I was paralyzed by emotion and indecision, and just about anything could trigger an emotional breakdown.

I was grieving a certain kind of loss, and I cried a lot and instantly felt guilty. But then it hit me . . . crying wasn't weakness, it was simply cathartic. Every tear tells a story. Tears are a way for the body to express itself when words aren't enough. They're a gift.

It's important to listen to what our tears are saying. They aren't arbitrary. Some *thing* in our home would trigger a memory that caused me to cry, then laugh almost at the same time. Though I felt crazy at times, I paid attention and began to understand what all those tears were telling me.

Selling our house is a threshold from one season to the next. It's a final letting go of one thing to be free to grasp another. These tears are evidence of a great love and for a life that has meant something special, even important.

A Moment to Breathe . . .

The physiology of tears is amazing. Did you know they're
protein rich and antibacterial? Let's begin to listen to our tears
and see them as evidence of a heart that loves and cares.

In Every Day and Every Season

BY LISA WHITTLE

*"But seek first the kingdom of God and his righteousness, and
all these things will be provided for you."* MATTHEW 6:33

WISDOM IS SENSING WHAT you need—or don't need—at the
specific time or season you're in and honoring it by not forcing the
perceived expectation upon yourself. I don't need the same thing
all the time. *Sometimes I need a sermon;* a preacher to preach to
me strong and tell it to me plain. My life is out of alignment. I need
the guardrails, the reminders, the insight. It's for my spiritual survival to hear the preacher preach.

Other times I need a book. I need the beauty in raw words. *And
then sometimes I just need to make everyone's opinion go away for
a while.* The older I get, the more I can't stand noise, and not just
the loud radio kind. Sometimes I need to quiet my spirit, go solo,
and rest. It's a need we all have. Otherwise, the loud finally gets to
be too much and we run away for good.

The trouble is, most of us don't stop to ask: *What do I need right
now?* For joy, peace, contentment. Too often we just keep doing the
same thing we always do, and the whole time it drives us mad. It's
crazy if you stop and think about it. We continue to do the same
things in every season, under every circumstance, and plug them
in methodically, as if they will work, every time. But life isn't a neat
and tidy formula.

Sometimes I have too many rules. What I expect myself to do and
what others expect me to do. After a while, though, I've noticed
that living like this takes away from my joy. Maybe our biggest
need is to give ourselves grace for new needs and seasons. So I'm
revolting against my own rules. And I'm asking you to join me.
Because breaking away from self-imposed rules helps us to be free.

A Moment to Breathe . . .

*Consider your daily habits. Which ones bring you life? Consider,
also, something new you might try today. A walk in a different
park, perhaps, or reading a less familiar passage of Scripture.*

Hurry, Climb Down

BY HILARY YANCEY

When Jesus came to the place, he looked up and said to him, "Zacchaeus, hurry and come down because today it is necessary for me to stay at your house." So he quickly came down and welcomed him joyfully. LUKE 19:5–6

IN COLLEGE, I HAD a list of theological books I thought would give me the best view of Jesus. I made lists in my notebook of famous things other people had said about God: His grace, His love, and His mercy. I rehearsed theories about the atonement in the empty dining hall on Monday nights as I studied at a quiet table, the window overlooking the front lawn of the chapel. This was my sycamore tree—if I climbed up the best theories and thinkers, I would be able to see Jesus passing by.

What I longed for was the glimpse from the safety of the tree branches, the ability to see Jesus without the big risk of welcoming Him, the frightening transformation that it requires, the openness of heart it demands. But when Jesus comes up to the tree where Zacchaeus is sitting, He doesn't just say, "Come down." Jesus calls up to him by name: "Zacchaeus, hurry and come down because today I must stay at your house." Jesus tells him to hurry and get closer, to hurry and join Him. Jesus is coming to Zacchaeus, and Jesus must come. So He offers Zacchaeus the chance to welcome Him with joy.

This is how salvation comes to Zacchaeus's house. This is how the message of salvation comes into our hearts—not by staying in the safety of the tree branches, but by hurrying down to the One who came to seek out and to save the lost.

After a semester of those Monday nights memorizing, I had climbed far up into the tree. And Jesus, in His grace and in His glory, came to me in the warm joy of summer, catching me off guard with the simplicity of His request: "Hilary, hurry and climb down, for I must stay at your house today." This Jesus longs to call us out of the tree, to come and abide with us, to bring us salvation.

A Moment to Breathe . . .

God wants to give us more than a glimpse of who He is. He wants to enter in, fully. Ask Jesus to reveal Himself to you today in a deeper way.

In Defense of an Ordinary Day

BY DAWN CAMP

Keep your life free from the love of money. Be satisfied with what you have, for he himself has said, I will never leave you or abandon you. HEBREWS 13:5

FIVE WEEKS AND FOUR days ago—not that I'm counting—my brand-new dishwasher decided to quit on me. Permanently, according to the repairman who's visited my home four times. I'm looking at a sink full of soaking dishes as I type. An installer should contact me soon to discuss delivery of a replacement unit, but until then, I'm up to my elbows in suds. (Feel free to laugh at me if you don't own a dishwasher, but then again, you probably have an established routine at your house. I have not.)

Recently, I've suffered from an assortment of skin allergies on my neck, chest, and face. Some I've identified and some leave me baffled. It's hard to make changes when you don't know what to change. There's no peace, waking or sleeping, when you are—quite literally—uncomfortable in your own skin.

As the mother of a large brood, I can tell you it's sometimes easier when your kids visit friends or family and you have fewer schedules to juggle and mouths to feed. Still, when your family is separated, your heart is divided. Last night the seven members of my family who still live at home spent the night in four different places spread over two different states. It always feels like someone is missing (because they are).

I will fall on my knees in gratitude when I've got a dishwasher that needs to be unloaded, skin that doesn't demand a layer of calamine lotion, and my children snug in their beds at home. In other words, my heart will sing with thankfulness for what I take for granted on an ordinary day. And on my better days, I'll praise Him when those ordinary gifts are absent. Now if you'll excuse me, I've got some dishes to wash.

A Moment to Breathe . . .

A broken dishwasher might not be the most calamitous thing to happen, but it can throw off our routine and undermine our peace. Let's give thanks, even when a part of our ordinary everyday isn't quite working.

When It's All Said and Done

TERI LYNNE UNDERWOOD

*When all has been heard, the conclusion of the matter
is this: fear God and keep his commands, because
this is for all humanity.* ECCLESIASTES 12:13

STOP BY THE PHARMACY. *Pay the utility bill. Pick up the dry cleaning.* When I looked at my to-do list for the day, I realized just how mundane my life can be. A sharp contrast from my childhood dreams of changing the world.

Some days, the most exciting task on my list is changing the sheets on all the beds. (I know you're tempted to feel envious . . . try to contain it!) Solomon's life stands in stark contrast to mine. A world leader, renowned for his wealth and wisdom, Solomon reached the end of life and landed here—the whole of humanity is about fearing and obeying God.

Sounds a lot like another Man, near the end of His life on earth, "Love the Lord your God with all your heart, with all your soul, . . . and with all your strength. . . . Love your neighbor as yourself" (Mark 12:30–32). From the Old Testament to the New, the priority for our lives is revealed: love God and love others. This is our purpose. This is why we're here, to love the Lord with abandon and to love others the same way.

It's easy to think I can't do much for the kingdom that impacts eternity. Do you ever have those same thoughts? What if we shift our focus? What if instead of seeing all the places, we choose to see the people? What if we stop focusing on the lists and start focusing on love?

The pharmacy, the utility department, the dry cleaners, even the grocery store move from mundane tasks on our to-do lists into missional opportunities to share the love of Christ with others. At the end of even the most uneventful days, we can rest in the assurance we've honored Him through our treatment of others. And when all is said and done, that's the most important task on any to-do list.

A Moment to Breathe . . .

*Imagine a conversation happening today that could impact a soul
for all eternity. That's what you get to do today. See each person
you meet today as a person you can love with Christ's kindness.*

On Pouring Out and Filling Up

BY ANNA RENDELL

"Look, I am about to do something new; even now it is coming. Do you not see it? Indeed, I will make a way in the wilderness, rivers in the desert." ISAIAH 43:19

I SET MY STEAMING cup of tea on an old apple crate beside my armchair. Soft piano music drifts from the other room. Crickets are chirping outside, and the birch trees across the pond rustle in a breeze. In this idyllic setting, I open my laptop and stare at the screen, blank and bright. The cursor blinks as if it's expecting the next move. Except I have no next move. I'm empty, spent. With not a word to be found in my brain or heart or fingers.

I clack away at the keys half-heartedly. This heart that has always penned its feelings is dry. There's been no great catastrophe, nothing life-altering to make my heart shrivel. I'm simply weary with the daily stuff of life—meetings and deadlines and full squares on the calendar.

There's no room to just be and I am dried up.

Feeling dried up scares me. And refueling my heart seems impossible because there's no time to sit in a quiet sanctuary, on a dock at a lake, in a field of wildflowers. The idyllic setting is fleeting. This is real life, and real life is messy and full of blinking cursors. Real life is loud, and I'm afraid that if I stop and be still, underneath the chatter, there won't be anything worth saying.

I forget that He calls us to stillness, to a deep sense of calm. That He speaks most clearly when I am most quiet. That even in my dryness, He shines clear. When we are most dried up, He is able to do some of His finest work. We may be scared to simply be still. We may not see the new works, the new pathways. But even then, He is at work—in us and for us. And in spite of the blinking cursor and dried-up heart, we can be still and know that to be truth.

A Moment to Breathe . . .

Look at your calendar. Find a date when nothing is scheduled. Then schedule it. Yep, schedule it with some "you and God time." And nothing more.

The Woman in the Navy Suit

BY STEPHANIE BRYANT

*Take delight in the LORD, and he will give you
your heart's desires.* PSALM 37:4

I WAS A FIFTH-GRADER laying stomach down, chin propped up with fists, when an airline commercial came on TV. I turned to my mom and said, "That's what I want to do."

Mom looked at me with a questioning stare, "You want to be a pilot?"

"No, Mom, I want to be her," pointing to the TV. The commercial had shown a woman in her thirties, dressed in a dark, skirted suit, briefcase in hand, boarding a flight for a business meeting. Now you have to understand, my mom had been a teacher in her "previous life" but never worked outside the home after I was born. My grandmothers and all other influential women in my life had made similar career choices. I'm sure she was wondering: *Where did she get such a notion?* Until that moment, I had no idea, but for the first time, I could see and respond to part of the vision God had planted in my heart.

I didn't realize what was happening, but my mom knew in that instant that something was taking place. She saw a vision being birthed: His vision in me. One that was different from her own but still valid. One she didn't quite understand but wanted to encourage. A vision she knew was planted while I was knitted in her womb.

My mom recently reminded me of this pivotal story in my life. Sometimes we forget how God has prepared us for the moments in our lives and need others to remind us. How does this story end? Well, I don't know. It's still unfolding. But I do know this: I have a passion for business and love to help inspire others.

God is faithful to plant seeds of a dream, sometimes years before they come to fruition. I know our stories will be different, but He has gifted each and every one of us, and His purpose for you is steadfast and sure.

A Moment to Breathe . . .

*Think about the dreams you had when you were little. How have
your dreams changed or stayed the same over the years? What
dreams do you have today? Share your dreams with a friend.*

By God's Design

BY JENNIFER DUKES LEE

"I have filled him with God's Spirit, with wisdom, understanding, and ability in every craft to design artistic works in gold, silver, and bronze, to cut gemstones for mounting, and to carve wood for work in every craft." EXODUS 31:3–5

I AM NOT A crafty person. A few examples to prove my point: the annual making of the elementary Valentine's box nearly sends me into anaphylactic shock every February. Also, knitting needles seem scarily pointy and dangerous. And back in my high school home-economics class, while learning to operate a sewing machine, I accidentally sewed my shirt to my project. I rest my case.

But over the years, some of my best friends have shown great prowess with all manner of craft projects. They are Pinterest ninjas, creating magical birthday parties for their loved ones. They are gourmet chefs and painters. One friend recently enrolled in a ceramics class.

There are two things I really love about my friends' creativity. First, I love tasting their edible creations and receiving their art as gifts to display in my home. But what I love even more than all of that? Seeing God at work in their creativity.

Truth be told, some of my artistic friends downplay their gifts. They don't always see the great value they bring to the world around us. The church tends to elevate people with gifts in teaching, preaching, and administration. But God gave the artists their gifts too. When I see my friends making art, I imagine them cocreating with our Creator God.

Maybe that's you. Maybe you're a baker, a poet, a scrapbooker, a woodworker, a quilter, or a floral designer. Don't underestimate the usefulness of your gifts in making this world a more beautiful place. With every stroke of the brush and every turn of a phrase, the Holy Spirit is bringing a fabulous dimension to your work.

A Moment to Breathe . . .

If you love making art, baking, or crafting, carve time out this week to cocreate with God. If you're not the crafty type, encourage someone else who is. Tell her how you see God at work, in her work.

It's Okay to Not Be Okay

BY KRISTEN WELCH

The LORD is my shepherd; I have what I need. He lets me lie down in green pastures; he leads me beside quiet waters. . . . Even when I go through the darkest valley, I fear no danger, for you are with me. PSALM 23:1–2, 4

I SAT ON THE edge of her bed, and she didn't even look up. I was visiting a friend who was not okay. It was more than a bad day, it was a sad season for her. But I wasn't deterred from my mission to cheer her up. And I tried *everything*. I suggested fun activities, reminded her of good times, quoted inspiring Scripture, and offered to play encouraging music.

I got an occasional head nod and a shrug. As I sat there in silence, I thought back to days when I haven't been okay. Some days I could name the pain I felt and others I couldn't. And then I remembered what I needed the most in those moments. Right then I did what I should have in the first place: I hugged her and whispered in her ear, "It's okay to not be okay." She sighed in relief. Permission to not be okay is sometimes exactly what we need.

Today, you might not be okay. You might be facing a mountain of sadness or impossibility. You might be walking through a valley of despair. You might not even know why you aren't okay. These are the moments we wrestle and exhaust every possible solution to resolve the struggle in our soul. But only one thing can refresh and renew and save our soul. And that's the Word. Yet, God's Word is often the last place we turn. It's crazy to think a Book with words can be the answer, but the Word of God is alive, and it cuts to the broken places and heals what we cannot. There's only one place to restore our soul and find comfort, and that's in the quiet place at His feet, where it's okay to not be okay. Because one day He will make everything okay.

A Moment to Breathe . . .

On a simple piece of paper write out Psalm 23. Slip it into your pocket or your purse. Or tuck it between your phone and your phone case. Then read it a few times throughout the day.

The Color of Courage

BY HOLLEY GERTH

Wait for the LORD; be strong, and let your heart be courageous. Wait for the LORD. PSALM 27:14

I'M SIX AND COURAGE is school bus yellow. I stand on the curb, holding my lunch, and wait for my first day of kindergarten. My sweet mom tells me again that she'll drive me to school (and she does every day after). But that morning I stubbornly put small feet in patent leather shoes on the steps to independence and ride.

I'm twenty-one and courage is wedding dress white. I wait at the end of an aisle to become a wife. In this crazy world I make vows that talk about for better or worse and wonder what the future may hold. I choose to risk for love.

I'm twenty-six and courage is pregnancy test pink. I stand in the bathroom and discover once again I'm ready to start our family but God has other plans. I learn to live in the waiting and discover sometimes bravery simply means remaining in the unknown. I'm still there now.

I'm thirty and courage is shiny laptop silver. I sit in coffee shops, at the library, and outside on our porch—writing. It feels like I'm putting my heart on display, like giving birth, like nothing and everything I'd hoped. And it scares me silly.

I'm here now and courage is summer leaf green. I stare out the window at the trees in my yard and hear God's whisper again, "Be still." So I stop my whirly-twirly life, let go of my insecurities, and try once more just to be. I once thought of courage as a single color—always fire engine red—blazing and bold. But I am finding it is more like a kaleidoscope. It changes with the seasons of our lives, with who we are becoming, with what God is asking our hearts to do. Just when we think we know it, the form alters and we find ourselves seeing it anew. And through all the shifting this remains . . . in every color, every life . . . courage is breathtaking.

A Moment to Breathe . . .

You don't often see courage paired with waiting. But waiting, and being still, takes some of the most courage of all. Whatever you're waiting for today, see it as an opportunity to exude courage.

I've Never Been Told That Before

BY JEN SCHMIDT

*Don't let your beauty consist of outward things like elaborate
hairstyles and wearing gold jewelry, but rather what is inside
the heart—the imperishable quality of a gentle and quiet
spirit, which is of great worth in God's sight.* 1 PETER 3:3–4

CLUTCHING THE NOTE, I held my breath as I reread the words
by my University's Admissions Director: "Jennifer, thank you for
your servant leadership this year on our Admissions staff. Your
hospitality welcomes each visitor, and your quiet and gentle spirit
blesses each one." I wept. I'd never been told that before. Since
childhood, that "quiet and gentle spirit" served as a reminder that
my extroverted and outgoing personality would never achieve that
elusive, godly disposition.

It started in kindergarten when that first progress report indicated
"lack of self-control" with the accompanying comment, "Jenny needs
to stop chatting with her neighbors," and so it began. An endless
cycle of second-guessing. By the time I could actually pen New Year's
resolutions, each year's list contained some form of "You'll be more
popular if you'd be like the quiet girls. Stop talking so much."

As my identity took shape, my tender heart failed to embrace the
other remarks. The ones where the teachers scribbled, "Jenny is
a friend to everyone. She always has a smile." Those words didn't
matter to me. I wanted to be one of those sweet, quiet ones. I saw
myself as a talker and didn't like it. I identified this "character flaw"
early on and wanted to stifle how the Lord had wired me.

I've learned, however, that this verse is not referencing a perfect
personality. It's a heart issue. It's the "why" behind the "who." My
desire is to love the Lord my God with all my heart, soul, mind, and
strength. That sometimes manifests itself through an outgoing personality, while at the same time demonstrating a meek and gentle
spirit. God desires for us to cast aside the labels we've carried far
too long, and embrace who we were created to be.

A Moment to Breathe . . .

*Whether your personality is quieter or chattier, see your personality
as a reflection of the Father's heart. Your beauty shines best when
you're most like Christ and the person He created you to be.*

When You Feel like Damaged Goods

BY RENEE SWOPE

You will be a glorious crown in the Lord's hand, and a royal diadem in the palm of your God's hand. ISAIAH 62:3

CAROL WALKED DOWN THE aisle of the discount grocery looking for a bargain she couldn't resist. Turning the corner, she noticed a bin labeled: "Damaged Goods." Filled with dented cans and unlabeled boxes, the collection of random items caught her attention. Although they were no longer considered shelf-worthy, an odd and aching sense of empathy washed over her, leaving her heart keenly aware of how it feels to be unwanted.

An unexpected divorce had torn her identity in half, leaving her with the unwanted label of divorce. She felt like she'd been tossed into a bin of damaged goods, no longer worthy of a place on the "Christian" shelf at church, in marriage, or in ministry. Unwanted. Unworthy. Unloved.

Perhaps you have experienced one or all of these as well. The deep pain we feel as a result of broken relationships can cause us to doubt we are valuable, or question if future relationships can be healthy, or if anyone would ever want us. Sometimes we start to see ourselves as disposable. Easily replaced. Not good enough.

But the truth is: Jesus paid the same price for all of us.

That day in the grocery store, my friend was determined to find something of value hidden in the rubble of rejected items. Something worth choosing in a bin filled with damaged goods. Leaning over the edge, she intentionally picked up a dented can without a label and purchased it. When she got home, Carol slid the mystery can under the edge of her can opener and removed the metal lid. Much to her delight, she discovered peaches! Not only was she thrilled to find her favorite fruit preserved inside, but it served as a "sweet" reminder that good things can still come from something that's been broken and damaged.

A Moment to Breathe . . .

Look for something old, or perhaps discarded, and find its hidden value. Maybe it's a lone teacup without a saucer or a chest of drawers in need of paint. See the beauty that's waiting to be discovered.

Walking Arm in Arm

BY DEIDRA RIGGS

The one who walks with the wise
will become wise . . . PROVERBS 13:20a

I SAT IN THE church pew with my friends—Michelle on my right and Lyla on my left—to sing the songs, eat the bread, drink the wine, pray the prayers, and listen to the message. I wanted to reach out and grab my friends' hands, but I didn't. Fear of freaking out my friends meant I kept my hands in my lap. Later, in the parking lot, I told them, "I almost reached out and grabbed your hands, but I didn't want to freak you out."

"You should have," they both told me. "It would have been fine."

When my husband and I visited Europe, we walked down street after street, in city after city, and saw pairs of women walking arm-in-arm everywhere we looked. They walked closely and it was clear their friendships were treasures. I said to my husband, "I'm going to do that when we get home. I'm going to walk arm-in-arm with my girlfriends."

Friendship is a gift. I've learned that the hard way. Finding someone who will talk you back from the edge, encourage you to follow your dream, stay up talking until 3:00 a.m., eat ice cream with you—straight from the container—hear your darkest confessions without flinching, and keep showing up anyway? That's a gift. No, a treasure.

If you've got one good friend, you've got a treasure, that's for sure. If you've got more than one good friend, you have what I've heard called an embarrassment of riches. I want my friends to know how much I love them. I want them to know they have saved my sanity on more than one occasion. I want them to know that sometimes my heart overflows with gratitude and love for them. So I'm turning a deaf ear to the voice that tells me I might just freak out my friends if I let them know how much they mean to me. A friend loves at all times. It's as simple as that.

A Moment to Breathe . . .

Decide today to become the kind of friend who hears
others' darkest confessions without flinching. Walking
together, arm in arm. A friend who loves at all times.

Peace and Thankfulness

BY ANN SWINDELL

Let the peace of Christ, to which you were also called in one
body, rule your hearts. And be thankful. COLOSSIANS 3:15

WHEN WE PULLED OUT of the driveway, heading toward seminary, part of me wondered if we were crazy. But we had prayed about this change for months and invited our family, friends, and church leaders into the discernment process. We felt sure of our trajectory, sure of where we were headed. The thing we were most unsure about? Money. My husband quit his job to become a seminary student; I quit mine to move. We knew we wouldn't have much money coming in for a while. But what we did have in front of us was a choice. Would we worry? Or would we choose thankfulness?

We had experienced lean times before and I had spent years worrying about paying the bills. This time, however, I made the intentional decision to say no to worry and yes to peace. To say no to fear and yes to thankfulness. It wasn't easy. I tend to be fearful rather than fearless. But I had walked the path of fear and worry before, and I didn't want to choose that path again. So I chose to be thankful for what we already had—our health, extra time together as a family, food on the table, the opportunity to learn to trust God afresh. And I found that choosing gratitude sustained my spirit over months of uncertainty. Focusing on God's provision for us, even in the smallest things, turned my mind to thankfulness and praise.

When I received a $50 check in the mail for some freelance work I had done several months prior, I found myself in awe of God's kindness—and timing. Choosing thankfulness has changed me. It's made me appreciate the ways, both big and small, that the Lord has cared for our family. And it also led me to peace in Christ's provision—one of the greatest gifts I've ever received.

A Moment to Breathe . . .

Choose today to see the things you do have, and show God
your gratitude for all the wonderful ways He has indeed
blessed you already by thanking Him out loud.

Opening the Ragu

BY KAITLYN BOUCHILLON

*"For my thoughts are not your thoughts, and your ways are
not my ways." This is the LORD's declaration. "For as heaven
is higher than earth, so my ways are higher than your ways,
and my thoughts than your thoughts."* ISAIAH 55:8–9

I PUSH DOWN AND turn it to the right. The lid still won't open.
So I try again. Push down. Harder. I scrunch up my face somehow
thinking the added effect will mysteriously help. I turn the cap
right and . . . nothing.

Child-proof locks kept me out for a long time. It took practice,
but after a while I learned how to open the Tylenol bottle and then
the Ragu jar. Sometimes the Listerine cap still gets me. As I tried
and tried again tonight to open the mouthwash bottle, I began to
realize that there's a lesson in all of this.

Children aren't supposed to be able to open certain things. Seat
belts are in cars for a reason. Electrical outlets are covered for a
reason when a little one is around. Protection. They're meant to say
"Keep Out!" But as children we go meddling with our little fingers,
twisting and turning until suddenly, the cap lifts off.

It's fascinating. But it's also dangerous. We do this as adults too.
We meddle with our words and our mouths. We stick our heads
into business that has nothing to do with us. We whine when we
don't have the answer when we want it, how we want it. We whine
when we get the "wrong" answer. It might seem harmless, but this
whining and meddling could be dangerous not only to us, but to
those around us.

The next time we're facing an obstacle, a closed door, maybe we
should just back away from the situation. Maybe it's like a child-
proof lock from our Father, and maybe we should just let it be.

A Moment to Breathe . . .

*Sometimes a closed door or a denied opportunity is meant
for your protection. Rather than lament your lack, trust
your Father is guiding you toward what is better.*

Your Life Is Never Too Small to Qualify for Big Ministry

BY LISA-JO BAKER

*Abram believed the LORD, and he credited it
to him as righteousness.* GENESIS 15:6

I'VE HEARD THE WHISPERS. The rumblings. Women with shy, embarrassed eyes pull me aside to share this worry that what they do doesn't count because what they do doesn't require a passport. Or because they think you need a pulpit for your voice to matter or make a difference.

Sister, don't tell me you don't make a difference, that your life is small. Don't tell me that pulpits are only found in churches and speeches only come from stages. Don't tell me that microphones are necessary to be heard. Don't tell me that Cheerios, diapers, laundry, and dishes somehow don't count as serious service.

I don't believe we are playing make-believe when we dress-up our daughters in all the courage and conviction to last a lifetime of love stories found in the pages of the only good Book that ever mattered.

Don't tell me that all the hours sown into sons between soccer practice and football matches, between trouble-makers and nay-sayers, pouters and bullies isn't wild obedience. Don't tell me that you aren't in ministry. Don't tell me that holy dirt beneath the fingernails doesn't look like blog posts, carpool, science projects, and teaching Sunday school. Don't tell me I need a platform to be seen when there are three sets of eyes looking back at me. Don't measure my meaning in stats; don't count my contribution with your calculator.

Because God has already credited our faith as righteousness. Me in the bathrobe at midnight with the undone dishes and raging fiery passion to encourage women who are too often convinced they don't count. Don't tell me we can't leave the back door open for that misunderstood word *ministry* to come quietly in. Along with the neighbor's kids. All the dirt in the backyard. And Jesus.

A Moment to Breathe . . .

*That seemingly ordinary thing you do? The way you serve and
give and sacrifice? It's ministry. Open your doors and your
heart wide to the ministry of small everyday moments.*

It's Not Too Late for You

BY ALIZA LATTA

"For I know the plans I have for you"—this is the LORD's declaration—"plans for your well-being, not for disaster, to give you a future and a hope." JEREMIAH 29:11

RECENTLY, I WENT CAMPING for the first time with friends. We took a cooler of sandwiches and iced tea and packed ourselves into the car to head toward the beach—driving with the windows rolled down and the music blasting. We toasted s'mores slowly by the fire, telling stories of the people we thought we loved when we were four years old. Later that night, there was a single layer of fabric between the stars and me. And I woke to the view of early sunlight peeking through the trees.

I think God gave me a fresh start on that camping trip—a fresh start I didn't realize I needed. There have been a series of firsts for me. There have been small things, like going camping or standing in the Pacific Ocean, but there have been larger things too, like buying my first car, finding a wonderful friend, and deciding, after waiting for four years, to attend college in the fall. God keeps whispering to me: *Aliza, it's not too late.*

It was pitch black and late when we decided to lay beneath the stars last weekend, so we took a couple of flashlights and walked through the woods, climbed down some rocks and lay beside the water. One of the things I love most about the sky is that neither a camera nor words can capture its glory. The sky is a secret love letter between you and God, and even when you try, you can't fully explain it to anyone. I laid my head against the ground and watched three stars shoot across the sky.

In the midst of my feelings of utter smallness and wonder and gratitude, I whispered back to Him: *Thank You for fresh starts and first times and people that keep showing me exactly who You are. Thank You that it's never too late for me.*

Friend, the same is true for you. It's never too late. Never.

A Moment to Breathe . . .

Fresh starts are always a gift—s'mores are too. Hear Him whisper to you today, that it's never too late for you. Not ever.

Above the Noise

BY ALYSSA DELOSSANTOS

On the last and most important day of the festival, Jesus stood up and cried out, "If anyone is thirsty, let him come to me and drink. The one who believes in me, as the Scripture has said, will have streams of living water flow from deep within him." JOHN 7:37–38

OUR HOUSE IS SITUATED slightly higher than the surrounding homes in our cul-de-sac. Because of its elevation, the view offers me ease in keeping a pulse on the comings and goings of my youngest son. When I need him, I step outside and call his name. Because I use a loud voice, it carries over the noise of childhood play. Whether I'm calling him in to work on homework, unload the dishwasher, or join us for dinner, his responsibility is to listen for the sound of my voice and respond when I call. It won't surprise you that sometimes my call is met with silence. As his mama, I know I'm calling for his benefit. Good things await his response, so I call again.

I love that Jesus used a loud voice to communicate the words in John 7. Jesus issued an invitation, in the middle of the commotion of a great festival, by speaking over the noise. He clearly desired to be heard.

We live in a noisy world with no shortage of distractions. Sometimes we need the loud to draw our attention away from the hustle and bustle. Deferring to loud implies a desire for every detail to be absorbed, whether near or far away.

My son is not always playing in our cul-de-sac so using a loud voice ensures he hears my call. He may not always see how responding to the call is to his benefit, but he has learned to trust the heart of the one who calls.

Jesus is calling us to eat, drink, rest, and be filled up. His invitation awaits our response. His offer is far better than the "noise" that fights for our attention and offers temporary satisfaction.

May we listen for the invitation of Jesus, come believing, trust the goodness of His provision, and find complete satisfaction in Him.

A Moment to Breathe . . .

Turn off all the sounds in the room you're in. Take a moment to bask in the quiet and ask Jesus to speak to your heart today.

On the Comforts of Home and Finding My Fit

BY AMBER C. HAINES

. . . grieving yet always rejoicing . . . 2 CORINTHIANS 6:10

I WAS BORN WITH a borrowed homesickness for Tennessee bottomland where my daddy grew up. We never stopped piling into a station wagon and winding the long way there from Alabama for weekends of lap-sitting, early biscuits, and percolated coffee. Is it any wonder I constantly long for the comfort of home? I moved from Alabama to Arkansas, and I do love it here, but it doesn't fit, and then the chilly edge of autumn undoes me. I'll wake one morning, uneasy, suddenly overwhelmed for home. I sling what I can into bags, load up the boys, and drive with my hand cupping at the air.

I wide-open sing. I stop in Memphis for the smell and imagine Mama waiting to greet us on the porch. I gather speed to climb the mountain, slow to admire change, straddle potholes in the driveway, and I'm home. Van door slung open, boys unleashed, I rush to my daddy's chest, shrinking small at the sound of his heart, the little girl in me recognized, pampered, and invited. And though it is very good, it's not long until I realize, as my daddy did, that no state here befits me. I'm realizing that I was really born into homesickness for the heart of God.

So I go there, to the God whose throne sits on my own heart, and I ask what keeps me from craving the comfort He offers. And I know the answer immediately. Sometimes I don't believe I can be "grieving yet always rejoicing." What the Spirit calls comfort is not what I call it, my giving my all, my whole complete self. Where I am serving the God of the universe in His Greatness, where I am giving Him my all, it is there I am overwhelmed with the tastes and sounds of home. And there, at His heart, is my only fit . . . and I realize contentment, how I'm the very apple of my Daddy's eye.

A Moment to Breathe . . .

Name the place you call home. Describe it to a friend. Reminisce the things that make it a refuge for your heart. Then think of God's heart, infinitely more inviting, making a space just for you.

The One Place That Has Taken Me the Longest to Call Home

BY CAROLINE TESELLE

Our citizenship is in heaven, and we eagerly wait for a Savior from there, the Lord Jesus Christ. PHILIPPIANS 3:20

IF YOU ASKED ME, "Where are you from?" my answer would include a pause, followed by: "Well, it's a long story but I live in Illinois now." After eight years you'd think I would call this home, right?

My entire life has been in a place of transition. From birth until today, I have moved twenty-three times. Half of those moves happened before I got married, and the rest have been with my adventurous husband. Looking back, it's no wonder it has taken me awhile to call this home, even though I've lived here the longest.

But here's the truth: This place really isn't home. Home isn't about the name of a town. It isn't about your mailing address. Home is about the people. With every move, my husband and I have said, "It's not about the place, it's about the people." Everywhere we've lived, we've met some incredible people. People we now call family. And this town we're in right now is the same.

Your roots grow where you're planted. Some places require a little more work—to prepare the ground for the seeds that will be sowed. Returning to a town we lived in once has had its challenges. The friendships we had before weren't the same—we weren't embraced by some people and that was hard. For the first time in the three years we've been back, I finally realized that I needed to let that go. Thankfully, God didn't wait for me to get my act together before bringing new people into our lives and giving us a renewed sense to embrace the ones who stuck by us.

And here's the biggest truth of all: Whether this place is our final destination or not, it's just a tiny glimpse of the place we will gladly call home forever—heaven.

A Moment to Breathe . . .

Count the number of homes you've lived in over the years. Then think about the places that have felt the homiest. Do one thing today to make your home feel homier, knowing that one day we'll be in the greatest home of all.

When You Need a Hug from God

BY DONNA JONES

"This book of instruction must not depart from your mouth;
you are to meditate on it day and night so that you may
carefully observe everything written in it. For then you will
prosper and succeed in whatever you do." JOSHUA 1:8

I WOKE UP IN a funk. Maybe it was the gloomy weather or the fitful night's sleep in a humid room. Have you ever been in a funk for no apparent reason? When I get in a funk, I am unproductive. My brain feels thick. I wander aimlessly from task to task, never quite landing on what it is I need to do. I'm emotionally vague. Not bad. Not good. Just directionless.

I unloaded the dishwasher, checked e-mail, and threw in a load of laundry. Finally . . . I paused. I knew something had to change and it needed to be me. I needed to get rid of the junk. So I pulled out my Bible, asked God to talk to me, read one verse, and wrote it down, word for word. As I continued this routine I've practiced countless times in the past, I felt my heart shift. I felt my burden lighten, my perspective change.

Hearing God speak to me through His words in the Bible feels like a giant hug from God. And all it took was ten minutes—tops. God's Word does that. This isn't just true for me; it's true for all of us. God promises that we'll find Him when we seek Him with all of our heart. Here's what I've found effective for me that can work for you too: 1) Open your Bible. 2) Ask God to speak to your heart as you read His Word. 3) Read a passage of Scripture. 4) Pick a verse or two that resonates with you and write it down, word for word. 5) Ask: *What does this verse teach me about God? About myself? About my circumstances?* 6) Ask: *Is there anything God wants me to know, to feel, or to do?*

Reading the Bible—and allowing it to transform your life—is this simple. And here's the best part—you don't have to wait until you're in a funk to do it!

A Moment to Breathe . . .

Open your Bible and read a psalm or start in Genesis or if
you're new to the Bible, read John. When we're in the Word,
spending time with God, it's like the best hug ever. I promise.

More Than What We See

BY JENNIFER J. CAMP

Therefore we do not give up. Even though our outer person is being destroyed, our inner person is being renewed day by day. 2 CORINTHIANS 4:16

IT'S THE CREASES AROUND my mouth I used to hate the most. One hand on each side of my face, I'd pull back my skin. The goal: making the two-mirror opposite "c's" on the sides of my mouth disappear. That has to be more like me, the real me, right? A face young and vibrant—that's how I feel inside. How did wrinkles and creasing and sagging become my reality? How could this aging body of mine, with all its weird bumps and lines, represent the beauty—the youthful energy—that God produces in my heart?

It doesn't. And I am learning it's okay. How do I appreciate these physical parts of me that are familiar and yet unfamiliar, too? How do I show kindness to this body that can do amazing things? Long legs that stride and strong arms that hold and nimble fingers that grip.

It's freedom I want—freedom from self-contempt, from comparison. I ask God for new eyes; I want to see how He sees. Purple varicose veins the reminder of carrying my sweet son in my womb. Brown sun freckles on my hands reminiscent of my beautiful grandmother's. Lines on my face testify to years of laughing and working, trusting and falling.

I want to turn this all upside down—take care of this body of mine and yet bless it too. I want to love it, be gentle to it—not get frustrated with it when things don't work as well as they did previously. My Father sees more than what I see. And He tells me, day by day—I am only just beginning to shine.

We grow more in our fullness in Christ each day when we trust, when we surrender. We become more of who we are created to be. Our physical selves might not show it, but our hearts do. And that is what I choose to have faith to see.

A Moment to Breathe . . .

Consider how you think about yourself. Ask God to show you what He sees when He looks at you. Be expectant. Be ready to be surprised by what He says. And then ask Him to help you believe it.

When You Need a Bigger Towel

BY MARY CARVER

He said to them, "Why are you afraid, you of little faith?" Then he got up and rebuked the winds and the sea, and there was a great calm. MATTHEW 8:26

WE'D BEEN AT A charity event downtown and had to park a block away. It didn't seem like such a bad idea when skies were clear. But as a huge storm blew in, we began to regret our walk back. The rain was insane! Finally, soaked and shivering, my brother and I jumped into my car. My brother reached for the napkins I keep in my glove compartment, and he handed me a single napkin. I was completely soaked, head to toe, down to my underwear, if you must know. And he handed me one napkin! I needed a towel, like the kind the store actually calls a "bath sheet." I needed a big, fluffy, extra-large bath sheet to soak up all that rain.

It's kind of like life, isn't it? Some problems can be fixed easily. Those types of problems cause inconvenience and frustration, sure, but they can usually be solved with a bit of time (and maybe some creative problem solving). But other challenges—other storms of life—require a lot more than the equivalent of a leftover napkin from last week's McDonald's run.

Sometimes our problems are bigger and deeper and harder than Sunday school platitudes and coffee dates and side hugs can fix. Like broken relationships and broken hearts, missed opportunities and the people we miss (the ones who are gone). A handful of napkins won't keep you from feeling like you're drowning. Sometimes we need help.

It's okay to say, "I need a bigger towel!" It's okay to ask for help, to seek wise counsel. Jesus assured us that this world would bring us trouble. He knew we'd face hard times, but He also knew He'd be right here beside us. He gave us this promise: "Take heart! I have overcome the world."

A Moment to Breathe . . .

When you're facing a storm that drenches your soul, don't be afraid to reach out for help. Don't be too proud to accept that help. And don't doubt for a minute that the sun will shine again.

The Worst Breakup

BY ANNIE F. DOWNS

They had such a sharp disagreement that they parted company, and
Barnabas took Mark with him and sailed off to Cyprus. ACTS 15:39

AS A SINGLE GIRL, I've had a few breakups. They're never fun. But you know what we don't talk about enough? When friendships break up. Of all the romantic breakups in my life, none have come close to hurting the way a breakup with a best friend hurts.

It all fell apart over a two-day period. Years of deep friendship ended and the ripping apart felt the way a sheet looks when it is torn in two. Shredded. Loud. Sudden. Jagged. After the dust settled, I didn't know who to trust and I didn't know what to feel. Isn't your best friend the one you talk to when things are broken? What do you do when things are broken with your best friend? How do you tell the other friends that a central friendship in your life is over without being gossipy? How do you process the hurt and pain without seeming overly invested and needy?

It's all very messy. I bet Paul and Barnabas would agree. Breakups are hard, but even Luke, who recorded the story in the book of Acts, shows us one thing we need to know: tell the truth, even when things rip to shreds. I can tell you this now, years later . . . I needed the ripping. While I hate how things ended, I don't regret what came of it. What it revealed in me when that friendship was stripped away was not healthy and Jesus needed a wide path in to heal some things in me. To make beauty from those ashes.

The more I say out loud, "the hardest breakup of my life was with a friend," the more nods and teary-eyes I see from other women. You are not alone if your heart is broken over a friendship. And you should talk about it. Let Jesus into the ripped places. He will show you a tapestry you could not see before. And somehow, in ways we don't get, it will be beautiful.

A Moment to Breathe . . .

When a friendship ends, go to Him and call it by name: a breakup.
Tell the truth, even when things break. Pick up a pen and journal
your thoughts and feelings and invite Him into the pain.

The Gaze of His Eye

BY KELLY BALARIE

*I will instruct you and show you the way to go; with
my eye on you, I will give counsel.* PSALM 32:8

I STOOD IN THE center of a kitchen that hadn't seen the likes of a mop for weeks. Crumbs scattered on the floor, goo stuck to the table, and something mysterious clung to the countertops. I felt like I might explode. *I can't do it all!* I thought.

The reality of my life—the countless needs and the never-ending feeling that life won't stop—made me wonder: *God, do You have more for me than nights of kitchen cleaning and mornings of kid-caretaking?*

My head spun. I had to fix my emotions. I needed God to answer. I prayed my heart out, as if my all-good effort would bring good results. At home, it usually does. No clean underwear? I'll do a load of laundry! Hungry? I'll make dinner! Sick? Let's get you to the doctor.

I waited. Nothing. I dropped my arms, wondering: *Where are You, God?* Letting my eyes relax, I found myself gazing out the window, into the density of night. There, a blur in the distance took shape.

The moon, I could see it. Strangely, it wasn't perfectly rounded, but imperfectly formed—shaped like an eye. All I could think was: *God, You see me. You know where I am going. You have a plan for me in my darkness. You have a way for me, in my wilderness, even when I can't see.* And in this, I can rest.

A Moment to Breathe . . .

*When the frantic pace of everyday life catches up with
us, let's remember to step outside at night and enjoy
the beauty of the nighttime landscape that God spoke
into existence. He sees us. He really does.*

Let Me Hide Myself in Thee

BY ALIA JOY

The LORD said, "Here is a place near me. You are to stand on the rock, and when my glory passes by, I will put you in the crevice of the rock and cover you with my hand until I have passed by. Then I will take my hand away, and you will see my back, but my face will not be seen." EXODUS 33:21–23

WE MAKE MEMORIES IN the spots on the calendar I've cleared. I have said no and fought off the filling of days so we could hike the wild trails of flowers growing along the river and jump with arms flung out wildly into the coldest of lakes. Every day the blessings pour down, dousing me with God's goodness.

These are the days of endless sunshine and the sugary scent of peaches and sticky-fingered children, barefoot and tanned. These are the days when hope rises up buoyant and I usually find solace from the weary days of winter. While my depression has been manageable at times, I've also seen it consume—tearing me and my world apart. But this week I am scavenging for another measure of grace. So I pray, "God, please, not now."

I'm always close to despair and nothing about this makes sense. But I've seen God in the dark night and the long loneliness that finds me when I cannot tell you why, when I have no answers for the sadness.

I've seen Him even when I cannot see, because I've penned my memories of His faithfulness. I am Moses glimpsing the back of God's glory as He passes me by, clefted in the rock under the hand of the Almighty.

Today, I push the covers back and seek out the squabbling kids. Should the battle come again, I'm bolstered by the remembrance that I need only to be still because my God will fight for me. And this is my yes. This is my choosing each day, my cup to bear, my thorn piercing deep. His strength made perfect because I am weak. So I answer with, "Yes, Lord, I am here. Your joy is my strength."

A Moment to Breathe . . .

You may not always see His face but His glory never ceases. Pray this prayer: Let me know Your joy, Lord, deep in my weary bones and let me see it with every counted thing.

When You Think You're Not Doing Enough

BY SARAH MAE

So if you have been raised with Christ, seek the things above,
where Christ is, seated at the right hand of God. Set your minds
on things above, not on earthly things. COLOSSIANS 3:1–2

THERE ARE SO MANY times I feel like I'm botching things up. Recently I have been struggling with fears that I'm not doing a good enough job discipling my kids. That maybe I'm failing them spiritually. So-and-so does nightly devotions with her husband and kids, and then they all pray together. So-and-so has prayer cards on their dining room table and they pray together every night. So-and-so writes beautiful letters to her kids that are so deep and thoughtful. So and so teaches her kids large portions of Scripture to memorize . . . and they do. And here I am, feeling like I can't seem to do enough.

So I emailed a former mentor of mine, someone from my college days, and asked her how she discipled her children, who are now grown. This is what she wrote back: "I usually read the Bible to my kids before going to bed. We never pushed them, but sometimes we would go out with them and have a special quiet time with them."

Hold up. That's it? She just read the Bible to them and sometimes took them out for special quiet times with them? I was expecting all the things. But this wise, godly woman who has discipled hundreds of women, who has led Bible studies and taught Scripture and co-led a ministry with her husband just "read the Bible" to them when they were young?

Sometimes we get super wrapped up on all that we're doing right or wrong and forget to set our minds on the things above, and the things above are the simplest: Jesus, the Word, and reading His Word. Yes. That's what I want to do. I want to stop setting my mind on my earthly fears and failures and set my mind on things above—on Jesus and His Word.

A Moment to Breathe . . .

Take a moment to sit down and simply read His
Word. Perhaps the rest of Colossians 3.

When You Feel like You Missed the Giving of Gifts

BY MELISSA AARON

And he himself gave some to be apostles, some prophets, some evangelists, some pastors and teachers, equipping the saints for the work of ministry, to build up the body of Christ, until we all reach unity in the faith and in the knowledge of God's Son, growing into maturity with a stature measured by Christ's fullness. EPHESIANS 4:11–13

I COME FROM A family of really talented, artistic people. Careers and livelihoods have been built on this talent. And while I've watched in awe and pride at their gifts, I've often been asked by others, "Are you artistic too?"

And I have to say, "Nope." I knew that Ephesians 2:10 proclaimed that I was His workmanship, created in Jesus specifically for these good works that God had prepared in advance for me to walk in. I noticed this person's gift, and that person's gift, and it seemed like everyone had some special gift except for me. I grew discouraged and kind of jealous too.

One day at a women's Bible study, one woman raised her hand and asked the teacher, "How do you really know what God wants you to do?" My heart skipped a beat because that was exactly what I wanted to know too, but I didn't want to ask; I was under the impression that everyone (except me) already knew the answer!

The teacher said, "God has already told you what He wants you to do. In His Word, He's given us very specific instructions to love and serve, to be a light, to refrain from ungodly behavior. If we focus on what He's already told us to do, we'll be better positioned to hear what else He wants us to do."

So I changed my focus from worrying about the gifts that others had and just started working on how well I could do what I know to do. Opportunities came that allowed me to serve, and in serving it became clear that God had made me especially for serving in these particular ways, and I realized I wasn't waiting anymore.

A Moment to Breathe . . .

List some of the special gifts you have. And if you're not sure, stop waiting and start serving. I'm willing to bet there are gifts inside you just waiting to be used.

The Value of Rest

BY ELISA PULLIAM

For the Lord God, the Holy One of Israel, has said:
"You will be delivered by returning and resting; your
strength will lie in quiet confidence" ISAIAH 30:15

IT NEVER FAILED, WHENEVER my mother-in-law came to town, she commented on how I would flit from one thing to another without ever sitting down. As a young bride, desperate for approval, I worried there was something wrong with the way I did life. I simply couldn't sit still if I knew there was a chore to accomplish. Of course, there was always another chore to do.

In the midst of so much doing and accomplishing, two very important parts of life can easily be eroded—rest and relationships. If I don't slow down, I won't be able to connect with the people God has placed in my life, nor will I find the refreshment needed to keep doing the holy mundane.

There is a type of "doing" that's an overflow of our passions, but even that "doing" can lead to burnout without rest. So we need to be intentional about finding rest, no matter our personality type or wiring.

By God's grace, He continues to lead and guide me in this process of learning how to put off the tyranny of the urgent. Sometimes it looks like leaving the laptop on the desk while I snuggle with my girls and listen to them pour out their hearts. Other times, it looks like playing a round of Uno with the twins (and I'm not a game person). Yes, I'm active, but it is rest for my soul.

I'll never be able to let go of the desire to finish whatever task is at hand. It's how I'm wired, but I don't want my life dictated by a never-ending to-do list either. Embracing rest means walking away from unfinished tasks while choosing to enjoy the present moments.

A Moment to Breathe . . .

If your to-do list is the boss of you, make a new to-do list and
write down things like: lay down for ten minutes, stand in the
sunshine for five minutes, sit down to drink a glass of cool water.

The Prayers We Neglect

BY JOLENE UNDERWOOD

You will call to me and come and pray to me,
and I will listen to you. JEREMIAH 29:12

I LOOKED AROUND THE room and asked the women present, "How many of you gather in a small group setting—perhaps a community or life group, a Bible study, or something similar?" Most nodded. Then I asked, "How often do your prayer requests include someone's mom, dad, grandma, grandpa, or another relative three times removed in another part of the country who has an illness, financial struggles, or a significant personal loss of some kind in their lives?" Most of the hands went up with a few knowing smiles and slight chuckles too. Then I asked the question I really wanted to ask, "How many of you pray for what's going on in your heart?" Not one single hand.

Every woman in that room lives incredibly busy lives, yet no one had a circle of friends to gather with to pray over their hearts. What if a woman in that room at that very moment was desperate to receive care from another human because her heart felt so shattered she didn't know what to do with it? Or better yet, what if you were experiencing a devastating situation? Would we create a safe place for individuals to vulnerably share? Would we pray together even when we don't have any answers?

We are so quick to ask for prayer for someone else's obvious need, which is easy to talk about. Yet, how often do we request prayer for the needs of our hearts to help us walk through life and grow in our faith? What steps could we take today to cultivate this kind of prayer among us?

The women, right then and there, clustered in groups of three to take turns sharing, listening, and praying. God will meet us in our darkest places when we cry out to Him in prayer. And He often chooses to do this through the gift of fellowship in community. May we pray for each other in the same way.

A Moment to Breathe . . .

Name the circle of friends you can turn to for prayer—for prayer about the deepest needs of your heart. If you can think of them right away, pray for them right now. If you can't think of who you'd call for prayer, ask God to bring women into your life you can pray with.

A Friend like Esther

BY BECKY KEIFE

The Spirit of the Lord God is on me, because the Lord has anointed me to bring good news to the poor. He has sent me to heal the brokenhearted, to proclaim liberty to the captives and freedom to the prisoners. ISAIAH 61:1

WHEN I APPROACHED ESTHER—the new, twenty-something, beautifully blonde staffer for our campus ministry—I didn't know exactly what it meant to be "discipled." But I knew the longing to grow. And wishing for someone to guide the way. We started meeting in my dorm room my sophomore year of college. We'd sit cross-legged on opposite ends of my periwinkle duvet for an hour of weekly "discipleship." I guess I expected to learn about God's Word and the how-to's of walking with Jesus. But what Esther really taught me was how to care for someone's heart.

The way she asked intentional questions and leaned in to hear the answer. The way she wasn't afraid of my messy past or confused present. Esther was just there, to be *with* me. She made space for me to explore who I was, where I had been, and where Jesus was leading me.

We had been meeting for several months when she pulled out a little fold-up keyboard and started typing. She said, "I usually take notes about our time together later, but what you're sharing is important. I don't want to forget it." I must have had a strange look on my face because Esther quickly added, "I want to remember how to pray for you and follow up later on what we've talked about. Does that make you feel uncomfortable?"

"No, not uncomfortable," I said while wiping tears. "It makes me feel seen. Loved. Invested in . . . Like no one ever has."

Sixteen years later and Esther has transitioned from a mentor to a soul sister and lifelong friend. I hope to be someone who influences many by influencing one—one woman on my block, one mom in my playgroup, or one college student at my church. May I share the love of Christ by caring for someone's heart.

A Moment to Breathe . . .

No matter what season of life you find yourself in, there's undoubtedly someone in your sphere who would love to have a godly woman invest in them. Pray about being that someone today.

Everyday Grace through Faith

BY KATIE ORR

For you are saved by grace through faith, and this is not from yourselves; it is God's gift—not from works, so that no one can boast. EPHESIANS 2:8–9

I BECAME A CHRISTIAN as a middle-schooler. In my teenage bedroom, I placed my faith in Christ as my only hope for salvation. Vividly aware of my sin and separation from God, I eagerly accepted the glorious grace so clearly pursuing me. That first moment of faith was so easy and clear and powerful. God loves me. Me! Christ died for me. Me! I had only to receive the gift of grace—eternal life with God through Christ.

Moving forward things were not so simple. I attempted to live out my new life of faith, but I was often confused as to what it should look like. I wanted to live big for God and become a strong woman of faith, and I thought drastic "faith-filled" decisions would prove my validity as a Christian. Slowly but surely, I felt I had to keep proving myself worthy of Christ's sacrifice.

Unfortunately, this led me to believing that God's acceptance of me was tied up in my performance. My relationship with God began by faith, but I moved forward by works. In doing so, I missed the point of grace. My journey with God started by God's grace, through faith. And my journey continues by God's grace, through faith.

All the power, action, and provision for my salvation was God's part. My part was faith—believing that the work was accomplished by a good and gracious God who loves me. The same is true for my everyday walk of faith. God continues the transformation He started in me that glorious afternoon in my bedroom. I don't have to keep trying to clean myself up. This is yet another gift of grace.

The work of everyday faith is drawing near to the presence of God, with complete certainty that He will accept me. Not because I have ever been good enough. Not because I ever will be. But because of Jesus on my behalf.

A Moment to Breathe . . .

Open your hands and turn your palms upward. Simply receive God's grace through faith. Tell God how grateful you are for His gift of grace.

When You Thought No One Was Watching

BY KAYLA AIMEE

Little children, let us not love in word or speech,
but in action and in truth. 1 JOHN 3:18

I CAME AROUND THE corner to see my six-year-old daughter doing the exact thing I had explicitly told her not to do only moments earlier. "Would you like to explain to Mommy why you were doing that after I told you not to?" I asked her. She sweetly replied, "Well, sure. The reason is because I did not know that you were watching me."

(I thought parenting was going to involve me imparting a lot of deep and meaningful wisdom to my children, but it turns out that it's mostly just me carefully composing my expression so that they don't know I'm laughing at them.)

I took in her innocent expression and kneeled down to look in her eyes. "It is important to do the right thing even when no one is watching," I told her.

The other day I was hosting a live seminar online when the video disappeared from the screen. I could not figure out what went wrong so I fretted about the room, checking cords and mumbling heatedly about technology. I may have growled at my computer. And also used a few choice words that I would never bandy about in polite company or dare to utter in the presence of my grandmother. It was most undoubtedly a grown-up temper tantrum.

That's when my phone dinged. I read the text message from my friend in horror. "Hey, I know you think your camera is off but it definitely is not and it definitely is still broadcasting you live on the Internet."

Bless my heart. I was appropriately mortified and admittedly a bit shamefaced that my lesson to my kindergartener had come back to haunt me. What we do in the quiet, unseen moments comprise our character. It's by our actions that we make known the truth. (And also because you never know when you might be accidentally broadcasting yourself live to the entire world.)

A Moment to Breathe . . .

Share one of your funniest, most embarrassing moments today with a friend. Go ahead and laugh. Even at yourself. It's good for the soul.

The View from My Window

BY HANNAH VAN DYK

"Provide justice for the needy and the fatherless; uphold the rights of the oppressed and the destitute. Rescue the poor and needy; save them from the power of the wicked." PSALM 82:3–4

I LIKE BEING COMFORTABLE. My favorite spot in my house is where my white chair sits by a window that overlooks my street. On sunshine-filled days, sitting in that spot with my coffee, my favorite quilt, and a good book is the best way for me to get outside of my head for a little while.

My setup at work is similar. My chair sits in front of a large window, overlooking our street, and the sunshine streams in, always with a cup of coffee beside me. But my work window seat leaves me feeling anything but comfortable.

I work and live in the inner city, and the reflective windows—the same windows that allow the sun's rays to stream through—are what people use as their mirror. There's a tent outside my window, too, made of yellow and blue tarps haphazardly thrown together for someone to sleep on the street. My heart becomes uncomfortably knotted every day, and the world's pain seems too overwhelming for any one person to make a difference to those people the world has deemed the least among us, to those among us hurting the most.

How do we serve, even when it seems too hard, even when it feels too uncomfortable, too inadequate? How do we move both individually and collectively, so our acts of service make the most difference for those whom Christ has created in His image?

We tune in so we don't avoid what makes us uncomfortable. We pray for our neighbors in Christ and also for our hearts to be moved to service. We listen to the needs of those in our community who are crying for justice. And we begin today, standing up for what is true and right, demonstrating Christ's love in action.

A Moment to Breathe . . .

It doesn't have to be big or grandiose. Just one small gesture. One simple act of kindness. Pray for the eyes of your heart to see the hurting around you and to know the one thing you can do today.

When You Aren't like Her but Wish You Were

BY ROBIN DANCE

Now as we have many parts in one body, and all the parts do not have the same function, in the same way we who are many are one body in Christ and individually members of one another. According to the grace given to us, we have different gifts: If prophecy, use it according to the proportion of one's faith. ROMANS 12:4–6

AS I READ HER words, the enemy hissed lies and I lapped them up like a ravenous kitten: *You aren't as good as her. You can't write as well as she can. Why do you even bother?* Waves of inferiority crashed over me. And it's 100 percent true: I will never write like her. That's how the enemy of our soul works; he mingles truth with lies because there's just enough truth to lend credibility to the lie.

You might not be a writer, but I bet there are ways your spirit receives a similar assault: I'll never cook like her . . . or dress like her . . . or deliver a public address like her . . . or excel at work like her . . . or be as Pinteresty of a Room Mom as her.

We torture ourselves with unfair comparisons because they don't tell the complete story. When we do this, we're only comparing one aspect of another's life to the whole of ours. It's illogical. I am a unique creature of God's careful design and He thinks I'm wonderful. So are you. I am the only me who has ever existed, who will ever exist. When God made me, He broke the mold. Same is true for you.

You and what you have to offer have immense and intrinsic beauty, value, worth, and desirability because you are created in the image of God. If you withhold what only you have to offer, you're withholding it from the body of Christ. Nobody can do something quite the way you can.

What if, when God made the rainbow, He made only bands of red? Oh, how we'd miss orange's flame, yellow's smile, green's signs of new life, blue's strength, indigo's charm, and violet's majesty! A rainbow's pleasure to the eye is its colorful diversity, true. But its treasure to the soul is its origin, its reason for being: a promise by a King.

A Moment to Breathe . . .

Lay aside any temptation to compare, and embrace the person God has uniquely created you to be. Name a gift or strength of yours and plan a special way to bless someone today with your unique gift.

I Number the Minutes

BY HILARY YANCEY

He counts the number of the stars; he gives
names to all of them. PSALM 147:4

I NUMBER MINUTES LIKE stars. The minutes Jack is in my arms. The minutes he sleeps while I monitor his oxygen levels. And the minutes of prayer.

Months ago, at the very beginning, when we didn't know anything but the need for a follow-up ultrasound, the need for a consultation, the need to see a more specialized doctor . . . I stood weeping and cradling my belly and asking Jesus again and again, "Where are You?" I wept and asked and begged Jesus, again and again, to do something. I believed and voiced to Jesus that where there was skin or muscle missing, He could build it.

Wasn't it His voice at the beginning, singing the world into being? Wasn't it His voice the wind and waves obeyed? Wasn't Jesus the one who spat on tongues and spread mud on eyes and put His fingers in ears and declared, by the words of His mouth, be opened? And wasn't it Jesus, reaching down into death, calling back Lazarus and Jairus's daughter?

Last night I looked again; my infant son has a mark from his IV in his hand and I am reminded of the scars on Jesus' hands—the hands that, even in these long minutes, I believe are holding my son. I cannot number all the stars or all the minutes. But the Lord can. He can count the stars and name them all.

Who am I, then, to think that Jesus has not been mindful of these minutes? Who am I, then, to think Jesus has not counted each one with me, His knowledge of them far more perfect than anything I could fathom? Jesus has seen each minute of prayer, of worry, and of desperate joy when my son is in my arms and I feel the weight of him, his hand grabbing my shirt, and Jesus is numbering the minutes with us.

Jesus knows each star, each minute. And He holds us, counting each breath.

A Moment to Breathe . . .

Just as Jesus knows each star by name, He knows
you by name too. Rest assured wherever you are, that
He sees you, and He's watching over you.

When God Anoints You
but Doesn't Appoint You

BY LISA WHITTLE

*Then the L*ORD *said, "Anoint him, for he is the one." So*
Samuel took the horn of oil and anointed him in the presence
*of his brothers, and the Spirit of the L*ORD *came powerfully*
on David from that day forward. 1 SAMUEL 16:12–13

"HE'S CALLING ME," SHE tells me on a drive in her car, and I can see how it pains her, how she feels called to things that her life, right now, won't allow. It's not that she doesn't love her life. She does. It's that God's pull is strong inside, and she doesn't know how to walk in a call she cannot, at this moment, fulfill.

Living in the space of not now is perhaps the hardest and holiest of all. It's a space of wrestling. It almost feels cruel for God to give us a sense of destiny and then not release us to walk in it right away. But the waiting is part of the plan too. The spiritual disciplines of surrender, trust, and faithfulness make us more like Jesus . . . more ready for the appointing.

The truth is, the anointing often comes before the appointing. Our job is to believe God and pursue holiness in the space in between. David was anointed the king of Israel, but then he had to wait fifteen years before he was officially appointed king! This was God's perfect plan. And all the while, David knew he had been chosen by God. He knew he was going to be the king. But he had to wait on God's perfect timing and learn to live in the space of not now. For him to do that, he had to trust God to complete that good work.

God knew what would happen if David became king before he was ready. God knew what he needed to learn, and how he needed to grow.

It's always the omniscience of the Father that saves us. So if you find yourself in that place now, in the holy hard space of waiting—for the anointed but not yet appointed—remember this: God knows what He's doing. And He is faithful. Every time.

A Moment to Breathe . . .

Grab a notebook and write out your prayers to God
while waiting. Because one day you'll be able to look
back and see how God's hand was there all along.

Show and Tell

BY JENNIFER DUKES LEE

He also said to them, "Is a lamp brought in to be put under a basket or under a bed? Isn't it to be put on a lampstand? For there is nothing hidden that will not be revealed, and nothing concealed that will not be brought to light." MARK 4:21–22

DO YOU REMEMBER "SHOW and Tell" in your kindergarten classroom? I do. I remember distinctly how we couldn't wait until it was our turn to bring something special to school. We'd bring stuffed animals, new basketballs, and trinkets from vacation. Quite often, we'd bring items we'd made with our own hands. Once, I carefully wrapped up a ceramic cat I had painted so I could take it to school. I still remember the quiet murmurs of appreciation from my classmates when I unwrapped the cat and held up my beautiful treasure.

After a few years, "Show and Tell" began to disappear—and not just because we graduated from kindergarten. It's because "Show and Tell" feels boastful. We think "Show and Tell" is the opposite of humble—and good Christian boys and girls should be humble.

Consider your own life for a moment. What are you making, doing, creating, or planning today—borne out of God's gifting in you—that you love? What is beautiful in your life? I'll bet you know the answers to those questions, but I'll bet you'd be pretty uncomfortable sharing your answers in front of a group of peers. Do you know that your gifts are the kingdom, shining in you? You are like a lamp. Some of us want to put our kingdom shine under the bed, thinking that's what humility means. But that's not humility; that's hiding.

Your light shows other people who Jesus is, and it shows people how to find their way to Him.

Your light comes in so many different forms: in your attitude, your kindness, your humility, and your generous heart. It also shines through the gifts that God has given you. You are free to shine for Jesus. Because of Jesus. Don't be afraid to let people see God's work in you.

A Moment to Breathe . . .

That gift you have? That special thing you offer? Share with someone today.

Work That Matters

BY ERIKA DAWSON

Let the favor of the Lord our God be on us; establish for us the work of our hands—establish the work of our hands! PSALM 90:17

FROM THE TIME I was eight years old (crimping my hair to impress the popular girls) to just this week (trying on five different outfits before choosing my clothes for church), I've spent too much time seeking the applause of people. This "approval addiction" runs deeper than my appearances. My insecurities come out in parenting, marriage, work, and even hobbies. But something changes when I'm confident about whose I am and what I'm called to do. I live differently.

Though he lived thousands of years ago under very different circumstances, Moses isn't entirely different from us. When God called Moses, a feeling of inadequacy flooded over him. Three times Moses questioned God. Who am I? Will they believe what I say? Why not someone else more qualified?

Instead of trusting the sufficiency of God, Moses obsessed over his own inadequacy. He questioned, he compared, and he hesitated. But when Moses stopped focusing on himself and started trusting God, God used Moses in history-changing ways. Moses became a man who met with God. He lived a life of faith and obedience, borne from knowing the heart of God for His people.

When we're focused on our deficiencies, comparing ourselves to others or trying to please people, we're not listening to the voice of the One who calls us according to His purposes. But as we rest our life on the love of Christ, our lives and our plans will change. When we live compelled by the love of Christ, we'll do work that matters, work that God establishes.

May we start every endeavor and each new day abiding in the love of God through Christ Jesus, satisfied, not by our effort, our work, or our possessions, but satisfied in the love of God. Only then can we do work that matters.

A Moment to Breathe . . .

Count the ways God has made you uniquely gifted. Go ahead. Count 'em. All the ways He's equipped you for a good work.

Use What You Have

BY MELISSA MICHAELS

*Just as each one has received a gift, use it to serve others,
as good stewards of the varied grace of God.* 1 PETER 4:10

YEARS AGO I WAS certain God was calling me to an adventure. But I spent an entire year in confusion, praying and wondering what was coming or where I was supposed to be going. God seemed pretty quiet. So I continued to pray about how God might use me. I knew increasingly that I wanted to encourage women, and perhaps God wanted to use me in that way. But I felt ill equipped, lacking in any sense of direction outside of serving my family. No flashing directional arrows, no answers.

Finally, after a long year of praying and waiting, the clouds finally parted and I could see more clearly. My confusion faded as I realized my passion, purpose, and direction for encouraging women had been right in front of me all along! I turned a "use what you have" style of decorating into a business because that's where my passion had been all along. I found it fascinating and even amusing that God would finally encourage me with the obvious answer: *use what you have.*

Sometimes I think we forget that God already gave us our unique gifts so we look high and low for the bigger passion and purpose out there in the flashing lights somewhere, only to discover that what we already have is all God wants.

Our stories aren't over when times are hard or things go wrong or when God seems quiet. Many exciting stories out there can make us all wide-eyed and in awe of what God can do for "some people." They can be inspiring stories. But they can also be perplexing when our story reads nothing like that. While we may want to rush to a flashy movie-ending conclusion of God's great provision in an amazing success story, we can miss out on the beautiful chapters where God is in the trenches with us, wiping the tears, carrying us across rising waters, and providing our daily bread.

A Moment to Breathe . . .

What would it look like for you to use what you have to serve others? What are some unique ways you can give to others?

Freedom

BY SANDY HAFEEZ

"Everything is permissible for me," but not everything is beneficial. "Everything is permissible for me," but I will not be mastered by anything. 1 CORINTHIANS 6:12

I WAS TIRED OF fighting. I wanted to be free; my soul ached for it. It was my birthright as a daughter of the King. My freedom had been paid for with the broken body and blood of Jesus. But in that moment I didn't feel free. I had chosen darkness, but no more, it was time to bring my sin to the light.

My friend encouraged me to call it out for what it was and what it is . . . sin. And as I confessed my sin, I felt the shame, guilt, hopelessness, and grief begin to fall like bricks.

In those moments, I tangibly felt the freedom and recognized the change. Letting the words come out and feeling the light slicing the dark. Letting the tears flow and feeling the comfort of a gracious Father. Letting the consequences be and knowing that our Father disciplines those He loves. Letting the weight be lifted and feeling the shackles loosed and the pathway to freedom ahead.

The journey was just beginning for me as I worked to get to the root of my issues, so I wouldn't return to old habits when life got hard. I walked through the process of learning my triggers and finding the accountability I needed. But once I tasted freedom—real freedom!—oh, how I ached for more of it. I was no longer feeling controlled by my own desires. What a gift we've been given to be able to confess our sins one to another. What a gift to have Christ-centered friends in our lives to walk with us and point us to the light. What a gift we have in Jesus!

A Moment to Breathe . . .

Confession frees you from the sin that so easily entangles. Receive God's grace and forgiveness today, knowing that you are deeply loved and free.

When You're Trying to Remember Who God Is

BY SHELLY WILDMAN

*"If the God we serve exists, then he can rescue us
from the furnace of blazing fire, and he can rescue us
from the power of you, the king."* DANIEL 3:17

"REMIND ME WHO GOD is." These words keep ringing in my ears, a mandate from a grieving friend as we stood near the casket of her twenty-six-year-old son. We hugged hard. She grabbed my shoulders and repeated her edict: "Remind me who God is."

I'm trying so hard to remember for myself who God really is. Who is God when real life comes knocking with a blow so forceful you can't stand against it? Who is God when everything you've planned for and dreamed of is altered, not just slightly, but forever?

Death. Divorce. Illness. Life has changed, and it will never look, feel, taste the same as it did before. Who is God through it all?

I do know this. It's okay to question and doubt. Throughout the Bible, examples abound of people who wondered about God. Wonder is okay. It may even be good for us.

I read the story of Shadrach, Meshach, and Abednego— Daniel's buddies who refused to bow down and worship King Nebuchadnezzar's golden statue. The king gave them one more chance to "do the right thing" and bow before his shiny likeness, but still the three refused. Their rationale? "But even if he does not rescue us, we want you as king to know that we will not serve your gods or worship the gold statue you set up" (Dan. 3:18).

But even if he doesn't . . . these words, strangely, have given me so much hope. They have strengthened my faith in the past and they help today as I process the death of a too-young man.

But here's what I know about God: He has not left our side. He is there, walking right beside us, weeping with us. He grieves with us. Because He loves us.

"Remind me who God is." I'm just beginning to remember.

A Moment to Breathe . . .

*Remind your heart who God is today. He is the God who
sees you and walks with you and grieves with you. He
is the God who will always and forever love you.*

Renewed: From the Inside Out

BY DENISE J. HUGHES

The instruction of the Lord is perfect, renewing one's life. PSALM 19:7

AS I WALK DOWN the grocery store aisle, the labels on various products call out:

Renew your youth!

Reduce those lines and wrinkles!

Look like a new-you in 3 easy steps!

One tiny jar says I could look ten years younger in just ten days. Imagine that.

I pass by the little jar of promise and look for the milk aisle instead. The truth is, I'm okay with my age, and I'm okay with the lines around my eyes. I've earned every crease at my brow with every story I've lived. My stories make up who I am—wrinkles and all.

I wouldn't trade my stories—my years—for anything. I've lived long enough now to see how God can use my life experiences to invite women to a place of deeper assurance. Not that every circumstance in my life has turned out peachy. Not at all. But has God shown Himself greater. And my trust in Him has grown, even as the lines on my face have lengthened.

My journey with God has taught me that renewal really is possible, but it's not the kind of renewal that's promised in a store-bought product on a shelf. Our journey of authentic renewal begins with soul surrender, yielding to the majesty of the Almighty. And with each day, our hearts are renewed as we spend time in the Word with the Ancient of Days, who is both matchless and ageless.

A Moment to Breathe . . .

Time in God's Word renews our hearts and prepares us for the coming day better than any jar of "miracle cream" from the store. Perhaps read Psalm 19 today and thank Him for the renewal He brings.

Heads Up

BY STEPHANIE BRYANT

If we live by the Spirit, let us also keep in
step with the Spirit. GALATIANS 5:25

MY DAYS ARE FILLED with puppy dogs and baby chicks, cuddling with a miracle daughter and planting seeds in our garden. We sit on the porch and pretend to play the harmonica. We go on tractor rides and take pictures of the pear trees we just planted. Sometimes I look at God's plans and marvel at how they're so different from the ones I had for myself. I never would have imagined the life I now lead.

The college-me wanted to climb the corporate ladder overseas. The single-me wanted to get married someday but couldn't fathom having kids. The married-me would never have thought about having a garden, much less a farm. The mommy-me thought I could juggle and do it all as a mom and the creative balance would easily transition.

I'm so thankful I was open to God's ideas, His desires and dreams for my life. I was frustrated as a young twenty-something that I had never heard God's voice. I wanted to know what to do and how to please God, but I came to know intimately the Holy Spirit that dwelt within me, and my life became worship instead of plans. Now God starts to change my heart, passion, and thinking and has the grace to make me aware of it. He begins to give me eyes to see He's doing a new thing in me.

God has transformed me as He's guided me. Right now? That looks like focusing on my daughter, learning how to be a farmer, and being set apart. I could look at my day-to-day and think it doesn't make much difference. That living as a salmon swimming upstream compared to our fast-paced culture is a waste. But then I would miss the opportunity to worship my God with my life, listen to His voice, and follow His lead. Because I love Him.

A Moment to Breathe . . .

Listen to His voice today. Lean into His Word and follow His lead.
Because He loves you and wants to walk each day with you.

Burden or Blessing

BY ANGIE RYG

*Indeed, we have all received grace upon
grace from his fullness.* JOHN 1:16

EVERY SUNDAY NIGHT, I packed my children's backpacks, tucked them in, said their prayers with them, and then proceeded to complain to my husband. "Oh, how I wish I didn't have to work tomorrow. I wish I could just stay at home, get all my errands done, go to Bible study, and be able to be only a mom!"

I said this every Sunday night. And not just on Sunday nights. I said it other nights of the week too. When I had papers to grade, I'd complain. When I didn't have time to go to the grocery store, I'd complain. It didn't matter that my job was teaching where my children went to school, I still complained.

Then, one day I was tucking my youngest son in and when he said his prayers I heard his tiny voice say, "And thank you, God, for Mommy being a teacher at school so I can hug her." My heart dropped. My tired eyes flew open and every blessing of me working came to mind: seeing my kids in the hall for a quick smile. Attending class parties because I was already there. Teaching about Jesus' love to kindergarteners. The way I got to know each of my boys' friends as they came to hang out in my room every day after school. Hearing the eighth graders chant my name when I got called to juggle at the latest assembly.

God wasn't punishing me. In fact, my job was a beautiful blessing that not only helped me pay for their tuition, but also allowed me a chance to interact with my children during the day! What I saw as a hindrance, God used to bless not only my kids, but me as well—with one blessing after another. I only needed to look for them.

A Moment to Breathe . . .

*Look for the blessings that may be hidden within the details of
a hard situation. Thank God for those blessings and ask Him
to help you to see them all the more in your life today.*

Filled with Wonder

BY KELLY BALARIE

*And [the Lord] replied, "My presence will go with
you, and I will give you rest."* EXODUS 33:14

I INHALED. THE AIR was crisp and my hands were cold, yet, before
long, my quick pace warmed me. I leaned forward with eagerness,
believing I was moving away from the battle and into something
better, something powerful. I needed this "something better,"
because, frankly, I was tired of the monotony: the repetitive days,
my continual lack of excitement, and other women's sparkling
success stories wrapped neatly in social media status updates. I
exhaled. The air took form as I hoped it would carry my frustrations
with it, then disappeared . . . not to be seen again.

What would happen if I disappeared? Would anyone notice?
Would anyone miss my love? Would it matter? I lifted my head,
observing the darkness above. It hung heavy, like a dome I couldn't
escape. It symbolized my feelings: I'm not valuable. Not worthy. So
I quickened my pace, trying to move past it. I wanted to move into
something new. I wanted to run, to hurry away and escape. But, as
always, there was no escape, nowhere to go, it seemed. The only
one thing left to do: look up and seek God.

So, I did. Literally. I looked up . . . and what I saw staggered me.
The clouds parted slightly and the sky opened slowly and small
rays of light cast down upon the earth, near the horizon. The beauty
of God's glory displayed through His creation beckoned me. It was
as if He was saying: *My daughter, move where I am, into the light
of My love. For under My light, you cannot be easily consumed by
darkness.*

Today, let's choose to dwell with God. Let's notice how God's
presence reminds us of His providence, His power, and His good
plan to help us, and be with us, wherever we go.

A Moment to Breathe . . .

*Step outside, breathe in deep, and look straight up. Tell Him
how marvelous He is and ask Him to fill you with wonder
at the beauty He bestows in the world all around us.*

Test for the True

BY DAWN CAMP

Test all things. Hold on to what is good. 1 THESSALONIANS 5:21

WHEN MY COUSIN AND I were kids, we swam at a large, public pool on hot summer days. It was a simpler time when people weren't afraid to drop off their elementary-age children for an afternoon of fun in the sun. Besides, my cousin was two years older and we thought we were practically grown.

Piles of T-shirts, shoes, discarded clothing, and other personal items lined the fence surrounding the enormous pool. Never much of a swimmer, I stayed near the shallow end, as far as possible from the cavernous diving pool. One day my cousin and I discovered that the stash of change we brought for the concession stand and hid under our pile of clothes was gone. Another child, who we believed to be a reliable witness, pointed to the thief. With righteous indignation, we reported the criminal and the crime to the proper (pool) authorities.

Only we were wrong.

Maybe our informant had a grudge against the other child. Maybe it made him feel important to solve the crime. The reason doesn't matter. What matters is that we publicly accused someone of something they didn't do, and it felt awful. I don't know if the child we blamed remembers this incident, but I have never forgotten it. All of my children know the story, because I remind them of it whenever they point fingers without the facts or speculate about what someone else has done, said, or intended.

This can be difficult for us as adults too. It's easy to make assumptions about people based on how they vote or where they live or how they choose to educate their children. But stereotypes rarely reflect people accurately; many of those associated with my choices don't apply to me. A painful childhood lesson taught me to trust what I see and hear firsthand more than what is related to me secondhand, and not to assume what I don't know to be true.

A Moment to Breathe . . .

Invite God to search your heart for any misconceptions or labels you're tempted to put on other people. Choose to give each other grace instead—and the benefit of the doubt.

This Is Your Life

BY DEIDRA RIGGS

Yet Lord, you are our Father; we are the clay, and you are our potter; we all are the work of your hands. ISAIAH 64:8

WHEN I WAS A little girl, I always asked this question: "What's it like to be you?" Somewhere early in my journey on this spiraling globe of a planet, I realized my life was unlike any other. And yours is too. Somehow I understood each life—yours and mine—is a note in the music of God's creation. We need each other. I remember asking my mom, "What's it like to be you? No, really. What's it like?"

One day, worn out by my tireless inquisition, my mom said to me, "You know, you should ask your teacher that question." The next day I waited until all my classmates filed out of the classroom and onto the playground for recess, and I stood next to my teacher's desk at the front of the classroom and asked her, "What's it like to be you?"

Teachers are beautiful people, walking around with an incredible desire to help, to provide the answer. My fourth-grade teacher was no different. I can't tell you what she said, because, quite honestly, what she said wasn't scratching where I was itching. What I can tell you is that's the precise moment—my teacher struggling to answer a question for which there really is no answer—I realized no one can fully articulate their existence in a moment-by-moment, blow-by-blow running account like the ticker at the bottom of a television screen.

Our lives are so much more than that. Your life is spectacular. Don't miss it by continually wishing you had someone else's. Don't miss the beauty of playing your one note in the symphony of God's creation. No one will ever be able to articulate your presence here the way you can. God isn't into mass production. You are a treasure—the only you there will ever be. We need each other, just the way God made us. Be you. Tell your story. Paint your canvas. Unlock scientific mysteries. Get dinner on the table. Create beautiful code. Because the way you do it is magnificent.

A Moment to Breathe . . .

Tell your story. Be confident in who God made you, and only you, to be. Because nobody will ever be quite like you.

An Easy Way to Bless Teachers

BY JESSICA TURNER

Let the one who is taught the word share all his
good things with the teacher. GALATIANS 6:6

TEACHERS PLAY A POWERFUL role in our lives. I can tell you the name of every teacher I ever had, as well as something about them. My second grade teacher, Mrs. Claas, was gentle and patient. My high school English teacher, Mr. White, pushed me to think about literature in new and deeper ways. My journalism teacher and mentor, Mr. Harrell, believed in me more than any other teacher.

I'm so thankful for the kind, wise teachers that God has placed in my life. I appreciate every one of them. Now as a parent I have an even deeper appreciation for teachers and the way they love the children they teach. The teachers there love on my children every day while my husband and I work. In some ways, they are an extension of us—loving, teaching, and shepherding our kids in our physical absence. I'm so thankful my children's teachers have loved them so well in their early years.

So I think a lot about how to bless the teachers at my children's preschool. Last year, my son colored cards to deliver to his teachers and his thoughtfulness was appreciated. This year, we decided to give each teacher a journal, wrapped with a tag of thanks, and they were something both male and female teachers could use.

As I wrapped the rope around the journals, I prayed for the hands that would receive the gift. That they would feel loved. That they would know that they are valued. That this small gift would minister to them. Honoring teachers doesn't require that we spend a lot (or any!) money. Something as simple as some homemade bread or a gift card for a cup of coffee is a thoughtful way to show you care.

A Moment to Breathe . . .

Think of the teachers who have made an impact on your life.
Let them know how much you appreciate their investment
in you. Send a note or a small gesture of thanks today.

Take the Training Wheels Off

BY KENDRA TILLMAN

*Peter began to speak: "Now I truly understand that
God doesn't show favoritism."* ACTS 10:34

OUR TWO OLDER KIDS were in preschool when we taught them to ride a bike—the kind without training wheels. For a few weeks we spent some time every day holding on to the backs of their bikes while running beside them. After several weeks of scraped knees and a few tears, we started to wonder if they would reach puberty before they got the hang of it.

Their upcoming preschool bike rodeo may have been part of our motivation for them to learn to ride their bikes without training wheels. At the rodeo all the kids would bring their bikes to school. The school encouraged the parents to get the kids to the place where they didn't need training wheels.

When the day of the rodeo came, our kids quickly realized there were very few kids still riding bikes with training wheels. Discouragement quickly set in. But then it set a fire under them. At home later that same day, they asked us to take the training wheels off their bikes. We were surprised, but we agreed and took the training wheels off. We went outside and did all the things we had done with them before the bike rodeo. They still fell. They were still afraid for us to let go at times, but they had a steady resolve. By the end of the day they were both riding their bikes without training wheels.

Watching their determination after school that day taught me a valuable lesson. After watching their friends succeed at something they had tried and failed at previously, their faith grew enough to believe they could do it too. (Their little competitive spirits probably contributed, as well.) God isn't holding out on us by playing favorites. Sometimes our faith is activated by witnessing success in someone else's life.

A Moment to Breathe . . .

*Name the thing you've deeply desired to do, but you've
been tempted lately to give up on it. Pray about it and
ask God to show you the next steps for you to take.*

Enough Light

BY KIM HYLAND

From the rising of the sun to its setting, let the
name of the LORD be praised. PSALM 113:3

MY PHONE SAYS THE sunrise is at 7:10. It's 7:03, and I look toward the mountains. There's no sign of the sun. It's dawn, and the light is rising. But thick, gray clouds cover the sky. I don't always wake up before the sun. But when I do, I anticipate its rising. Something in me derives an inordinate degree of satisfaction from saying I saw the sunrise. It's kind of like getting the cool 10K T-shirt before the race. I already have bragging rights.

So sitting here in the gray dawn sans sun . . . well, it's like checking in at the race and finding out they ran out of shirts. Major bummer. I want to see the hot orange promise of a fresh new day, warming me to all the inevitable challenges that will rise with the sun. Yeah, I know it's there either way. The light testifies to that. And I ask myself if I can be content with light.

My Bible sits open on my lap beside my current study and pencil. Each time I open it I have hopes of seeing the sunrise here too. And many days I do. It crests between the words and begins to glow. My heart feels the warmth and my mind wakes up with the illumination. By the time I'm done, it's a bright new day, and I'm feeling pretty awesome about Jesus and me.

But some mornings, it's just light. Enough to chase away the dark, but the sky is still gray. And I ask myself: *Can I be content with light?* No warm fuzzy feelings. The chill of life's trials right there beside me on the couch. Light undeniably right there in my lap. Truth illuminating the gray just enough for me to take the next step.

It's 7:20 now. I take one more hopeful look out my window to the east. And my day begins.

A Moment to Breathe . . .

Set your alarm to rise before the sun tomorrow. Then place your Bible
next to your alarm. Plan to spend tomorrow's sunrise with Jesus.

The Table

BY KIM MARQUETTE

When the hour came, he reclined at the table,
and the apostles with him. LUKE 22:14

THE TABLE . . . SO MUCH energy is exuded when making this decision on what is basically four legs with a slab of glass or wood on top. Square, rectangle, or round—there's not much creativity in geometry there. Of course this four-legged thing needs chairs, and they're usually a separate purchase. Such a racket. Chairs with arms or no arms? Chairs with cloth or wood? In our house with little ones, it's always safest to go with wood, preferably dark wood, without decorative scrolls for the back. Mac and cheese will surely find its way to those crevices.

Then we have to find a place for it in the dining room. And someone actually thought carpet in the dining room was a good idea? The most herculean task of all is when we have to convince the family to leave the screens and sit at said table for a meal. Sometimes I'm tempted to forget it and just turn the dining room into an office.

But after more than three decades of marriage and almost as many years raising a family, I can tell you one thing I have learned: the table is the most precious piece of furniture you will ever own. Something amazing happens at the table. Those four legs with a flat slab on top pulls itself up strong and straight as you set her. With either china or plastic, home-cooked or take-out, the table hosts your conversations.

The table hears it all. The heated arguments and celebrated announcements. The table remains steadfast and silent at the telling of the most heart-wrenching story, and she releases no squeal of delight at the most exciting news shared. The table simply stands, waiting for you to gather around and share life. For the sweetest moments in life happen there.

A Moment to Breathe . . .

Think of the memories at the table as you've gathered
with loved ones around her. See your table as the host
of both precious conversations and simple delight.

Reaching across the Divide

BY KIMBERLY COYLE

"If a kingdom is divided against itself, that kingdom cannot stand." MARK 3:24

I STEPPED THROUGH THE doors of the Pantry and entered a hive of activity, alive and buzzing with purpose. An elderly black woman manned the front desk, a middle-aged white man stocked shelves in the pantry, and a young Hispanic woman walked the halls with a determined step and a stack of official papers. All around me, men and women of all ages and races came together with a singular goal: to feed local families in need.

The Pantry opened after local houses of worship united their food assistance programs—recognizing the need was too great and their resources too small to make an impact if they remained divided. Together, they cast a vision for something greater, a vision that required setting aside individual goals in order to reach their neighbors in need.

"Neighbors helping neighbors." These words guide the mission of the Pantry. As Christians, we know that feeding the hungry is kingdom work. The volunteers and staff are the hands and feet of Jesus. They are the Good Samaritan who bent over the body of a man in need and recognized his own face in the broken and bruised flesh.

As believers, the words "neighbors helping neighbors" should guide our lives too. But it often feels as if the gap is too great. We find ourselves staring across the great divides, of age and race and economic status, and feel unable to cross them. Rather than see a neighbor in everyone we meet, we see a stranger stranded on the other side.

If we are to bring the kingdom of God here on earth, then we must reach across with eager hands to bridge the gap. When we join hands, we become braided together with a common purpose gathered from the strands of neighborly love. We become a cord that cannot be broken.

A Moment to Breathe . . .

Find a local community outreach near you and inquire about the possible ways you could contribute.

Friends Don't Let Friends
Tell Themselves Lies

BY MARY CARVER

For I am the LORD your God, the Holy One of Israel, and your Savior. I have given Egypt as a ransom for you, Cush and Seba in your place. Because you are precious in my sight and honored, and I love you, I will give people in exchange for you and nations instead of your life. ISAIAH 43:3–4

IT'S BEEN A ROUGH season for me in the friendship arena. I've felt rejected, disappointed, deserted, and excluded. I have definitely experienced a few flashbacks to those middle school years. The ones where I desperately wanted to be liked by the cool girls. Not because they were popular, but because I genuinely liked them. Okay . . . maybe just a little bit because they were popular. But they didn't, or they didn't for long. And that's been a little bit how I've felt recently.

I don't know about you, but when I struggle with friendship and community, it's way too easy for me to move from thinking sad thoughts about the situation to thinking sad thoughts about myself. *If I were cooler . . . If I were thinner . . . If I didn't make so many stupid jokes . . . If I had more time or more money . . . If I weren't so me . . .*

When I start thinking that my lack of friends or hurt from friends is a result of my inability to measure up, I open God's Word for a dose of reality and a reminder of who—and Whose—I am.

In Christ, I am enough. In Christ, I am loved.

The mighty God of this universe would do anything for you, for us—and He has. And when we forget that—because, let's be real here, we probably will—let's point each other straight back to the truth. We can't let each other sit in fear and doubt and insecurity, half-truths and pretty lies. We must be a community that points, pushes, drags each other to truth. Let's not dwell in the lies any longer, friends. Let's run, not walk, "do not pass go" back to the Truth. I'll meet you there.

A Moment to Breathe . . .

Remind your heart of the truth in Isaiah 43 today.
Then remind a friend of this same truth.

The One Sure Way They'll See Jesus

BY ABBY MCDONALD

No one has ever seen God. If we love one another, God remains
in us and his love is made complete in us. 1 JOHN 4:12

THERE'S SOMETHING DISCONCERTING ABOUT sitting half-naked in a sterile room while someone prepares to stick a huge needle in your back. I was about to have my third C-section, and the fear hit me all at once. My husband, who was my rock and my calm, was not allowed in the operating room until anesthesia was administered.

Waiting, I sat there trying to be patient when the nurse noticed my anxious look.

"How you holding up, hon?" she asked.

I tried to keep it together. I took a deep breath and exhaled shakily. "Okay," I lied.

She saw the wetness in my eyes. "It won't be much longer. Waiting is the hard part."

I agreed with a nod. She and the doctor left the room, promising to return a few minutes later when the anesthesia team made sure I was numb. All I wanted was to see my daughter. To hear her first cry and smell the sweetness of her. What I didn't know was that while I was being pricked and prodded, the nurse and the doctor were talking to my husband. He was waiting impatiently down the hall. I couldn't see him, but he was giving them advice to help calm my nerves.

When the doctor returned, he grabbed my arm tight where I still had some feeling left. The firmness of his grasp reassured me. He talked to me about my boys, bringing a smile to my face. Even though my husband wasn't in the room during those moments before surgery, his presence was still there. And when we love others in a way they can see and grasp, Christ is there too.

Our communities are looking for God, often in places where they'll never find Him. But we have the opportunity to show them His presence here on earth. We don't have to complicate it or water it down. We can simply love. It's the one true and perfect way.

A Moment to Breathe . . .

Find creative ways to tell the people you love how much
you're thinking of them, even from afar. Whether it's a text
or a note, tell someone today how much you care.

The Difference That Makes All the Difference

BY RENEE SWOPE

Therefore I, the prisoner in the Lord, urge you to live worthy of the calling you have received, with all humility and gentleness, with patience, bearing with one another in love, making every effort to keep the unity of the Spirit through the bond of peace. EPHESIANS 4:1–3

ONE MORNING I WAS working from home, alone. The house was quiet, and I was feeling all kinds of productive. That week marked the final stretch of a big project, and I had planned a fun family dinner and game night. Life was peachy. And I felt like such a good mom.

Then my kids came home from Grandma's house, earlier than planned, and one of them did something that was not-so-peachy! A few minutes later, my other child did *not* do something I asked him to do. All of a sudden I lost my peace and patience right in the middle of my kitchen. Our family dinner and game night didn't go so well.

Later that night as I tried to fall asleep, a regret-filled soundtrack of harsh words replayed in my head. Guilt convinced me I was a terrible, horrible, no-good parent who had permanently damaged my kids' emotional well-being. Shame pointed its finger in my face and told me I was the worst mom on earth.

In the past, I would have shook hands with shame and agreed with guilt, but something was different this time. I had come to know the difference between conviction and condemnation. Condemnation comes with cruel broad-sweeping statements: *You're so hypocritical, Renee. You are never going to change.* But God's conviction is specific and points me toward love and relational repair: *Your words were harsh, Renee. All you need to do is apologize and ask for forgiveness.* Condemnation says we'll never change. But godly conviction shows us how we can.

The next morning, I apologized to my kids and asked them to forgive me for losing my patience with them the day before. And we did a make-up date of our failed family game night. I'm so grateful for grace that convicts me and helps me put back the pieces of my broken attempts to be humble, gentle, patient, and kind.

A Moment to Breathe . . .

Thank the Father for the loving conviction He brings and the sweet gift of His grace.

Meeting God in the Silence

BY DIANE W. BAILEY

He said to them, "Come away by yourselves to a remote place
and rest for a while." For many people were coming and
going, and they did not even have time to eat. MARK 6:31

I WALKED INTO THE house and allowed the plastic bags filled with groceries to fall to the floor with a thud. The dinner hour neared, and I realized I hadn't eaten breakfast or lunch. Mentally and physically I had given all I had that day, and I needed to stop and collect my thoughts.

A cold glass of sweet tea accompanied me to my white wicker rocker beneath a fan on the back porch. My breathing slowed as a cool breeze came off the pond, and I was suddenly aware of silence all around me. It was the most profound silence I had ever heard. And my mind began to rest as my spirit began to revive.

Sometimes it feels like God isn't near. The truth is, His Spirit is within us at all times, but the problem is we don't stop often enough to recognize Him. God has called us to a great adventure—a journey of unpredictable adversity, as well as God-sized victory. The only way to be faithful to His call is to find time each day to sit in the profound silence of heaven intersecting earth and listen to His Holy Spirit speak.

Jesus called His disciples away to a quiet place to rest because ministry without pause can bring both weariness and waywardness. Jesus' example of coming away to rest can be difficult for those of us who pride ourselves on productivity. I'm like a young child who's been told it's nap time. I throw my head back and protest, "But I'm not tired!"

Do you have trouble with taking time to rest? I do. So to help me with my need to achieve, I bring God's Word and a journal to my time of rest. Then it's not long before I sense the Lord's presence speaking to my soul. Rest time isn't a place to achieve; it's a place to receive.

A Moment to Breathe . . .

Pour yourself something cold to drink and sit in the silence. Open His Word and allow the words on the page to speak to your heart today.

Chasing Space

BY EMILY P. FREEMAN

You are my hiding place; you protect me from trouble. You surround me with joyful shouts of deliverance. PSALM 32:7

FIVE ADULTS AND FOUR children gathered around two square tables pulled together with plates, food, and napkins piled high. My husband and his brother returned with drinks, only to find us all settled in our seats. The only two chairs left were right next to each other, nestled between a four-year-old on one side and me with our not-so-small son on my lap on the other. No one could possibly expect these two over-six-feet-tall men to squeeze into this tiny space, much less eat there with all the elbow action and room a man needs to consume food properly.

They needed space. Technically speaking, the space was there. They could have sat next to each other. They could have made it work. But there would have been no room for a dropped napkin under the table or simultaneous bites, not to mention comfortable conversation. There would have been no room to breathe.

When it comes to a meal, I can squeeze around the table just fine. But when it comes to my schedule, I need space in my days and weeks and months to think and mull and ponder. Because when I don't get that, I start to wish for a faraway land to live in. I want to walk barefoot in the grass and read stories. I long for money and chocolate to grow on trees. I consider buying a new toilet instead of cleaning my old one. I dream about having lots of space. And in all of that dreaming, I find myself beginning to worship space and chasing after it—and all the while it seems to become more and more elusive.

In my quest to experience space for my soul, to pin it down and plan for it, I'm hearing a voice remind me that it isn't simply space I want. It's Jesus. I want the calm and strength and understanding only He provides. I want to be known fully, loved wholly, accepted unconditionally. That is really what I want.

A Moment to Breathe . . .

Make your home a place that feels safe for all who live there. This kind of safety begins in the heart. With intentionality, set the tone of your home to be the safest place in the world.

Releasing Expectations and Finding True Friendship

BY JACQUE WATKINS

Dear friends, let us love one another, because love is from God, and everyone who loves has been born of God and knows God. 1 JOHN 4:7

I HADN'T HEARD FROM her in over a month. And I didn't feel a release to send another message until she responded. Sometimes in friendship, we need space. We need to process all that's happening inside and respond when our heart is ready—when we have something meaningful to say. So I waited. And I prayed.

I hoped to hear from her soon. It was hard because I wanted the friendship on my terms. I wanted interaction and connection now. I longed to hear her heart, and deeply desired her to hear mine. Because to me, that's what friendship does. But until someone decides to reply, there's not much one can do. A relationship can only be vibrant, close, and growing, when both people mutually give. And sometimes, that dance takes a long time to learn.

This morning her words finally came. And with them a release, as I read the words she had typed and sent to me. Words of love and care. Of concern and thanks. Of reassurance and hope for the newness of our friendship once again.

Friendship is complex. Fluid. And no one relationship is alike. Each one has its own unique dance—with steps and moves and music and rhythm. And it's not until we lead and follow, and then follow and lead, that the dance becomes graceful, elegant, and smooth.

In friendship our hearts need to breathe and figure out how to respond to each other. And sometimes we need a break to sort things out.

And sometimes the space and in-between moments make our renewed connection all the sweeter when it finally comes around again.

A Moment to Breathe . . .

As you move with the ebb and flow of friendship, bring each name of a friend before the Father, asking Him to bless her now, in this moment.

The Mentors We Need

BY KAITLYN BOUCHILLON

*In the same way, older women are to be reverent
in behavior, not slanderers, not slaves to excessive
drinking. They are to teach what is good.* TITUS 2:3

"WHAT CAN ONE GENERATION do for the next one to come?"
Over coffee a friend and I talked through this question, and long
after the coffee was gone, neither of us wanted to leave. We shared
about the women who had poured into us and one name immediately came to mind.

When I think of those I most want to model, Kelli is one of the
first people to come to mind. She has taught me, by example, what
it looks like for one generation to pour into the next. These are a
few of the things I (and you) can begin to emulate as we grow and
mentor younger women:

1. Invite her out for coffee. Conversations over coffee cultivate
   relationships.
2. Ask her how you can pray for her. Then follow up, days later,
   and ask how she's doing in that area.
3. Refuse to settle for the answer of "I'm fine." Ask again.
4. Share your story and what you're learning in your own life.
5. Write a card for her and include a verse of encouragement.
6. Do you have children? Invite her to tag along next time you
   go to the park. Everyone needs some sunshine, and it's a great
   break from studying or job searching.
7. Keep the lines of communication open. Time and again, Kelli
   has told me I can text or call her any time of the day or night.
   Something as simple as, "I knew you could do it! I'm proud of
   you!" speaks volumes.

Most of all, don't try to have everything together before inviting
someone into your life. Trust that she wants the friendship just as
much as you do.

A Moment to Breathe . . .

*No matter the stage of life you're in, there's probably someone
in your neighborhood or your church who would really love
to get to know you. Pray about who that might be today.*

This One Is for All Us Expert Worriers

BY LISA-JO BAKER

*Because of the LORD's faithful love we do not perish, for
his mercies never end. They are new every morning;
great is your faithfulness!* LAMENTATIONS 3:22–23

MOST MORNINGS WHEN I wake up and stumble to the bathroom
to put in my contact lenses and step on and off the scale and then
move to the kitchen to figure out how to prepare breakfast without
using the leaky sink, I'm not thinking about Christ's mercies. The
ones that are new every morning. I'm thinking about my to-do list.
I'm thinking how my hair has more gray in it than I remember from
last month. I'm googling YouTube videos to figure out how to fix the
leak underneath our kitchen sink.

My mornings don't involve a list of God's mercies, they involve
a list of my own worries. I can rattle off all my very specific fears
and worries without even having to think very hard. There's the
old white minivan with the flat tires that require pumping every
morning. There's the mouse who must have moved in while we
were on vacation because the brand-new bathroom mat I bought
has long shreds chewed off it.

I can sit in the house of my dreams and miss it all because I'm so
busy counting worries. And then that old hymn rolls around in my
head. The one from Sunday school. The one about His great faithfulness. And the new mercies I see. But that "all I have needed" part
is what makes me stop. I come to a complete standstill. Do I really
believe that?

Of course, there are the big things like a home and clothes and
warm food. But I'm waking up more to the little things—the ordinary
glory of walks to the mailbox. Fresh chocolate chip cookies. Bike
rides. New markers. Clothes warm out of the dryer. His faithfulness
is new every morning in a hundred different ways. On the stormy
days as well as the mild ones. It's the one thing that doesn't change.
And I so desperately want to become an expert at believing *that*.

A Moment to Breathe . . .

*Wherever you go, first thing in the morning, tape a list
of the mercies you want to see each day, and then sing a
song of thanksgiving. Yep, sing. Sing of His mercies.*

When Grace Chases

BY NASREEN FYNEWEVER

Send your light and your truth; let them lead me. Let them bring me to your holy mountain, to your dwelling place. PSALM 43:3

I AM STUCK. THE air is thick and the weight is burdensome. I twist left only to see dark and I scurry right to seek help, yet I am alone. It's not a panic attack or a moment of anxiety. It's my identity—I feel like it's been lost.

The search is visceral and daily. Sometimes it's a dream, sometimes a reflection. And sometimes it appears as scribbles on a journal page. I look and I look, and I begin to feel small for my wandering. My mind is confused by the juxtaposition of feeling stuck while actually moving away from my Keeper, my God.

But grace chases. It finds the orphaned in me—the battered, the outsider—and grace shows up every time. It whispers worth. The edge of light can slip around the bent brokenness to tap me gently on the eyelids. They flutter open with expectancy to see danger or isolation, but my eyes take in a beautiful me surrounded by His majesty.

Not all of me is restored, but for that which reflects the Creator, a song plays in the storm. It beckons me to the truth of being known and feeling held, instead of alone and stuck. Although I don't always understand my purpose or potential, I trust that He does.

The search for me is exhausting and at times thwarted by depression or triggers from the past. Yet the search ends when my Comforter draws near while I cry. His care is evident as the Spirit intercedes. He stands in the gap when humans fracture my spirit. He draws me close and into sacred space where all my divots are filled, all my canyons of hurt are held by His holiness.

He lights the way. He cares for me. I rest in being His. There, on His holy mountain, I find identity and true peace.

A Moment to Breathe . . .

The world cannot dictate your worth or claim your identity. Only your Maker can tell you who you are and whose you are. Say it now: I am His and He is mine. He calls me His beloved.

It's All about Perspective

BY RACHEL ANNE RIDGE

You will indeed go out with joy and be peacefully guided; the mountains and the hills will break into singing before you, and all the trees of the field will clap their hands. ISAIAH 55:12

A FEW YEARS AGO, I was absolutely enchanted with the aspen forests in Colorado, displaying their glorious fall foliage on the mountainsides. Each turn of the road revealed new vistas of trees in blazing colors—as if they were on fire! I couldn't wait to get out of the car and experience it from underneath the incredible leaves.

The floor of the forest was so much more open than I expected. From the road—a far-off vantage point—this same forest looked massive and formidable. I couldn't see the individual trees, just a bright wash of color. But up close, I could see how each aspen had its own space, its own uniquely patterned trunk. And high above, their branches touched and interlocked to create a shimmering cathedral ceiling.

While standing there, I was reminded how, in life, a vantage point makes all the difference. As they say, it's easy to miss the forest for the trees. I took a deep breath of the crisp air and thought of the times I've been so focused on the obstacles I faced that I missed the grace God was providing for me to get through them. I'm forever thinking tasks are so big, so intimidating, that I don't see the small, simple things I can do to accomplish them.

Forests. Trees. So often I'm blinded by one for the other. Perhaps you're facing something that seems just too big to handle and you can't make any sense of it. You can see the forest in front of you, but not the trees it will take to make it through. Let's step back for just a moment and ask God to help us see beyond it in order to focus on the work He is doing. Changing our vantage point will give us new perspective and will lighten the burden we're carrying because we'll be able to see a bigger picture.

A Moment to Breathe . . .

Whatever situation you find yourself in today, ask God to show you His different perspective. Trust Him to give you a grand view of what He's creating in and through you.

Stop Waiting to Be Ready

BY ANNA RENDELL

"For you are a holy people belonging to the LORD your God. The LORD your God has chosen you to be his own possession out of all the peoples on the face of the earth." DEUTERONOMY 7:6

I'M A PROJECT-PUTTER-OFFER. I prefer a project to be complete before beginning another one. My train of thought goes like this: "I want to paint my desk, but I can't do it until we clean the deck so it can sit out there. And we can't clean the deck until the kids are in bed because they love playing out there." Can you guess what piece of furniture in my office still isn't painted? It happens with other stuff too. Like starting a book club or scheduling coffee with that new friend. My good intentions never turn into action.

I've heard the "wait till you're ready" argument used for getting married, buying a home, or changing careers. These are huge decisions, and there are steps to take before diving into some things. But there are other things we simply can't be ready for, and that's okay because it leaves us open to the path God has prepared for each of us. If we wait until everything is in place, we might miss it.

In Scripture we see that David chose to fight a giant. While he knew the odds weren't on his side, David trusted that God was with him. David was neither trained nor ready, but he was victorious—because of God. And then there's Rahab, a prostitute who risked her life to help a couple of Israelite spies and was used by God to further His kingdom. And here's the thing about Rahab: she didn't wait to clean up her life to do God's work. She accepted the opportunity before her when she could have said, "No thanks. My life's a mess."

We, too, can choose to follow God's call in our everyday-yet-extraordinary ways—despite our lives being messy. We may not be ready, but He is. So let's take the risk. Give a *yes*. And paint that desk.

A Moment to Breathe . . .

Whatever thing you want to do "someday," do it today. Whether it's a desk that needs painting or a speech that needs writing. Stop waiting to be ready and get started right away.

The Gift of Presence

BY BECKY KEIFE

Now when Job's three friends—Eliphaz the Temanite, Bildad the Shuhite, and Zophar the Naamathite—heard about all this adversity that had happened to him, each of them came from his home. They met together to go and sympathize with him and comfort him. JOB 2:11

MY DAD'S HIGH SCHOOL yearbook told the story of a popular teen with the world at his fingertips—track star, editor of the school paper, class council president. So full of promise and potential. But that's not the story I knew. Nor the one reflected at his memorial the day we gathered to mourn my father.

Had someone asked my dad's friends back then what his funeral would be like someday, I'm sure they would have described an auditorium packed with old classmates and friends eager to pay their respects. The line to greet the family would be long, but everyone would wait because that's what you do to honor an extraordinary man.

When we gathered on that somber morning to pay tribute to my father, I think I could count on one hand the people who were there just for him. His life didn't turn out the way everyone expected. Yes, he had worked his way into a high-paying management position. He got married and had three beautiful daughters. But the majority of his adulthood was marked by pain and broken dreams. He distanced himself from everyone, except for my sisters and me, because we worked hard to continue a relationship with him.

But the sanctuary was not empty that cold February morning. Rows and rows were filled with friends and loved ones—of mine. Of my sisters. They came to give a gift—the gift of their presence. When I stood behind the wooden podium next to the big floral wreath to share about my dad, I looked out and saw not only my husband and sisters, I saw my community. There was nothing left for them to say or do. Just be there. And that is one of the greatest gifts we can give someone on the journey of grief. We can give the gift of our presence.

A Moment to Breathe . . .

If you have a friend going through loss or grief of some kind and you're not sure what to say or what to do, it's okay. Just be there. Give her the gift of your presence.

When He Calls You Beautiful

BY ALIZA LATTA

As it also says in Hosea, I will call Not my People, my
People, and she who is Unloved, Beloved. ROMANS 9:25

YOU DON'T FORGET THE first time a boy calls you beautiful. You don't realize until years later that when he was whispering those words, he was permanently engraving them deep inside of you. You don't perceive the power that handful of syllables has. Before he tells you, he looks at you. His eyes peer into yours, causing your face to flush red down to your toes. You half wonder if he's aware of how he makes you blush. You don't comprehend what's happening. You don't think. You just watch him while he speaks the words, "I think you're beautiful."

You lean into how you're feeling: you're a wildflower, freshly plucked. You're a dainty ballerina. You're a fuzzy Polaroid picture, the edges blurred, still in the midst of focusing. You are feminine and beauty. Of course you are—he just said so himself. "You do? You think I'm beautiful?" the stuttered questions come out before you can stop them, and you turn your face down shyly, away from him. You want him to think you're confident, not insecure. Then he's grasping your chin with his long fingers, turning your face back up to look into his eyes. He repeats what he told you before, "I do. I think you're beautiful."

The power of his words—they changed everything for you. Years later, when you finally understand that what the boy said about you doesn't determine who you are, you think about Someone else's words. So often we forget how Jesus calls us beautiful. We forget that His fingertips formed ours, and His breath seeps from our lungs, and it's His love that whispers . . . "I think you're beautiful. I do. I think you're beautiful."

He's not a boy who makes you blush, or turns you shy, or calls you pretty. He's the Poet who created the universe. The Artist who made you worthy. The Writer who authored the story you're living. And He calls you beautiful.

A Moment to Breathe . . .

Tell at least three people today that they're beautiful. You may need to repeat yourself. Because, too often, these words have a hard time sticking. So say them again. And, for fun, once again.

Daughters of the King

BY RACHEL C. SWANSON

"No one has greater love than this: to lay down his life for his friends." JOHN 15:13

EVERYTHING WAS UNFAMILIAR TO me. The sounds. The smells. Even the people seemed different. I didn't know a single person in this new city with fast moving cars and people rushing to get from one destination to another. There were millions of us, like scattered ants on a hillside, busily doing, hardly noticing, barely looking up to acknowledge another person's existence. Now, staring at all the empty moving boxes that I had unpacked in my tiny apartment, I couldn't help but feel a little empty myself.

I needed a friend, at least one person I could connect with. God has crafted us as women to desire fellowship with other daughters of the King. It's necessary for our survival. We are meant for community. So I prayed: *God, please, I need a friend.*

When I visited a new church that following Sunday, I was surprised. My church back home had about 100 people attend the weekly service, but here, thousands of people have congregated to praise Jesus with upright hands in pews. You'd think that would give me hope for finding just one friend in this crowd, but instead I felt overwhelmed, with a sense of despair enveloping me.

Then across the sanctuary I thought I recognized someone and wondered, "Can it be?" She looked toward me and our eyes connected. A spark of remembrance flashed behind her eyes! A long-lost girlfriend, from four years earlier when we both worked on staff at a Christian summer camp. A friendship I thought was lost long ago was now rekindled, and she continues to be one of my truest, most trusted friends to this day.

In that moment, when I first saw her at church, God reminded me how much God sees us and He answers our prayers. I had regained a friendship, but more importantly, I remembered the everlasting friendship I already have in Christ Jesus.

A Moment to Breathe . . .

Think of a long-ago friendship in your life and ask the Lord if there's something you could do today to reach out across the miles and perhaps rekindle a friendship.

God Isn't Afraid of Our Big Feelings

BY ALIA JOY

*God, hear my cry; pay attention to my prayer. I call to you from the
ends of the earth when my heart is without strength. Lead me to a
rock that is high above me, for you have been a refuge for me, a
strong tower in the face of the enemy. I will dwell in your tent forever
and take refuge under the shelter of your wings.* PSALM 61:1–4

I'VE STRUGGLED WITH MENTAL illness for most of my adult life.
First, the postpartum depression ripped the joy from the births of my
children and left me reeling with feelings of hopelessness, fear, and
isolation, even as I rocked them in my arms. Later, the depression
would come and blot out the good in the world until all I felt was the
cold insides of a dark and unrelenting shadow life. I often felt like I
was grasping onto the ends of the earth as my strength failed, trying
not to let the world topple me while I cried out for God to rescue me.

The Psalms were a balm to my battered and weary soul. Because
the Psalms aren't afraid to admit how empty and scared and tired
we become. The Psalms aren't afraid of our humanity and neither
is Jesus. My faith in Christ helps me get the help I need because I
know I'm not alone in my pain.

Scripture reminds us we are never alone. Not in our frustrations.
Not in our loneliness. Not in our fear, or anxiety, or sadness. We are
never too far from the shelter of the Almighty and sometimes, when
it feels like the world has dimmed and grown dark and weary, we
remember that our refuge and shelter is under the shadow of His
wings. When I cannot see the light, I'm reminded that God is with
me in the shadows and His mercy never comes to an end. Even
when I fail to feel it, He holds me to Him like a mother rocking her
babies through the night.

God hears our cries and is attentive to our prayers. When we are
overwhelmed and it feels like our hearts might falter, remember,
God hears our cries, shelters our hearts, and isn't afraid of our feelings. Take refuge, friend, for you will find rest for your soul.

A Moment to Breathe . . .

*It's okay to be honest about our feelings—even the big,
scary feelings. Whatever you're feeling today, lay it
at His feet. God wants us to bring it all to Him.*

God Is in Control

BY JEN SCHMIDT

Jesus Christ is the same yesterday, today, and forever. HEBREWS 13:8

"HONEY, GO HOME," MY husband murmured. "You haven't slept more than a few hours. Surgery is scheduled for 8:00 a.m. I'll stay with him." Our five-day-old son snoozed soundly in his crib at Children's Hospital. Diagnosed with the congenital birth disease, Hirschsprung's, our pediatric surgeon explained that I couldn't nurse our babe again until they completed his colostomy in the morning.

My emotions whirled from the day's diagnosis, but at least we finally had answers. "Lord, I beg You. Calm my wavering heart. Help me focus my attention on Your many gifts," I exhaled as I processed through my short, choppy prayer. Exhausted and broken, I gathered my belongings and trudged to the parking structure. All the "what-ifs" danced through my mind. Pulling onto the highway, I cranked the local Christian music station knowing that praise music would help squelch the impending darkness. A brand-new song by Twila Paris, "God Is in Control," rang out. The tears flowed.

As I wept, the Spirit of the Lord descended into that car and whispered: *Remember, your son is Mine.* I didn't hear God audibly, but I heard the one true living God speak truth straight to this momma's heart in the middle of a crisis. My Savior loves my tiny babe more than I ever could. He always has and always will. God is the same yesterday, today, and forever. He does not change. How quickly I forget.

God's creative medium that particular day? A song. The outcome? A life change. As I finished my drive home, His peace enveloped me. I can't explain it, but on one of the scariest evenings of my life, I set my alarm and slept soundly. So often it's in the ordinary, everyday, simple moments of life when He chooses to reach out and minister to us. I love that He uses so many creative mediums to do so. We just have to quiet our hearts and listen expectantly in order to hear what He has to say.

A Moment to Breathe . . .

Turn on some praise music. Listen to the words. Dance to the beat. Remember how much He loves you. He loves you the same—yesterday, today, and forever.

From the Old to the New

BY JUDY WU DOMINICK

Then he said to them all, "If anyone wants to follow after me, let him deny himself, take up his cross daily, and follow me." LUKE 9:23

I RECENTLY MOVED TO a new city. In my old city, I had a career that gave me a tremendous sense of importance and influence, as well as a reputation I had built over many years through various means. I had roots—a history of conversations and shared experiences. I felt known. And the familiarity afforded by an established history was—I now realized—a comfortable and constant companion.

In a new city, I felt strangely emptied. I found myself in a place where I had no career, no reputation, and no history. And as I met people, I struggled with waves of insecurity, with a desire to be respected, admired, and accepted. Even though I made this move with a positive attitude, I became increasingly nostalgic of my old life. Mentally and emotionally, I reached for those things that once gave me such a sense of significance.

All those things that were a part of my life previously weren't bad things. Actually, they were very good things. Most of them involved serving and being involved with others, both at work and at church. But my flesh took great pride in them and caused them, over time, to swell my vanity. And it became a stumbling block to me.

God disrupted my complacency in order to move me forward. I never would have chosen this kind of change for myself. But He is good. I've seen it in myself and others time and time again. As long as we feel adequate in ourselves, we won't reach for God to make us complete.

The grace of Christ that had seemed so small when I was craving the approval of man now seemed infinitely sufficient. Don't get me wrong. I'm not completely well yet. I still feel those idols tugging on my heart from time to time, but I'm thankful for pruning. It's the way we're transformed—from the old to the new—as we grow into the likeness of Christ.

A Moment to Breathe . . .

Take an inventory of the things in your life that give you a sense of significance. Ask God to reveal to you any things in your life that could be an idol.

Remain in Me

BY KIMBERLY GILLESPIE

"Remain in me, and I in you. Just as a branch is unable to produce fruit by itself unless it remains on the vine, neither can you unless you remain in me. I am the vine; you are the branches. The one who remains in me and I in him produces much fruit, because you can do nothing without me." JOHN 15:4–5

IN DESPERATE DEFIANCE I declared a month-long fast to finally be loosed from the burden of fear and anxiety that had plagued me for years. One month later, on the first leg of a flight headed from Oakland to Chicago to attend my beloved grandfather's funeral, I had my first panic attack. I cried in the airport bathroom, frustrated that I simply could not make the connecting flight for fear that I would surely die en route.

I was heartbroken that God had not delivered me. At my next doctor's visit, words like "anxiety, grief, and rest" swirled around me. But then I heard in my spirit the gentle whisper: *rest, abide, and remain.* I covered my ears and continued the hustling, the striving, and the doing. I did everything but obey the whisper in my soul. And the panic attacks continued, joined by days-long insomnia, neck spasms, and headaches. Dejected, I limped to the doctor's office, begging this doctor to do something, anything. With no additional questions, she looked into my eyes, then wrote a script. This time words like *anxiety* were joined by *follow-up* and *increases.* My eyes welled.

But then I heard: *Abide. Remain in Me.* And this time I listened.

Sure, our attempts at serving, working, mothering, and living in our own strength and power produce some fruit. But it is subpar and low-hanging. We want more. Need more.

More is found in remaining in Christ, choosing to spend time in constant prayer, reading His Word, and interacting with it. Asking Him before committing to (or rejecting) something. Staying connected to Him—and true to Him, and focused on Him. In Christ alone this is where freedom and fruitfulness reside.

A Moment to Breathe . . .

Consider areas that are bringing you angst. Confess those struggles out loud to the Lord, trusting Him with the burdens. Remain in Him.

What Jesus Prayed for You and Me

BY STACEY THACKER

Sanctify them by the truth; your word is truth. JOHN 17:17

I SIGNED UP FOR a mission project the summer after my soph-omore year in college. My youth director at church sensed my excitement mingled with fear and invited me to the Sunday night service for a time of prayer. I thought that sounded like a great idea considering my wave of emotions.

Toward the end of the service, I was asked to come to the front of the church for prayer and I quietly sat down on the front of the platform. My worship pastor made his way toward me and did something I will never forget. He kneeled in front of me. Filled with father-like compassion, he put his hand on my shoulder and bowed his head and began to pray not just for me, but over me. The tenderness and power of his words broke my heart completely open. I could not stop the flow of tears nor did I want to.

I imagine a similar tender scene in John 17 when Jesus, with head bowed low, prayed on the night of His betrayal. He prayed for many things that night, but He did something that also breaks my heart wide open. He prayed for you. He prayed for me. He asked His Father to set us apart (or sanctify us) with truth. He knew His Word would reform and revive our souls and He wanted us to be immersed in it. He not only prayed for this to be true, He made a provision as well.

We read in His truth-filled Word, "I am the way, the truth, and the life. No one comes to the Father except through me" (John 14:6). His Word was the truth tool always pointing to Him. He is that truth. What He prayed for us that night changed our lives forever. It's meant to. Let's sit at His feet and let it do just that.

And that summer mission? It ended up changing my life in so many ways. God's faithfulness was evident and He delighted in answering this prayer.

A Moment to Breathe . . .

You can always pray while walking or driving or sitting. But today, if you're able, kneel to pray. For your outward posture is a way of demonstrating an inward posture of the heart, kneeling before Him.

No Longer Afraid

BY CHRISTIE PURIFOY

*There is no fear in love; instead, perfect love drives
out fear, because fear involves punishment. So the one
who fears is not complete in love.* 1 JOHN 4:18

I WATCHED MY SON begin to die in a suburban Florida frozen yogurt shop. Two bites in to his dairy-free frozen treat and some trace contamination caused his throat to swell shut. I realized what was happening in the same second that I realized I had forgotten to carry his epi-pen. A stranger in that shop saved my son's life when she pulled an epi-pen junior from her purse. She had curly red hair and two kids by her side. I struggled to uncap the pen because my hands would not stop shaking.

My son recovered so quickly he didn't even need to ride in the ambulance that arrived a few minutes later. But it took me longer to recover. It took a long time for my hands to stop shaking and an even longer time to realize that all the fear I had carried since my son's first allergic reaction was gone. I felt sad and guilty and shaky, but I was no longer afraid. I understood that I could never keep my son perfectly safe. I understood that life and death are so much more than the love a mother has for her child, and that both, life and death, are held in someone else's hands.

I have seen how God carries us through the very thing we imagine we cannot endure.

It is written, "Perfect love drives out fear." I have read those words and imagined this love like something familiar, something sweet like the candy hearts my children have been eating for days. But fear is powerful. Enormous. It takes a very big love to drive it out. I don't know if this love causes terrible things. I don't know if this love allows terrible things. All I know is I cannot look at the terrible thing without also seeing love.

A Moment to Breathe . . .

*Fear is real, but so is love. And love is more powerful. Tell God
your fears. Every one. And ask Him to flood your heart with
His love, so much so, that there's no room left for fear.*

The Courage of No

BY JENNIFER DUKES LEE

For every one of God's promises is "Yes" in him. Therefore, through him we also say "Amen" to the glory of God. 2 CORINTHIANS 1:20

WITH ONE FOOT, I bounced a fussy baby in her bouncy seat. My unbrushed hair threatened to stretch itself into the next city's zip code. Meanwhile, my yoga pants were wondering why they'd never actually been to a yoga class. That's when the phone rang. I recognized the name on the caller ID. She was a well-known woman from our community who ran a sizable nonprofit. And she was calling *me*!

Mrs. Very Important called to see if I might be interested in serving on the nonprofit's board of directors. She was in a pinch because someone had resigned unexpectedly and my name had come up as a possible replacement. She asked if I would let her know my answer within the week. A huge part of me knew that my answer should be "no." I was a busy mom. I was trying to manage several freelance projects. And I already had several obligations in my community.

But two days later, I called her with my "yes."

I served out my board term, but a part of me suffered because I gave time away that God intended me to use elsewhere. The organization may have suffered, too, because I was not as engaged as I should have been. I learned a lot from my mistake. I learned that God never intended us to say yes to every good thing that comes our way. I also learned that it takes a lot of courage to say no to an enticing offer.

I am older—and hopefully wiser—these days. Courage looks different depending on the circumstance. Sometimes it sounds like a "yes" while other times it sounds like a "no." And I want to encourage you toward a courageous "yes" if you are being called to step outside of your comfort zone. But if you need to say "no," I want to cheer you toward that response because there's another kind of courage—the courage of no.

A Moment to Breathe . . .

As hard as it is to say no, it's also hard to hear no. Determine today that the next time someone tells you no, you will be their biggest cheerleader, and you will affirm the courage it takes to say no.

Fixin' My Stinkin' Thinkin'

BY DONNA JONES

Now the mind-set of the flesh is death, but the mind-set of the Spirit is life and peace. ROMANS 8:6

I SENSED SOMETHING WAS wrong. Let me rephrase that. I smelled something was wrong. And the odor in question came from somewhere in my youngest daughter's room. A quick look, though, seemed to indicate everything in her bedroom was fine. So I opened the closet doors. Nothing. I peered under the bed. Nothing there, either. I opened each drawer. Still nothing. Until I saw an odd-shaped thing, sticking up from underneath a sock.

Slowly, I lifted the sock to reveal a half-eaten piece of pizza and Styrofoam cup, half full of a moldy strawberry smoothie. Ewww! And right there next to her dresser was her trash can! What was she thinking?

We laugh about the incident now, but this story reminds me of how often we tidy up the outside while holding on to emotional or relational garbage—stashing it away in places others can't see unless they do a little digging. I call this stinkin' thinkin'. We hold on to thoughts that stink up our hearts, our relationships, and our peace of mind, when all it takes is a little effort to toss them in the trash.

We all struggle with stinkin' thinkin'. It's part of our fallen human condition. But we can, and should, do something about it. What controls my thoughts controls my feelings. And what controls my feelings controls my joy.

The easiest way to know whether a thought should be tossed or kept is how you answer this question: Does this thought bring life and peace or does it bring death? Death of peace. Death of hope. Death of confidence. Death of faith. Death of unity.

When we realize we're holding on to stinkin' thinkin', let's do the one thing that makes sense: let's throw it in the trash.

A Moment to Breathe . . .

Take a little inventory of your thoughts, either from today or earlier this week. Wherever a root of envy or bitterness or unforgiveness or smugness threatened to seep in, take it to the "trash" by asking God for His forgiveness.

Focus and a Yellow Rolling Pin

BY EVI WUSK

Rejoice always, pray constantly, give thanks in everything; for this is God's will for you in Christ Jesus. 1 THESSALONIANS 5:16–18

THE LONG YELLOW ROLLING pin swirled in an almost-circle on the hard wood floor. I wondered if the short flecks of brown dog hair on the tile would stick to my ten-month-old's slobber on the end of it. I'd given my son the rolling pin as something to play with, a new shape to occupy his ever-curious little mind. As soon as I handed it to him, my two-year-old came running in from the other room, suddenly disinterested in the Daniel Tiger cartoon she just *had* to watch minutes before.

"But I want the rolling pin, Mama!" she wailed as tears streamed down her cheeks.

Let's be honest. A yellow rolling pin is a little cool, but not really. It's not even a toy, and yet she was wailing for it like a possessed hyena.

How often do I focus on, and therefore magnify, what I don't have? I see it in my daughter as she hears a toy commercial in the morning and then mentions at suppertime how she "would like to have one of those." What if, instead, I magnify the things I'm-glad-I-have, and not always even things, but the small joys that come my way each day if only I would open my eyes and notice.

What if I move my gaze from the mess on the carpet to the built-in bookshelf that I love? This might feel like work, at first, but then I see the sunroom differently later that day. The thanks come to me, and later the same day my eyes draw up to notice the little spiral light fixture in our high-up hallway ceiling. It is beautiful, quirky and unique. Why hadn't I seen it before? How is it that even the tiniest things can start to shimmer when we stop and say thanks?

Were they shimmering the whole time?

A Moment to Breathe . . .

Look up. Look around. Take notice of the things you see—the things that are there but so often obscured behind the veil we call ordinary. Delight in the small. Smile at the quirky.

Keeping Guard

BY KRISTEN STRONG

*LORD, set up a guard for my mouth; keep watch
at the door of my lips.* PSALM 141:3

IF YOU COULD'VE PULLED back the curtains on my growing up years, there's one thing you would have seen the teenage-Kristen doing all too often—arguing. Especially with those chief authority figures known as parents. You would've seen my dad shaking his head while reiterating one classic response, "Kristen, never become a lawyer because every judge you encounter will hold you in contempt of court for disrespect."

Oh, what "fun" my parents had raising me! Yes, I liked to argue my position ad nauseum because of one chief reason: I wanted to be right.

As an adult, I'd like to think I've abandoned such immature, prideful ways, but I still see within my heart the desire to be right. Where the heart leads, the mouth follows, and before long I'm falling into old habits by explaining away my position when I really should keep quiet. I want to follow Jesus' command to die to self, especially die to the desire to be Ms. Right all the time. But in the moment, with all its flailing emotions, it's hard.

Psalm 141:3 offers a literal picture of a guard placed in front of my mouth. Generally speaking, a guard is used not only to prevent any harm from coming in, but also to prevent anything harmful from coming out. So if I sense the Holy Spirit telling me in a particular situation I need not justify myself, I imagine that guard preventing the escape of my own retaliatory words. And I find rest in Christ's opinion of me—the only one that matters.

When frustration causes regretful words to spill over, let's speak them vertically rather than horizontally. Let's share them with our Father who isn't put off by our honesty, nor is He unfamiliar with our struggles. Then let's rest knowing our defense and reputation are right where they belong: right in the hands of Christ.

A Moment to Breathe . . .

Literally picture a guard over your mouth! Metaphorically, that is the prayer of this psalm, for the Lord to set a guard over our mouths. How much healthier would our relationships be if we could do this today?!

A Solid Foundation

BY GRACE CHO

"Therefore, everyone who hears these words of mine and acts on them will be like a wise man who built his house on the rock." MATTHEW 7:24

EVERYTHING TAKES A BEATING when storms hit. The incessant drops are powerful enough to create landslides and floods, their accumulated weight crushing roads and breaking up foundations. The same seems to happen in life. Financial troubles, relational tensions, mental illness cause rifts that seem irreparable and shake the faith we once thought was solid.

In the midst of those stormy seasons of life, I often wonder if my faith will endure. Will it hold me steady when I can't seem to catch a break or when the light at the end of the tunnel mocks me with its distance? Will it withstand the instability of my circumstances and the lack of control I have over them? Will the things I profess to be true in my faith *prove* to be true when the rubber meets the road?

The longer I journey with God, the more I learn that faith is not only given to us by grace but is also built through obedience. Each act of trust, each act of obedience is a brick laid. It's a slow process of knowing God's character, becoming familiar with His ways, listening to His voice, and then actually doing the things He tells us to do. And like the muscles that grow in our bodies with intention and care, faith becomes strengthened by practice over time.

Whenever I tell the Lord I love Him, I now hear Him say this back to me with tenderness wrapped in love, "If you love me, you will keep my commands" (John 14:15). Friends, if we love Him, we'll obey Him. The little yeses we say now in the mundane rhythms of our lives will eventually help us to stand firm when we face the raging storms.

A Moment to Breathe . . .

Genuine faith leads to love-filled obedience. Is there an area of your life where God is calling you to greater obedience? Take the first step of obedience today.

Why We Don't Have to Feel Ready

BY HOLLEY GERTH

"For the eyes of the Lord roam throughout the earth to show himself strong for those who are wholeheartedly devoted to him. You have been foolish in this matter. Therefore, you will have wars from now on." 2 CHRONICLES 16:9

I'M AN AMATEUR EAVESDROPPER. I often work in coffee shops where conversations swirl around me as thick as the scent of espresso. Most of the time I'm able to tune them out but sometimes one makes my head snap up from my laptop. I've heard scandalous confessions of love, details of doctor's appointments, and workplace complaints of all sorts. This morning I found myself the recipient of some unsolicited wisdom.

A young man and his mentor sat next to me talking about faith. Apparently they've been meeting awhile because the young man asked, "When am I going to be ready to help someone else?"

The mentor paused and then answered, "I think you're asking the wrong question. Because as long as you ask 'Am I ready?' then you'll always be able to find a reason you're not. The better question to ask is, 'Have I received something?' If so, then you have something to share. When is the best time to start passing it on? Yesterday."

I looked over for a second just to be sure he wasn't talking to me. Because I have wondered this as well. Haven't we all? Here is a secret of faith I'm learning: We never feel qualified. We never feel like professionals. We never feel like we've got it together enough to really make a difference. And maybe this is a good thing. Because the only folks who seem to have believed otherwise were the Pharisees.

God isn't looking for perfect examples. He is looking for ordinary people willing to just love one another. He's calling the messy, the broken, and the incomplete. This is good news for all of us. It means our role isn't to show off; it's just to show up. He gives to us, then He gives through us.

A Moment to Breathe . . .

Write down all the reasons you're unqualified to serve or lead. Then crumple up the list and throw it away. God is looking for willing, obedient hearts—not people with perfect pasts.

When Her Life Is Better Than Mine

BY KRISTEN WELCH

Don't you know that the runners in a stadium all race, but only one receives the prize? Run in such a way to win the prize. 1 CORINTHIANS 9:24

I HAVE A FRIEND. She lives in an amazing house. She has well-behaved children and more than enough money for every need and want. Oh, and she's beautiful. And if all that isn't enough, she's a wonderful person who gives to the poor, defends the weak, and serves others. I used to think her life was better than mine. You don't have to be a genius to realize that some people have it better than you. You only have to be human.

It's in our nature to compare our bodies, our hair, our homes, our lives to others. Women compare. We compete. We covet. And we grieve God when we do. The cost of comparison is high. When I compared myself to my friend, it only magnified my own insecurities. It only left me feeling discouraged. It created a desire in me to be something other than I am. There is only one me. I wasn't designed to look or act or be my friend. God created her and called her to something, just as He created me and called me to something.

As believers, we're all in a race. But we think a race signifies a competition, one against another. But we aren't competing against other believers for the prize. We're running toward the prize of Jesus. There isn't a trophy for first, second, and third place. We're all first-place winners by finishing the race.

I'm never going to have a house like my friend. And no matter how much I try, I'll never have her body. But that's okay. It turns out that her life isn't really better than mine. It's just hers. A year ago, she started a blog, but didn't write on it once. After a few months, she emailed me and said, "I wanted to have a blog like yours. But I just can't do it. It's not me." She has her job and I have mine. I wouldn't trade our lives for anything.

A Moment to Breathe . . .

You know her name—the one who seems to have the perfect life. Ask God to fill your heart with love and appreciation for her, and also a renewed passion for the life He wants you to live today.

Abundantly and Lavishly

BY MARLENA GRAVES

*Both were righteous in God's sight, living without blame
according to all the commands and requirements of the Lord.
But they had no children because Elizabeth could not conceive,
and both of them were well along in years.* LUKE 1:6–7

NOT LONG AGO MY anxiety revealed a pent-up sin—envy. In my affliction, I blurted out to God: *I wish I had her life. I've loved You and obeyed You all these years, and this is all I get? Nothing? It seems like You love her more than me!*

I was feeling sorry for myself and anxious because I did not think I had the privileges and opportunities I felt I deserved. I knew better than to pine away for another person's life, but knowing better didn't prevent my pining.

We see that Elizabeth and her husband Zechariah were righteous people, yet Elizabeth was unable to conceive—a sure sign in her culture of God's punishment and a source of tremendous suffering for her. Eventually, God allowed righteous Elizabeth and Zechariah to miraculously conceive John the Baptist—the joy of their lives. God had finally blessed them! Maybe Elizabeth, who was once the object of gossip and scorn, was now the object of envy.

Christianity is not formulaic; obedience to God seldom entails worldly success. Throughout Scripture we see those closest to God, including Elizabeth and Zechariah, suffering greatly. Yet when we don't get what we think we deserve, we accuse God of being stingy with us and become jealous of His generosity to others.

Scrolling through the virtual lives of others on Facebook, we tend to see only people's good experiences. Very few advertise their anguish. With our eyes on other people, we fail to see God's lavish generosity on our behalf even amid this world of trouble. Once I put my eyes back on Jesus, instead of my perceptions of my Christian sister's life, I was able to accept God's Word to me: "Everything I have is yours" (Luke 15:31).

A Moment to Breathe . . .

*You know the one who seems to have it all? Yeah, her. Ask God
to bless her, abundantly and lavishly, and while doing so, ask
God to replace any shred of envy with a heart of joy for others.*

When Jesus Wore Camouflage

BY MEI L. AU

The God of all grace, who called you to his eternal glory in Christ, will himself restore, establish, strengthen, and support you after you have suffered a little while. 1 PETER 5:10

WE STOOD IN LINE waiting to pay for our meal at our favorite Mexican restaurant. My husband, Darren, had just returned home after a six-day business trip. The demands and weariness of the past week still weighing heavy on his shoulders. In front of us, I noticed a couple with three young children.

"I left my wallet in the van," said the mother as she shifted the baby in her arms while herding the other two little ones. The man gave his wife an exasperated glare and headed out the door. As Darren stepped up to pay our bill, he leaned over to me and said, "I think I'm going to pick up theirs."

"Sure, but hurry up before he comes back," I told him. I didn't want to draw attention to us. As Darren was signing the receipt, I saw the father coming towards the front door. Hastily, we made our getaway.

"Walk fast!" I said to my accomplice as we headed across the parking lot. Suddenly, we hear the man's voice. "Sir, sir." We pretended not to hear. "Sir, sir!" The voice got louder as he got closer. Darren turned around. He had caught up to us.

"Did you pay for our meal?" said the big burly man. Dressed head to toe in hunter camouflage, the husky man with a thick beard seemed to tower over my tall husband. As the two strangers spoke, Darren extended his hand. The man, however, was not content with a handshake. So there, under the glow of a business sign, I watched as two brawny guys embraced. Time stood still as I was struck by the tenderness of the moment. With genuine authenticity, the men acknowledged their mutual brokenness and each became wrapped in the arms of Grace.

In our stress, in our struggles, in our suffering, Jesus meets us . . . sometimes wearing camouflage.

A Moment to Breathe . . .

The next time you're at the grocery store or the coffee shop, maybe right now, or later today, take a look around. Spy someone in line and quietly pay their tab.

Trusting God in the Terrible Seasons

BY TERI LYNNE UNDERWOOD

*Give us aid against the foe, for human help is worthless. With God
we will perform valiantly; he will trample our foes.* PSALM 60:11–12

"WHY IS THIS HAPPENING?" my friend choked through her tears.
Over the previous two years, it seemed every dream and plan she
had for her family had slipped away or fallen apart. After months of
putting on a brave face, her faith wavered.

I didn't know what to say; how to speak hope into her heartache. As we sat together in the silence, I too wondered why. Before
leaving, I prayed for my friend to know the nearness of God and to
know His peace in the middle of her circumstances.

David's words in the first verse of Psalm 60, "God, you have
rejected us; you have broken us down," resonated with me in light
of my friend's circumstances and our conversation. Maybe they
resonate with you too?

At some point, we all experience seasons when it's difficult to
remember that it's God who will tread down the foes (v. 12). But,
friend, He will! He is our Deliverer. And His timing is perfect. When
I get lost in the situations around me, I need to be reminded of His
sovereignty.

It's easy for us to look for someone to save us—to fix the problems
we see around us. But the salvation of man is vain (v. 11). May we
remember there is Someone who has come and will one day come
again. He came to bring our salvation and when He returns, He
will bring restoration and judgment and healing and wholeness.
All will be made right. He will deliver us fully from the heartache
and sorrow of this broken, sinful world.

When I met my friend for coffee a few days later, I shared these
verses with her, as a reminder we cannot put our hope in anyone
or anything other than Jesus. Whatever your situation, Christ is the
hope and assurance of God's presence and power.

A Moment to Breathe . . .

*Write out Psalm 60 and tuck it into your purse. Save it as a psalm
for a rainy day to remind your soul that God will come to your aid.*

Kicking Guilt to the Curb

BY SARAH MAE

*Therefore, there is now no condemnation for
those in Christ Jesus.* ROMANS 8:1

I USED TO FEEL guilty all the time. Mainly, mother guilt. But I've had wife guilt, house-cleaning guilt, homeschooling guilt, eating guilt, and a slew of other guilt, if you will. In fact, I would say that for most of my adult years I've lived in a perpetual state of guilt. The I'm-not-doing-enough-and-I'll-never-get-it-together kind of guilt.

It's a plague, really. A plague I've not only allowed, but invited. I've let the guilt in to do its dirty work, to make me feel worthless, to keep me down, to keep me looking down instead of up. And there it is, the trick of that slimy, slithering devil, always tempting us, teasing us, encouraging us to look down. Down to our weaknesses. Down to our struggles. He wants us bound up, not free and wide-open, head back, gazing up.

Oh sure, there is a built-in conviction that is good and of God and that shows us the way when we forget His goodness and we try *our own way*. But I'm talking about the guilt of always feeling like a mess. Like someone who lives in fear that she will damage her children and will never get intimacy right or who still has clothes piled up in the corners of her bedroom.

And it all may be so, but that is humanity. It's our personality and quirks and bents and strengths and weaknesses wrapped up in a flesh that will struggle until that glorious day when the struggle will be gone. We're never going to get "it" right on this earth, but we have a God who is willing to live inside us, to guide us and comfort us, and He's perfect. When we keep our eyes on Him, we can let go of the guilt and start really living. We're not meant to wear those guilt shackles. We're meant to live free. Jesus gives freedom, the real kind. Be free.

A Moment to Breathe . . .

*Conviction leads to repentance and forgiveness and freedom.
But condemnation leads to guilt and shame and more guilt. That
thing you feel guilty about? Is it conviction or condemnation?*

Looking for God in a Billboard Sign

BY KRISTIN A. SMITH

Then he said to him, "If I have found favor with you, give me a sign that you are speaking with me." JUDGES 6:17

I SAW A MOVIE once about a guy who was trying to find love and somehow had a "talking billboard" that helped guide him along the way. I haven't ever forgotten that movie because I can relate with the desire to have a message spelled out for me, in big letters—an unmistakable message from God. How easy would that make life? Driving down the road in prayer, asking God for direction, and then you pass one of those electronic billboards and—*voilà!*—your answer appears. How could I argue God's direction if it were plastered on a billboard just for me?

While that scenario might seem perfect, what happens to our faith and trust? Those times I have faced the unknown—when I trusted God's love and provision although I couldn't see it or feel it right at that moment—those are the times I have been closest to God. It's in those desperate moments, those intimate moments, those on-my-knees-grateful and shaking-my-head-in-disbelief moments that bring me to the feet of my Savior.

When I look back at all the times I cried out to God and didn't get my answer plastered across a billboard, that's when I found myself clinging to a hope. Hope that He would make sense of it for me some day. Time and time again God has taken the darkest moments of my life and transformed them. If He had flashed an answer saying that everything will be okay, would I have missed the beauty in the journey?

While an electronic billboard sign might be the easy way out, ultimately the journey to the discovery of all that God has planned for us would be so much less sweet. When we look for who God is in His Word, we find all the answers we need.

A Moment to Breathe . . .

Do you ever wish for a billboard sign to point you in the right direction? Open His Word and seek Him there. Because He promises you'll find Him when you seek Him with all of your heart.

The Best Way to Know What to Say

BY LISA WHITTLE

"But store up for yourselves treasures in heaven, where neither moth nor rust destroys, and where thieves don't break in and steal. For where your treasure is, there your heart will be also." MATTHEW 6:20–21

IT'S A HOT TEXAS day, I am twenty-two, and I've just returned to my small apartment from a long day at seminary. I've barely changed clothes when someone bangs on my door and yells, "Fire!" I don't think. I just grab the two things I value most and run out the door. Carrying them down the stairs, I see the girl next door dragging her big flowered couch down the same concrete steps. Even with skinny arms, she is determined. Two guys run up the stairs to help.

"Grilling accident," I overhear someone say, and I glance over just in time to see a guy with scared eyes holding a spatula. The flames from his apartment are spreading, inching closer to my cute little home on the third floor, and I am grateful my wedding dress and my Bible have made it out of there intact. Thankfully, the firemen put out the fire right before it reaches my apartment, and the scary event comes to a close.

Looking back, that moment of crisis revealed to me what I most valued and also shaped the message I'm now committed to live and share. Because the truth is, our message—that one that burns deep inside—is best discovered by determining what life lesson we most value. It's the lesson that has taught us the most and is still teaching us, the lesson we know will help others because we've seen them struggle with it, too. It's the one question we must ask ourselves: *What would I grab in a fire?*

In the same way, we can also ask ourselves: *If I could only say one thing to people for the rest of my life, what would it be?* It's simple, really. If the stopwatch said you only had time for one sentence. If you had enough breath to preach one final thing. *What would you preach?* One sentence. Your core message. Your most treasured thing. It's the best way to know what to say on any given day.

A Moment to Breathe . . .

As you grow and change, your core message may grow and change too. But right now, answer this one question: If I could only say one thing to people for the rest of my life, what would it be?

Because of Jesus in You

BY STEPHANIE BRYANT

*Jesus knew that the Father had given everything into his hands,
that he had come from God, and that he was going back to
God. So he got up from supper, laid aside his outer clothing,
took a towel, and tied it around himself. Next, he poured
water into a basin and began to wash his disciples' feet and
to dry them with the towel tied around him.* JOHN 13:3–5

SOMETIMES, I FEEL LIKE I take care of enough already, so the needs flashing on my newsfeed can make me feel like I'm not enough to help those in need. Are you too tired or overwhelmed to know how to serve those in need? Do you wonder what ability you really have to make a difference?

Because Jesus knew who He was—secure in God the Father's love—He could love the utmost and serve the lowest. Because Jesus knew this world was not really His home, He could humble Himself to obey washing stinky man feet without thinking it wasn't grand enough to make a difference. Because Jesus knew whose He was, Jesus could listen to the whisper of God's voice and know His response was to obey, serving those who loved and hated Him . . . even if there were many more seemingly important needs at hand.

God has to do a miracle inside us to produce His character in us. The Holy Spirit produces the same character and confidence of Jesus in us. We can rely on Jesus to empower us to do the good works He has prepared in advance for us to do through the power of His Holy Spirit. Not everyone's good works, just ours.

I can't count on myself, but I can rely on Jesus to empower me to take the hard steps the Holy Spirit is calling me to. Then, I will grow closer to Jesus and become more like Him—having life to the full.

Because we can be secure in the Father's love, we are enabled to be led by the Spirit, hear clearly His moment-to-moment instructions and glorify God by our service.

A Moment to Breathe . . .

*Washing people's feet isn't part of our daily culture anymore,
but there are still so many ways to serve others. Look for ways
to serve someone—especially someone who least expects it.*

Sometimes Friendship Is a Piece of Cake

BY ANN SWINDELL

"Now, may the LORD show kindness and faithfulness
to you, and I will also show the same goodness to you
because you have done this deed." 2 SAMUEL 2:6

I'VE SPENT MOST OF my life being the pursuer in female friendships. In junior high and high school, I was the one who invited girlfriends over to my house. In college, I was the one who invited other women to coffee dates. Even now, I'm the one in our circle of friends who plans the get-togethers.

The other day, when I mentioned scheduling another dinner, one of my friends laughingly responded, "I was just thinking to myself—Ann needs to organize another girl's night!" And I don't mind it really. I like bringing women together, creating a space in which we can rest, reflect, and laugh together. But sometimes I forget how special it feels to be pursued by other women in friendship. Last week, I was reminded.

While planning a weekend retreat for the college students at our church, a friend had asked me if she could bring something by my house. When she knocked on the door, she was standing there holding a piece of cake. But not just any cake . . . my favorite flavor from my favorite bakery in town. She smiled and said she knew we had a big weekend coming up and just wanted to "drop a little something off." She told me she was praying for us.

I enveloped her in a hug and laughed. She had me pegged; chocolate is one of my love languages and a swift way into my heart. More than that, though, I felt loved and known by her.

She is a new mom with a job; she is busy and tired, as we all are. But she had taken time out of her day to drive across town, pick up a piece of cake, and bring it to my home. It was a small gesture, but it meant a lot. It meant that she valued our friendship, and she was, in a real and tangible way, pursuing me.

A Moment to Breathe . . .

Pursue a friend this week with something fun—just for her.
A cookie. A cupcake. A cup of coffee with all the fixings.
Share a smile with a friend and let her know you care.

When God Writes Your Story

BY BRITTA ELLIS LAFONT

Your eyes saw me when I was formless; all my days were written in your book and planned before a single one of them began. PSALM 139:16

MY FRIEND JODI IS a scrapbooker—a diligent keeper of stories. She treasures special moments by taking pictures and keeping the photos organized. She saves up these memories in neat little boxes. She buys special tape and fancy scissors, and she collects just the right stickers and papers.

When she finds a few hours to craft, she lovingly arranges the pictures so they retell those memories . . . she curates her family's story.

I'm not a great scrapbooker. Crafting isn't really my thing. But my friend has inspired me to think about some ways I might become a curator of my story.

The Lord is the best keeper of stories. He is the Author of all of life, knows us so well, and plans our special moments before we are born. He sees all the messes we are going to make, even before we make them, and He loves us anyway. In fact, God sent His Son to make sure that all of our stories, even the hard ones, are used for His glory.

Do you ever think about how God wrote your story? Next time you take a few pictures and share them on social media—pictures of your family vacation, or dinner with friends, or your new haircut—remember that every bit of your story was written before you were born. God has left nothing to chance. The apostle Paul says we can have peace with God because of what Jesus Christ our Lord has done for us (Rom. 5:1).

God is always at work to fulfill His plans for us. He makes it so we can grow in wisdom and love and peace. He invites us to walk with Him closely, each and every day. And He will stop at nothing to meet you, right where you are today.

A Moment to Breathe . . .

Whether you're crafty or not, consider some ways you might curate your own story. How might you keep a record of the story God is writing in your life?

Getting Nudged Out of Our Comfort Zones

BY MARY CARVER

This is love: that we walk according to his commands.
This is the command as you have heard it from the
beginning: that you walk in love. 2 JOHN 6

I HAVE THIS CAT, Peanut. And she's really sweet and affectionate. But the thing that drives me nuts about Peanut is that she's stubborn. Or lazy. Or both. I'm not really sure where the issue stems from, and I don't have time for kitty therapy. All I know is that when I try to make her move—off my spot on the couch, off the dining room chairs at dinner time, off my leg when I'm trying to sleep at night—she refuses.

I know! She's a cat! How can she refuse to do what I tell her?

I might be crazy, but I do really like cats, especially my own. So when I want Peanut to move, I'm gentle. I nudge her with my foot or pat her nicely on the back. And, well, I suppose it's a lot how I behave when God asks me to move. Get up early to read my Bible? Reach out to that person who makes me feel uncomfortable? Apply for that job? Quit that job? Start that project? Move to that city? Stay here? Try this new thing? Go to a new place? Talk to a new person? But, but, but . . .

It doesn't really matter what God asks of me. From small changes to big risks, my first instinct is to dig my claws into the couch and stay put, so to speak. Change is hard, and my comfort zone is soft and safe. So when He asks me to follow, my immediate response isn't always one of obedience. But no matter what feels safest to me in any given situation, my calling—to love Him, to follow Him, to trust Him, to obey Him—is more important than my comfort. It's not easy, and sometimes I still act like my grumpy, stubborn cat. But I want to move *with* God, instead of making Him resort to pushing me off my proverbial couch.

A Moment to Breathe . . .

Have you ever struggled to respond to God's nudging? What thing is God asking you to do today? Think of one thing you can do today that would be a step of obedience toward Him.

When There Are Eggshells in Your Washing Machine

BY KAYLA AIMEE

For you were called to be free, brothers and sisters; only
don't use this freedom as an opportunity for the flesh,
but serve one another through love. GALATIANS 5:13

MY MOTHER WOULD DUTIFULLY empty the pockets of every pair of pants in the basket before she ran them through the laundry. She kept the forgotten money she found in a green glass jar and called it a laundry tax. Now that I am responsible for serving my family through the art of sorting and folding, I am of the mind that a laundry tax should be mandatory, if only I could remember to check pockets.

I am not as meticulous as my mother in my housekeeping. Some might say I'm a little lax.

My lack of attention to detail when it comes to my housekeeping skills is why I just spent twenty minutes vacuuming approximately one billion broken bits of eggshell out of my washing machine. (I also wish I knew why my kindergartner had entire eggshells stuffed in her pockets.) It was not my idea of a fun afternoon, not to mention that you can't buy a latte with eggshells. A vinegar rinse through my front-loader was not ever how I envisioned a life of service. I kind of imagined my gospel-sharing self as a bit of a jet-setter—and also imagined myself with really great hair and a delightful accent. (I've had very grounded daydreams.)

I have learned that we can't put "serving one another through love" in a nice little box and assume it looks the same for everyone. Today I'm sorting laundry and spreading peanut butter on bread for our lunch and my daughter is beside me on a step stool to reach the counter, doing the same. She slips sandwich after sandwich into a brown paper sack and then we stop and start on the afternoon drive, delivering them for the local food pantry. Today love looked a lot like eggshells, broken up bits of ourselves wrung out in the rinse cycle and strewn throughout the world.

A Moment to Breathe . . .

Look for the small, the mundane, as an invitation
to serve quietly, knowing He sees it all.

Drawing Near

BY MEL SCHROEDER

But as for me, God's presence is my good. I have made the Lord
GOD my refuge, so I can tell about all you do. PSALM 73:28

I REMEMBER THE NIGHT my phone dinged. A text from her happened almost every day, but my heart sank and tears filled my eyes as I read this one. A dear friend was facing something scary, and I felt helpless. Between swallowing the lumps in my throat, I tried to pray, but it had been a long time. Too long. Without meaning to, I'd let the busyness of life take over. Most days I struggled through the crazy and sometimes-survival mode of parenting, and I hadn't carved out those desperately needed moments with God like I should have.

There was a physical ache in my chest that night as I poured out my heart to God. Over and over, I begged Him to make everything okay. I told Him how sorry I was that He'd come last. I tried to thank Him for the blessings. And then I begged some more.

That text began several weeks of waiting and praying . . . and it also began a journey that would change my heart. I started talking to Him more; sharing with Him all throughout the day. While I was driving, while I was cleaning, even while I was feeding my baby boy at midnight. I'd look for detours, just for the chance to pray.

And in that difficult season of leaning into my Father, I also began to crave more time with Him.

My friend ended up getting good news, and believe me, I celebrated with her and thanked Him over and over. I still do. But whenever I think about that hard time, I'm humbled . . . because it was in that painful, uncertain season that my Father became my refuge and showed me just how good it is to be near Him.

A Moment to Breathe . . .

Rather than waiting until something hard happens before reaching
out to God, talk to Him right now. Tell Him about your day. Invite
Him into your daily thoughts and choices. I promise He's interested.

Just Me and Him

BY MELISSA AARON

After dismissing the crowds, he went up on the mountain by himself to pray. Well into the night, he was there alone. MATTHEW 14:23

MY HUSBAND IS AN active duty sailor in the US Navy. I am regularly flying solo, raising our kids while he's on a ship on the other side of the world. When he's away, I tend to overcompensate for his absence, trying to ensure the kids aren't feeling the stress of his absence in a detrimental way. The kids' success at school and them feeling the love and care of our whole family are two key goals of mine.

I'm exhausted more often that I'd like to admit. I find myself lonely in an over-stimulated world. And sometimes I'm fearful and uncertain of what lies ahead. But what I've found to be absolutely crucial, especially during my husband's absences, is carving out precious time with my Father.

I'm so grateful for Jesus' example of separating Himself from the crowds and getting alone to be with the Father. His ministry must have been draining—carrying the good news, healing the sick, combating opposition on every side. Four instances of Him stealing away for a few quiet moments immediately come to mind, although there were likely more:

- Before His temptation while fasting in the desert
- After the death of His cousin, John the Baptist
- After He'd been speaking to the masses during the height of His ministry
- In the Garden of Gethsemane before He faced His Passion

My day-to-day can in no way compare to Jesus' burdens. But I too find myself burdened and seeking out time to be alone with the Father. I don't feel guilty about this time away, though, because . . . it was modeled by Jesus. It's my time to sit at His feet and feel His love and care for me. To be enveloped in peace and quiet where my empty cup can be refilled so I can go back to the work He has given me to do.

A Moment to Breathe . . .

Take a few moments to sit at His feet right now. Quiet the noise. Open His Word. Be in His presence.

Tangled and Tied

BY SUZANNE ELLER

Woe to those who drag iniquity with cords of deceit
and pull sin along with cart ropes. ISAIAH 5:18

SOMETIMES WE GET ALL tangled and tied up and we wonder how we got there. One time my kids and I were having a blast on a yellow Slip 'N Slide in the backyard when some visitors showed up, and suddenly there I was, tangled and tied up. My house was a mess and my stretch marks were glaring for the entire world to see.

But if I could go back, I'd gently tell my young-mom-self that one day her kids would be grown. They'll pull their own babies onto their lap and tell fun stories—like the adventure with the yellow Slip 'N Slide—and that they don't mention one thing about the visitors because those visitors didn't register in their memories. All they remember is the joy of sliding down a sudsy Slip 'N Slide. They remember a mama throwing her head back and laughing.

Goodness girls, we've got to give ourselves some slack. You know that old lady in the store that gives you advice when you don't ask for it? I don't want to be her, but I am reaching for every woman out there and I'm telling you something I wish I'd known a long time ago.

Don't spend one more minute tying yourself in knots over things that don't matter in the long run. The sweet memories you make messing up the kitchen as you make cookies with your kids are greater than the dishes in the sink afterwards. In the long run, you realize that perfection was never a worthwhile goal.

Let's provide room for mistakes and growing through them. Let's choose which things matter and not worry about what others may think. Let's give each other a little grace and while we're at it, let's pour some over our own heart too.

A Moment to Breathe . . .

Nothing tangles you up more than trying to keep up a certain
image for others. But that always leads to a weary soul. Be
yourself instead and allow the grace of God to cover you.

Our Response Matters

BY CAROLINE TESELLE

Enter his gates with thanksgiving and his courts with praise.
Give thanks to him and bless his name. PSALM 100:4

EARLIER THIS WEEK I was driving home after dinner with a dear friend when someone in another car decided to sideswipe mine on the interstate—just because he was about to miss his exit! Instead of slowing down to go behind me, he sped up to pass me to go in front of me but failed and hit my car. While going 65 mph! He didn't slow down or pull over. He just hurried away, barely making his exit. This could have been a horrible accident, but thankfully Benny (my truck) only suffered a few scratches.

Many of the things that happen to us are beyond our control. I was just driving along and *wham!* What matters is how we respond.

My initial response of yelling and honking my horn (even though he couldn't hear me) was understandable. I didn't want to crash! And if I'm completely honest, I wanted to chase him down (scenes from cop movies flashed through my mind!) but I was way past the exit. Besides, who am I kidding? I probably would have caused an accident myself trying to chase him down.

I didn't pull over to see if Benny was okay because she was driving fine and she wasn't making any crazy noises. So I just drove home.

I pulled into my driveway and the anger I felt the previous ten minutes was quickly washed away with gratitude. I was so happy to be home and not stuck in what could have been a crashed-up Benny on the interstate. Overwhelmed with gratefulness and relief, I walked in my house, hugged my husband, and kissed my kids goodnight. Home is where everything comes back into focus.

A Moment to Breathe . . .

The next time you walk through your front door, remember
to say a quick prayer of thanksgiving. You're home.

The Secret of the Secret Place

BY FRANCIE WINSLOW

Tie them to your fingers; write them on the
tablet of your heart. PROVERBS 7:3

HAVE YOU EVER WONDERED how to multiply your peace? Peter seemed confident of how and where to find more peace when He wrote this: "May grace and peace be multiplied to you through the knowledge of God and of Jesus our Lord" (2 Pet. 1:2). Our peace is multiplied in the knowledge of Him.

Not a "heady" or academic or textbook knowing, but a spirit knowing. A closeness. A confidence. He is the One who made us, knows us, and loves us. It only makes sense that in knowing Him, we find the peace we were created for. It's the (not so) secret of the secret place.

In high school, I taped Scripture to every surface of my life: my mirror, my desk, my door, my car dashboard, and my journals. I recently found stacks of index cards that were wrapped neatly in rubber bands and put in a box from years of Him exciting my heart with truth and love.

As these verses jumped off the pages of the Bible, I just had to write them down to allow them to be written not just on the pages and cards, but on the tablet of my heart.

God wooed me to Himself through His Word. He showed me His love, His nature, and His heart as I spent time with Him and He revealed Himself through Scripture. He showed me that His Word is worthy of my trust. Not because I understood everything in the Bible. But because He met me and spoke to me as I sought Him. He made Himself real to me in the most tangible way I can imagine. He transformed my mind with truth as He washed me with His Word.

This is the secret of the secret place, of finding peace—that we know Him, and as a result, grace and peace are multiplied in our lives, extending to those around us.

A Moment to Breathe . . .

Pick up a journal or a notebook and write out 2 Peter 1:2. Yep, simply
write it out and ask God to grow His peace in your heart today.

When You Don't Feel the Love

BY ROBIN DANCE

Love is patient, love is kind. Love does not envy, is not boastful,
is not arrogant, is not rude, is not self-seeking, is not irritable,
and does not keep a record of wrongs. 1 CORINTHIANS 13:4–5

THERE'S LITTLE DOUBT THAT familiarity breeds contempt, but recently I wondered if familiarity can breed contempt even when it comes to Scripture. It's not a matter of disdain or unbelief, but more a case of having read or heard certain "go-to" passages so many times it's easy to gloss over them or think there's nothing new to learn because you already know it all.

That's how I was thinking about 1 Corinthians 13—the greatest treatise on love ever penned. But there are important things we need to know about love. Try to read 1 Corinthians 13:4–5 as if you're seeing those verses for the first time.

Throughout the entire chapter, love is seen through the lens of demonstrable action, not emotion.

Love is something we do, not just feel. This is a game changer. Paul provides a beautiful way for the church to love others when we've been wronged. Love—when companioned by emotional attachment, affectionate connection, and deep feeling—is a precious thing. It's what first draws us to our mate. It's what binds us to our children. It's the thread that knits together the most special of friendships.

But at all times we're called to love others. And not just others, we're called to love our enemies! How loving do you feel when your teenage children defy and disobey you? When a friend betrays your confidence? When a coworker undermines your decisions? When your spouse leaves your marriage and your family in shambles? How can you love then?

Now reread 1 Corinthians 13:4–5 and practice the ways you can show love to the hurtful people in your life. Thanks be to our Lord who loves us enough, not just to command us to love others, but to make a way for us to love people, and in doing so, live out the gospel.

A Moment to Breathe . . .

Read all of 1 Corinthians 13 and ask God to show you how you
can demonstrate His love toward a difficult person today.

Because You Just Never Know

BY DENISE J. HUGHES

*"For you will be judged by the same standard with
which you judge others, and you will be measured
by the same measure you use."* MATTHEW 7:2

EVERY SUNDAY MORNING I made an extra effort to walk up
and down the aisles at church. Since I was new on staff, I wanted
to shake hands with the adults, smile, and say hi. All the church
members received me with cheerful greetings and friendly hugs.
All except one. This one lady never reciprocated any warmth
toward me. Each week I'd say hello. But she'd only mumble a
weak "hi" in return. And sometimes she'd just give me this blank
expression . . . and walk away. I kept thinking: *What's wrong with
her? She's not friendly at all. In fact, she can be quite rude! What a
terrible example of Christ! Hmph!*

One Sunday I sat next to a new friend and whispered, "Gee,
she's not very friendly, huh?" I nodded in the direction of the
grumpy lady.

"Oh, that poor woman," my friend replied, "she lost a young
daughter a few months back, just before you arrived. It was so
tragic."

I felt convicted. My conclusion about this person was based solely
on what I could see with my eyes and hear with my ears. She was
grieving—struggling to breathe. It must have taken every ounce of
energy just to get out of bed, get dressed, and show up at church.
I asked God to forgive me and to bring her face to mind whenever
I meet someone I'm tempted to judge after a first impression. You
just never know what heartache another person might be going
through.

After this misguided judgment call, I decided I'd rather be easy
on people. I'd rather give grace. Because you just never know . . .
maybe the woman in desperate need of an added measure of grace
. . . is me.

A Moment to Breathe . . .

*Think of that hard-to-love person in your life and ask God to
help you grow in grace for that person today. Because you just
never know what another person might be going through.*

Storing Up Grace

BY ANNA RENDELL

*Mary was treasuring up all these things in her
heart and meditating on them.* LUKE 2:19

I WAS IN SEVENTH grade homeroom when she approached me with a smirk. "What brand are your jeans?" she asked. "Where did you get them?" Those jeans were my best-kept secret, my "please-make-me-cool" prayer. My mom and I were thrilled when we found the knockoff denim, identical to the expensive brand we couldn't afford.

But with one glance, she knew, and she carved me with her simple question, asked with smug intention. I stammered out an answer, cheeks burning and eyes downcast, and she grinned and went on her way. That morning has never left my heart.

Now the mid-thirties me wonders what the other girl was storing up in her heart. I wonder what fed her, what gave her joy, what made her celebrate and smile. And I wonder why it's so much easier to store up words and experiences that hurt rather than treasure the ones that reward eternally.

I recall with clarity and swiftness the cruel, sarcastic, and plain hurtful comments that I've been on the receiving end of, but I have to dig deep to dredge up the kindnesses—the compliments, the gifts of good and real friendship, the examples of grace.

As a college-age camp counselor, we began each day with declarations. We'd gather around the flagpole, plant our feet, and loudly declare, "I am a child of God! I am more than a conqueror! I am beautifully and wonderfully made!" It was the best way to start a day—with truth stored up, spoken aloud.

Today, let's choose to fill our hearts with truth and grace, to forget the old and ugly, and to treasure and ponder that which He says we are: Blessed. Loved. His.

A Moment to Breathe . . .

*Store up grace—for yourself and others—by treasuring
the truth and beauty that's found in God's Word.*

How to Recognize the Glorious Ordinary in Your Life

BY LISA-JO BAKER

Don't neglect to show hospitality, for by doing this some have welcomed angels as guests without knowing it. HEBREWS 13:2

IT'S RIDICULOUS HOW MUCH of our lives we consider ordinary. But Wednesdays are holy nights in our family because we offer an open call for our kids to come into our bed, mostly to try and keep them out of it the other nights. So my husband crams himself into the bottom bunk next to our middle boy, and our oldest crawls into the big bed next to me. Of course, they never go straight to sleep. Because it's there under the blankets they'll ask you if their breath really does stink or if you've ever flown through the Bermuda Triangle.

Their questions will surprise you, and if you're not careful you'll find your mind wandering to the emails you haven't returned. But if you pay attention, you'll find that you're living the *extra* part of your ordinary. Right there at 9:15 p.m. on a Wednesday night. You watch as his hair falls just so across his eyebrows—it probably needs to be cut again. And you can't even believe these tall, gangly limbs were once folded in prayer inside your belly. And here it is—the real-life living answer to those prayers. He's lying across from you in the rumpled bed and you dared to think your life ordinary?

No, these are the moments for kneeling in mystery and delight as you absorb every nuance on the face that can split your gut in ridiculous jokes one minute and crunch your heart the next with disrespect and frustration. This is living. It's the people that make us extraordinary.

I have a tray in my house with the words from Hebrews 13:2. Too often I've kept one eye on the door, waiting to be amazed by the strangers in my midst. When, really, it's those I know best—the ones I most take for granted. Don't believe ordinary for a minute. Life is so full of glory it will weigh you down if you just stop to let it sink down deep into your here and now.

A Moment to Breathe . . .

Take the most seemingly ordinary part of your day, washing the dishes or brushing hair, and see it as a gift of extraordinary glory, a sweet glimpse of life so full, to be cherished today.

Set Apart

BY SHEILA DAILIE

"Tell the Israelites: This will be my holy anointing oil throughout your generations. It must not be used for ordinary anointing on a person's body, and you must not make anything like it using its formula. It is holy, and it must be holy to you." EXODUS 30:31–32

ANISE. GRAHAM FLOUR. DARK syrup. Raisins. Browned hamburger. These ingredients probably sound as strange as the items God listed for the holy incense. But for our family, these ingredients come together to make our traditional pancake breakfast.

Every year my mom would plot ways to improve the flavor in her secret recipe. She treated each concoction like a secret formula, examining the batter, adding a bit of water or a handful of flour, and heating the griddles just so. Then, every year after lively debate, my family would finally agree to disagree whether to eat with syrup or without—since dark syrup was an ingredient.

Unlike my family's top-secret recipe for homemade pancakes, God's recipe for incense was not to be altered. This anointing oil was to cover everything in the Holy of Holies to set it apart for the Lord, including the ark of the covenant. Anyone using it for personal consumption would be cut off from the community

This anointing oil was used to cover everything.

The ark of the covenant was the place God said "I will meet with you there." Once a year, a priest representing the people would enter the Most Holy Place where the ark resided. Everyone else stood outside, and waited.

Jesus changed all of this with His own blood of the new covenant. It was no longer necessary for the incense recipe to be guarded. The Most Holy Place is now open to everyone who calls on His name. Now you and I are the dwelling place of the Most High God. And He still meets us at the mercy seat because He is holy, just as you and I are holy.

A Moment to Breathe . . .

Thank Him for His abundant mercy. And ask Him to show you how you can invite others to meet God at the same mercy seat.

Why It's Okay to Not Be Enough

BY AMBER C. HAINES

Concerning this, I pleaded with the Lord three times that it would leave me. But he said to me, "My grace is sufficient for you, for my power is perfected in weakness." 2 CORINTHIANS 12:8–9

WHEN THEY TOOK MY Titus to another room to insert the feeding tube, I felt flush all over, green. My milk wasn't enough. The food wasn't enough, and so they called it "starvation mode" and "failure to thrive," his one-year-old body the size of a four-month-old. In the hospital, I had to hold Titus's feisty arms down so he didn't pull out the tube. We had an intense, demanding job in that little room, and suddenly we were the needy ones. We couldn't care for our other boys. We couldn't water the tomatoes or go make a pot of coffee.

One of the things I've been asking from God is that He would make me a servant. Then He allows me to be in a position where I'm able to do nothing. He surrounds me with dearest friends and family, some of whom have the very least in time, physical stamina, sleep, emotional wherewithal, or material possessions. He shows me how they stop and sit with me and my children in their own not enough-ness.

Sometimes I think about Paul's thorn, how he must have thought, *If only it were gone, I would finally be enough.* If only my milk were better. If only I read more. If only my kitchen were bigger or we made more money. But God's response? "My grace is sufficient for you." When He says this, it's the same as saying, "Don't give Me your excuses," while simultaneously saying, "You're not the one doing it anyway."

I suddenly feel so free to shirk the pretense that I could possibly have anything together, and I'm learning that boasting in this weakness—it's the gospel. My temptation is to say that if I nurse him more or read the Bible more or pray harder, I'll be enough—that my works are sufficient. But when the mighty fall, when the rich go bankrupt, and the greatest dreams land broken, we can say to ourselves and to the world what is true . . . His grace is sufficient.

A Moment to Breathe . . .

Think of a weakness you wish you didn't have. Then thank Him that His strength is made perfect in our weakness, that His grace is sufficient for all we lack.

When Prayer Goes Unanswered

BY KELLY BALARIE

The LORD of Armies has sworn: As I have purposed, so it will be; as I have planned it, so it will happen. ISAIAH 14:24

I STARED OUT THE window. My eyes squinted. Not because the sun was blinding me, but because I was furious with God. He failed me. And from where I stood in that moment, my view wasn't pretty. For the past six months I had pleaded with God to no end and I believed God was going to come through for me, and then I was left looking at a pile of nothingness. God not only didn't come through, He hurt me. So, like any good Christian girl, I went to church. And when they sang, "How great is our God," I lip-synced.

Have you ever felt abandoned by God? Maybe someone is still sick. The spouse is still mean. A child won't return. Your finances are in the dumps. A friend has hurt you. Your car keeps breaking down. Whatever is going wrong, it's because God has gone rogue, right? Oh, I know these feelings. But looking back, years later, I see things through a different prism, a different angle.

Sometimes we don't receive the lesser prayer because God is answering a bigger prayer. And the waiting produces patience. Patience actually equals faith. It is in the wait we learn faith. It is here where we either stick with God, or we bail.

What looks like rejection is often protection. We see life horizontally, but God sees life horizontally, vertically, cross-diagonally, and inside out. He sees how Person A affects Person B and how Person B may know Jesus if Person A goes here or there. He also sees how closing a door may prevent our foot from getting jammed in it.

God hasn't given up on you. Just as He hasn't given up on me. He doesn't discount our prayers as frivolous or worthless. God loves us and He has a plan. Just wait and see.

A Moment to Breathe . . .

Remember back to a situation when things seemed awry, but in hindsight you can see God's hand, evident and present. Tell Him, this moment, that you trust He's present today too.

Sinners in the Hands of a Loving God

BY ALIA JOY

But God proves his own love for us in that while we were still sinners, Christ died for us. ROMANS 5:8

WHEN I WAS A girl I would diligently go forward for every altar call. Every time a preacher asked who was ready to accept Jesus into their hearts, I would raise my tiny hand as if I was a student waiting to be picked for my right answers. I would repeat the sinner's prayer with my eyes squeezed shut and hope that this time it took.

I was afraid I didn't do it right. Later, I'd fight with my brother, think mean or envious thoughts, or I'd disobey my mom. I thought this disqualified me from God's love and I vowed to try harder next time. I thought my performance was somehow tied to Jesus' willingness to go to the cross on my behalf.

In my teen years, when I wasn't walking with God, I'd imagine Him a distant and angry taskmaster who was waiting to smash me like an ant for all the wrong I did, for all the wrong I was.

Looking back on those years, I realize how mistaken I was and how distorted my view of grace was, and yet sometimes I find myself slipping back to that place where I refuse abundant grace. Because I somehow still think I need to earn it and that it's possible for me to lose it. Sometimes I am still that little girl with her arm raised and her heart thumping, hoping to be seen and loved by God. Sometimes I still think I must initiate love from Jesus.

But it doesn't start with me. God's love has already been demonstrated on the cross. While we were sinners, with tempers that flare and petty thoughts that run through our minds, with insecurities and worries, with the need for approval and selfish intentions, with bad mom days and flesh that often wills against God, Christ died for me.

I can put my hand down and rest in the arms of my Savior.

A Moment to Breathe . . .

"Even while I was yet _____, Christ died for me and His grace covers me." However you might fill in this blank, know that His grace is enough. Christ is enough.

Saying Yes to Courage

BY ALIZA LATTA

*"This is what the LORD says: 'Do not be afraid or
discouraged because of this vast number, for the battle
is not yours, but God's.'"* 2 CHRONICLES 20:15

I WAS PETRIFIED. I hadn't been to college before, and there I was
. . . my first day of school. I was going to college four years later
than my friends, and I was certain everyone in my program would
immediately know I was different. Maybe I could pretend I had just
graduated from high school or something.

I arrived an hour early that first morning. The sun had just risen,
a pinky-orange sky stretching above me. I sat in my car for a few
minutes, gathering the courage to go find my classroom.

What if I fail? I thought to myself. *What if everyone hates me?
What if I forget how to write a thesis, or study for exams, or read
a textbook?* It was fear, I knew, trying to tangle its way inside me
and snatch away my new experience. Fear often does this when
I'm experiencing something new. I felt the same way when I went
on dates with a boy I was fond of. I almost said no about a hundred
times when he asked me.

When I went to Africa, I was terrified. I was scared of missing out
on what was happening back home, scared of falling too deeply in
love with a continent, and I was petrified of snakes. I can remember
thousands of times when fear tried to snatch my experiences from
me. But in almost every case, I said no to the fear, and yes to the
experience. I said yes to going to college four years later. I said yes
to Africa, and yes to the boy, and yes to being scared, and yes to
choosing bravery.

I want to keep saying yes. Yes to Jesus, and yes to courage, and
yes to opening my hands and letting go of the fear I feel. I'm still in
college, but I'm not scared anymore. I want to go out and face it. I
want to keep saying yes to courage and no to fear.

A Moment to Breathe . . .

*Where has fear tangled you up with a no? Where is a
yes knocking on the door of your heart? Ask God to
show you the yes He wants you to make today.*

Slowing to Listen

BY BECKY KEIFE

For just as the sufferings of Christ overflow to us, so also through Christ our comfort overflows. 2 CORINTHIANS 1:5

AS I'M WATCHING MY boy hang up his backpack and run off to the playground, the lovely mom I'm chatting with mentions the daughter she lost last Christmas. I look at her beautifully pregnant belly and her toddler playing with his pacifier in the stroller and her kindergartener with pretty blonde hair and pink bow skipping toward the playground. I see a mom who looks like she has it all together and never in a million years would I have known the grief and sorrow she has lived. Never would I have known her full story.

She's smiling as she talks about the light and joy her little girl brought to her family for nearly three years. She gently touches the life swelling within her and tells me how her eldest is excited to have a sister again. "It's hard," she says, "I never imagined it would happen to us, but we are so blessed by the time we had with her and the time we now have with these little ones."

I want to weep right there in front of Room 3 and hug this woman I've just met. I want to grab hold of my son with the missing front teeth and not let him go to the tricycle calling his name. The morning bell rings, and as the children freeze in mid-play motion, my heart wants to freeze time, yet somehow also turn back the clock and change its course for this other mom's broken heart. I can't do either.

"We still miss her beyond words," my new friend says, "but we know we'll be with her again one day, and there is so much hope in that."

I say goodbye at her car and keep traveling the sidewalk alone, passed manicured lawns and then two turns toward home. I thank God for the gift of this startling glimpse into another woman's story. A glimpse of His grace. I walk to my front door—filled with sorrow, filled with hope.

And thankful for home.

A Moment to Breathe . . .

Take the people you love most and wrap your arms around them. Right now. In the kitchen. On the porch. Wherever. Tell your loved ones how much you love being around them.

What Jesus Means by Salt

BY DAWN CAMP

*"You are the salt of the earth. But if the salt should lose its
taste, how can it be made salty? . . . In the same way, let your
light shine before others, so that they may see your good works
and give glory to your Father in heaven."* MATTHEW 5:13, 16

I TOLD MY KIDS I'd make brownies for them this week. Mentally I
added it to my try-not-to-be-a-loser-mom-on-spring-break strategy.
So last night after supper I pulled out *Down Home Cooking* and
found my favorite brownie recipe. Our home filled with the lovely
smell of butter and melted chocolate and the sound of children
counting down the numbers on the oven timer. After a long fifteen
minutes of cooling in the pan, plates were passed, bites taken, and
confused and disappointed faces seen. Apparently I forgot the salt.

Have you ever omitted the salt in a loaf of homemade bread or
a batch of brownies? I've done it just enough times to realize my
mistake when I take the first bite. As soon as I sheepishly said,
"Oh, I left out the salt," voices throughout the kitchen exclaimed,
"That's the problem!" and "Oh! She forgot the salt!" and "That's
what's wrong!" Plates were immediately pushed to the side and no
one took another bite. Because three sticks of butter, three cups of
sugar, and seven squares of baking chocolate cannot make up for
the absence of that teaspoon and a half of salt.

When Jesus tells us to be the salt of the earth, He's not talking
about a little seasoning sprinkled on the side. He's talking about a
living, breathing faith that permeates everything we say and do—a
light that cannot be hidden, a tangible hope.

I was determined not to let three sticks of butter and seven
squares of baking chocolate go to waste in my kitchen, so I continued to nibble on those brownies and grimace. And I took this
clear lesson to heart, glad that Jesus can use even my failings in the
kitchen to help me see Him more.

A Moment to Breathe . . .

*Bake a fresh batch of brownies. A little sweet something to
share with your loved ones. But . . . don't forget the salt!*

No Regrets

BY DONNA JONES

*When I was a child, I spoke like a child, I thought like
a child, I reasoned like a child. When I became a man,
I put aside childish things.* 1 CORINTHIANS 13:11

"WHAT SHOULD I DO?" My plea sounded more like a whine when I asked my dad this question back in college. But he wouldn't tell me what to do. It was time to make my own decisions. Even the tough ones. I felt frustrated. And confused. Looking back, I realize I wanted to shift the burden of decision-making off my shoulders and onto his. I thought I was seeking wisdom; now I realize I was avoiding responsibility.

Have you ever felt like your heavenly Father responded like my earthly one? Have you ever been in the midst of a decision-making process and prayed something like, "God, just tell me what to do! Show me in neon lights!" Then . . . crickets.

Frustrating, isn't it?

It may be because God knows. He knows the Bible studies you've been in, the sermons you've heard, the worship songs you've sung, the deep conversations with Christian friends you've had, and the passages of Scripture you can recall. If God seems radio silent, it may be because He has already given you the wisdom you need, and it's time to apply what you already know.

I love the passage in 1 Corinthians that says we've put away childish things once we became adults. We're not children anymore. Even though we don't know everything, we know enough to do something. What information do we have that's enough to make a right choice today?

God rarely reveals His plan to us in neon lights. Instead, He asks us to seek Him through His Word. The question, "What should I do?" has one primary filter: Does this express my love for God and does it express my love for others? If I'm seeking to please God and extend love to others, then I do right. But if I rush into a decision with no regard for God or people, the rightness of my choice comes with no guarantee.

A Moment to Breathe . . .

*Make this filter your own whenever you have a tough decision to
make: Will my actions show love for God and others? If the answer
is yes to both, then you know you're going in the right direction.*

There Is No Safe Gospel

BY HILARY YANCEY

*"Again, the kingdom of heaven is like a large net thrown into
the sea. It collected every kind of fish, and when it was full, they
dragged it ashore, sat down, and gathered the good fish into
containers, but threw out the worthless ones. So it will be at the
end of the age. The angels will go out, separate the evil people
from the righteous, and throw them into the blazing furnace, where
there will be weeping and gnashing of teeth."* MATTHEW 13:47–50

I'M IN A CIRCLE of thoughtful and kind people, and I've been
asked to read the gospel lesson. I read that there will be a separating of the righteous and the evil, that there will be weeping and
gnashing of teeth. God's Word is living and active, but this is an
uncomfortable parable. *Why did I have to read that parable? Why
couldn't I have read the one about the pearl of great price or the
mustard seed or the treasure in the field?*

It isn't just that I wonder why Jesus teaches in parables; it's that
I don't really want to proclaim the teachings I don't like or understand. I don't want to be linked to something uncomfortable. I don't
want to be that close to some of the teachings, because speaking
them out loud makes *me* uncomfortable.

There is no encounter with the Word that will leave us comfortable. Comforted, perhaps, but only first through the upheaval of
our worlds, the collapse of our presuppositions, the relinquishing of
our desire to have the easiest story to tell. We cannot claim *Behold,
the Lamb of God who takes away the sin of world* if we are clinging
to a tamer, easier version, without the uncomfortable parables or
the uncertainties or the radical promises or the hardest questions.

I'm still wrestling with the parable of the nets. But it's in the midst
of my wrestling—not on the other side of it, not beyond it—that I'll
learn what it means to preach this life-changing gospel in my life,
in my heart, in the world.

A Moment to Breathe . . .

*When struggling through certain parts of the Bible, ask God
to reveal Himself to you, to open the eyes of your heart that
you might see Him more clearly—as He is, rather than the
comfortable version of Him we try to make Him out to be.*

Tied to the Dock

BY KATIE ORR

He is like a tree planted beside flowing streams that
bears its fruit in its season and whose leaf does not
wither. Whatever he does prospers. PSALM 1:3

I GREW UP ON the water. As a kid, I loved to sit at the front of the boat, hands gripped to the sides, my nose stretched out past the front of the boat. Boats are not like cars, which stay put when you turn them off. When you're in the water, if you aren't tied to the dock, the boat will float away—even in the smoothest of waters.

The Bible says there are two paths in life. Either I'm following Jesus, or I'm not. Either I'm allowing God to permeate and affect every area of my life, or I'm holding the control in my own hands. There is no in-between in the kingdom of God. Either I'm tied to the dock, or I'm drifting away.

We can learn much from the person in Psalm 1. Scripture speaks of him as blessed. Because he walked with intention and treasured God's Word. He lived his life like a tree planted by water. He paid attention to where he was walking, standing, sitting. He didn't allow his life to drift, like an unfettered boat.

The written Word of God brought this man delight. When I think of the things that bring me delight, I think of getting to sleep in, treating myself to a pedicure, and indulging in my favorite two-raw-sugar-no-foam-with-whip-latte drink. A facial? Yes, please! These are all things that bring me pleasure. Though I must ask myself: Do I delight in God as much as these? Do I delight in His Word as much as these?

We're blessed when we're in His Word every day. Because God's Word is the truest anchor, preventing us from drifting with the currents of cultural trends. Blessed is the woman who is tied to the dock.

A Moment to Breathe . . .

List three things that bring you delight. Set a time to do one of
those things today. Then ask the Lord to increase your delight
in His Word, for that's when we experience the deepest joy.

Catching the Next Wave

BY KIM MARQUETTE

I am able to do all things through him
who strengthens me. PHILIPPIANS 4:13

UPON ARRIVING IN FLORIDA for a family getaway, we unpacked the minivan and headed straight to the beach for some boogie boarding. With a boogie board strapped to my wrist, I'd position myself to literally "catch a wave." I'm quite sure I never really figured it out, but every so often, I'd hit a wave just right and have the ride of a lifetime. It was pure excitement.

Of course it always ended the same way . . . The force of the water would land me facedown at the water's edge with a mouthful of sand. But the moment of defeat, with a mouthful of sand, was not the place I intended to stay. I wanted back out there for another chance at victory. So I grabbed my board and waded back out for the next wave.

The rhythm of boogie boarding soon began to shed light on my parenting, with moments of defeat and victory alike. Wading into the adventure of potty-training, I remember the moment she finally got it. Victory! Next moment, a note was sent home from school for biting! A mouthful of sand. Wading into the adventure of elementary school, I had an advanced reader. Victory! Next moment, he was suspended for bullying. A mouthful of sand. Wading into the adventure of teen years, I had an employed teen, with a bank account and a debit card. Victory! Next moment, overdraft notices start pouring in. A mouthful of sand.

Parenting—like life—is a lot like boogie boarding. With moments of victory and defeat. But I did figure one thing out. The mouthful of sand moments would not be the place I'd choose to live. Instead I'd address the failure (spit out the sand) and then move on (wade back out to catch the next wave of victory). We would live in the victory!

A Moment to Breathe . . .

When you feel like you're having a "mouthful of sand" kind
of moment, remember it's just a moment. It's not where you
have to stay. Keep going and catch the next wave.

Why God Allows Change

BY MELANIE DAVIS PORTER

*There is an occasion for everything, and a time for
every activity under heaven.* ECCLESIASTES 3:1

"HEY, MOM, I'M LEAVING," he said.

Looking up from a book, I see my twenty-one-year-old son with a backpack and pillow under his arm. Confused by the time, I glance at the clock. "Where are you going at this late hour?"

"I moved into the new house today," he said. His wedding day was less than a week away and suddenly I realized he'd spent his last night sleeping under my roof. In the weeks and months that followed, I experienced more change. I met the unexpected loss of my father, and the company I loved working for shut their doors forever. Yeah, I wanted my old life back.

Perhaps you're wrestling with some big changes right now, but with every life change that brings pain, God is allowing something new to be born. It's okay to grieve or regroup, but let's not linger too long there. If change wasn't a part of life, there would be no long summer evenings on the porch. We wouldn't have the glorious splendor of fall to look forward to. There would be no winter for the earth to rest. And without the rest, spring can't bring new life.

The same is true in our spiritual life; trusting Jesus to transform the shades of our faith, making them more brilliant, no matter what season we are in—be it the hurts or the joy. In time, my empty nest became a place of beauty. I found new purpose and went back to school at the age of forty-eight. My retired husband and I found a new depth of love and joy in our relationship. And surprisingly, God has taken away the fear of change. I've finally realized that every season the Lord brings into my life is lovingly filtered through His precious fingertips.

A Moment to Breathe . . .

Find an old photo album and savor the sweet memories of seasons past. When you turn the last page, ask God to fill the "new pages" of your life with sweet new memories.

Friendship Heals Our Broken Hearts

BY DEIDRA RIGGS

*"Don't let your heart be troubled. Believe in
God; believe also in me."* JOHN 14:1

FOR AN ENTIRE YEAR, when we found ourselves in our new church, I began each Sunday morning with a panic attack. Sitting on the bed with a towel wrapped around me from the shower, I tried to remember how to fill my lungs with air. Sometimes I'd walk across the room and turn on the box fan in the window, or flip the switch to the exhaust fan in the bathroom, all to drown out the sound of my heart pounding loud in my ears.

I'd been down this road before, and every time I'd had my heart stepped on by women who shared my faith in Jesus and who loved Him big time and for real. Every time, it caught me off guard and sucked the air out, leaving me flat and empty and sore. I don't know why we break each other the way we do.

We carry the glory of God in earthen pots with dirt caked on, and He trusts us to let Him shine through all the broken places. He knows how prone we are to wander, to crush and be crushed. And He has this uncanny way of bringing glory out of ashes, grace transforming dis-grace, and healing banishing dis-ease.

Eventually, I found a way through those panic attacks. I opened up my heart to women over coffee or tea or a good book. I kicked off my shoes and tucked my feet under me at the end of the sofa and leaned in to hear the stories other women shared. And eventually, my heart got stepped on because that's what happens. It's true. But also? This heart, all tender and broken and split wide open, has been filled with breath and life and hope—hoisted on the shoulders of women who love well with bruised hearts of their own. The good with the bad, and God right there in it, working it all for His good.

A Moment to Breathe . . .

*Pick one woman you can open up your heart to today.
Over coffee or tea or a good book. Or pick several
and start intentionally spending time together.*

Holding on to Hope

BY KRIS CAMEALY

Now in this hope we were saved, but hope that is seen is not hope, because who hopes for what he sees? Now if we hope for what we do not see, we eagerly wait for it with patience. ROMANS 8:24–25

I CAN TELL HE'S nervous by the way he's hopping back and forth, from one foot to the other. My son's skinny arms are tight at his sides, like a little soldier, but he's out of formation with that nervous jig he's dancing. I notice how he didn't volunteer this time to go first. I remember that fear.

He steps onto the diving platform and I can see his growing muscles tense, but then . . . he leaps. We rally and clap for him as he emerges and I can see his grin from across the pool. His chest swelling with the triumph of having overcome. The satisfaction of having been willing radiates in his confident steps as he walks the pool deck. He did it.

Watching my boy step up to repeat the move, my lungs empty in a heavy sigh. I remember all the times I was his age and all of the moments of stepping up, taking that leap. And I wonder if I will ever stop being afraid.

Faith cancels fear. I learned this recently, and God repeats the lesson almost daily. Constant opportunities present themselves. To choose fear or faith. I'd like to say the choice is simple. Sometimes it is. I'm still neck deep in learning how not to fear. In fearing, I lose hope. I'm still ripping the seams of this suffocating pride that snuffs out those flickers of faith. I'm still reminding myself every day that hope overcame death, so that I could live constantly under hope's wings.

I am learning, like my boy, to step up, to believe that when I leap, God will catch me. I am learning to hold fast to that hope because it does not disappoint. I know I cannot do any of it myself and yet this human heart tries. I'm learning to trust and believe that with hope in the cross, in the saving grace of Christ, I can overcome, not by my own strength, but by His.

A Moment to Breathe . . .

Name the thing for which you're afraid to hope. Then place it at the foot of the cross. Let Him be your Hope. By His strength, we can learn to hope—and breathe—again.

To Believe the Best

BY LISA WHITTLE

"Do not judge, so that you won't be judged." MATTHEW 7:1

I HAVE A FRIEND who feels discouraged, labeled, and misunderstood. One time he did something some people didn't like. And now, years later and with long memory, some people have decided he is not a good person. And no matter how much he comes to the table with a pure heart, they do not believe the best about him.

I have another friend who is sure things are not going to work out. That God doesn't want to use her like He does others. That she is never going to be what, as a little girl, she always dreamed of being. It's the human reality that all of us at some point struggle with—to believe the best, even about ourselves.

But when we don't believe the best, in others or ourselves, we're really saying to God: *I do not believe You. I do not believe people can change or grow or be considered as worthy, unless I deem them to be.*

To choose not to believe the best, in others or ourselves, is the stuff of humans. To believe the best—even in our unseen, unclear, unknown situations—is the stuff of God. He's the Maker of all things new, the Knower of the heart, the Turner of things around, and He never throws anyone away. God asks us to believe the best because what that really means is we place our faith and trust in Him without trying to put that job in our own hands.

And if that person does disappoint us, we will have honored God by believing the best. And if our life doesn't turn out to match our dreams, it will have been beautiful anyway with a hopeful, positive outlook. We all have past moments we're not proud of. Everyone has been less than faithful, less than honest, less than good. And yet, God doesn't give up on us. Shouldn't we then, too?

A Moment to Breathe . . .

Think about a time someone gave you the benefit of the doubt, someone believed in you. As you move through the day, give the same benefit of the doubt to each soul you come in contact with.

Play Your Note

BY ALYSSA DELOSSANTOS

For just as the body is one and has many parts, and
all the parts of that body, though many, are one
body—so also is Christ. 1 CORINTHIANS 12:12

IN ELEMENTARY SCHOOL I remember wanting to read, write, and draw like Grace Su. She could do all those things and more. I partnered with her for a "Young Authors" contest, and it was the only year my entry received recognition. (Thank you, Grace, for letting me ride your coattails.)

Middle school and high school ushered in more opportunities to examine what I lacked. From best friends to book smarts, from the right clothing to a cool hairstyle . . . I was mostly a day late and a dollar—or $20!—short.

Inadequacies and mistakes, failures and fears regularly find their way into my thoughts. Not measuring up—not being enough—has been reoccurring in my thoughts for as long as I can remember. So familiar, they can creep in and linger undetected.

When I became a mother, a gift I deeply treasure, a new layer of presumed inadequacies developed. Comparing sleep habits, feeding schedules, and milestones was a real issue. I had to fight against comparison because it only left me feeling disappointed and fearful. But I decided to say, "Enough!" I pulled the plug on the scarcity treadmill.

I have a friend who encourages me by saying, "Play your note." It's easy to get sideways about the notes that others get to play and forget that I have a note to play too. And so do you. The song is better when I add my note—and when you add yours—by exercising the unique gifts and talents given to each of us.

Together, let's say, "Enough!" Let's walk confidently in the "you-niqueness" we've been given by God. When we're each playing our note, we bring God the greatest glory.

A Moment to Breathe . . .

Name the thing you love most to do. Name your note. Then play
it. Share the sweet note of who you are with those around you.

The Ballfield

BY DIANE W. BAILEY

The righteous one will live by his faith. HABAKKUK 2:4

YOU COULD FEEL THE heated friction of competition in an already blistery June afternoon on the softball field. It was the state playoffs and my daughter was running hard. As she kicked one knee up and extended the other leg, she slid into home plate. Red dust rose from the Alabama clay and covered home plate. The catcher lost her balance, and instead of tagging her with the ball, she fell on Megan's extended leg. With Megan's first step, we could tell she was injured, but she insisted on finishing the game.

When it came time for Megan to bat, it was clear she would not be able to run. The decision was made for her to bat, but another girl from the team would be a pinch-runner in her place—a partner for a batter when she is unable to run around the bases. The girl they chose wasn't great at fielding or batting so she didn't see much playing time. But when Megan hit the pitch, her friend began to run. Around first base, then second, then third, then home! We all realized she had an amazing talent to run. Once given the opportunity to show her hidden ability, her confidence grew because she saw that she had value. Megan and this girl bonded as friends. And their new bond opened the door to us inviting her to church.

It's hard to understand God's plans for achieving eternity. It can sometimes appear as if He's being unfair to us. But it could be that He is using our afflictions to work out eternity for us, or perhaps to work out eternity for others through our wounded places. So we trust that He sees more than we ever could and we trust that His purposes are good. In this way, we choose to live by faith.

A Moment to Breathe . . .

A delay here. A detour there. You never know what things the Lord may use to steer eternity to fulfill His purposes. Accept a delay or detour as a way God may be working out eternity on behalf of you or someone else.

Saying Yes to Hospitality

BY JESSICA TURNER

. . . I opened my door to the traveler. JOB 31:32

LAST WEEK, WE HAD family in town for a visit. With my due date just two weeks away, I was a little overwhelmed by the thought of a family of five staying with us, but our time together was wonderful. Our kids played well and we made amazing memories. After they left, I thought about how glad I was that we flung our door open wide, blew up air mattresses, and made everything work.

The following day I planned to take it easy, maybe do a few loads of laundry, and work on some writing. But then I got a text from a friend who was unexpectedly in town with her family, asking if we wanted to get together for lunch. "Yes" was the only option. Though I was still pretty worn out physically from the previous week's company, I knew that seeing her would be such a gift.

Instead of going out to lunch, which I knew would be tough and not as relaxing or as fun for our six kids, I invited them over to our house. I warned them that the state of my house was chaos, but that as long as that was okay, we would love to have them over. Of course they didn't care about our house. They didn't want to come over to see a dust-free mantel or a spotless living room. We spent more than two hours together and our time was rich with conversation. We kept lunch simple—just cold cuts, fruit, and chips. The kids played and everyone enjoyed one another's company.

When they left, I was again reminded that hospitality is not about the condition of our homes, but the condition of our hearts. Hospitality is about saying yes. It's about honesty, not about perfection. Life can be so busy; it's easy to miss out on opportunities to demonstrate hospitality. But let's not miss those chances. Let's be the friend who invites others in.

A Moment to Breathe . . .

Let the dishes sit awhile longer. Let the dust in the corner be. Open your door—the one in your home and the one in your heart—to a friend when she calls.

How to Pour Coffee like a Believer

BY EMILY P. FREEMAN

"In fact, God knows that when you eat it your eyes will be opened and you will be like God, knowing good and evil." GENESIS 3:5

REACHING FOR THE CREAMER, I realize it's lighter than usual and there's only a small amount left in the bottom of the container. A voice in my mind shouts two words—*not enough!* I do love cream in my coffee, but those words come too fast. They reveal a belief I don't even realize I'm holding on to: *there will never be enough.*

Do you ever have these types of thoughts greet you in the midst of everyday moments? Maybe you're waiting for the coffee to brew and then a thought comes up you didn't even know you've been carrying.

Today, those words—*there will never be enough*—they haunt. But they don't come out of the clear blue. I've actually been feeding that thought for a while now. The whispers grow and sound something like this: "If you work faster, then you'll be more successful. If you had more time, then you'd be a better mom. If you were thinner, then you'd be enough."

I'm all too familiar with "if-then" theology. It started back in the garden, with a liar who said: *If you eat this fruit, then you will be like God.* It's a lie that tells us we have to *do* something in order to *be* something. And we've been buying it ever since. We all have our own if-thens, don't we?

After pouring my coffee, I spend a little time in my chair by the window, allowing all the if-thens to float to the surface and letting Jesus still those voices on my behalf. He has redeemed those false if-then statements. And He replaces them with new ones that depend not on me being enough of something, but on God Himself. Because the one who lives under the protection of the Most High dwells in the shadow of the Almighty.

A Moment to Breathe . . .

What "if-then" statements are you holding on to? Invite God to replace those false statements with His truth.

Clothed in Strength and Dignity

BY JENNIFER DUKES LEE

*Strength and honor are her clothing, and she can
laugh at the time to come.* PROVERBS 31:25

OUR FAMILY VISITED AN amusement park every summer when I was growing up. My favorite ride was a rollercoaster called the Tornado. Ironically, it was also the ride I dreaded the most. When I stood in line with my dad, I lived in the tension of wanting to get on the ride, but fearing I would literally plummet to my death if I did.

When we reached the platform, I could see the sign for the Chicken Exit—an escape for anyone who decided, at the last minute, that they didn't want to ride the Tornado after all. I usually considered walking through, but I never once took the escape. With Dad at my side, I felt brave. I'd step into the rollercoaster car and we'd *click-click-click* up the first hill, and then plunge straight to earth, before rocketing up another hill, and then another. Dad and I would laugh through the whole ride. When it was all over, I'd beg Dad to get back in the line again.

Now that I'm an adult, I see how life is a lot like waiting in line to ride the Tornado. We *want* to live life with adventure, but we feel the pull of the nearest Chicken Exit. Yet Scripture says God gives us strength for this adventure called life. God even gives us the ability to laugh in the face of our fears!

I am not naturally brave. When I think about the future, I sometimes want to take the easy way out. But then I remember what I learned on those July afternoons with Dad at my side. If I took the Chicken Exit, I would have missed out on the adventure my father intended for me. The same goes for you. Your heavenly Father is inviting you to take a seat next to Him. If you step into the adventure, He'll guarantee you the ride of your life. And then, you might even hear yourself say to your heavenly Father: "Let's do it again, Dad!"

A Moment to Breathe . . .

*Bravery looks a lot like trust. When you're not feeling
brave, ask God to help you trust Him even more. Then
throw your hands in the air in praise, knowing your
Father has an adventure waiting just for you!*

When You Wonder If You'll Ever Measure Up

BY KRISTEN WELCH

It is not that we are competent in ourselves to claim anything as coming from ourselves, but our adequacy is from God. 2 CORINTHIANS 3:5

I DON'T REMEMBER THE first time I felt it. It could have been in the third grade when I was the last one picked for the kickball team. Or maybe when I opened my mouth to sing like my musically talented brother and sister only to discover I was tone deaf. Not being enough has sort of been a faithful companion in my life . . . always there, reminding me of ways I didn't fit in or belong.

I don't remember the first time I didn't measure up. But I do remember the first time I stopped measuring. I was a freshman in college, rooming with my twin sister. I called my mom on the phone and said, "Mom, did you know I'm petite?"

She laughed at my crazy question and said, "Of course, honey. You're 5′ 2″. That's petite by most standards. Why are you asking?"

I replied, "But Mom, I'm the big twin. I had no idea I was petite!"

This new realization was remarkable to me. I had spent my entire childhood being compared to my twin sister. We were born five minutes apart and I towered over her 4′10″ frame. I was shocked when someone referred to me as petite. But that's because I was measuring myself by the wrong perspective. And that's what comparison does: it skews our view of ourselves and we begin to believe the lie that says we aren't pretty enough or smart enough or stylish enough or skinny enough or tall enough or young enough or whatever enough.

We can never be all those things and certainly not at the same time. But that's okay. We don't have to be enough. Because Jesus is. All the time. And even better—through Christ—we are enough. He takes our inadequacies and unrighteousness and exchanges it for His perfection. When we don't measure up, He does. And that is enough for all of us.

A Moment to Breathe . . .

Whisper a prayer of thanks—that Jesus takes all our "not enough-ness" and He makes up for everything.

From Heaven, with Love

BY MEI L. AU

*See what great love the Father has given us that we should
be called God's children—and we are!* 1 JOHN 3:1

WHEN MY MOM LOST her battle with breast cancer, my office gifted me a beautiful bright pink orchid. I was in a busy season of life—me changing jobs and a son graduating from high school and going off to college—so I didn't have time to research how to care for an orchid.

To my surprise, the flowers lasted a long time. Then my husband accidentally bumped into the stem and cracked it off. I continued to water it sporadically, if I remembered, but we were convinced we killed it.

A couple of years later I considered throwing out this barren plant. It was showing no signs of life. But I couldn't. Then one day I noticed a new shoot growing out of the base. After a few weeks the new growth starting shooting up and tiny buds appeared at the tips.

I came downstairs one morning and was greeted by two full fuchsia blooms, proudly standing at attention. I smiled and thanked God for the brightness it brought to a dreary winter day.

As I sat down to spend time with Him, He gently reminded me what the date was—the fourth anniversary of my mom's homecoming to heaven. I blinked back tears as I reflected on the tenderness and goodness of our Father's heart. That He would reach down from heaven to remind me of my mom's new life in eternity.

Sometimes God smiles at us from heaven and reminds us that He never forgets and He is always bringing forth new life.

A Moment to Breathe . . .

*Give a single orchid or a small potted plant to a friend
today as a gentle reminder that you see her, you
know what she's going through, and you care.*

Confidently Going in the Right Direction

BY ROBIN DANCE

"Do not remember the past events, pay no attention to things of old." ISAIAH 43:18

WHEN MY SON WAS born, my husband planned a special date night with our daughter. She wasn't yet two, and *The Lion King* would be her first theater outing. I can still see her racing to tell me all about it afterward. Fizzy and breathless, she explained that Simba was the "Kine King," and her favorite part was "popcorn and Pepsi." Eventually I'd get to see it, too, once it was finally released on video. If you polled any member of our family today, it still ranks as one of our all-time Disney favorites. The music, story, and characters have sweet universal appeal.

When we first meet Timon and Pumbaa, a fun-loving duo in the form of a banded mongoose and warthog, Simba is depressed, wrongly believing he is responsible for the death of his father. Well intentioned, Pumbaa advises for him to put his past behind him, and then launches into a spirited performance of "Hakuna Matata."

The sweet characters of Timon and Pumbaa make an important point, a lesson that serves us well to learn early: we can't change our past. It's futile to dwell on it. I think it's even dangerous to be anchored to our past. It's a form of bondage holding your future hostage.

Regrets. Bruised feelings. Bitterness. Anger. Grudges. Even if you were wronged by no fault of your own, holding onto the past is limiting and unhealthy. If we're only looking in the rearview mirror, we won't be able to move on to all the Lord has for us.

A Moment to Breathe . . .

Take some time to consider if anything from your past is keeping you from the perfect place God has for you. Pray for the Lord's leading and strength to let go of what lies behind, and keep your eyes on Christ as your prize.

Celebrating the Middle

BY BRITTA ELLIS LAFONT

*Whatever you do, do it from the heart, as something done
for the Lord and not for people.* COLOSSIANS 3:23

I WALKED UP THE stairs and saw her, out of the corner of my eye, sitting at her computer. She was muttering to herself and shaking her head.

"What's wrong, sweetie?" I asked.

My sixth grader fumed, "Mom, I just want to hurry up and get all my work done, so I can have some fun."

Everyone likes to have fun, but my child has always loved school too. What happened?

Instantly, I knew where she learned this way of thinking and it stopped me in my tracks. It's me. I'm the one always rushing. I'm the one always hurrying.

Let's get our reading done so we can relax! Let's finish our home-work early so we can meet our friends at the park! Let's hurry up and do our chores so we can bake!

I explained to her that much of life is work, and if we can't see the value in it, then we are missing our calling to honor the Lord in all we do. As I turned to walk back downstairs, I repented of my own haste. I don't want to model a life of hurry.

Do you ever find yourself rushing ahead? Wanting to get to the next place? Or move straight from "before" to "after" without spending the time in the middle? That day on the stairs got me think-ing. We don't enjoy cleaning, but we love the shiny, sweet-smelling result. Most of us don't really love exercising, but we usually feel better when we lace up our shoes and do it.

What if we realized that most of life is lived in the middle? What if we took a moment, just to recognize that God wants to meet us right in the middle of whatever we're doing, right now, wherever we're at.

A Moment to Breathe . . .

*What "middle" do you find yourself in today? Invite God
into your middle moments. Let Him meet you there.*

Even When We Can't Be There, God Still Is

BY HOLLEY GERTH

*God is our refuge and strength, a helper who is
always found in times of trouble.* PSALM 46:1

I ANSWER THE PHONE and hear the tears in her voice. I close my eyes and wish I had wings to fly the many miles to her side. I read the hurt in the email that makes its way to my inbox. As I respond, I want to reach through the screen and put my arm on her slumped-with-discouragement shoulders. I see the status update on Facebook and whisper a prayer with the hope she'll somehow sense it.

I want to be there for the people I love. I imagine you do too. I don't like the idea of missing even a moment when they might need me. And yet I realize making this happen is impossible. How do I live with that reality? How do I know they will be okay anyway? The answer came to me through Psalm 46:1. God is an ever-present help in trouble. He is on the other side of the phone line after she hangs up. He is right beside her when she reads my email reply. He is with her in every event on her Facebook time line.

There is never a time when God will not be with the people we love. They are not alone even when we can't be with them. They are not without help even when we can't do all we'd like to serve them. We don't have to bear the weight of believing they can't possibly make it unless we're there every second. And the same is true for us. As much as the people in our lives care for us, they can't always be there for us either. Sometimes they'll be busy. Or they may simply be unable to meet our needs. But God is always available. He is with us even when the room is empty. He's not even a phone call, email, or hug away—He's with us right now, right here, every moment of every day.

A Moment to Breathe . . .

Whisper a word of thanks that God is with you always. No matter where you go or what you do, He is with you.

Let the Music Play

BY NASREEN FYNEWEVER

*Sing to the LORD with the lyre, with the lyre and melodious
song. With trumpets and the blast of the ram's horn shout
triumphantly in the presence of the LORD, our King.* PSALM 98:5–6

MUSIC IS MOVING. IT connects us across the centuries and binds
people together in profound ways. It takes practice to get it right
and dedication to learn it well. It is beat, melody, and harmony all
in one. Art claims it, humanity is touched by it, and our souls are
the holder of it.

Silence has its place and for those moments, be still. But if it's a
time for the music to play, let it. If someone loved you, love out loud.
If someone mentored you, pour out. If someone taught you, teach
others. If someone gifted you, pay it forward. For tragedy and joy
are some of the greatest complexities in life, we are intertwined
with both daily.

When tragedy shatters the stained glass window around you and
the piercing sun blinds your eyes, keep breathing, keep living. Let
the notes of courage and providence carry you to the next measure.
Weep to the slow, riveting sound of the low tones and know this
too is music. Heartbreak is still worship, in the wrestle and the raw,
faith laid bare, do not mute the music now.

When joy gives pacing to your heart's arrhythmia and the care
from others brings your quality of life to notable goodness, keep
living. Let the notes of confidence and community carry you to the
next song of beauty. Sway to the rhythm, the momentous pulse of
the strong tones and know this too is music.

Hope is worship, not for you alone but also for those you can
bless. Don't mute the music now. For tragedy and joy are some of
the greatest complexities in life, we are intertwined with both daily.
For both, I stay on my knees; join me. For all you enjoy and for that
which calls you to endure, let the music play.

A Moment to Breathe . . .

*Press play. Turn on the music to your favorite worship
chorus and sing. Sing in the kitchen, in the bathroom,
in the car. Sing His praises wherever you are.*

The Importance of Sharing Our Stories

BY SHELLY WILDMAN

This will be written for a later generation, and a people who have not yet been created will praise the LORD. PSALM 102:18

WHEN MY MIDDLE DAUGHTER was four years old, she was nearly killed by a falling tree in the middle of a tornado. When my youngest daughter was born, she had a collapsed lung and pneumonia, causing her to spend a week in the NICU. Several years ago I spent twelve days in the hospital, eventually undergoing a serious surgery that saved my life.

These stories are told at birthdays, and we share them with friends and family. We return to these stories, again and again, because they remind us of God's faithfulness.

God told His people, the Israelites, to share their stories, to write them down, to remember. These weren't just feel-good stories that helped bolster the faith of the Israelites in that day, although they were that indeed. God had a purpose for the writing down of these stories: so that future generations would praise the Lord.

I hope someday to have grandchildren, and I hope to tell them all the stories of how God has intervened. I hope that one day, because of all of our family stories, my grandchildren (and dare I say great-grandchildren?) will also know and follow Jesus better.

All of us can share our stories so that future generations will praise the Lord. Perhaps we could share our stories with other women at church, the coffee shop, or the park. When we share God's goodness with those in our lives, we all are encouraged to give Him the praise.

A Moment to Breathe . . .

Make a list of all the times God has intervened on your behalf. Then look over that list and praise God for His provision. Ask Him to show you someone you could share your story with today.

Less Words, More Presence

BY SANDY HAFEEZ

If anyone thinks he knows anything, he does not yet
know it as he ought to know it. But if anyone loves
God, he is known by him. 1 CORINTHIANS 8:2–3

IN THE PAST, I worked hard to encourage my friends, especially in the hard times. Even when I sensed that my words weren't resonating or helpful, I would persist. I searched my brain for more examples, more analogies, more personal experiences, but to no avail. The countenance of a friend's face would remain unchanged. None of my examples or life experiences would bring contentment or peace. I felt helpless to help.

I was trying to be a savior. How arrogant of me to try to soothe anyone's ache with my own logic.

Coming face-to-face with my own inadequacy—my own lack— was demoralizing. But take heart, sister. When we come to this point, that is when we get to enter in with our friends. For that is when we become two broken daughters on a journey to live in this world, loving God and loving each other, but knowing that neither of us have the strength alone to do it well. As we fall to our knees in humility, the pride of trying to be someone's savior falls too.

But we are not alone. Christ is in us and we can be His arms to hold others close when the tears flow and the grief is thick. We can listen to Him, using His discernment for the right words, for sound counsel, and most importantly, for more prayer.

A text on my phone read, "Thank you for being present, for understanding and being helpful this morning . . . thanks for your encouragement, wisdom, and prayer!" A smile made its way across my face and gratitude filled my heart. This was the sweetest compliment to me because it confirmed God's continued grace and growth in my own life. This is the dearest gift we can give each other—less words, more presence.

A Moment to Breathe . . .

Enter in with those who are struggling with fewer words,
with less of ourselves. Simply be present and let the
real Savior do the work of healing and comfort.

The Canopy

BY STEPHANIE BRYANT

"Everyone must appear with a gift suited to his means, according to the blessing the LORD your God has given you." DEUTERONOMY 16:17

THE FURNITURE SALESMAN ASKED my dad, "How can I help you today? Looking for anything particular?"

My dad grinned and motioned for the man's attention to head my direction. In my small hands were new bills, recently exchanged from quarters that were saved, birthday checks from Aunt Sue, and little tuck-ins that Meme made sure I had on the everyday-normal kind of days. I unfolded the ad ripped from a magazine and carefully showed it to the man—a white four-poster bed with hand-painted flowers on the headboard and a beautifully adorned gauzy canopy had been my dream bed for over a year.

Fast-forward more than twenty-eight years and I still love that bed. It's traveled with me from my parents' house to my first home, to the storage shed after I married. Now after our last move, it sits in our garage next to my car. I convinced myself that someday I would give it to my daughter. But I'm sure that would be like giving a faded wedding dress that was worn thirty years ago to a newly engaged bride-to-be. Not exactly her taste.

The other morning I pulled into our garage and glanced at the four posters sticking up over cardboard. For the first time I realized that its purpose was being wasted, so I started to pray for God to show me what to do with this bed, plus the matching desk, chair, and side table. (My parents bought the rest of the set after I purchased the bed.)

It's funny how God prompts us to pray. How He orchestrates timing and reasons that are beyond our imagination. A day later, in our church bulletin, there was a small announcement for a Furniture Loan Program to international students at our local university. But it's a gift, not a loan. And God will answer my simple prayer through it.

A Moment to Breathe . . .

Ask God to show you one simple way you could be a blessing to someone else today.

How Great Thou Art

BY TERI LYNNE UNDERWOOD

The LORD is great and is highly praised; his greatness is unsearchable. One generation will declare your works to the next and will proclaim your mighty acts. PSALM 145:3–4

WE GATHER EVERY MONTH in the yellow community room at the nursing home. They're a beautiful bunch, this gathered assembly. As we sing about the "sweet by and by" and the "lily of the valley," some join in while others simply nod along as the familiar words touch a soft spot in tired hearts and worn bodies. Their mouths gently form the words of their beloved youth.

As we begin to sing "How Great Thou Art," a gentleman stands slowly, a grin on his face as he pulls out his rusted tambourine and the tiny cymbals mix with the out-of-tune piano and the voices of those who have lived long and known both joy and sorrow. And together we sing strong and pure. As the last note ends, the tambourine player bows his head low, and I steal a glance to see his face . . . and it's glowing. A man whose thick tongue makes his words difficult to understand had used his constantly shaking hands to worship.

Then we sing about being glad to be a part of the family of God, and as I look around the room with withering bodies and faltering minds, the tears slip from my eyes as I whisper a word of thanks for being in such a holy place. The gift of this day isn't us being here . . . it isn't even the man who played the tambourine . . . it's the sweet presence of God in this place. So real you could almost touch it. We pray one more time and then stand, all who could, to sing the last precious hymn.

Amazing grace, how sweet the sound, that saved a wretch like me . . .

Afterward we shake hands and thank our friends for letting us come and share their morning, and I realize once again how much God sees each and every one of us, and how He calls us to love.

A Moment to Breathe . . .

If you're not sure of all the lyrics, google "How Great Thou Art" and sing the hymn, right where you are. Sing with all your heart to the greatness of our God.

The One We Should Go to First

BY ANGIE RYG

Then the king asked me, "What is your request?" NEHEMIAH 2:4

"DO YOU GUYS WANT to go out with us on Saturday night?" I asked my friend.

She answered quickly, "Well, I need to check with my husband, but it sounds fun!"

I walked away thinking either she was just using that as an excuse and she really didn't want to go out with my husband and me or she actually meant what she said. She ended up saying yes and we went out to dinner and I asked her about it. She told me that she always asks her husband about everything from weekend plans to activities for the kids. That got us started on a whole conversation about who we ask for advice.

For advice I realized I often go to my husband, my sister, my brother, my parents, and even my sixteen-year-old daughter. But going to God was often a last resort. If I'm confused about something, I'll go to my close friends or family. Most of the time, I'm seeking affirmation of decisions I already made! If I'm worried, I'll talk over the best-case scenario with my mom and the worst-case scenario with my husband. Prayer often comes after I have talked to everyone else.

When Nehemiah needed to answer the king's question, Scripture tells us that he said a quick prayer to God. How many times would my decision-making seem clearer if I went to God before I asked other people? Or maybe just offering a quick thank-you could change my thinking? How easily I forget that I have a God who has everything in control and wants to hear me ask about decisions, share about my day, and come to Him with any worries or questions I have. He is in control over everything!

A Moment to Breathe . . .

Purpose in your heart to go to God first. With your questions and your worries. Seek Him in His Word and be willing to wait to hear Him speak.

When Healing Brings Hope

BY ELISA PULLIAM

"Be strong and courageous; don't be terrified or afraid of them. For the LORD your God is the one who will go with you; he will not leave you or abandon you." DEUTERONOMY 31:6

I KISSED THE KIDDOS goodbye and watched them drive off with their daddy to a brand new school. It was a new season for all of us, in a new home and a new town, with new rhythms and responsibilities, and I was feeling just a tad bit overwhelmed.

Adjusting to a new life is hard when you only remember the good of what you left behind and long for your friends from back home. Isn't it easier to remember the highlights of the past instead of clinging to hope in the present moment? Like the Israelites in the desert, I too easily forget the details. There are moments in this new everyday that feel like the wilderness and I pine for the good of what was. Except, what "was" was never perfect. Neither will this new life be perfect. But then again, moving wasn't about leaving the bad and finding the better. It was about obedience. We asked and God answered. God led and we followed.

So while I cry out to the Lord for understanding, as to why He would relocate us in the midst of all that seemed so good, the response I get isn't about my circumstances. It's always about Him. My heavenly Father gently whispers to my soul . . . "I've got this. I've got you. I'm doing a new thing. Just abide in Me."

Maybe that's the answer to my "why" question. Maybe He's orchestrated all of this so I'll lean more on Him and less on myself. Maybe it's about not clinging to anyone, anything, or any idea, and learning how to cling more to Him alone.

A Moment to Breathe . . .

Wherever you find yourself today, remember that He wants you to lean on Him. When the everyday feels overwhelming, He simply wants you to come and abide in Him.

The Rules Are Tools

BY KELLY BALARIE

"For I am commanding you today to love the Lord your God, to walk in his ways, and to keep his commands, statutes, and ordinances, so that you may live and multiply, and the Lord your God may bless you in the land you are entering to possess." DEUTERONOMY 30:16

"MIKEY, DON'T STAND ON Maddie's stroller. Mikey, step down. Michael, now!" He looks at me and steps up higher until he loses balance. The stroller tips backward and through tears he asks, "Mommy, why did you let me fall?"

I want to grab him and yell, "Why didn't you listen to me?" But instead I say, "I'm sorry you fell. I love you, little Mikey. It's important to listen to Mommy. I'm watching out for you when I tell you things. I want you to be safe." I give him a hug.

How often are we like Mikey? How often do we push the boundaries just a little bit more? We think: *I can get away with this; I'll be okay.* We want to do things our way. We fool ourselves. We think God won't punish us. We think that grace will cover us, so we're okay. But, even though His grace secures us in eternity with Him, our actions have consequences. We often look up at God and say, "Why God? Why did this happen? Why did You allow it?"

God lovingly laid down directions for our lives to keep us in areas of safety. He gives us a roadmap so we can move forward with an idea of where we are headed. He informs us of the places we shouldn't venture. Why? Because we may get hurt, we may get stuck. We may even miss our destination entirely if we go our own way. His directions keep us from shame, guilt, and regret. Even more, they offer us joy, fulfillment, and purpose.

If only we would see God's commands as tools instead of rules. Tools to help us and guide us. To keep us in places of contentment and peace. When we live within the boundaries He has set, we'll live lives that are focused and purposeful. Let's walk hand in hand with God toward the destination He has set before us.

A Moment to Breathe . . .

God's Word is like a "roadmap" of sorts. His commands show the way to go, the way to live. Spend a little time soaking in His Word today.

The White Space Challenge

BY MELISSA MICHAELS

As a deer longs for flowing streams,
so I long for you, God. PSALM 42:1

ONE NOT-SO-FINE DAY I woke up to catch my computer deleting all my photos. One by one, *gone*. My son's birthday party? Poof! My daughter's graduation? Goodbye! Our family's Christmas brunch from last year? Deleted!

My computer had been telling me my disk was full for *ages*, but I was "too busy" to figure out what I needed to do about it. Hitting "OK" to get that pesky error message to go away allowed me to get back to all the more pressing things on my to-do list.

The next morning I hoped that simply shutting down my computer for the night would solve all its problems. It didn't. In my panic to restore everything, I pushed all the buttons! I googled "SOS! White screen of death!" I was hoping beyond all hope that some really smart guy at Google would offer me the right answers.

As an interior design blogger, the worst possible business move is to lose all your photos. As a mom, you are supposed to protect every single memory stored in that computer. Fortunately, this disaster ended well, offering me more than just a restored computer. After finally taking the time to free up space on the startup disk, my photos miraculously returned safe and sound.

Just as I needed to heed the early warnings to free up disk space on my computer to avoid calamity, I must also get better at building intentional white space into my day. I'm a *doer*. I thrive when I'm busy checking things off my list and doing as much as possible, until it all crashes in around me. My soul craves slowing down to simply *be*. No amount of "doing" will ever satisfy. I need quiet moments with God—that free white space to refocus, to reboot, recharge, and rejuvenate my life and my soul.

A Moment to Breathe . . .

Look at your calendar or day planner. Mark out certain
days and times for intentional white space in your life—
time when you can be quiet in God's presence.

The Answer God Gives

BY ELISE HURD

Now these three remain: faith, hope, and love—but
the greatest of these is love. 1 CORINTHIANS 13:13

"MOM, WOULD YOU PRAY for me?"

I looked up from the dish I was scrubbing, "Of course. What's going on?"

She hesitated. "I just don't want to do my schoolwork. Could you pray and ask God to give me the desire to do my school?"

I smiled and nodded. "I will pray, but you should pray too. God likes for you to talk to Him directly."

Her eyes remained hopeless. "I will, but I don't think He's going to do it."

I smiled again, as I continued to rinse off the dishes I had no desire to clean, from a meal I had no desire to make.

"No, He may not give you the desire to do your schoolwork," I said, "but you know what? When you ask Him for something good—like the desire to do something you know is right or healthy or necessary—and He doesn't answer your prayer the way you hoped, He's giving you a huge compliment and a great opportunity. When God doesn't give you a good desire you pray for, He's indicating you are mature enough to choose what is right and best whether you feel like it or not. He's giving you the opportunity to grow in maturity . . . to choose not to follow your feelings. Our feelings will take over our lives, if we let them. But feelings are meant to be indicators, not dictators. A 'no' to a good desire means a 'yes' to the gift of perseverance."

Her eyes locked with mine and we shared a hopeful smile. Then she faced her books and turned the page, pencil ready for the next challenge, as I scooped up the basket of overflowing laundry and prepared to bear the weight up the stairs, one step at a time.

A Moment to Breathe . . .

After asking God to give you the desire to do the right thing,
step forward in obedience, trusting the feelings will follow.

Our Identity in Christ

BY ALIZA LATTA

I chose you before I formed you in the womb; I set you apart before you were born. I appointed you a prophet to the nations. JEREMIAH 1:5

MY IDENTITY ISN'T WHAT I thought it was. I am one month into college. Currently I should be writing two papers, creating a film, studying for a test, researching a prominent Canadian figure, reading my textbooks, and making a hefty amount of artwork so I actually have something to sell at my second art show.

Identity is a funny thing. People ask, "What do you do?" Before school, I felt as though I had nothing to say. But now I have something. Now I can tell them, "I'm a journalism student. I am learning to be a truth-teller in all I do. Also, I am very tired." I can easily wrap myself around the idea that being a journalism student is who I am because it's currently what I do.

The other day I received a mark on an assignment I had finished. It was a terrible grade. And get this—it was for a writing class. I saw the mark and instantly wilted. I'm supposed to be good at this. I'm supposed to be a writer. People have told me I'm a good writer, and if people tell you that, it has to be true, right? If I get a bad mark in a writing class, does that prove I'm a bad writer? Am I in the wrong program? Why am I taking journalism if I can't actually write?

It's astonishing what can happen when you make what you do into who you are. When your identity is something shakable, a feather can touch you and you'll fall apart. I'm a writer, even after that bad mark. But it's what I do, not who I am. I am a journalism student, but it's what I do, not who I am. I am an artist, but it's what I do, not who I am.

So who am I? I am one who is deeply, immeasurably loved by the God of the universe. This is who you are too.

A Moment to Breathe . . .

What "labels" do you wear for an identity? What would it be like if you laid your labels down? What if you saw yourself simply as a daughter of the Most High, deeply and immeasurably loved?

Louder Than Nutella

BY ANNIE F. DOWNS

Who do I have in heaven but you? And I desire nothing on earth but you. My flesh and my heart may fail, but God is the strength of my heart, my portion forever. PSALM 73:25–26

I TAP MY FINGERS on the table and check my phone again. Nope, I hadn't missed a text or call. He said he would call today. He hasn't. Another day has started and now it's trying to end and my phone still hasn't rung. I'm still alone. I feel un-thought-of. So I walk to the kitchen and pull a spoon out of the drawer. Just one scoop of Nutella will get my late afternoon back on track.

I pause at the cabinet. My counselor says I should determine a reason before I eat. Yep, I see a counselor, and yep, we talk about food. I usually bulldoze through that question, but in this moment, I actually stop. I stood there, spoon in the left hand and cabinet handle in the right hand. "I'm not hungry," I say in the emptiness of my kitchen, "I'm just sad, and I'm about to eat this Nutella because something in my brain says it will satisfy this hurt." My grip tightens on the spoon and I slowly close my eyes. "God, You're gonna' have to be louder than this Nutella."

I turn away from the cabinet and keep talking, saying the deep hurts of my heart and the disappointments and all the ways I wish my life was different. When I finish, nothing happens. My phone doesn't ring. I don't see an angel. I don't feel some supernatural strengthening in my soul. I just put the spoon away and remember Psalm 73:25–26. My flesh and heart feel like they're failing, but He is the strength of my heart, my portion, forever.

And it's true. I need Him more than anything. I'm so quick to heal all my hurts in other ways when I should just go to Him. My phone is still the quietest piece of technology in this whole house and I'm annoyed about it. But for today, my vice loses, my God wins, and somehow, my heart will survive it all.

A Moment to Breathe . . .

Nothing wrong with a spoon of Nutella or peanut butter or whatever you fancy most. But tape the passage from this psalm where you'll most need to see it the next time you feel discouraged.

To Know Him More

BY RENEE SWOPE

*Those who know your name trust in you because you have
not abandoned those who seek you, LORD.* PSALM 9:10

I USED TO BE afraid to trust God. And it bothered me. I wanted to slip my hand in His and let Him lead. I wanted to put my concerns in His capable arms and believe He could take better care of them than I could. I wanted to have more faith. But I didn't.

One day I realized it's hard to trust someone we don't really know. Therein was the reason for my heart's hesitancy to fully rely on God.

You see, I knew a lot about God but I didn't really know Him. So I decided to start spending time with Him like a friend, getting to know Him. Talking to Him with conversational prayers. Listening to Him through the promises in His Word. Depending on Him in different circumstances. Relying on Him in faith as I struggled with different fears.

Over time my trust in God grew stronger. And my dependence grew deeper as I leaned on Him and found He is dependable. What about you? Have you ever struggled with trusting God, like really trusting Him and fully relying on Him to meet your needs?

One thing that has helped me get to know God and push through my fear of dependence is remembering the names of God and giving Him a chance to show me the faithfulness of His character through the power of His names. The truth is, we can't know God as Jehovah Jireh, our Provider, if we aren't in need. And when we are, we can learn to trust Him as we depend on Him to meet our needs. The more we do this, the more our trust will deepen and our relationship with Christ with be strengthened.

A Moment to Breathe . . .

*For your trust in God to grow, pray this simple prayer: Lord,
I want to know You more each day, and I want to trust You
in deeper ways. Thank You for hearing me when I pray.*

Small Is the New Great

BY ANNA RENDELL

The LORD had done great things for us;
we were joyful. PSALM 126:3

I'M A SUCKER FOR Christmas cards. I love creating one each year, and I love receiving them from friends and family. Annual Christmas letters that some tuck into the envelope—a simple page full of the good, the sad, and the joyful from the previous year—are a fun, general update to receive as well. Catching up with friends and family via their own words is a gift I cherish, so of course I write an annual letter as well.

The first year I sent such a letter was the first year we were married. We'd read Psalm 126:3 during our wedding, and I included it as a sendoff in our letter.

It's been over ten years since that first letter went out, and Psalm 126:3 has been in the closing of each one. Not because every year has been sunshine and rainbows (there have been years with tragedies and struggles and hardships), but because there have always been great things—the births of our babies, God sparing us from some things and exposing us to others, and financial blessings that came in the nick of time.

But even more precious are the small, everyday things that may not make the annual letter but bring great joy. Like sunshine in February. Hot coffee in the morning. Time with girlfriends. Wispy baby curls. Clean sheets.

Small can be great. Small just may be the new big. Joy can come from the smallest of places and it can fill our whole hearts and it can be the theme of our years, no matter what.

A Moment to Breathe . . .

Take note of small joys on this very day. Take stock of these
small great things, and let them fill you with joy.

Put Me Back Together

BY EVI WUSK

For God has not given us a spirit of fear, but one of power, love, and sound judgment. 2 TIMOTHY 1:7

I REACH UP INTO my mother's dish cupboard, past the stacks of Corelle plates and bowls. *Got it,* I think as I slide my fingers around the canary yellow ramekin. *This will be perfect for the olives.* But somewhere between the "perfect" in my head and the grip of my hand, I fumble. The dainty cup with ruffled edges smashes to the tile floor and spreads out in shards like a firework.

I clench my fists and thoughts together, knowing I cannot undo this mess. My mom reassures me with words of love and forgiveness. "I got it on sale," she says, "It doesn't matter."

But to the voice in my head it matters: *How could you do this? You are always screwing things up, always leaving a mess for someone else to clean up.*

The thoughts spin, an old record I recognize.

I breathe in the fear I feel and speak back in prayer, "My spirit is one of power, of love, of sound judgment," I pray in a small voice held up by a big God. In spite of my shortcomings, God's love meets me in this place. So I start small and whisper back to the fear, and then speak, and then know. This love really is for me too.

I look at the clean kitchen floor, thankful for my dad who ran to get the vacuum as I stood among the mess. The broken yellow ramekin is now safe in the belly of the vacuum, somehow all together again. I reach up in the cupboard once more, praying that I might keep reaching, keep taking the courage offered me . . . even when I can't believe the mess I've made, or the far-reach of the love that comes for me again and again, always ready to clean me up.

A Moment to Breathe . . .

Think of a moment in time when you made a giant mess, literally. Tell that old-mess-making-you that there is grace for that mess, just as there is grace for any mess today. Then thank God for abounding grace.

When Mercy Found Me

BY JACQUE WATKINS

*I waited patiently for the LORD, and he turned to me and heard
my cry for help. He brought me up from a desolate pit, out of the
muddy clay, and set my feet on a rock, making my steps secure. He
put a new song in my mouth, a hymn of praise to our God. Many
will see and fear, and they will trust in the LORD.* PSALM 40:1–3

AS THE KIDS PLAYED soccer in the sunshine, I sat in my Suburban
eager for some quiet time to read. I didn't think twice when another
mom walked to my window. We weren't close friends, but we
weren't strangers either. She wasted no time.

"One of the moms in our group has a problem with you, and—
just so you know—I already defended you because I really do like
you. But I can see her view, and wanted to ask you something."

"Sure," I said.

"Why is it that you chose to lie and have an affair, yet you get to
have a nice family and be happy? While I've stayed faithful to my
cheating husband and tried to work it out, yet my family is struggling and my marriage is a mess? It's like you did wrong and got
rewarded for it. It's just not fair."

In a split second my heart flooded. Failure. Guilt. Shame. Regret.
It had been over fifteen years since I dove into that desolate pit.
But her words made the memory as crisp as the blue sky. While it's
true I dove in, in time I did get out. But I wasn't capable of getting
myself out. And I didn't deserve to be brought out. At the bottom I
had no one left. I'd ruined everything.

But God heard my cry. He turned to me. He rescued me and gave
me new life. God's mercy found me. On the one hand, my friend
was wrong. There is no reward for sin; the natural consequences of
sin are real. But at the same time, my friend was also right. God's
love is so great that He chooses to lavish His mercy on those who
don't deserve it. All we can do in response is thank Him.

A Moment to Breathe . . .

*Take a moment to reflect on the mercy you've received from
God. Count the ways He's brought you out of your own pit.
And in those moments when you're aching for justice, ask
Him to give you a heart of compassion and mercy.*

My One-Word Vocabulary Shift

BY JEN SCHMIDT

*I say, "The LORD is my portion, therefore I will
put my hope in him."* LAMENTATIONS 3:24

AS THE SUN SET on our back patio conversation, my friend paged through her journal, sharing glimpses of private thoughts. She said, "Jen, my relationship with the Lord is stronger now than it was thirty-one days ago." I had no words. Just a month ago, her eldest, the nineteen-year-old son who made her a mom, went to be with the Lord. "God is still good," she reiterated, "and I want the other kids to know that."

On the morning of the funeral, it hit me. My son stumbled down the stairs airing his bad attitude. Eggs greeted him, but he didn't want eggs. He wanted pancakes. Yet, as he grunted his way to the table, I knew my precious friend would give anything for the same, disrespectful morning greeting. She would gladly be a short order cook one more day. For the rest of her life, she'll daydream about past breakfasts gathered at the table. Tragedy opens our eyes to perspective changes, and in that moment, the simplicity of a one-word vocabulary shift marked me.

This making of meals and tending to wounds and continuing on when I'm tired and worn out and really don't want to—it's a privilege. I don't *have* to, I *get* to. I don't have to tackle the world's largest load of laundry, I get to, because it means we have plenty of clothes to wear. I don't have to go to work, I get to because it means we're employed and there's a paycheck coming. I don't have to pay the electric bill, I get to because it means that we have heat on chilly nights.

Whether married or single, mothers or not, this one-word gratitude challenge impacts how we do life. We can all press in and learn to love what must be done, regardless of how we feel. It's the choice we get to make.

A Moment to Breathe . . .

*Think of the one thing today you're really not looking forward
to. Then swap the words. "I don't* have *to; I* get *to."*

The Imago Dei

BY KIM HYLAND

So God created man in his own image; he created him in the image of God; he created them male and female. GENESIS 1:27

IMAGO DEI. WHAT WOULD it look like if we really lived like we truly believed every human being was created in the image of God? Including the guy who cut you off in traffic. The boss intent on making your day miserable. The child breaking your heart. Again. The former friend doing her best to ruin your reputation. The church member rubbing you the wrong way. That dishonest business that's trying to rip you off and winning. Your political opponents. Your negligent landlord. Your obnoxious, scary neighbor. Your ex. And his girlfriend. All of them knit together in his or her mother's womb by the same Artist that spoke the universe and all its varied wonders into being. All of them created and cherished.

It's a risky proposition. Our vulnerable hearts are intent on dividing humanity into neat categories with hidden titles—love, like, tolerate, dislike, can't stand. Protecting ourselves behind a carefully crafted shield of neglect, indifference, and even hate. Not my religion. Not my denomination. Not my political affiliation. Not my type. Not my friend. Not my people.

But protection is a deceptive illusion and is ultimately destructive. When we construct fences and build walls to "protect" our neat categories and hard hearts, it's like stepping on our oxygen line. Because love is like air.

Inhale. Exhale. Both directions. And it better not stop, or you'll pass out. We're made for love. Sure, there's plenty of hard work involved. But when we choose to set aside our prejudices and silence the anxious judge and jury of our minds, we find that we hold two things fundamentally in common with everyone: 1) the image of God and 2) our need for His grace. Suddenly, we are the acquitted and the only justice is to share the unmerited favor we've received. And love becomes simple.

A Moment to Breathe . . .

Imago Dei. All of us. Created in God's image. Ask God to open your eyes to see all people the way He does, to love the way He does.

The One Thing We Should Never Hoard

BY LISA-JO BAKER

Then God said, "Let there be lights in the expanse of the sky to separate the day from the night. They will serve as signs for seasons and for days and years." GENESIS 1:14

IT'S NOON AND I'M jumping in the car to go grab a spur-of-the-moment donut. Boston Crème. And I get a text message from a new friend. I'm in the drive-thru when I hear her voice pop up on my phone and she wants to know what I'm doing for lunch tomorrow. She suggests sushi. I do not like sushi. Not even a little bit. I don't like to feel like my food may be making eye contact with me.

But I like my friend and getting to know her is one of my favorite things. I remember this when she texts me again, "All I want is your time. I want to talk about God and life and success and failure and moving on and being strong." And there it is. It was never about the sushi. It was about the raw time. The biggest gift we can give each other. Being willing to spend uninterrupted hours together. Because we'll all starve on a diet of 140-character tweets and Facebook updates.

It's about being able to sit across the table from each other and talk about what success and failure mean and how we survive both. It's about being able to dig into our lives and sift through the ordinary in order to really connect beyond the default, "I'm fine." It's about being willing to be interrupted.

How easily I forget that my relationships thrive on time and that it wasn't even mine to begin with. God spoke days and nights and seconds and hours into being and then He gifted them to us. I don't want to hoard my time. I want to be generous with spending time on the people in my life. I get that we won't have time for everyone every day. But we all know who the specific few are that we've been entrusted with. So let's spend our time on them. Generously. The more the better. For both our sakes.

A Moment to Breathe . . .

Name those you want to generously spend your time with. Then make a plan. This week. A coffee date with a friend. A game night with the kids. Or maybe something else. Make it a date.

Hope Beyond the Pain

BY MELISSA AARON

For I consider that the sufferings of this present
time are not worth comparing with the glory that
is going to be revealed to us. ROMANS 8:18

EARLIER THIS WEEK MY daughters and I were watching a sitcom and the mom on TV was having a baby. She was doing the stereotypical heavy breathing and moaning that is associated with dramatic (and comedic) television births, so my daughters began to question me about the validity of pain and childbirth.

They were horrified when I confirmed that, yes, women do typically have a great deal of pain associated with childbirth. And I may have mentioned Eve and "the curse." They started having second thoughts. I assured them that they have plenty of time to worry about birth. At least fifteen years or more! They still need to finish their education and get married first.

I also shared that a lot of women (myself included) report that—while childbirth was painful—I don't really remember the specifics of that pain. "Why else would people have subsequent children?" I joked.

I assured them that the pain of childbirth isn't comparable with the joy that comes with the birth of a child. It's not that you completely forget the pain, but the newfound joy overshadows the pain. The pain, in fact, is "worth it" when all is said and done, which is really a beautiful metaphor for the trials of life. Thankfully, even our omniscient God chooses to forget some things. Jeremiah 31:34 says He forgives our sin and remembers it no more.

But God is faithful to remember His promises to us. He commands that we remember too. God calls us to remember our trials and pain. To remember how He brought us through. Because He will continue to bring us through, again and again, until finally, He brings us home. In Christ, there is always hope beyond the pain.

A Moment to Breathe . . .

Recall a time when the trial was hard, the pain was real.
Remember, too, how Jesus pulled you through. Because
of His faithfulness to us in the past, we have confidence
that He'll be faithful in our present and future too.

The Soil of Friendship

BY BECKY KEIFE

A friend loves at all times . . . PROVERBS 17:17

ONE MONDAY MORNING I received a simple text from a friend: "How was your weekend?" I chose to be real and reveal that the weekend in fact didn't go so great. My two-year-old woke up in the night with a sudden onset of croup. Unable to breathe, I rushed him to the ER where we spent an unpleasant four hours. "We didn't get home till after 3:00 a.m., so now I feel like Zombie Mommy. But thankfully, he's doing much better and I'm hopeful for the chance to take an afternoon nap."

Without skipping a beat, she replied back, "Oh, no! Can I bring you dinner?" In that moment, I faced a decision: decline help because I could handle the day on my own or accept dinner and be tangibly blessed while deepening our friendship. Yes, I would be fine without help. But what if being fine isn't the point? I accepted my gracious friend's offer.

A few hours later, I heard a soft knock and opened the door to arms full of delicious delights: shredded barbeque chicken with soft rolls for sandwiches, tender-crisp green beans, sliced strawberries, olive oil chips, and Caesar salad. A little "Get Well" balloon peeked through the spectacular smorgasbord. I grew giddy when I spied a box of Magnum Mini ice cream bars, because apparently Zombie Mommies need dark chocolate to survive. As I thanked my friend, the light in her eyes beamed a genuine pleasure for the opportunity to help.

Over the past few years—on my journey from isolation in a new city and new life-stage, to thriving in a community of do-life-with friends—I've learned that meaningful friendships are forged in the soil of service. We are meant to come alongside. To lean in and be held up. To do the holding. It's in needing one another that relationships bloom. Later, my friend arrived again, this time with a basket of fruit . . . and a bouquet of sunflowers.

A Moment to Breathe . . .

Sometimes it's the smallest things that say, "I care." Put a few sunflowers in a mason jar and surprise a friend with a bright hello.

The Name That Defines Me

BY ABBY MCDONALD

*"Look, I have inscribed you on the palms of my hands;
your walls are continually before me."* ISAIAH 49:16

THE FIRST TIME OUR eight-year-old realized I had a name other than "Mama," we were sitting at the dinner table and my parents were visiting. Of course, they do not call me "Mama." We could see the lightbulb moment in his expression, but I made sure he knew that to him, my name would always be "Mama" or "Mom." But never "Abby."

I wear the title proudly, and yet, at the same time, I don't let it define me. At times I have to remind myself that my identity exists outside the wonderful roles of wife, mother, and friend. These different roles shape me and mold me, but they don't determine who I am.

My search to discover who I was began after I became a mom. Everything about my supposed birth plan failed. Then after my family left and my new baby and I were alone, we cried together as I tried to cling to something stable. My former labels—student, worker, daughter—were eluding me. Now as a wife and mother, I felt like I was failing miserably at both.

Somewhere in my darkness I sent up a simple prayer, "Lord, help." And over time, God showed me I would never know who I am until I learn who He is.

The more I learned about Him, His love, and His unchanging character, the more I discovered my own identity. I learned these different hats I wore—mom, wife, friend, employee—were meant to enhance, but never define. If we hang our identity on a finite role, we will never discover who we are as an eternal being. He created each one of us to leave an eternal mark. And while our families are a huge part of that, they are only one part. It's up to us to discover the distinct gifts He gave to each of us to reflect His glory.

A Moment to Breathe . . .

*List all the different hats you wear—the many different
roles you fill. As beautiful, and even God-ordained as
these roles are, our identity is in Christ alone. Thank Him
today for making you His daughter, for eternity.*

A Different Way of Looking at Success

BY DENISE J. HUGHES

Tell Archippus, "Pay attention to the ministry you have received in the Lord, so that you can accomplish it." COLOSSIANS 4:17

GROWING UP IN MY family meant being fiercely competitive when it came to board games. I loved staying up till 2:00 in the morning with my brothers, trying to take over the world, in the game of Risk. Our favorite games involved strategy—like Chess, Stratego, and Empire Builder. I loved it whenever my big brother agreed to play chess with me—even though I posed no challenge to him. He patiently taught me how to move each piece and checkmate the other person's king.

The queen might be the most powerful piece on a chessboard, but I liked the knight. I thought it clever how the knight could move in little L-shapes, so I played my knights exclusively until they died. Then I played my bishops, sliding across the board in grand diagonals. Meanwhile my brother methodically moved various pieces into position for checkmate. Game after game my brother won, but I managed to stay alive a little longer each time. That was something.

What I learned playing chess is that I can't become so fascinated with one piece and one move that I neglect the others. Each piece has a part to play, working together for a common goal. The church is like that too. We come together, with each person doing the thing we do best.

When I think of success, I think of a mostly unknown man in the Bible named Archippus. Near the end of Colossians, Paul stops to speak directly to him. Archippus received a call from God for a specific work. We don't know what he was supposed to do, but whatever it was, we know he needed to finish it. That's my definition of success: being obedient to complete the work God has called me to do.

A Moment to Breathe . . .

You know that long list you have of things to do? Pick one. Just one. And complete that one thing today. Then exhale.

Home Is Where You Feel Wanted

BY DONNA JONES

*How good and pleasant it is when brothers
live together in harmony!* PSALM 133:1

WHILE IN COLLEGE, I found it odd that a childhood friend visited my family before her own when she returned to town during university holidays. One day she confided, "When I walk into your home everyone gets up, greets me with a warm 'hello!' or 'hey!' and wraps me up in a bear-sized hug. Your family makes me feel like a big deal."

I was blessed to be raised in a home where I was made to feel like a big deal. My communications professor taught that the first three minutes of every human interaction—the first three minutes of the morning, the first three minutes at the office, the first three minutes of when a family member comes home—these 180 seconds set the tone of your communication for the rest of the day. It's not that a negative tone can't be course corrected—it can—but it's a lot harder to make a negative interaction positive than keep a positive interaction positive.

No matter what time Dad came home, we'd hear his key jingling in the lock, followed by a booming "Hello!" as he entered the front door. Mom always answered with a cheerful "Hey!" It's not that their lives were perfect. They occasionally argued, like all married couples do. But in the midst of it all, they never stopped making each other feel welcome and wanted. And they never stopped making others feel that way too. Because home is not merely where you're welcome; home is where you feel wanted.

Maybe God created homes so we'd get a glimpse of who He is. Our Father in heaven opens His arms wide and lovingly invites us in. Best of all, God's welcome lasts longer than the first three minutes. His welcome lasts forever.

A Moment to Breathe . . .

*Begin today. If the first three minutes of interaction
sets the tone, commit to giving others your best—
smiling and saying a cheerful "Hello!"*

The Strength of Our Lives

BY ERIKA DAWSON

The LORD is my light and my salvation—whom should I fear? The LORD is the stronghold of my life—whom should I dread? PSALM 27:1

AFTER A PARTICULARLY CHALLENGING day, I abandoned the laundry, the dishes, and most of my responsibilities and retreated to a mindless binge of reruns on television. Avoidance comes naturally to many of us. Friends confess a dependence on food, alcohol, shopping, and even exercise to buoy them up in tough times.

We spend most of our lives trying to be strong. We muster courage, try harder, grin and bear it, and make the best of a situation. But sooner or later, we discover that behind the mask of strength, we hide a broken, fearful heart. Rather than addressing our weakness, we avoid it or cover it up. But as believers in Jesus, we can live differently! When we make the Lord our light and our salvation, we no longer have reason to avoid or be afraid, for the Lord becomes the strength of our lives! Through Jesus, we no longer live a life of self-reliance but of God-dependence.

He is our stronghold—our refuge, our protection, our strength! Whatever we face, whatever honor or heartache, dream or disappointment, no matter the reception or rejection, the step up or setback, may we look to the Lord as our refuge, depend on Him as our strength!

This strength comes not from Christ beside us, but from Christ in us. He is not merely the shield that encloses us; He is the internal foundation upon which everything else is built. He is not our exoskeleton, but the very bones inside of us, the endoskeleton upon which our whole lives hang!

When we can't, He can—in us and through us. In Christ we live and move and have our being. In Christ all things hold together. In Christ we can do all things because He is the strength of our lives!

A Moment to Breathe . . .

You know that thing that's your favorite go-to? Food? Shopping? Television? Today let's make God's Word our favorite go-to. Let's go to Him when we need strength and encouragement.

Jesus and Road Maps

BY HANNAH VAN DYK

Lord, lead me in your righteousness because of my
adversaries; make your way straight before me. PSALM 5:8

LATELY I'VE BEEN ASKING for Jesus to show up with directions on Google maps because I'm really not sure where I'm going these days. I want something like a neon billboard because I need a glaringly obvious sign. And if He's going to show me a road map, I'd like it to be one that reflects who I am and what I'm already doing.

I keep thinking I'm the first one to experience any of this. And then I think of all the characters in the Bible who had Jesus show up for them, but He never showed up with a road map. I love the story of Jonah, because he was a prophet. And when he received his call—or his road map, to continue the metaphor—Jonah ran away. He saw the destination of his road map—Ninevah—and ran away. (This is probably why Jesus isn't showing up with a road map for me.)

When Jonah was in the midst of a storm and couldn't change what he was supposed to do, God showed up for him, even after Jonah ran away from Him. God didn't show up with a neon billboard or a road map that gave detailed directions, but rather, He came with a whale.

Maybe I need to be swallowed by a whale? I don't know these days. But what I do know—even though I've tried to run away from this truth—is that Jesus always shows up. He may not have a road map, but He knows where He's going. Because He knows the name of every star He's placed in the sky. Just like He knows how many stitches were used when He bound up the scars on my heart. And today, that's enough for me.

A Moment to Breathe . . .

Walking with God means trusting Him to lead the
way. Every day. Beginning today. Ask Him to help you
grow in your trust as He leads you day by day.

How to Be Worry-Free

BY JENNIFER DUKES LEE

"Therefore don't worry about tomorrow, because tomorrow will worry about itself. Each day has enough trouble of its own." MATTHEW 6:34

IT WAS 11:58 P.M. on December 31, 1999. Most people I knew were just minutes away from "partying like it was 1999." It was New Year's Eve, baby. And it was a big one. Meanwhile, I sat at my work desk on full alert, eyes glued to my computer screen. I sat in a newsroom full of other reporters, waiting to see whether our world would collapse under a predicted technological catastrophe. It was the year of the "Y2K bug."

Many people believed that when the calendar switched from 1999 to 2000, computers all over the world would glitch out. Doomsdayers warned that this glitch might just end civilization as we know it. You know, like grocery stores couldn't keep bottled water and canned goods in stock. So we reporters were called in to wait, watch, and then report. While I sat at my desk, the clock struck midnight. And? Nothing happened. All that worry . . . and it never came to pass.

I thought about that moment last night. Because it reminded me of the unproductive nature of worry. And I've been such a worrier lately. Most of you have your own personal worries that keep you awake at night. I get it; it's definitely possible that one's worst fears will come true. I've had some of my deepest fears unfold into reality.

But it's just as true that our worst fears will never come to pass—kind of like the Y2K catastrophe that wasn't. Worrying about what might happen *tomorrow*, does little more than distract us from what God is doing *today*. In the end, this truth remains: We can't fix outcomes, but we *can* fix our minds on Christ. God must have known we'd face times like these, because He gave us words of hope, on nearly every page of Scripture, to keep us grounded when things get out of hand. Today, let's keep grounded. Let's listen to the Master of Hope instead of the worry on the news cycles.

A Moment to Breathe . . .

Uproot worry by fixing your mind on Christ through His Word.
Open the Bible to Matthew 6 and read the whole chapter
where we find this nugget of wisdom about worry.

When No Means Yes

BY KRIS CAMEALY

And my God will supply all your needs according to his riches in glory in Christ Jesus. PHILIPPIANS 4:19

MY THREE-YEAR-OLD WOULD SURVIVE on crackers alone if I would let her. To say she is a picky eater is an understatement at the very least. She would be the happiest little girl in the world, if only I'd stop pushing disgusting vegetables (oh, the horror!) and chewy meat (oh, urp!) at her, at every dinner.

And, well, to be honest, I'd probably be happier too, because then we could forgo the tears, and forced gagging that ensues when we encourage her to eat a few tiny bites of any meal. The reality is, that while her mood would undoubtedly be better, her body would indeed suffer in the long run. And I'm more concerned with her health than her mood.

This is similar to how our heavenly Father cares for us. We want "crackers" all day long. But perhaps He says no. Maybe He nudges the plate of "vegetables" a little closer, while the "crackers" are getting harder and harder to reach. How many times have I sought something in prayer, without really knowing or considering the long-term effects of my request? How many times have I pushed Him for my will be done, not His?

I'm not so different from my toddler. Sometimes I'm after that which is not ultimately what is best for me. And God says no. He loves me by offering up something better—His best, for my best. That's when I recognize that His no's are a gift, because it means He's sparing me from something outside of His will.

God's no is really a yes to something else, something better. So I am learning to give thanks for the no's, reminding myself that Abba knows best and He will provide everything I need to navigate this life.

A Moment to Breathe . . .

The prayer that hasn't been answered. That no you've heard again. See it as God's provision, disguised as a withholding. And trust He has your best at heart.

In Every Season God Is Enough

BY LOVELLE GERTH-MYERS

*I know both how to make do with little, and I know how
to make do with a lot. In any and all circumstances I have
learned the secret of being content—whether well fed or
hungry, whether in abundance or in need.* PHILIPPIANS 4:12

I'VE SEEN A LOT in the few short years I've been on this earth. I've
felt pain almost unbearable that was associated with choices others
made that were not in my best interest. I've been homeless and
hungry, scared and worried. Most of all, I felt hopeless.

Somehow God found me in the midst of my hardship. There I
was, trudging through life with no hope when God grabbed ahold
of my situation and my heart. He taught me that everything I go
through has a purpose. And that I am not defined by my baggage.

I learned quickly that I am not promised an easy life on this earth,
but when I seek Him for my contentment in every season that life
throws at me, I will come out on the other side as an overcomer.

Flash-forward a few years, and here I am . . . stable, out of
poverty, and prospering in ways I never thought possible. I was
adopted at the age of twenty-one. I now have parents who love
me so well and they are worth every bit of pain I endured prior to
knowing them. I am married to an amazing man and have a baby
on the way. God is using every bad experience I have ever walked
through for His glory.

The Lord is faithful. I've learned the hard way that I can't get
through this life on my own. I will make mistakes, but have learned
to seek His Word and embrace each season knowing He is with me.
In the end, I will walk with a better understanding of who He is and
who I am in Him.

A Moment to Breathe . . .

*Look back over the seasons of your life and give every difficult
circumstance to God. Ask Him to take the hard and redeem it
for a purpose greater than any human mind can imagine.*

We All Break Differently

BY MARY CARVER

LORD my God, I cried to you for help, and you healed me. PSALM 30:2

THE SUNDAY AFTER WE left our church plant, we returned to our previous church home. We immediately began trying out Sunday school classes, looking for a new way to get involved. I joined the choir and began attending rehearsals every Thursday night. When we talked to friends who had left the church plant a few months earlier than us, they were surprised to hear that we'd jumped right back into church after the deep hurts we'd experienced.

Our friends were taking some time off from church—time to process and to heal—as were several others involved in our church plant. And who could blame them? What we went through was traumatic and exhausting and life-changing. So why weren't we doing the same thing?

Though our eventual exits took place at different times and with different reasons, we all experienced many of the same challenges and hurts while planting that church. We all poured our hearts and souls into it. We all wrestled with the decision to leave. And in the end, we all left with regrets and heartache. And yet, we all reacted to the end of that season differently.

To be clear, my way of coping wasn't any better than anyone else's. I jumped back into church life right away, but it was years before I felt safe enough to let a church family back into my heart. We all break differently. We hurt differently. We react differently.

In crisis, every person will feel differently. And even if two people share the same feelings, their responses to those feelings will be different, just as the long-term life-change they endure as a result of that crisis will be different. I think this is a lesson we all need to learn: We break differently and that's okay. God made each of us unique, so we need to give each other grace when we go through tragedy together.

A Moment to Breathe . . .

Share with your closest friend what "breaking" looks like for you. Then ask her what it looks like for her. Together, commit to being there for one another when either one of you has a moment when you're breaking.

Consider It Joy

BY ALIA JOY

*The LORD is near the brokenhearted; he saves
those crushed in spirit.* PSALM 34:18

I AM SPECTACULARLY CLUMSY, so while I was in Kenya, I had to pay close attention to my feet in relation to the world around me. I traveled from an insulated world where possible injury comes with prerequisite signage and safety rules. American to-go cups warn me the contents are hot and may burn me. And I cannot turn on my car without the annoying *ding ding ding*—chiding me to fasten my seat belt. But Africa hasn't the time to be concerned with my hot beverage or the possibility of a seat belt when sharing a vehicle with fifteen other people, a few chickens, and a goat.

I returned to my insular world and wondered if maybe the North American church has missed out on a deeper relationship with God and each other because we're so surprised by injury and inconvenience, by suffering and circumstances. We have taught a tidy life. But the reality of following Christ is there's nothing tidy about it.

We've reduced our gospel to a formulaic set of rules whereby the faithful sidestep the pitfalls of this broken world and instead float unscathed and isolated through their good life. We offer a discounted gospel when we say it will fix your problems, ease out the wrinkles of your day, give you shiny full-bodied hair and perfectly behaved children. We want a warning sign or someone to blame when things get broken.

But if we fail to dig into a theology of suffering and the way we as Christ followers will hurt right alongside a broken world, we write off people's trials as an anomaly or a reaping they had coming instead of a place we connect with God's solace and peace and even our purpose in walking with and weeping with those who weep. For what does the gospel offer us in our pain if we cannot be people who grieve even while we believe?

A Moment to Breathe . . .

Pour the oil of gladness and praise from your lips, but never forget the wails and cries and pounding fists, because God sees those too and He's close to the brokenhearted.

For Unbelief, God, I Give You Thanks

BY CHRISTIE PURIFOY

We love because he first loved us. 1 JOHN 4:19

I REMEMBER THE DAY I stopped believing. I see that day now for what it was: a doorway. Nothing would ever be the same for me having passed that threshold. I thank God every day for leading me to that place, for giving me the courage to do what I had never yet done. For the first time, I doubted Him.

Growing up, they told me God is love and I believed them. And then I stood in church one Sunday and sang some song about God's love. I was in pain and saw no evidence that God had noticed, so I stopped singing the song. I no longer believed in a God who equals love. I no longer believed this love saw me. Here is the thing about unbelief: it's like a fire. It burns away the truth, yes, but it also burns away the lies. What is left is a heart like a dead, blackened field. In other words, what is left is the perfect ground for new life.

I do not want to idolize unbelief, no more than I would want to idolize certainty. All I want is to say: Do not be afraid. On the days when you believe, the days when God is near, do not be afraid. Do not imagine it is up to you to keep the feeling going, like a bicycle that might disappear the moment you become too exhausted to keep peddling. And the dark days when belief is difficult may be painful, but they, too, can be a gift.

Which came first, my love for God or His love for me? Before I stepped through the door of this day, I'm not sure I could have answered the question. My view of divine love was a mixed-up mess of lessons I'd been taught, songs I had sung, parents who loved well, and my own lonely efforts to be a good person. Maybe that has been the greatest gift of unbelief. Embracing it, I let go of everything I thought made me lovable. And then love found me.

A Moment to Breathe . . .

Picture yourself riding a bike. Then picture yourself too tired to keep peddling. The bike keeps moving. That's a picture of God's grace, carrying us through when moments of doubt seep in.

The Wide Open Shore

BY JENNIFER J. CAMP

If I live at the eastern horizon or settle at the western limits, even there your hand will lead me; your right hand will hold on to me. PSALM 139:9–10

WE GRASP HANDS AND lean back, digging our toes as deep as we can into wet sand. The waves crash against our legs and the sea water splashes into our open, smiling mouths. We stand side-by-side, heads back, delighted by our ability to not fall despite the surf's resolute heaving of itself onto shore.

This is the best. I don't want to miss it. So I don't take many photos, just a few. And then I put the camera and phone away. To look and to see, to listen and to hear, I have to fight against every distraction, every obstacle threatening my awareness of love, joy, beauty. I struggle with the tension of wanting to remember moments like this—filled with love and God's presence and glory. My heart needs to remember, needs to see, hear, be.

A phone, an Instagram feed, a Facebook post, a journal description—none of this can adequately capture what God is doing in us, this moment: Me. My daughter. Standing barefoot with waves crashing, the sun bright and hot on our tangled hair, our bare skin. I am practicing deeper awareness, for I'm hungry to experience life.

There is something that is born in us—and killed in us—when we recognize that there is something we are probably worshipping more than Jesus. For me, it was other people's approval. And my own approval, too. Striving toward anything but Jesus is wasted time.

Anything good we do must have Him at the center. Otherwise our own heart, born in Him, is crushed with the weight of our own attempts at earning and chasing and pleasing. So we run to the beach this morning with no plan, no agenda. Because we, His daughters, want to open our hands, our hearts, our lives to more freedom, more joy, more life. More of Him.

A Moment to Breathe . . .

Put the phone away. If just for an hour. Take in the scene—of God's beauty all around you—without a camera in hand, but with the eyes He made so you can see His beauty.

Living beyond the Bubble

BY SUZANNE ELLER

*"You are the light of the world. A city situated on
a hill cannot be hidden."* MATTHEW 5:14

A CONCERNED PERSON PULLED me aside after church and said, "Do you know what your daughter is doing?" I waited to hear, holding my breath. She continued, "Your daughter is hanging out with people who aren't Christians."

Oh, that. I sighed in relief. Yes, I knew about that. Because they hang out at our house too. My daughter invites them to come over often. They spend the night. I know their names and some of the details of their lives because my daughter has shared them with me. When I explained this, the woman at church was a little affronted.

Huge bubbles are created when we put up boundaries around things that aren't sin, just in case they *might* lead to sin, and we become hyper-vigilant to make sure that everyone stays within that self-designed bubble. Yes, we want to be wise, and we understand that it's good to surround ourselves with people who share our love for Christ. But if Jesus is our example—and He is—then I'm not sure we should live in self-made bubbles.

Jesus burst bubbles right and left. He loved people who were different from the traditional crowd. He believed in people discarded by others. He listened to people and saw them, which demonstrated how sometimes those things led them straight into the arms of the Father. Jesus engaged in long conversations over debates. He walked straight into crowds where people adored Him, mocked Him, and were curious about Him. He showed compassion that was the lasting impression in every one of those encounters.

Jesus remained true to Himself and His mission. He spoke truth, and had very clear and honest words for those who lived in a bubble and demanded that others live there too. Jesus came to rescue humanity and we are part of that plan.

A Moment to Breathe . . .

*Open your circle to include people who are different from
you. Listen to their stories, even if you don't agree. Have
honest conversations filled with truth and light.*

Read and Repeat

BY KIMBERLY COYLE

These words that I am giving you today are to be in your heart.
Repeat them to your children. Talk about them when you sit in
your house and when you walk along the road, when you lie down
and when you get up. Bind them as a sign on your hand and let
them be a symbol on your forehead. Write them on the doorposts
of your house and on your city gates. DEUTERONOMY 6:6–9

HE STUTTERS A LOT. Over most sentences and in every conversation, the words come labored and slow. It breaks his mother's heart, and she watches him regress and fall behind in his ability to manage every day activities. They've taken him to specialists, and hope to find one who will discover the key to unlocking his speech so the words begin to flow.

He's an adult now, and everything he says and does is on constant repeat. Because of his other disabilities, he must work twice as hard.

So my friend prints out Scripture and hangs it all over her house, and she quotes it daily until the words take root in the hidden places of her soul. Her grown son sees the words hanging, and she asks him if he wants to learn Scripture with her too.

They memorize the verses together, read and repeat, read and repeat. He's already good at repetition, and the words take root in him too. These are the only ones he speaks without a stutter. He quotes Scripture loud and clear, speaking the truth of God without pause.

Scripture is the key that unlocks the twisted tongue, just as it is the key that unlocks the twisted soul. He still stutters in conversation, but his mother holds close to hope. She's seen the transformative power of the Word of God, and while the effect on his speech may be temporary, these are the words that set his spirit free.

And so they walk around the house . . . and they speak life together . . . to one another. Read and repeat. Read and repeat.

A Moment to Breathe . . .

Write Deuteronomy 6:6–9 on several notecards and post them around
your house. Make Scripture repetition part of your everyday moments.

From the Overflow of Our Hearts

BY SARAH MAE

*"A good person produces good out of the good stored up in his heart.
An evil person produces evil out of the evil stored up in his heart,
for his mouth speaks from the overflow of the heart."* LUKE 6:45

COZIED UP UNDER MY covers with my head nuzzled into my pillow, the thoughts rolled silently on my tongue. I was swearing and there was bitterness and jealousy. Even though these words were whispers to myself, they were there. This was the overflow of my heart. I can't tame my tongue because this is a heart issue. My ugly is coming straight from inside my soul. So instead of praying, "Lord, help me tame my tongue." I'm praying, "Lord, give me a pure heart." Because if my heart is cleaned out and I submit to the work of the Holy Spirit, then the overflow will be good, uplifting words.

As I was pondering my heart, I thought about why it's so important to focus on our children's hearts instead of trying to tame their tongues. Whenever I hear one of them say something that's filled with an edge, I'll automatically respond with, "We are not going to talk like that; it is not okay." And I'm trying to tame the tongue, but really, I need to pull my child aside and ask, "What's going on? Can we talk about these words and what is maybe behind them?" It might sound like I'm overdoing it, but when I see past the attitude, I see stress or tension or built-up resentment. When I take the time to gently prod the heart, I find the root of the overflow. If I can help my children untangle the roots, then their words will change because their hearts will mend.

Whether we're big or small, we must do this over and over again, because sin is always lurking; the flesh is always ready to try and dominate the spirit. When left to myself, I follow my sin nature. When I'm not reading God's Word, I'm not thinking on good and lovely things. But when I pour God's Word into my heart, every single day, then His goodness is what pours back out.

A Moment to Breathe . . .

The next time you hear a harsh word—or speak one—consider the heart. What might be lurking beneath the surface of the words? Make all of Luke 6 the words you pour into your heart today.

Duped by Darkness

BY KELLY BALARIE

Your word is a lamp for my feet
and a light on my path. PSALM 119:105

DARKNESS CAN BE ALLURING. It calls to us saying, "You won't get hurt. Come and see what I have for you. No one will ever know." Too often the carefully-hidden things in our lives bite us when we least expect it. I, once, carefully hid a secret. Instead of eating in public, I didn't. And instead of eating in private, I also didn't eat. I starved myself. Little by little, I died internally, all the while trying to prove to the world I had everything together.

I lost so much weight I could hardly breathe, hardly sleep, and hardly survive. My mind felt much more comfortable in the dark than in the light, in lies than in truth, and caught in a series of mistakes than in a posture of repentance.

We often are aware of our mistakes, but hide out of embarrassment. God doesn't desert us though. He loves us too much. He sees us hiding. He always has. And He illuminates our escape. He shines His light on the path to take.

God's Word is that light. Through His Word, God leads and guides. Today, the light may seem dim, but it's still there, ready to lead us to hope, encouragement, and restoration. No matter what darkness you find yourself in, His light is there, waiting.

Jesus didn't choose to abandon us on the cross and He won't abandon us today. He is with us. And His glory and light extend far beyond the shadows, and far beyond the words attempting to lure us back into darkness. He calls us to safe pastures. He calls us to truth. He calls us to light.

A Moment to Breathe . . .

Look up the verse from today's reading in Psalm 119.
Read the entire psalm. It's all about God's Word—the
lamp that lights the path for us to take.

What It Means to Be Winsome

BY DAWN CAMP

"By this everyone will know that you are my disciples, if you love one another." JOHN 13:35

THE SPRING BEFORE I began tutoring high school students, I observed another tutor's class for a day. The most memorable lesson came during a debate when the tutor challenged the class—and subsequently, me—to think about what it means to be winsome. I'm sure I sneaked a peek at the dictionary app on my phone as I analyzed this unfamiliar word. *Winsome* means innocently charming. The tutor stressed being winsome as more important than winning.

Sometimes my debate students don't know which side of an issue they'll argue until the day of the debate. It forces them to be fully prepared, to understand both sides and be able to defend either one, a skill which helps not only in debate, but also in life. Although they may not agree with the position they're ultimately asked to support, they know both sides inside and out. Can you imagine how that level of understanding could benefit us in our everyday lives with people whose opinions differ from our own?

The desire to win serves us well if our only concern is a judge's scoresheet, tally marks on a page, or getting the last word. But the desire to be winsome serves us well if we want to convert others and win them to our point of view. It's the mark of an evangelist or peacemaker.

I heard a speaker recently. He commanded the attention of the crowd and the respect of many simply by his presence. But when he opened his mouth the words were tinged with disdain for those who disagree with him. Even when his words rang true, his tone repelled. It was the opposite of winsome. To be winsome is to be persuasive, to win people to your side.

Although eternal salvation is accomplished through the shed blood and finished work of Jesus Christ on the cross and the quickening of the Holy Spirit, we can touch lives here and now when we live ours joyously, as winsome ambassadors for Christ.

A Moment to Breathe . . .

Be winsome at home, at work, at church, and in your neighborhood. Be an encourager and a supporter. Delight in the success of others. And play and laugh a little more too.

Shaped Not Scorched

BY JOLENE UNDERWOOD

"I will be with you when you pass through the waters, and when you pass through the rivers, they will not overwhelm you. You will not be scorched when you walk through the fire, and the flame will not burn you." ISAIAH 43:2

DID GOD REALLY SEND us? It's a question I returned to periodically after showing signs of anxiety and depression from obeying His call. An "intense season of serving" had marked me. I'll never be the same.

Others have asked if maybe I misunderstood what seemed so clear at the time. I don't think so. When we moved our family to live on a ranch and foster many children, the decision was so beyond what I would have dreamed to do on my own. The multiple opened-doors along the way were unmistakable. Still, our experience left me utterly depleted.

My mind and body wore out. My soul wrestled through the forging that suffering tends to ignite. Every day we faced a surreal number of challenges. Breakdowns occurred in material possessions, physical health, spiritual stamina, and emotional capacities. Perhaps the biggest challenge of all was coming face-to-face with my inability to make it on my own. My new normal became the cry, "Lord, I need You." This sentiment changed everything in me. Never before had I needed to trust God so completely . . . so implicitly. Desperation led me to a kind of brokenness only God could carry.

Looking back, it's easy to question our decision. Did we miss something? Why was it so hard? Today, I see God's presence where He once felt distant. God walked us through far more than we ever thought we could handle and showed us His ability to do so tangibly.

Though I felt overwhelmed, I came to know a sense of being overawed. Where I felt scorched, I was being shaped. Times of fiery trials are not times of God's neglect, no matter how we feel. They are times when we learn to trust His ways.

A Moment to Breathe . . .

Whatever you're facing today, or may face tomorrow, know that He promises to be with you. When you look to Him to guide you, He will walk you through.

With Broken Hearts and Wings

BY KAYLA AIMEE

"Consider the birds of the sky: They don't sow or reap or gather into barns, yet your heavenly Father feeds them. Aren't you worth more than they?" MATTHEW 6:26

I BECAME A MOTHER on a cold night in November, cut hip to hip in trauma, and we both bear the scars. They strap your arms down for an emergency C-section, and it's unnatural because all of motherhood is spent reaching, hands unconsciously hovering to catch, to cuddle, to soothe.

Later, when one pound eight ounces grows into an indomitable three-year-old and the days are spent long in time-out—one for her for throwing things and one for me to count to ten before I start throwing things—there my arms are again reaching out for wisdom because from beginning to now, motherhood has been hard. Yet, from the harsh beginning, it has also been beautiful. From the moment I saw her still-fused-shut eyelids struggle to catch her first glimpse of the world outside the womb to last night, when her lashes fluttered against my shoulder.

Every year a bird builds a nest in the rafters of our porch. And one day we see the momma bird hovering with frantic cries. Our eyes transition to the tiny, broken bird, fallen from the nest too soon. I pull on gloves and tuck in the feathered baby as a tiny voice pipes up behind me, "Maybe God and da doctors can help the baby birdie, Mommy."

We pray for it as we rock to sleep that same evening. I trace the edges of the scar that winds long around her back, the one from the day they cut into her heart and simultaneously sliced mine open as I sat anxious in a waiting room, waiting for the doors to open with assurances that hers never stopped beating.

I have no idea what I'm doing, but after so many hours spent sitting next to her tiny bedside, when she was closer to there than here, I know for certain that I'm grateful every single moment I have to look my little legacy of love in the face and teach her to fly.

A Moment to Breathe . . .

Our scars tell a story. Share with a friend the story of one of your scars, whether seen or unseen.

The Friends We Invite

BY KIM MARQUETTE

"It is not those who are well who need a doctor,
but those who are sick." MATTHEW 9:12

I CAN'T FIND HOSPITALITY at the local bookstore. All I can find are cookbooks, lots and lots of cookbooks with a tiny section on etiquette. I was also directed to the decorating magazines by a very helpful clerk. When I google the word *hospitality*, I find images and links for hotels and restaurants. I understand that cooking and decorating help to set the stage for hospitality, but we're more likely to find a perfectly decorated table with a perfectly balanced meal in a hotel.

Hospitality, it seems, has been relegated to a lost art, a long forgotten practice, an old-fashioned notion. And it's been replaced by Pinterest perfection and chic coffee in shops instead of people who gather around tables. But what about true, biblical hospitality? I long for a place in time when people were the point not perfection. When open homes and crowded dining tables demonstrated love one for another.

The word for hospitality in the Greek—*philoxenia*—literally means "lover of strangers." In a nutshell, Scripture calls us to love strangers and to bring them into our family, to receive and embrace those who do not share our faith and our values.

When was the last time I hosted someone different from me? Different skin color? Different first language? When did I last host a smoker? (Do I even own an ashtray? Should I?) An unwed mother? A Buddhist? An adulterer? A Muslim? When is the last time I hosted someone who did not look, think, or act like me? When indeed?

When did I last embrace, listen to, take by the hand, receive, and accept someone who does not share my faith or my values? When was the last time I invested in someone before they were all cleaned up? Jesus did this, many times. In fact, He invited me to have dinner with Him, long before I was all cleaned up. And, of course, I'm still in process.

A Moment to Breathe . . .

Thank Him for loving and pursuing you. Ask the Lord to place a name, or even a few names on your heart—some friends you might invite over for dinner, friends who maybe are different than you.

Redemption for the Nice Girl

BY KRISTEN STRONG

*And we exhort you, brothers and sisters: warn those
who are idle, comfort the discouraged, help the weak,
be patient with everyone.* 1 THESSALONIANS 5:14

I DO A DOUBLE take when I read the words on the screen, the ones that compliment a writer for being both nice and smart, calling this a rare combination. I wanted to ask point blank, "What in the Sam Hill do you mean both nice and smart is a rare combination? We have to choose one or the other?"

A short time later, I leave a comment on a blog post written by a friend, and she replies saying, "Kristen, you're the nicest girl ever." And I roll my eyes. For the love, quit calling me nice! Sinking back in my chair, I realize I've bought into the lie—that if you think I'm nice, maybe you don't think I'm smart or strong.

Sometimes nice doesn't feel like enough. Nice feels like a pushover, a doormat, the one you can't take too seriously. The nice one is the shy one standing in the corner. She isn't owning the dance floor all wild and witty. Nice is vanilla-flavor boring. But then again, for the person receiving the "niceness," such kindness tastes like double-chocolate heaven. Nice is powerful. Nice is the way hope turns its face to you, often unexpectedly. Nice leaves you breathless. Nice is the cool drink of water that lingers on dry hearts in need.

If you're one of the nice ones, don't eclipse your light by believing nice isn't enough or by pining away for a personality other than the one God gave you. An infinitely creative God makes room for infinitely creative personalities. They're all equally valuable and equally needed. Regardless of personality type, we need those who aren't afraid to confidently be who God created them to be. And this includes those like you, the one who knows nice isn't just something you do, but something you are. This is the truth: nice Jesus-loving folks are love-spreaders, grace-sharers, and gospel-livers. And living the gospel? Now, that's always a smart choice.

A Moment to Breathe . . .

*Take nice a step further today. Go ahead and practice super
niceness everywhere you go. I'm talking the kind of nice that
makes people do a double take. Be a sister in Christ who is nice.*

A New Creation

BY KRISTIN A. SMITH

Therefore, if anyone is in Christ, he is a new creation; the old has passed away, and see, the new has come! 2 CORINTHIANS 5:17

I WAS TWELVE YEARS old when I first heard another woman share her testimony. I was captured by her stories of pain and heartache and rejoiced at God's redemption through it all. I can't recall the specific details, but I understood that God could do amazing things if we only asked Him to be a part of our lives.

At the end of the talk, the woman invited those who didn't know Christ in a personal way to pray a short prayer with her. My eyes squeezed shut and I fervently prayed. I knew that I was a sinner and I wanted so badly to be "fixed." Maybe this Jesus could do just that. I expected something to happen, anything really. I had been passionate in my prayer, that's for certain. But I didn't feel anything. Maybe I had done it wrong? Confirmation came when the sin that continued to entangle me, reared its ugly head once again.

So the next month, when yet another woman shared how God had changed her life and we were invited to pray, I once again begged God to come into my heart and change me too. I must not be a new creation if the sin remains, or so I reasoned.

Whenever I read 2 Corinthians 5:17, I was only able to see my failure. Somewhere along my journey I held onto the lie that if I was truly saved I also must be "perfect." We all know that isn't possible, but I spent the better part of thirty years working really hard at making myself perfectly presentable before God.

Only recently was I able to truly grasp the gift of salvation that has been mine all along. Such a burden was lifted when I finally stopped doing, doing, doing, and started resting in the gift of Christ. I am fully flawed, yes, but because of Jesus, I am made new.

A Moment to Breathe . . .

Have you ever shared your story? Or written it down somewhere? If not, write it out today. Pray and decide who may need to hear your story and then go share.

What Lies Ahead

BY KENDRA TILLMAN

*Brothers and sisters, I do not consider myself to have taken hold
of it. But one thing I do: Forgetting what is behind and reaching
forward to what is ahead, I pursue as my goal the prize promised
by God's heavenly call in Christ Jesus.* PHILIPPIANS 3:13–14

OVER THE YEARS, I'VE set goals and even planned toward their
success, yet they've always seemed just beyond my reach. Lots of
prayer and tears and more prayer followed as I've tried to figure
out the underlying reason. I've read the books that say: *Write it
down. Put the goals where you can see them. Choose the high
payoff actions first. Prioritize. Ask for the support you need. Don't
be Superwoman.* I know intellectually what I need to do, but none
of it has been enough.

Sometimes, when I get bored or tired of the discipline, I simply
default to what I've always done. But then I ask myself, "Why do
I continually, habitually do the things that take me in the opposite
direction of my goals?" The answer: escapism.

When feeling the pressure of all that comes with being a wife,
a mother, a business woman, a volunteer, and all the other hats I
wear, I attempt to escape the realities of the work that is required to
reach goals and realize dreams. Instead, I look through the refrig-
erator or skim through emails, trying to find a way to escape.

In Philippians 3, Paul encourages us to press on—forgetting
what lies behind us, and focusing on what lies ahead of us. So I am
making a day-by-day, moment-by-moment conscious decision not
to allow myself to escape when I feel the pressures of my responsibilities. I will keep pressing on, with my eyes on the joy waiting
before me. I will disregard the discomfort I feel. I will think of my
Savior, and I will look to Him when I grow weary. With His help and
by His grace, I will not give up.

A Moment to Breathe . . .

*What does "escapism" look like for you? What if you ran to His
Word when the pressure is high? Meditate on Philippians 3:13–14
and ask Him for strength to focus when you feel distracted.*

God Wants Your Surrender, Not Your Strength

BY ALIA JOY

Youths may become faint and weary, and young men stumble and fall, but those who trust in the LORD will renew their strength; they will soar on wings like eagles; they will run and not become weary, they will walk and not faint. ISAIAH 40:30–31

I HAVE BEEN IN bed for five days now. Getting up only to change into a different T-shirt and pajama pants or hobble to the bathroom. I have a cup of water lingering on my bedside table. I take small sips through a straw when I have to take my medicine.

We all know to hold still when it hurts. It's our first instinct to pull into ourselves and try to brace that broken part. We protect our pain like a broken-winged bird, shielding our wings from flight. We know we are bound and we want to fight against it but for the brokenness.

I've always had restlessness in me. Stillness doesn't come by me naturally. I am frenzied or fatigued, but the stillness it takes to heal is elusive. I can quiet my limbs and my lips but not my mind. My mind always fights the seeking when I'm backed into involuntary stillness.

Sometimes I wonder if I'm more afraid of the quiet from God or of the surety of His voice when He does speak.

In the chaos that surrounds being still, when the world moves on at a steady pace and you cannot keep up, it's hard not to push through the stillness. Stillness often means waiting. No one wants to be a burden. No one wants to be passed. No one wants to feel like they're going nowhere. But sometimes God is telling us to be still. Because He's healing broken parts. He's building our strength while we wait on Him; we need only be still.

So many of us are limping along, and we've put on our brave face and determined to at least make some valiant effort on God's behalf. But really, God isn't asking for our tenacity as much as our surrender. He's asking to carry us.

A Moment to Breathe . . .

Surrender to the arms of the Almighty. Be carried along, find your strength in the stillness. For soon, you will be renewed, you'll find your wings and take flight again.

Enough Is Enough

BY KIMBERLY GILLESPIE

*Who can separate us from the love of Christ? Can affliction
or distress or persecution or famine or nakedness or danger
or sword? . . . No, in all these things we are more than
conquerors through him who loved us.* ROMANS 8:35, 37

I WAS EIGHT YEARS old the first time I heard I wasn't "enough."
I wasn't enough to hang with the cool kids or play on the best
team in gym class—thus began my journey of striving to feel like
"enough."

This journey has been a precarious one—paved with lies and
insecurities often laid by people haunted by the same struggle.
And when comparison joins in as a constant companion, it is never,
ever, ending. Comparison taunts:

"You are not enough."

"You aren't a good enough wife, mother, friend."

"You aren't smart enough or rich enough or spiritual enough."

"See? You aren't enough to be chosen by that company, that
man, that friend, that group."

The more you strive to feel like you are enough, the more miserable you become as you realize that no success is enough to quiet
comparison's nagging voice. She will always point out someone
smarter, brighter, more talented, and better qualified.

So your pursuit is not to feel as though you are enough. That is
elusive. God wants you to know that He is enough for you both. All
your days were ordained by Him. He will complete any good work in
you because He is enough. God wonderfully made you, then delivered
you from darkness and provided a way into His kingdom. God loved
you enough to forgive you, seal you, and fill you with His Holy Spirit.
He is enough, and He sustains you through whatever may come.

Christ loved us enough that, even though He knew every single
thing we would do to break His heart, He still died for us. And
nothing can separate us from His love.

A Moment to Breathe . . .

*Recall those times in your life, past or present, when
you felt as though you were not enough. Replace those
lies with this truth: in Christ we are enough.*

Trusting His Purpose

BY ANN SWINDELL

I call to God Most High, to God who fulfills
his purpose for me. PSALM 57:2

I'M IN A SEASON of life where a lot of things are up in the air. My family just moved to a new city, and while our home is cozy and our family is healthy, everything else feels challenging. We're trying to make friends, find our place at a new church, and figure out rhythms and schedules. I know what I need to do every day—love and care and provide for my family's needs—but sometimes I still feel a little untethered. Confused. Lost. All of the externals in my life are in place, but inside, I feel kind of purposeless.

Psalm 57:2 reminds me that the Lord knows the exact details of our current situations. When David wrote this psalm, he was in a challenging situation, and he knew that only the Lord could fulfill the purpose he was created for. And as the psalm continues, David thanks God and praises Him. He declares God's love and faithfulness. Ultimately, David believed that God was the one who would complete the work that needed to be done in his life.

This, too, is how we can learn to live with purpose, even when life feels unclear. We cry out to the Lord, asking Him to fulfill His purposes in us. We thank Him, praise Him, and declare who He is. And in the process, we turn our own hearts to worship, trusting in the God who made us and loves us completely. Even when we feel adrift, God is secure in who He is and in who He has created us to be. His purposes for you always stand firm.

A Moment to Breathe . . .

Take a moment and worship God. Declare who He
is—the Creator of all things, the Redeemer of all
humanity, and the Fulfiller of all His purposes.

On Giving My Heart a Good Scrub

BY ANNA RENDELL

Who is a God like you, forgiving iniquity and passing over rebellion
for the remnant of his inheritance? He does not hold on to his
anger forever because he delights in faithful love. MICAH 7:18

WE'RE GETTING READY TO sell our house. To help our chances, we've been working on projects. We've had to replace, repaint, and repair places in our home we've gotten so used to that we don't even see them anymore. The carpet that's ridiculously old and worn. The handle-less deck door. The screen door that the previous owners painted purple.

These quirky little places—ones practically invisible to us—in our home stick out like a sore thumb to potential buyers. As we clean up years of life lived within these walls, I'm finding that, along with my kitchen cabinets, my heart also needs a good scrub and purge. To toss lingering hurts and replace with forgiveness. To spackle up the cracks with gentle love notes from Scripture. To donate good deeds and kind words. To clean out the dark corners long neglected, and give them a good scrub to let light shine in.

What in my own heart and life have I grown so accustomed to that I don't even see anymore, but may stand out to others? Only when I look at myself from the outside in am I able to name (more than) a few. I can see my first instinct is to defend myself instead of defending others. I can see the small chips on my shoulders have grown deeper, etched further into the bone. I can see that what I view as weariness, others may receive as complaint.

These quietly ugly characteristics have been given room to lurk, to settle in comfortably like an old broken-in pair of shoes, and it's time for them to leave. They need a kick to the curb. God isn't dwelling on the dusty, stale parts of my heart and I don't need to either. It's time to make the place sparkle . . . and I want that for my heart too.

A Moment to Breathe . . .

Take an inventory of your heart. Any lingering hurts? Any
leftover unforgiveness? Invite God into those crevices in
your heart, asking Him to give your heart a good scrub.

Mountain Whispers

BY BECKY KEIFE

For his invisible attributes, that is, his eternal power and
divine nature, have been clearly seen since the creation of
the world, being understood through what he has made.
As a result, people are without excuse. ROMANS 1:20

I LACED UP MY tan hiking boots, coated my pale skin with bug repellant, and loaded my backpack with just the essentials: water, Bible, pen, and journal. I tucked the trail map in my pocket and closed the door to my mountain dorm. I was off on another adventure. Just me and God.

My ears were tuned to the tiny songbirds perched on spindly branches of the red manzanita. My nose was tuned to the melodic fragrance of woody sequoias mingled with sweet wildflowers and musky earth. And my heart was tuned to hearing God's voice through it all. My eyes continually scanned the landscape ahead for the prize of every hike: a huge off-trail boulder with a scenic view. Once I found it I veered off course and scampered up the hill, unmindful of the undergrowth, eager to get to my perch.

Three months spent working and ministering in Kings Canyon National Park right after my freshman year in college turned out to be a summer of learning. Learning how to do everything as unto the Lord during long shifts as a thankless "bus boy" at the mountain village diner. Learning how to work with teammates so unlike me as we pooled our minimal experience and resources to put on Sunday worship services for park visitors. But more than anything, it was the summer I started learning to awaken to God's wonder through creation.

The difficulties of that summer paled in comparison to the vividness with which I experienced God. At every turn I heard His whispers. Often I would come back from those nature treks sun burned and bug bitten (because that repellant never really worked). My tummy was usually grumbling and my palate parched from not enough water. But none of it mattered. Because I was awake to wonder.

A Moment to Breathe . . .

Plan a hike in nature's wilderness. Walk with God in the lush
surroundings of His creation and sense the majesty of His goodness.

When You Worry You're Disqualified from Being Loved

BY LISA-JO BAKER

Love consists in this: not that we loved God, but that he loved us and sent his Son to be the atoning sacrifice for our sins. 1 JOHN 4:10

MY DAUGHTER COMES TO me with snot and tears streaked down her face and asks between wails, "Do you still love me, Mama? Even when I'm crabby?"

I take her small frame onto my lap and wipe the hair out of her eyes. I slowly pet her back and say, "Zoe, I love you when you're crabby, and I love you when you're happy. I love you just as much when you're mean as I do when you're kind. Mamas always love their girls." And I hug her tighter. I want her to know this deep, reassuring promise of a love that isn't conditioned on good behavior. This love that doesn't keep a list of all she got wrong.

Because it's easy to keep our own score, isn't it? Yesterday I was late getting the kids up, I lost my temper, and we didn't properly hug good-bye, so today I'm a bad mom and don't deserve to be loved. Or today everything ran smoothly and kids laughed and leaned through the minivan window and kissed me good-bye, so today I get to feel worthy.

Maybe for you it's keeping score of which days you lost your temper and which you didn't. Or which days you managed to put up with your boss with a good attitude and which days you snapped at that coworker. Or which days you read your Bible and which days you forgot. Again. Or which days you managed not to take a drink and which days you woke up in a bed you didn't recognize.

We're good at keeping tabs on ourselves. But that kind of list-keeping isn't love. God's love burns our lists to the ground. His love looks at everything we are and everything we've done and chooses to purposefully love us through it all. Because nothing can disqualify us from how Jesus loves us.

A Moment to Breathe . . .

Whatever list of things you've done that make you think you're unworthy of being loved—yes, even that really horrible thing—throw the list away. All of it. Receive the grace that God gives.

One of the Most Important Things to Remember

BY ROBIN DANCE

Then my enemies will retreat on the day when I call. This I know: God is for me. PSALM 56:9

THE SCOTTISH THEOLOGIAN IAN Maclaren shares one of my favorite life philosophies: "Be kind, for everyone you meet is fighting a hard battle." We've inherited a world marred by sin, which leads to brokenness. Believers and non-believers alike are walking wounded. I often find myself asking, "How can I be like Jesus?" whether in this circumstance or within the context of that relationship. Sometimes it's easy, but other times it's downright hard.

Loving others well is a daily offering and requires prayer. I know I cannot accomplish it apart from the holy work of the Spirit. Any good in me is only God, all glory and thanks to Him. The reason I beg God to continue this transforming work in me is because I long to be treated the same way.

I, too, am walking wounded. Unless you're trusted and close, though, you don't get to see beyond my mask. I'll wear that smile and tell you I'm fine, while sometimes secretly feeling misunderstood, betrayed, or forgotten. The worst is when the offender is someone I care about, but it still hurts when anyone treats me badly. It's tempting to gossip about how I've been wronged. And while I don't have the power to change others' behavior, I can control my response.

My deepest desire is to honor the Lord, which demands I respond like Jesus. In the wake of atrocities committed against Him, the likes of which we'll never fully grasp, He always loved first, quickly forgave, and was for the very people who hurt Him. May we follow in His footsteps and learn to do likewise.

A Moment to Breathe . . .

When the world feels like it's against you, remember what you already know: God is for you! Pray for Him to tender your heart toward those who've hurt you, and for your response to glorify Christ.

The Key to Successfully Handling Change

BY DONNA JONES

Then I heard the voice of the Lord asking:
"Who should I send? Who will go for us?"
I said: "Here I am. Send me." ISAIAH 6:8

THE HOUSE IS QUIET. It's a foreign sound. For decades my house has been full of voices, laughter, music, and the occasional sibling squabble. We affectionately call ourselves "The Loud Family." Not one of us is an introvert. And then, just like that, they're all on their own. And tonight, there are no sounds from other parts of the house. No one bounding down the stairs. No one hugging my neck. Only the silence greets me.

What do I do now? is all I can think. With each changing season, we're faced with this question. It's scary and a little sad, but it's also brimming with new possibilities. My new normal doesn't have to be bad. It's just different. And change can be good in a different sort of way. In fact, with the right attitude and a plan of action, it can be great.

I wish I could say I've always known how to handle change in a positive, healthy way, but the truth is, I haven't. As a new mom I sometimes longed for the days when I could grab my purse and be out the door in two minutes flat. When the kids were in preschool, I wondered how my wardrobe suddenly morphed into sweatpants central, and I secretly envied women who actually got dressed in outfits that required heels. When we moved to a new area, I longed for the familiar, even though our new city meant new opportunities.

But I learned the key to successfully handling change is to look forward with anticipation and look back with gratitude. I had to stop saying, "I wish it was . . ." and start saying, "I'm glad it is . . ." So whether you're a new graduate, a new mom, a new employee, or a new empty nester, embrace the new season, thanking God for every moment of the old one.

A Moment to Breathe . . .

Begin to look at every season of change as an opportunity to look back
with gratitude, and also to grow and ask God how He wants to use
you in this new season. Say to Him today, "Here I am. Send me."

The Delight You Bring

BY ALIZA LATTA

He brought me out to a spacious place; he rescued
me because he delighted in me. 2 SAMUEL 22:20

THE FIRST TIME SOMEONE told me they delighted in me, I didn't understand what they meant. "What do you mean?" I had asked.

"I delight in you," the person replied. "I see you, and I know you make mistakes and are flawed, and I delight in you anyway."

That was a powerful moment for me because it reflected God so clearly. If a human could delight in me this way, wouldn't God's delight be even greater? And it is. God sees us, exactly as we are. He sees our flaws and our strengths, and He takes all of that and delights in us.

What comes to mind when you think of delight? For me, it's sitting on a lawn chair in my hometown watching fireworks pop overhead. Or laying a blanket out in a field, so I can lie down and watch the stars. Or holding my nephew while spinning him faster and faster, with his laughter echoing across the room before we collapse together on the ground. All of these instances are sources of delight that make sense to me. What doesn't make sense to me is the thought of me being the source of God's delight.

How am I—a girl who is utterly imperfect, often screwing up and making innumerable mistakes—the source of the Almighty God's delight? It's an idea that doesn't compute in my brain.

But this is the truth: you and I bring God delight. Think of your greatest moments of pure joy . . . holding your baby in your arms for the first time, seeing your to-be husband at the end of the aisle, receiving your degree that you worked so hard to attain, or a hundred other moments. All of those pale in comparison to the delight you bring God. He looks at you and sees a treasure, someone worthy and whole. Someone worth rescuing, something worth delighting in. *You* bring God delight. You are the source of His deepest joy.

A Moment to Breathe . . .

Later tonight (or any night), take a blanket and go outside. Lie down on the blanket and gaze at the stars. Tell God how much you delight in Him, and thank Him for how much He already delights in you.

The Purpose of Loneliness

BY AMBER C. HAINES

For who has known the Lord's mind, that he may instruct him? But we have the mind of Christ. 1 CORINTHIANS 2:16

MUSIC OFF, TELEVISION OFF, phone left on silent, I've been dabbling with the quiet because I need to hear from God, but the truth about the quiet is that it has opened me up wide, turned on my dulled senses, and faced me toward my rawest, loneliest places. It is a constant struggle for me to not reach for my phone, always at my side. With my mouth I say I want to walk with God, but with my actions I crave a culturally acceptable numbness that keeps me from pain.

We start to feel the quiet working on us, and so we reach for the phone and scroll through Instagram. I'm finding, even as I pursue the presence of God, that the quieter it gets, the lonelier I feel and the more I am left to deal with my own thoughts and what I really believe about God. I'm beginning to see how I've discounted that I have the mind of Christ and that I am actually supposed to be able to hear myself think.

I've started asking . . . how lonely was Jesus in His flesh? I imagine the internal communion Jesus kept with His Father, the kind of communion I want with Him too. Because of Jesus, I'm starting to embrace the lonely, not hiding from it anymore, and rather asking Jesus into it with me. Only then do I find myself truly not alone.

Even with our most favorite sisters, in huge crowds, we find ourselves deep in the crevices of loneliness. Community can point us in the right direction, but it still won't fix us. We find ourselves feeling exposed and unfixed because there is no people fix, no earthly father, no covering that will do other than the covering Jesus gives, the messianic fix.

What if we allowed the quiet, faced the lonely, and sat in it a bit? Might that lonely place be exactly where the door is, the one on which we knock, the one Jesus promises to open?

A Moment to Breathe . . .

Turn off the radio, the TV, and yes, even your phone. Turn off every noise or potential noise you can think of. Then turn to Him, invite Him into your quiet, and listen for that still, small voice.

Dwelling in the Rhythm of Grace

BY STEPHANIE BRYANT

I have asked one thing from the LORD; it is what I desire: to dwell in the house of the LORD all the days of my life. PSALM 27:4

MY FAMILY OF THREE moved to ten acres with a farmhouse this year. We're overflowing with ideas. I can see all this place can be and I want to share it. So I figured God would be saying: *Lots to do, girl. Let's get busy.* Instead, God has whispered to my heart: *Dwell.*

Dwell means to abide, nest, reside, and inhabit. God takes my hand like a patient Father and slows my pace to His as we walk in the garden. He's not in any hurry with His vision, and I feel grace pouring down, like a much-needed summer rain.

Dwelling means rest. But dwelling is not an easy word for a woman with vision. I'm excited to be on the other side of the Jordan and into our Promised Land. So, dwell? It can sound like defeat in our day of hustle. But dwelling implies harmony, not isolation. God wants us to *be* with Him. To dwell in the house of the Lord forever. To be about one thing—His heart.

I'm learning that to dwell feels a lot like art. Absorbing colors, making memories, stepping into the picture God is painting, while choosing not to be so worried about framing it up for presentation. The point of a promised land is to dwell, to allow God to reign, and for the world to see us living differently. Dwelling is a little piece of heaven on earth.

I desire to be at rest in the pace God has placed me in, becoming vital in the role between vision shared and vision experienced. I'm called to find a rhythm for our daily lives and get in sync with what God has already done for us and what He is about to do. So I'm working at being still to embrace the grateful heart God is trying to instill in me. I will dwell in the house of the Lord, forever. There's no rush.

A Moment to Breathe . . .

Inhale deeply, slowly. Then exhale with thanksgiving. Savor the sweetness of His presence. And determine in your heart to dwell in the Lord's house forever.

Author Bios

Abby McDonald. Writer, wife, and mom of three who seeks the hope of Christ in life's messes. abbymcdonald.org ~ Days 48, 122, 169, 240, 332

Alecia Simersky. Writes to encourage Christians to live differently because of the grace we've been shown through Jesus. aleciasimersky.com ~ Days 52, 137

Alia Joy. Coffee dependent, grace saved, wife, and mom who writes the reminders of God's goodness and mercy. aliajoy.com ~ Days 8, 88, 178, 211, 253, 289, 341, 355

Aliza Latta. Canadian writer, journalist, and artist who is a huge fan of telling stories. alizanaomi.com ~ Days 3, 93, 202, 251, 290, 321, 363

Alyssa DeLosSantos. Jesus lover, hope hunter, storyteller, collector of old doors, and occasional blogger. alyssadelossantos.com ~ Days 74, 127, 151, 203, 301

Amber C. Haines. Poetry lover from the dirty South. Author of *Wild in the Hollow*. Finds community with the broken. amberchaines.com ~ Days 26, 98, 204, 287, 364

Angie Ryg. Bible teacher who is passionate about equipping women to encounter the beauty of the gospel in our everyday lives. angieryg.com ~ Days 39, 118, 146, 230, 316

Ann Swindell. Author of *Still Waiting: Hope for When God Doesn't Give You What You Want*. annswindell.com ~ Days 33, 83, 199, 273, 357

Anna Rendell. Social media coordinator at (in)courage. Latte lover. Speaker. Author of *A Moment of Christmas*. girlwithblog.com ~ Days 21, 92, 191, 249, 284, 324, 358

Annie F. Downs. Best-selling author, speaker, and podcast host based in Nashville, TN. anniefdowns.com ~ Days 6, 100, 209, 322

Arlene Pellicane. Speaker and author of *31 Days to Becoming a Happy Mom* and *Calm, Cool, and Connected.* arlenepellicane.com ~ Days 63, 136

Becky Keife. Writer, speaker, and editorial coordinator for (in)courage. Three wild boys call her mom. beckykeife.com ~ Days 11, 97, 216, 250, 291, 331, 359

Bev Rihtarchik. Founder and president of Redeemer Christian Foundation, Inc. Ministry. Writer at: walkingwellwithgod.blogspot.com ~ Days 75, 149

Bonnie Gray. Speaker, retreat leader, and the author of *Whispers of Rest* and *Finding Spiritual Whitespace.* thebonniegray.com ~ Day 46

Britta Ellis Lafont. Loves to curate the good. To discover, collect, and display evidence of God's goodness. brittalafont.com ~ Days 49, 116, 177, 274, 309

Cari Trotter. Known as an enthusiastic, relatable speaker that brings real life to the feet of Jesus. caritrotter.com ~ Days 80, 170

Caroline TeSelle. Dream encourager. Marriage mentor. Virtual assistant. Writer. Lives in Chicago with her husband and four kids. carolineteselle.com ~ Days 65, 134, 205, 280

Christie Purifoy. Wife, mother, writer, and gardener. Author of *Roots and Sky: A Journey Home in Four Seasons.* christiepurifoy.com ~ Days 18, 162, 258, 342

Dawn Camp. Wife, mother, and editor/photographer of *The Beauty of Grace*, *The Gift of Friendship*, and *The Heart of Marriage.* myhomesweethomeonline.net ~ Days 27, 126, 148, 189, 232, 292, 348

Deidra Riggs. Serves people who are totally over shame, blame, and guilt. Helps them turn division into unity. deidrariggs.com ~ Days 7, 106, 198, 233, 298

Denise J. Hughes. Lover of words and the Word. Author of *Deeper Waters* and editorial coordinator at (in)courage. denisejhughes.com ~ Days 4, 81, 184, 228, 283, 333

Diane W. Bailey. Wife, mom, Gigi, and friend. Also storyteller, lake-dweller, life coach, author, and speaker. dianewbailey.net ~ Days 37, 112, 168, 242, 302

Donna Jones. National speaker. Author of *Seek: A Woman's Guide to Meeting God* and a normal gal who's married to her pastor. donnajones.org ~ Days 78, 105, 206, 260, 293, 334, 362

Elisa Pulliam. Life coach, teacher, and writer. She inspires women to live out their God-given callings. elisapulliam.com ~ Days 44, 124, 154, 214, 317

Elise Hurd. Personal trainer for your faith. Wife. Mom of five. Tiny house living, big personalities. Jesus keeps her sane. littlelunchmaker.com ~ Days 29, 176, 320

Emily P. Freeman. WSJ best-selling author of four books including *Simply Tuesday* and *A Million Little Ways.* emilypfreeman.com ~ Days 20, 144, 243, 304

Erika Dawson. Writes at FaithfulMoms.org sharing biblical teaching and practical tools for moms. erikadawson.com ~ Days 64, 224, 335

Evi Wusk. Teacher and writer who loves faith, family, gratitude, and guacamole. eviwusk.com ~ Days 76, 119, 166, 261, 325

Francie Winslow. Passionate about growing in intimacy with God. She lives with her husband, Wyatt, and their five kids. franciewinslow.com ~ Days 31, 131, 281

Grace Cho. Wife to a chef. Mother of two littles. Mentor. Lover of feeding bellies and souls around the table. gracepcho.com ~ Days 38, 145, 263

Hannah Van Dyk. Canadian fundraising professional. Passionate for sugary coffee, semi-colons, and Jesus' life on earth. ~ Days 61, 138, 219, 336

Hilary Yancey. Loves to write, study philosophy, and learn to fall more gracefully in beginner ballet. She lives in Waco, Texas. thewildlove.wordpress.com ~ Days 53, 99, 188, 221, 294

Holley Gerth. Author, encourager, life coach, follower of Jesus, and friend to you. holleygerth.com ~ Days 1, 84, 195, 264, 310

Jacque Watkins. Jesus follower. Mama to five. Mercy Lover. Podcaster. Labor and Delivery Nurse. Tea Drinker and Friend. jacquewatkins.com ~ Days 57, 109, 161, 244, 326

Jen Schmidt. Host of the Becoming Conference and author of *Just Open the Door*. beautyandbedlam.com ~ Days 10, 94, 196, 254, 327

Jennifer J. Camp. Co-founder of Gather Ministries and author of Loop Devotional and *Breathing Eden*. jenniferjcamp.com ~ Days 60, 133, 207, 343

Jennifer Dukes Lee. Author of *The Happiness Dare*. She and her husband raise crops, pigs, and two humans on an Iowa farm. jenniferdukeslee.com ~ Days 16, 96, 193, 223, 259, 305, 337

Jessica Turner. Speaker, blogger, and author of *The Fringe Hours: Making Time for You*. themomcreative.com ~ Days 42, 113, 171, 234, 303

Jolene Underwood. Writer and blogger, who writes regularly and has been featured on GraceTable, iBelieve, and (in)courage. joleneunderwood.com ~ Days 72, 129, 160, 215, 349

Judy Wu Dominick. Atlanta-based writer helping Christians engage better across social divides. lifereconsidered.com ~ Days 77, 147, 255

Kaitlyn Bouchillon. Loves iced coffee, good storytelling, and laughter. Author of *Even If Not*. kaitlynbouchillon.com ~ Days 62, 111, 132, 200, 245

Karina Allen. Devoted to helping women live out their unique calling and build community through practical application of Scripture. forhisnameandhisrenown.wordpress.com ~ Days 73, 165

Katie Orr. Author of the FOCUSed15 Bible studies that provide a deep time in God's Word in just 15 minutes a day. katieorr.me ~ Days 43, 120, 143, 217, 295

Kayla Aimee. Finds her joy sharing stories of hope + humor. She is the author of *Anchored* and *In Bloom*. kaylaaimee.com ~ Days 35, 121, 152, 218, 276, 350

Kelly Balarie. Speaker, blogger, and author of the book *Fear Fighting: Awakening Courage to Overcome Your Fears*. purposefulfaith.com ~ Days 32, 87, 210, 231, 288, 318, 347

Kendra Tillman. Wife. Mom. Encourager. Founder of the StrongHer Women's Event and author of *You Are Stronger Than You Think*. strongher.me ~ Days 34, 181, 235, 354

Kim Hyland. Kim loves to encourage women by sharing her imperfect path and God's perfect plans. winsomeliving.com ~ Days 50, 130, 174, 236, 328

Kim Marquette. Loves Jesus, her big family, and coffee with a brownie on the side. Her motto: Live deliberately ~ Finish strong. kimmarquette.com ~ Days 79, 114, 175, 237, 296, 351

Kimberly Coyle. Writes, raises three kids, and revels in a perpetual state of wanderlust on the East Coast. kimberlyanncoyle.com ~ Days 51, 110, 150, 238, 345

Kimberly Gillespie. Writer. Storyteller. Wife. Mother of three. Bible-teacher. Joy-chaser. Atlanta-dweller. thingsithoughtidnever.com ~ Days 56, 125, 159, 256, 356

Kris Camealy. Author of *Come, Lord Jesus: The Weight of Waiting* and *Holey, Wholly, Holy: A Lenton Journey of Refinement*. kriscamealy.com ~ Days 24, 107, 183, 299, 338

Kristen Strong. Wife to her retired Air Force veteran, mama to three priority blessings, and author of *Girl Meets Change*. kristenstrong.com ~ Days 19, 91, 185, 262, 352

Kristen Welch. Founder of The Mercy House and author of *Rhinestone Jesus* and *Raising Grateful Kinds in an Entitled World*. wearethatfamily.com ~ Days 12, 90, 194, 265, 306

Kristin A. Smith. Wife and mother but most importantly a daughter of the King. She's redeemed by God's grace and grateful for it. therichesofhislove.com ~ Days 67, 128, 167, 270, 353

Lisa Whittle. Wife, mom, lover of laughter, Bible teacher, and author of six books including her latest *Put Your Warrior Boots On*. lisawhittle.com ~ Days 14, 86, 187, 222, 271, 300

Lisa-Jo Baker. Best-selling author of *Never Unfriended* and *We Saved You a Seat*, and the community manager for (in)courage. lisajobaker.com ~ Days 2, 85, 201, 246, 285, 329, 360

Logan Wolfram. Plate-juggling mom, wife, speaker, and author of *Curious Faith: Rediscovering Hope in the God of Possibility*. loganwolfram.com ~ Days 54, 172

Lori Harris. Jesus follower. Wife. Mom. Writer. Podcaster. Urban missionary. Church planter. Chief of sinners. loriharris.me ~ Days 25, 141

Lovelle Gerth-Myers. Mom to a spunky little girl, a wife to a wonderfully nerdy husband, and a mentor to some crazy-amazing teenagers. lovellegerthmyers.com ~ Days 58, 179, 339

Marlena Graves. Author of *A Beautiful Disaster: Finding Hope in the Midst of Brokenness*. ~ Days 17, 153, 266

Mary Carver. Writer and speaker who loves sharing truth found in unexpected places. marycarver.com ~ Days 5, 101, 135, 208, 239, 275, 340

Mei L. Au. Bible study teacher and contributor for Deeper Waters, the Consilium, and Flourish Motherhood. belovedandredeemed.com ~ Days 45, 123, 142, 267, 307

Mel Schroeder. Jesus follower. Wife to Tobin. Mama to Mae and Mac. Friend. She loves coffee and lots of it! barefootmel.com ~ Days 66, 158, 277

Melanie Davis Porter. Blogger, playwright, and drama director. Ministry and family are her passions. melaniedavisporter.com ~ Days 68, 155, 297

Melissa Aaron. Cancer survivor, military spouse, and mom to three (one in heaven and two here on earth). casadeaaron.blogspot.com ~ Days 55, 108, 213, 278, 330

Melissa Michaels. Author of *Love the Home You Have* and the award-winning home blog The Inspired Room. theinspiredroom.net ~ Days 47, 140, 225, 319

Myquillyn Smith. The Nester. Home stager. Re-designer. Design school drop-out. Author of *The Nesting Place*. thenester.com ~ Day 40

Nasreen Fynewever. Educator. Writer. Speaker with messages of hope, advocacy, adoption, and mental health. nasreenfynewever.com ~ Days 22, 163, 247, 311

Rachel Anne Ridge. Artist, author, and stray donkey owner in Texas. rachelanneridge.com ~ Days 23, 173, 248

Rachel C. Swanson. Author, speaker, and accredited life coach. Creator of *Big and Little Coloring Devotional*. rachelcswanson.com ~ Days 71, 180, 252

Renee Swope. Word-lover, heart-encourager, and grace-needer. Author of *A Confident Heart*. reneeswope.com ~ Days 15, 102, 197, 241, 323

Robin Dance. Wife, mama, and curious believer. She cares deep, loves wide, laughs often, and makes a wicked apple pie. robindance.me ~ Days 13, 103, 186, 220, 282, 308, 361

Sandy Hafeez. Passionate about discipleship and equipping local church leaders. sandyhafeez.com ~ Days 69, 115, 156, 226, 313

Sarah Mae. Author of several books, including *Desperate*. Her ministry is to encourage women to keep on and begin again. sarahmae.com ~ Days 9, 95, 182, 212, 269, 346

Sheila Dailie. Lover of music and words. Raising her four daughters to be God-honoring women is her joy. ~ Days 70, 164, 286

Shelly Wildman. Wife, mom, and former professor. Author of *First Ask Why*. shellywildman.com ~ Days 59, 117, 157, 227, 312

Stacey Thacker. Wife, mother to four awesome girls, blogger, and runs on grace and coffee. Author of *Fresh Out of Amazing*. staceythacker.com ~ Days 30, 139, 257

Stephanie Bryant. Co-founder of (in)courage. Courageously passionate about God's heart and His vision for His daughters. bryantfamily.farm ~ Days 28, 104, 192, 229, 272, 314, 365

Suzanne Eller. Bible teacher, international speaker, blogger, and a Proverbs 31 Ministries writer. tsuzanneeller.com ~ Days 41, 89, 279, 344

Teri Lynne Underwood. Lopsided-living encourager. Girl mom cheerleader. Author of *Praying for Girls*. terilynneunderwood.com ~ Days 36, 82, 190, 268, 315

Scripture Index
(By Verse and Page)

Proverbs

Ecclesiastes

(in)courage

FIND YOURSELF AMONG FRIENDS

TO SAY WE LOVE COMMUNITY MIGHT BE AN UNDERSTATEMENT.

At (in)courage, our hearts beat for strong, healthy, God-honoring friendship. Nothing brings us more joy than watching like-hearted women connect. Connecting with others lightens the load and adds space for more laughter—and healing—because we know we aren't alone.

JOIN US at **www.incourage.me**
and connect with us on social media!

@incourage

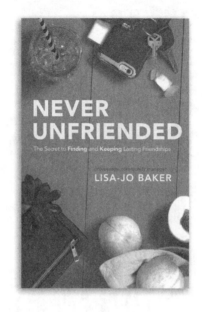

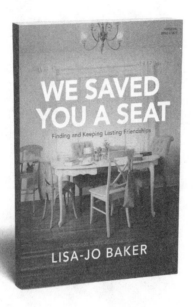

THE BIBLE STUDY TO FIND

YOURSELF AMONG FRIENDS!

God wants us to pursue friendships just as we are with the people He's placed in our lives. This 7-session Bible study explores our relationship with Jesus as a model for friendship—the kind that shapes us into the image of Christ.

WeSavedYouASeat.com

30 *Challenges*
for Real-Life Engagement

Join as (in)courage writers share real-life stories, practical Scripture application, and challenges to help you connect with God, friends, and community.

CravingConnectionBook.com